DATE DUE

MAY 2 2 1989		
MAY 2 2 1992		
NOV 1 6 1992		
JAN 1 1 1993		

DEMCO 38-297

MACRO

MACRO

A Clear Vision of How Science and Technology Will Shape Our Future

FRANK P. DAVIDSON

with John Stuart Cox

PHOTO RESEARCH BY VINCENT VIRGA

William Morrow and Company, Inc. | New York 1983

To the Dutch, who engineered a nation out of the turbulent North Sea, and to the Romans, whose legions taught them how to build dikes and, on another continent, demonstrated that the Sahara Desert is not invincible. *Ars Celere Artem.*

Library of Congress Catalog Card Number: 83-62049
ISBN: 0-688-02182-4
Printed in the United States of America
First Edition

1 2 3 4 5 6 7 8 9 10

BOOK DESIGN BY LINEY LI WITH FLORENCE BERLIN

Grateful acknowledgment is made for permission to reprint the following:

FRONTISPIECE: *"Le Réalisateur"* by Charles Despiau. The Metropolitan Museum of Art, Edith Perry Chapman Fund, 1953; from the Museum of Modern Art, Gift of Mrs. John D. Rockefeller, Jr. (53.140.7).

CHAPTER 1
Portions from "Macro-Engineering: Its Social Implications," by Frank P. Davidson, reprinted with permission from *Technology in Society*, Vol. 1 No. 3, copyright © Autumn 1979, Pergamon Press, Ltd. Photographs of Camp William James and the early volunteers for Camp William James courtesy of Argo Books, Norwich, Vt. Photographs of the Civilian Conservation Corps reprinted courtesy of the Library of Congress, Prints and Photographs Division, Washington D.C. Photograph of William James reprinted courtesy of the New York Public Library. Photograph of the California Conservation Corps from *The Moral Equivalent*, prepared and published by Ideas in Motion (San Francisco, Calif.), copyright © 1983; reprinted by permission. Photograph of farmland engineering at Wilson Farms reprinted by permission from *American Vegetable Grower*, Vol. 31, No. 2, February 1983. Photographs of the Erie Canal reprinted courtesy of the Canal Museum, Syracuse, N.Y. Photographs of the *De Witt Clinton*; the first locomotive to cross the Alleghenies; the Lehigh Valley train in Sayre, Pa.; the reenactment of the driving of the Golden Spike; a trestle near Portland, Ore.; and a train rounding Dry Fork Bridge reprinted courtesy of the Library of Congress, Prints and Photographs Division, Washington, D.C. Photographs of the Shinkansen high-speed train reprinted courtesy of Japanese National Railways. Painting of Captain Prince's aerial ship reprinted by permission of the Metropolitan Museum of Art. Photographs of a Zeppelin gondola; the *California Arrow*; a toy airship; the grand salon of the R 100; the R 100 moored to the mast; the *Los Angeles* at Lakehurst, N.J.; and the *Graf Zeppelin* reprinted by permission of the Library of Congress, Prints and Photographs Division, Washington D.C.. Photographs of Dr. Robert H. Goddard; Dr. Goddard and his team; the Goddard rocket; Dr. Wernher von Braun; Neil Armstrong; Michael Collins; the moon; Commander John Young; and *Apollo 17* reprinted courtesy of NASA.

CHAPTER 2
Photograph of the Colossus of Rhodes reprinted courtesy of the New York Public Library. "The Tower of Babel," painted in 1563 by Pieter Brueghel, reprinted by permission of the Kunsthistorischesmuseum, Vienna, Austria. Photograph of the arm of the Statue of Liberty reprinted courtesy of the Philadelphia Free Library. Photograph of the temple at Aswan reprinted courtesy of the government of Egypt. The map of Alexandria in Antiquity, as reconstructed by Duruy, reprinted courtesy of Collection Roger-Viollet, Paris. Photograph of the lighthouse of Alexandria reprinted courtesy of the New York Public Library. Photograph of Vitellius Aulus reprinted by permission of the Library of Congress, Prints and Photographs Division, Washington D.C. Photograph of the Appian Way reprinted courtesy of the Italian Tourist Office, New York City. Photograph of the Appian Way reprinted by permission of Adolfo Tomeucci, Rome, Italy. Map of the roads of Rome by Tom Stalker-Miller, from *The Roads That Led to Rome* by Victor Von Hagen, reprinted by permission of George Weidenfeld and Nicolson, Ltd. and World Publishing Co. Photographs of a Roman aqueduct, Hadrian's Tomb, and the Baths of Caracalla reprinted by permission of the Italian Government Tourist Office. Drawing of the view from the north of Chichén Itzá by R. Proskouriakoff and the photograph of the "Acropolis," Copán, Honduras, reprinted courtesy the Peabody Museum of Archaeology and Ethnology, Harvard University. Photographs of Aigues-Mortes, Carcassonne, the ruined bridge at Avignon, Mont Saint-Michel, the Chartres spire, and the Chartres window reprinted courtesy of the French Government Tourist Office. Photographs of the arch under the "New River," the map of the New River, the modern map of the region, and Sir Hugh Myddelton taken from *Lives of the*

Engineers by Samuel Smiles (London: John Murray, 1861). Photograph of King James I of England reprinted courtesy of the Library of Congress, Prints and Photographs Division, Washington D.C. Photographs of Versailles reprinted courtesy of the French Government Tourist Office. Photograph of "Cholera Protests to Haussmann" from *L'Illustration* (Paris, 1869) taken from *Napoleon III and the Rebuilding of Paris* by David H. Pinkney (Princeton University Press, 1958). Photographs of the Boulevard Haussmann, the Rue de Rivoli, and the Bois de Boulogne reprinted courtesy of the French Government Tourist Office. Photographs of the George Washington Bridge, the Goethals Bridge, and the Triborough Bridge reprinted by permission of the Library of Congress, Prints and Photographs Division, Washington D.C. Photographs of the Aswan High Dam reprinted courtesy of the Egyptian State Tourist Administration.

CHAPTER 3
Aerial view of Abuja from *How Big and Still Beautiful?* reprinted by permission of Westview Press (Boulder, Colo.). Photographs of an "inselberg," a major highway entering Abuja, Abuja's National Legislative Building, and the master plan for Abuja provided by Dr. Andrew C. Lemer of the Planning Research Corporation, McLean, Va. Schematics of a Nuclear-Powered Agro-Industrial Complex from *Nuclear Energy Centers: Summary Report*, National Bureau of Standards, U.S. Department of Commerce, Springfield, Va. "Great Lakes" plan for South America by Vake Karishjian for *Fortune*, December 1967; reprinted by permission. Photographs of the Osaka Artificial Island Concept and the Alternative Plan, New Island, Osaka, reprinted courtesy of The Kozai Club, Tokyo, Japan. Photographs of the Sea City wall section, the Sea City diagram, and the Sea City model reprinted by permission of Pilkington Glass. Plan for New Island, Port of Osaka, reprinted by permission of the Port and Harbor Bureau, City of Osaka, Japan. ICONN-ERIE offshore island concept provided by Mr. Nigel Chattey of ICONN-ERIE, Inc., New York. Photographs of the Erie Canal Lock at Little Falls, N.Y., the lock before Lake Ontario, and Lock 11 in Amsterdam, N.Y., reprinted by permission of the Library of Congress, Prints and Photographs Division, Washington D.C. Photograph of submerged caisson system reprinted courtesy of Mid-Channel Access Corporation. Photographs of the Seikan Tunnel reprinted courtesy of Professor Manabu Nakagawa of the Japanese Institute for Macro-Engineering.

CHAPTER 4
Photograph of Tubexpress prototype reprinted courtesy of Tubexpress Systems, Inc., New Jersey. Photograph of the "Subterrene" from the slide collection of Dr. Robert Salter. Photographs of World Planetran Route from *Macro-Engineering and the Infrastructure of Tomorrow* reprinted by permission of Westview Press. Photographs of test trains at Myazaki reprinted courtesy of Japan National Railways. Photographs of Amtrak by John Stuart Cox. Ship railway plans for Tehuantepec Isthmus taken from *Scientific American*, December 27, 1884. Model of an above-ground high-tech canal courtesy of Lilian Kemp Photography. Photographs of the Panama Canal reprinted by permission of the Library of Congress, Prints and Photographs Division, Washington D.C. Photographs of Jubail reprinted courtesy of the Royal Commission of Jubail and Yanbu and the Bechtel Corporation. Drawing of colony on the moon by Joan Joos. Drawing of Experimental Model of Mars Rover, CSDL No. 56225 copyright © 1969 Charles Stark Draper Laboratory, Inc. Photographs of space shuttle and space station reprinted courtesy of NASA. Drawing of Atlantic tube or tunnel by Joan Joos from a cartological study by J. Vincent Harrington; reprinted with permission of J. Vincent Harrington and Joan Joos. Drawings of trans-American bikeway route, the Appalachian Trail, and the trans-Australian canal by Joan Joos; reprinted by permission.

CHAPTER 5
Photographs of the solar-power satellite, its receiving station, and the city it serves provided by Dr. Peter E. Glaser. Photographs of the Great Wall of China and Sacshuaman reprinted courtesy of Ramón Barquín of IBM World Trade Corporation, Hong Kong. Photographs of junks reprinted courtesy of the Mansell Collection, London. Photograph of the Grand Canal today reprinted courtesy of Jacquie Kay. Photographs of the Shasta Dam under construction and the Imperial Dam of All-American Canal reprinted courtesy of the Library of Congress, Prints and Photographs Division, Washington D.C. Photographs of St. Lambert Lock on the St. Lawrence Seaway and its reopening reprinted with permission from United Press International. Photograph of the 1956 construction of the seaway reprinted courtesy of Ontario Hydroelectric Authority. Photographs of the James Bay area reprinted courtesy of La Société d'Énergie de la Baie James, Montreal, Quebec. Photographs of the GRAND Canal scheme of Professor Kierans and its North American distribution from *Macro-Engineering: The Rich Potential*, edited by Salkeld, Davidson and Meador, copyright © 1982 by Salkeld, Davidson and Meador (New York: American Institute of Aeronautics and Astronautics); reprinted by permission. Maps of river flowing north to the Arctic in Northern Russia and Russian river-diversion plan from New York Times News Service, copyright © 1983 by the New York Times Company; reprinted by permission. Photograph of geothermal power project of U.S. government laboratory in Sandia, N.M., reprinted by permission of the Sandia (N.M.) U.S. government laboratory. Photograph of solar-power array at Barstow, Calif., by Kim Steele. Photograph of French tidal-power plant on the Rance River in Brittany reprinted courtesy of French Embassy Press and Information Division, New York.

CHAPTER 6
Photographs of Fonserannes locks, map of Canal des Deux Mers, photographs of Pierre-Paul Riquet, Béziers, and Toulouse with the Canal des Deux Mers from *Le Canal du Midi* (Marseilles: Éditions Rivages, 1983); all rights reserved, Odile de Roquette-Buisson for the text, Christian Sarramon for the photos; permissions arranged courtesy of Madame Jean Pellotier, Paris. Photograph of Ferdinand de Lesseps from *Vanity Fair*, November 27, 1869. Photographs of Thames Tunnel banquet and disaster from *The Tunnel* by David Lampe (George C. Harrap & Co.), 1963; reprinted by permission. Engraving of the diving bell by George Cook from *The Tunnel* by David Lampe reprinted courtesy of the Bermondsey Public Library. Photographs of the Thames Tunnel, Brunel, the *Rover*, the *Flying Dutchman* at Worle Junction, the Box Tunnel, Maidenhead Bridge, the Clifton Suspension Bridge, the *Great Eastern*, the launching, the interior of the *Great Eastern*, the *Great Eastern* taking on cable, towing the cable, the upper deck with machinery, and passing up the cable from below decks from *Isambard Kingdom Brunel* by L.T.C. Rolt (London: Longmans, 1957); reprinted by permission. Aerial view of PREVI from *Macro-Engineering and the Infrastructure of Tomorrow*, edited by Davidson, Giacoletto, and Salkeld; reprinted with permission of Westview Press. Photographs of expandable house at PREVI, interlocking

concrete blocks, and typical PREVI plaza reprinted courtesy of Professor Peter Land, Illinois Institute of Technology. Photograph of PREVI street from *Macro-Engineering and the Infrastructure of Tomorrow* reprinted by permission of Westview Press.

CHAPTER 7
Photographs of World War I battle plane, Curtiss Racer, Pan American's *Christopher Columbus*, American Airlines' DC-3 (1937), Lockheed XF-90, and the De Haviland Comet III reprinted courtesy of the Library of Congress, Prints and Photographs Division, Washington D.C. Photograph of the Concorde SST reprinted courtesy of Ramón Barquín, IBM World Trade Corporation, Hong Kong. Photograph of the space shuttle *Columbia* blast-off reprinted courtesy of NASA. Photographs of solar-power satellite concept and the "mass driver" in action reprinted courtesy of Rockwell International. Photographs of the torus-shaped space colony and the interior of a larger space colony reprinted courtesy of NASA.

CHAPTER 8
Photographs of the channel tunnel, De Gamond's tunnel scheme of 1856, an 1890 scheme for a bridge, Colonel Beaumont's tunneling machine, and the survey vessel *Ajax* from *The Channel Tunnel* by Slater and Barnett (London: Wingate Ltd.); reprinted by permission. Article by Winston Churchill appeared in *The Daily Mail* on February 12, 1936. Conceptual drawing of loading cars provided by Channel Tunnel Study Group. Photographs of the founders of Technical Studies, Inc., and terminal area as seen in automated model prepared by British Railways from "Tunneling the Channel," *Technology Review*, Vol. 76, No. 7, June 1974; reprinted by permission. Route map reprinted courtesy of Aktieselskabet af 1966 til fremme af Bro-og Tunnelbygning. Painting of concept of Gibralter bridge by Julian Allen for *Esquire*: reprinted by permission. Sketches of twin stateroom and promenade deck of proposed macroairship by Dr. Francis Morse from *How Big and Still Beautiful?* reprinted courtesy of Westview Press. Outside view of the Morse airship reprinted courtesy of the Boston University Photo Service. Photographs of building dikes near Enkhuizen and constructing the Barrier Dam copyright Luchtfoto Bart Hofmeester, Rotterdam; reprinted with permission. Photograph of motor highway atop the Barrier Dam copyright Frans Popken; reprinted by permission. Photographs of Block van Kuffeler and view of lakes between polders copyright Luchtfoto Bart Hofmeester, Rotterdam; reprinted by permission. Photograph of concrete piers by Avk Arslanian for *Fortune*; reprinted by permission.

ACKNOWLEDGMENTS

The present book is an outcome of a series of seminars on macro-engineering conducted at the Massachusetts Institute of Technology from 1970 on, and sponsored successively by the Urban Systems Laboratory, the Program for Social Applications of Technology, the Department of Mechanical Engineering, and the Sloan School of Management. While the views set forth herein are entirely the responsibility of the author, many of the insights reflected in the chapters that follow owe much to the collaboration of faculty and students. In this connection, I would like to mention with particular appreciation intellectual debts owed to Professors Gordon S. Brown, John F. Collins, Jay W. Forrester, Mel Horwitch, Charles Miller, Thomas B. Sheridan, David G. Wilson, and the late Carroll L. Wilson. Former students who have made impressive contributions to macro-engineering studies include Beverly Bugos, Stephen C. Ehrmann, Andrew C. Lemer, Mats G. Lindquist, C. Lawrence Meador, and Michael L. Telson.

Dr. Jerome B. Wiesner, former president of M.I.T. and former science adviser to the President of the United States, provided vital insights. And no one working in a new interdisciplinary field at M.I.T. can fail to be appreciative of the encouragement of the institute's president, Dr. Paul L. Gray.

For the original suggestion that led to this book, I am sincerely obliged to Owen Davies. I wish to salute also, and with every expression of the highest esteem, the editor who has seen this volume through the trauma of design, development, and final realization: Without Maria Guarnaschelli's patience, judgment, and persistence, this would have been but one more project, a "mini" one at that, without the "unacademic" anecdotes that add color and conviction to general ideas, and very likely without the opportunity of standing, in print and illustrated, before the bar of public scrutiny at a critical moment in history. And it was through Maria Guarnaschelli that I met my "coach" and mentor, John Stuart Cox, the veteran and professional wordsmith who not only prepared a first draft on the basis of my miscellaneous written ramblings extending back over a period of fifteen years, but collaborated unselfishly in the selection of illustrations and in the myriad details that preceded delivery of the manuscript to the printing press.

That the field of macro-engineering was taken "under the wing" of the American Association for the Advancement of Science was surely due to the initiative of Dr. Ernst Weber, former president of the Polytechnic Institute of New York, and Dr. A. George Schillinger, an outstanding Polytechnic faculty member who is also Distinguished Visiting Professor at the School of Organization and Management at Yale University. Articles on this new interdisciplinary field of study have appeared from time to time in *Technology in Society*, a quarterly journal edited with much flair and sophistication by Dr. George Bugliarello, the youthful and dynamic president of the Polytechnic Institute of New York, and by Dr. Schillinger. Having had the honor of serving for a term as adjunct professor of macro-engineering at Polytechnic, I can attest the quality of the interest at this fine institution in the complex problem of preparing the engineer-managers of the future.

To the quarterly journal *Futures*, published in Guildford, England, I wish to acknowledge the publication in Volume 1, Number 2, dated December 1968, of the article entitled "Macro-Engineering: a Capability in Search of a Methodology," one of the earlier systematic discussions of the issues elaborated in this volume. To Dr. Frederick Praeger, the wide-ranging publisher of the Westview Press, and to Dr. Kathryn Wolff of the Publications Office of the American Association for the Advancement of Science, I offer sincere thanks for sponsorship and vital assistance in arranging the publication of symposia held in 1978 and 1979, thus laying the basis for subsequent publication of work in the field. The Westview Press has graciously permitted use of some of my opinions and remarks included in introductions to the three volumes that they have published, which are listed on the page of this book entitled "Selected Readings."

To Earl Nelson, a graduate student in classical studies at the University of North Carolina, I am indebted for detailed information about the situation in North Africa when the 3rd Augusta Legion waged and won its greatest campaign—against the Sahara Desert! Professor Manabu Nakagawa of Hitotsubashi University, Tokyo, has been a source of constant inspiration—and information. As founder of the Macro-Engineering Association of Japan and of a whole congeries of organizations formed to develop this new field of inquiry, he has been a loyal and ingenious colleague and friend. I wish to record also the services to the field of Professor Uwe Kitzinger, C.B.E., director of the Oxford Centre for Management Studies, and chairman and founder of the Major Projects Association in the United Kingdom. And to Professor Jack Ives, Dr. John Cool, and my other colleagues in the International Mountain Society, I am grateful for the deepening awareness that if fragile ecosystems are to survive, we must indeed do our engineering and interdisciplinary homework, and bring the full resources of modern technology to bear, with sensitivity and with courage, lest environmentalism become a shibboleth rather than a common cause around which all people of goodwill can rally.

During the writing of this book, I have been considerably helped by the encouragement of my wife and three sons, who have had to put up with a "closed door" during the long weeks of preparation of the manuscript. For the typing, the usual polite word of thanks will have to be foregone: I typed the pages myself, with the moral support, however, of our cat, Boadicea, who made herself quite comfortable in the box of typing paper on my desk.

CONTENTS

Infrastructure, Public Works, and an Intersectoral "Moral Equivalent of War"

WHEN, IN 1973, THE LATE E. F. SCHUMACHER CHOSE THE TI-tle *Small Is Beautiful*[1] for an extended essay on the dilemmas of scale, it was perhaps inevitable that the public would be more impressed by the phrase emblazoned on the cover than by the thoughtful and balanced analysis appearing inside. Dr. Schumacher had been economics adviser to the Coal Board, probably the largest single industrial organization in the United Kingdom, between 1950 and 1970; he had observed firsthand the shortcomings of bigness. His argument for small and "inter-mediate" technology struck a responsive note; but he never claimed that large-scale engineering is always and inevitably "in-appropriate." "It depends," he wisely pointed out, "on what you are trying to do."

I met Dr. Schumacher, a rumpled German-born former Rhodes Scholar who had taught economics at Columbia Univer-sity, at a hurried lunch in the downtown Manhattan headquar-ters of America's largest investment banking and brokerage house: Merrill Lynch, Pierce, Fenner, and Smith. Our host was Wallace O. Sellers, the innovative executive who then headed the firm's Municipal Bond Department. Mr. Sellers mentioned that today's successful big businesses had started as small businesses, but that the companies that remained small were not necessarily more efficient or even more socially useful. Dr. Schumacher smilingly agreed: Big, too, could be "beautiful."

Today, ten years after that luncheon conversation, the United States faces an immense task of rebuilding its economy. This book argues that, to accomplish the task in the most satisfactory manner, we shall have to resort to large-scale projects and programs, and that in doing so we can preserve and enhance individual liberty, the public health, and the amenities of social and environmental well-being. It is time to "go *macro*," not only at home but abroad as well. And we must act with adequate knowledge of the history—and the risks—of large-scale engineering as well as a vision of what supertechnology can accomplish for the United States and its trading partners. If the Republican party has often appeared as a spokesman for "Big Business," the Democratic party has been dubbed a defender of "Big Government." Modern science, meanwhile, has added the armory of advanced technology—the new capabilities of computer science, telecommunications, ballistics, and so on—to humankind's ancient ability to organize masses of people for large-scale work; if we are to benefit from the consequent increase in the scale, range, and impact of "Big Technology," there will have to be a transformation in our behavior, our institutions, and—not least—in our vocabulary. We shall have to abandon the sterile political rhetoric of "public sector" *versus* "private sector," and learn instead the neglected arts of intersectoral harmony and collaboration.

To those who remain suspicious of all attempts to apply large-scale solutions to endlessly repeated local or private problems, it is worth glancing back at the record of the Civilian Conservation Corps. Established by an executive order of President Franklin Delano Roosevelt in the depths of the Great Depression, the CCC offered millions of young men gainful employment in thousands of camps throughout the nation's countryside. Each camp dealt with specific local problems identified by the Forestry Service, the Soil Conservation Service, or county or state agencies. It has been said that half the trees planted since the founding of the Republic were planted by enrollees of the Civilian Conservation Corps. Obviously, the CCC was using "low" or "intermediate" technology. But we must not become the victims of terminology: "High tech" cannot be sustained in a country that cares neither for its youth nor for its natural patrimony.

For more than twelve years, I have served as chairman of the Steering committee of the System Dynamics Group at the Massachusetts Institute of Technology. The director of research and the leader of the studies and the policy of this remarkable team is Dr. Jay W. Forrester, inventor of the memory core of the digital computer. It has been a "high tech" operation from the outset, concerned with the software of analysis and simulation, so that computer models may give us a better understanding of how our society really behaves, and which remedies are least likely to be counterproductive. Forrester was raised on a cattle ranch in Nebraska. He likes to tell of his early life, and of the debt he owes to stern parents who expected hard work and straight thinking. Nor do I wish to forget my own youthful experiences, which included a full year as a hired hand on Arthur Folsom's backhill dairy farm in Tunbridge, Vermont, and a term as a volunteer enrollee in the Civilian Conservation Corps.

American farming may not seem the most logical introduction to a volume whose theme is macro-engineering. But the farmer is misunderstood if his methods and thinking are seen only as opposites of the engineering mentality. Correctly viewed, farming is nothing other than the application of science and "know-how" to the land for the purpose of raising crops; the American farmer is truly an engineer—versatile, efficient, innovative, tenacious. And in the fostering of American agriculture, the federal government has been a benevolent partner, not least through the Morrill Act which, in 1862, in the midst of the Civil War, provided for Land Grant colleges to improve the practice of "agriculture and the mechanic arts."

Rhode Island's Senator Claiborne Pell, a century later, followed the precedent set by Vermont's Senator Justin Morrill by persuading the Congress to establish "Sea Grant Colleges" or to confer this status upon existing institutions in return for knowledgeable attention to the arts of naval architecture and marine engineering. It is to be expected that in due course a proposal will arise for "Space Grant Colleges," so that the enormous momentum in space science resulting from the successful Apollo Program inaugurated by President John F. Kennedy is not dissipated in a confusion of policy and rhetoric.

We remain the world's leading industrial power, but friends and opponents alike are puzzled by our lack of direction. With former preeminence gone or challenged in steel, textiles, automobiles, railways, shipbuilding, and other traditional areas, there has been an effort to "paper over" evident failures of foresight and management by pointing to the promising "new wave" industries: computers, avionics, telecommunications, and genetic engineering, among others. But is a "post-industrial society" such a desirable goal? Will the United States feel secure when, in addition to our substantial present dependence on imports of minerals, we may have to rely on foreign sources of supply for industrial equipment as well? It would be closer to the mark to accept the new slogan "reindustrialization." Advanced technology will not be a self-replicating phenomenon if it cannot be applied to more humble tasks. What is the sense of being a leader in computer controls if we do not apply this knowledge to machine tools, transport, and communications?

In truth, all our industries and services ought to be reequipped so that they can benefit from advances in technology. Ever since the first prehistoric man shaped a stick or a horn for digging, improvements of tools have tended in the direction of "automation." A larger percentage of the population will evidently be concerned with the new gadgetry of "high tech" as industry moves in the direction of the automated factory and the automated office. Our educational system (a "system" by courtesy only) does not offer a general foundation for the understanding of the sciences and the letters. Despite numerous and honorable exceptions, the nation's public schools do not provide the training, in the elementary and high school grades, that a modern nation requires if it is to maintain, renew, and improve its physical infrastructure. Even among well-endowed colleges and universities, there remains the bias against science and engineering best summed up in the old British adage, "experts on tap, not on top." The decline of British industry should be ample evidence that a modern industrial plant cannot safely be entrusted to the kind of manager who is completely ignorant of what the plant makes or how it is made.

Wealth is a result of engineering; it does not spring full-born like Pegasus from the Medusa's blood, out of a "science" of economics. More of the engineering mentality must now enter into the old "liberal" professions, so that discussions of public policy—and of private investment—may be reality-oriented. There has been much discussion in recent months of the deterioration of America's infrastructure, that is, of the basic services of water supply, roadways, communication lines, and energy transmission, without which no extended community can continue to exist. Renewal and upkeep of the country's infrastructure require steadiness in policy and investment. When a portion of New York's West Side Highway collapsed through over-age and under-maintenance, it became obvious that public policy had lost touch with reality. If the public safety can be neglected to the point where structures disintegrate under normal loads and use, then the public has a right to expect some new ideas and some more reliable principles from persons aspiring to leadership.

Where is the money to come from? In times of military emergency, nations appear to be capable of raising unheard-of sums in the interest of survival—and "glory." The repair and improvement of public facilities must be accorded an honorable priority, or the public will have to pay a far higher price at a later date. But infrastructure engineering must also occupy the best minds in the country: Thanks to advances in science and engineering, we can often do better than the mere maintenance of an obsolete system. It is the obligation of government—and always has been—to think in long-range terms and to provide the underlying conditions for "the public safety and convenience." Now, thanks to a cascade of progress in applied technology, the rebuilding of infrastructure can be dramatic, innovative, and of the highest public utility.

One of the great strengths of a free society is the ease and openness of communications across geographical, professional, and hierarchical lines. Although each of us necessarily lives and works in a setting somewhat preordained by law and custom, the different sectors of our society *can* cooperate and even devise new instrumentalities whenever a novel public need is perceived and articulated, and when enough people are convinced that a stated objective is worth attaining. At twenty-three years of age, I was persuaded by a group of friends to see President Roosevelt[2] and ask him to set up a "new model" camp for the Civilian Conservation Corps, with the idea of establishing a *permanent* service that in good times and bad, would allow all our young people, rich and poor, urban and rural, to have a half-year or year of outdoor work and training in the conservation and development of natural resources. The year was 1940. Mr. Roosevelt not only took a great personal interest in Camp William James; he devoted the necessary time to make sure that his wishes were in fact carried out. Only the lengthening shadows cast by World War II led to the end of this seminal experiment—and to the gradual demise of the entire Civilian Conservation Corps as a whole generation joined the armed forces.

It is typical of American folkways that now, two generations after the Civilian Conservation Corps was inaugurated by President Roosevelt, our Congress is concerned with its reestablishment. To be sure, times have changed. For one thing, a CCC would almost certainly be open to young women as well as to young men. And we have the experience of the California Conservation Corps, the first state-sponsored body of this nature, which has been in operation for several years, thanks to the initiative of the American historian, Page Smith, who was the first general manager of Camp William James. But will a reborn Civilian Conservation Corps be seen in narrow terms as a mere receptacle for the unemployed? Will applicants be required to pass a humiliating "means test" as a precondition to acceptance in the Conservation Corps?

The administration and the Congress could usefully consult Professor Smith and others who lived through the debates of the early 1940's as to the best formula for recruiting corps members. Camp William James had been established initially, in Norwich, Vermont, as a private embodiment of the suggestion that had been made by the philosopher William James in his famous 1910 essay, "The Moral Equivalent of War." Two of the three sons of the philosopher attended the opening ceremony, and volunteer CCC enrollees joined male college students to constitute, at the camp, a veritable cross-section of American society. If conservation is indeed in the national interest, why should admission to a Conservation Corps be less honorable than service in the United States Marine Corps—or in a local fire or police department? And, this time around, should there not be access by enrollees to technical training and eventual supervisory positions?

President Roosevelt was a master of improvisation. Two weeks after he promulgated the initial order, the army was setting up the first camp, and specialists from the Departments of Agriculture and the Interior were planning the program of outdoor work. But with years of experience available, it is not excusable, in 1983 and—yes—in the dread year 1984 so publicized by George Orwell—to repeat errors that were understandable when precedents were lacking and the economic crisis was far more serious than today's. That the Civilian Conservation Corps met such evident needs and received such unanimous public acclaim made it difficult to legislate improvements. But throughout its history, the early CCC operated without any civilian equivalent of the Code of Military Justice of the United States Army. That more injustices did not occur was due to the humanity and common sense of all concerned. but an organization with the twin objectives of environmental enhancement and the education and sustenance of our youth should not be put together with such haste that major issues are not even considered, let alone resolved. A new Conservation Corps ought to be a permanent service (like the U.S. Forest Service or the Soil Conservation Service); admission should be open to all young Americans; and there should be a code of conduct governing the relations of Conservation Corps members and their supervisors, with adequate provisions for on-the-job training and for promotion to supervisory and technical positions on the basis of merit.

It is one thing to legislate a new service for youth and conservation. It is quite another thing to overhaul a congeries of educational institutions that are short of the mark and that represent a waste of resources and a brake on the nation's future. In Massachusetts, there is strong backing for a new forty-million-dollar education and research center for microelectronics, to be jointly funded by the state and by private industry. Such centers of excellence can act as magnets to attract talented young people, dedicated teachers, and the necessary wherewithal. If many public schools are not up to par, the only remedy is an aroused and insistent public opinion. In the "information society" of the future, a major national resource must continue to be our schools and colleges. If we are indeed a community, then all elements in our society must work together to make public and private schools more worthy of the confidence reposed in them. And even wealthy and reputed institutions of higher learning must make some difficult adjustments: The effective management of technology will require a new kind of engineer-manager trained not only in technology, but also in the legal and administrative traditions of our country.

In June of 1980, the American Society for Engineering Education held a memorable session devoted to "Education for Macro-Engineering." Under the chairmanship of Dr. George Bugliarello, the dynamic president of the Polytechnic Institute of New York, there was a lively discussion of the need for people with the experience and maturity to handle jobs whose sheer scope could not have been dreamed of a generation ago. American designers and managers have now been given responsibility—often in developing countries—for vast new cities, agro-industrial complexes, and infrastructure developments costing many billions of dollars. Cordell W. Hull, the engineer-lawyer-banker who is vice-president and chief financial officer of the Bechtel Group, described the complexity of organizing the finance and the contractual undertakings for the vast projects now under his aegis. Typically, both government agencies and private banks and industries are involved in "macrofinance." The entrepreneur of such a multinational enterprise must have resilience, stamina, the ability to make decisions under conditions of fatigue and pressure, and the patience of Job.

I remember, several years ago, receiving a telephone call from a former student of the Macro-Engineering Seminar at M.I.T. Andrew C. Lemer had been quiet and diffident, and it was a moment before I could visualize the face at the other end of the line. After receiving a doctorate in civil engineering, Andrew had gone to work with a consulting firm near Washington, D.C. He and a small group of young engineers were encouraged by the firm to enter a competition for the design of Nigeria's new capital. Dr. Lemer had called me because, quite unexpectedly, his team had won the international design contest, in which more than three hundred firms from all over the world had participated. And the new capital, Abuja, is now under construction; it is probably the largest single civil engineering project in the whole of Africa. Designed to relieve pressure on the over-crowded port city of Lagos, and deliberately located in the center of the country, in a tribally neutral area, Abuja is expected to contribute to the resolution of long-standing logistical, cultural, and political conundrums.

It is the developing countries—the "Third World" if you will—where macro-engineering projects have been most conspicuous and most welcome. During the decade of the 1970's, as Dr. Kathleen Murphy and her associates demonstrated in a landmark study for McKinsey & Company, investment in large-scale projects skyrocketed. As Dr. Murphy has explained:

> Viewed within the context of a single developing country, macroprojects tower above all other enterprises by virtue of the investment they represent for the country and the impact that their presence has upon the local economy. Whether a $100 million mine in West Africa or a $5 billion liquid natural gas processing plant in the Middle East, the projects challenge the capabilities and strain the resources of the developing nations . . . Projects planned or underway had increased more than thirtyfold during the decade, ranged in size from $100 million to over $1 billion, and represented a total investment of more than $1,000 billion.

By 1981, the prevalence of the ultralarge, multinational technical project had become so evident that special associations were formed to study the phenomenon. In the United Kingdom, a Major Projects Association was put together on the initiative of Uwe Kitzinger, C.B.E., the dapper and brilliant director of the Oxford Centre for Management Studies. With the enthusiastic aid of Allen Sykes and Derek Fraser, both trained by Willis Faber & Dumas, a leading firm in Lloyds of London, an elite list of industrial and commercial companies, together with some senior government agencies, joined in providing the association with a "war chest" and a series of highly focused seminars. I was privileged to address the group's organization meeting in Oxford and, two years afterward, to sit in on a businesslike discussion of the management and finance of new oil fields in the North Sea.

Meanwhile, Professor Manabu Nakagawa, who had attended the first Macro-Engineering Symposium held by the American Association for the Advancement of Science (in 1978, in Washington, D.C.) formed the Macro-Engineering Association of Japan as well as a Major Projects Research Society and a Japan Institute for Macro-Engineering. When, in 1981, Professor Kitzinger and I, together with C. Lawrence Meador (my fellow coordinator of M.I.T.'s Macro-Engineering Research Group) made a macro-engineering lecture tour of Japan, we noted with surprise that the top leadership of Japanese industry and government were represented at our numerous assemblies and seminars. Patently, Japan's success since World War II has been in the field of what we might call "microengineering," that is, in the precision industries of watchmaking, television, computer components, and in the older industries of shipbuilding, steelmaking, and automobile manufacture. What does this new interest in macro-engineering portend? Will the completion of the great undersea tunnel between Honshu and Hokkaido serve as a precedent for macroventures beyond the home islands?

My own view is that Japan, having now accumulated capital and confidence, is ready to become an equal investment partner with the United States and Europe in very major projects of common interest. I had concrete evidence of this trend in a private interview accorded me in Tokyo by the venerable Shigeo Nagano, honorary chairman of Nippon Steel Corporation and the effective head of the Japanese Chamber of Commerce. Mr. Nagano would like to join with the United States and other legitimately interested countries in designing and building a second trans-isthmian Canal in or near Panama. Having myself led a private-enterprise delegation to Panama to discuss this very question a generation earlier, I was delighted to know that the United States could count on the entire "establishment" of Japan as a partner in an enterprise of such historic importance to the United States Navy and to our own trade and commerce. There are fascinating technical and geographical options to explore in this matter; what is encouraging is that the State Department,

now under a Secretary of State with "hands-on" experience in large-scale projects (he was, after all, president of the Bechtel Corporation before migrating to "Foggy Bottom"), has set up a joint study group and is pursuing this potential project with sympathetic understanding.

Macro-engineering presents the United States with major opportunities in foreign as well as domestic policy. We are entering a new age of technological diplomacy where joint ventures will include not only large corporations from a number of countries; there are a few areas that remain so sensitive and vital that governments themselves will wish to call the tune, although private enterprise, under an enlightened policy, may play an increasing role. Space industrialization is one such area. And the solar-power satellite may offer a tempting case for decision.

The idea of capturing power from the sun on orbiting reflectors and then beaming the power to earth via microwave was first conceived and put into patentable form by Dr. Peter Glaser of Arthur D. Little, Inc., a century-old "think tank" in Cambridge, Massachusetts. Peter Glaser was the first guest lecturer in one of my early macro-engineering seminars at M.I.T., and I have admired the patience and persistence with which he has developed and promoted his singular invention.

In 1981, the United States National Academy of Sciences sponsored a review of the proposal and concluded that, for the present, it was too costly a scheme to justify a continuing government program of research and development.[3] If indeed this remains the policy of the government, then the door would appear to be wide open for *internationalizing* the preparatory work. Dr. Makoto Nagatomo, in a persuasive paper entitled "Japanese Motivation to Develop Solar Power Satellites," reviewed the special reasons that have led to the active interest of the Institute of Space and Astronautical Science in Tokyo: Japan is overwhelmingly dependent on imported oil and coal for its energy; in the long run, a steady supply "up there" would be a good insurance policy for Japan. And with the United States having the capability to contribute decisively to the planning and construction of such a system, it appears that a modern diplomacy would explore in detail the possibility of a firm, international long-term

agreement to develop and test a prototype of an orbital or lunar-based solar-power facility.

A small but useful step forward was taken in Vienna, in the summer of 1982, when the United Nations held a well-attended conference, "UNISPACE," on the subject of space industrialization. Professor Kitzinger, Professor Nakagawa, and I joined with Dr. Glaser as sponsors of a special session, under the Non-Governmental Organizations rubric, devoted to the solar-power satellite. The discussions aroused interest among developing nations as well as among the delegations of the industrialized powers, and Rashmi Mayur, the ebullient representative of India, insisted that his country would wish to participate fully in the eventual development of a power source that would free the Indian subcontinent from its inordinate dependence on Middle East oil.

How Metternich must have turned in his grave! What a ragged lot we would have seemed to him: scientists, professors, bureaucrats from the world's space agencies, rushing off between sessions to peer at technical exhibits garishly displayed in tents or hallways preempted by the principal space-exploring nations. But diplomacy itself is changing so rapidly that even its practitioners must be taken aback: Along with the old-fashioned disputes about borders and fishing rights, there is a whole new catalogue of subjects for foreign secretaries and ambassadors—the allocation of telecommunication frequencies, protocols for joint finance of extraterrestrial enterprises, and covenants on liability for accidental crashes of space orbiters that unexpectedly come home to roost.

In this new context, it is hardly surprising that the National Science Foundation, wishing to explore the problem of "Federal Policy and Macro-Engineering for Energy," has turned to Dr. Glaser's team for analysis and guidance. Assisted by Dr. P. K. Chapman, himself a former astronaut, and a topflight crew of young planners and researchers, the forthcoming report by the Arthur D. Little group should provide policy guidance for a basic turning point in government attitude and emphasis. The solar-power satellite symbolizes the new era of macro-engineering possibilities; but it remains only one of literally hundreds of interesting proposals for applying technical knowledge on a very

large scale to the solution of perceived human problems. Faced with such a plethora of alternatives, do we have the people, the procedures, and the policies to make appropriate decisions?

Since the dawn of history, bureaucrats have avoided making unpleasant decisions by deferring choices through the artifact of "further study." Unfortunately, our own administrative habits have become so fixated on the mysterious activity called "research," that we now have few hesitations in studying the same problem over and over again, as a substitute for clear thinking and responsible action. Although "R & D"—that is, Research and Development—has become a passport to modernity, it is necessary to point out that "R" can be the enemy of "D": If America is to remain a dynamic world leader, we shall have to go beyond mountainous reports, however expert and wise, and assume the risks of action. President Kennedy might have been forgiven if he had decided that the risks of going to the moon were too great—and besides, the benefits and the mission itself could only take place long after his own presidency. But he opted for a decision, and the American people followed his lead.

The space program of the United States must be viewed in the context of large-scale engineering and must be treated as part of normal life, not as an exceptional occasion for mere entertainment and adventure. Dr. Stewart Nozette of the California Space Institute has outlined a series of steps that the United States government could now take, in order to set in motion a space development program that would have a good chance of earning its own way. A first effort, based on the University of Arizona's NASA-supported program for a more powerful Spacewatch Camera, will endeavor to identify a number of asteroids with commercially useful minerals; then, in ten years or so, we can begin mining the asteroid belt—and perhaps the moon—to provide the funds without which the American public may simply tire of huge expenditures that bring little identifiable return except information absorbed by the minority of scientists in the population. Stewart Nozette represents the coming breed of engineer-manager: aware of public opinion, competent in the minutiae of technology and science, and able to navigate in the arcane spheres of budgets and graphs. His concept of a Southwest Institute for Large-Scale Engineering and Space Development has already attracted more than regional attention. Here is another case where the universities, together with private industry and finance, can attract government participation in an endeavor that promises long-term benefits for the whole nation.

America has a tradition of great endeavors: The West was, after all, opened to settlement and development first by the Erie Canal, on which De Witt Clinton staked his political future in the 1820's, and later by the Union Pacific Railroad. One year after the War of Independence, General George Washington made the difficult journey up the Hudson River and across northern New York to Schenectady, Fort Schuyler, and Oneida Lake. Asked about a canal from the Hudson River to Lake Erie, Thomas Jefferson had replied, "Little short of madness." But De Witt Clinton, the leader of the Democratic party who had lost the presidency to James Madison, succeeded in convincing the New York legislature that it should raise six million dollars to build the canal. And in the period 1817–1825, "Clinton's ditch"—364 miles long, with 83 locks—was completed and open to traffic. It made so much money for the state that, in 1883, tolls were eliminated. And just before World War I, in an "engineering operation greater than the building of the Panama Canal,"[4] the channel was deepened to twelve feet, and locks were lengthened to accommodate vessels three hundred feet long.

The continent was finally spanned, not by a canal (as Calhoun had advocated—joining the Missouri and Columbia Rivers), but by a railway. Despite his preoccupation with a series of defeats of the Union Armies, Abraham Lincoln supported and signed the Pacific Railway Act on July 2, 1862; on May 10, 1869, the Golden Spike was driven home at Promontory Point, Utah, thus providing uninterrupted rail service from coast to coast. The full import of this event was highlighted on the back cover of Robert West Howard's *The Great Iron Trail: The Story of the First Transcontinental Railroad*[5]:

> The perilous sailing trip around Cape Horn took from four to six months; the plague-ridden shortcut across the Panama Isthmus required five weeks; on the trails crossing the 2,000 miles of "The Great American Desert," stagecoaches and

prairie schooners faced a deadly gamut of Indian attacks, starvation, fevers and blizzards.

In the field of foreign affairs, the United States showed that it appreciated the relevance of large engineering works when, under the impulsion of President Theodore Roosevelt, a Republic of Panama was hastily recognized after Colombia, from which the new republic was carved, had proved too reluctant in granting a concession for the Panama Canal. In a more cooperative vein, the United States joined with Canada to design and construct the great St. Lawrence Seaway and Power Project.[6] The Grand Coulee Dam, the Tennessee Valley Authority (TVA) hydroelectric schemes, and the Interstate Highway System are all symptomatic of the American taste for large-scale, efficient engineering projects. Curiously, after World War II, when our country stood in a preeminent position of power and wealth, the nation's self-confidence went through a period of wavering and decline. Prosperity had not erased urban blight or inequalities; the sixties were a tumultuous time, with inner-city riots and student unrest, with President Johnson's "Great Society" plowed under by the controversies surrounding U.S. intervention in Vietnam. With a bewilderment that spread throughout industry and academia as well, and with adverse impacts from a few major projects (such as St. Louis public housing) drawing media attention, the public welcomed Mr. Schumacher's plea for small and intermediate technology.

Senator Claiborne Pell of Rhode Island had introduced the first congressional resolution, in 1962, calling for studies of the potential of high-speed railway transportation; this led to the High-Speed Ground Transportation Act of 1965. I remember feeling elated when the Secretary of Transportation invited me to serve, with Donald Douglas and one or two others, on an Advisory Committee for High-Speed Ground Transportation; mysteriously, the committee never met. In 1975, again on Senator Pell's initiative, a Northeast Corridor Authorization Act was passed—and signed into law by President Ford. The act provided $1.7 billion for improvements to the Boston-New York-Washington, D.C., service. Additional funds were committed in

1980, but anyone who has traveled on the railways of Europe or Japan can testify that the end result has been so picayune that, to this very day, passenger railway service in the United States constitutes a national disgrace.

As early as the mid-1960's, Richard Rice, a professor at Princeton University and later at Pittsburgh's Carnegie-Mellon University, had demonstrated to the hilt the advantages of high-speed rail service. This was the period when William Miller (later Secretary of the Treasury in the administration of President Jimmy Carter) had joined with General Doriot, Judge Byron K. Elliott (then chairman of the John Hancock Mutual Life Insurance Company) and others to form a broadly backed Geo-Transport Foundation of New England, Inc., to provide inputs from the private sector. Senator Pell and several other proponents of American technological leadership gave unstinted support to this effort, in the launching of which I played a small role; but the Department of Transportation in Washington was never able to set its mind to the development of a modernization plan that would enlist the latent energies of both the private and the public sector.

While the American effort at rail improvement slowed to a halt, the French were laying the groundwork for their "TGV" trains (*Trains de Grande Vitesse*—trains of great speed), now in service between Paris and Lyon at speeds in excess of 200 mph; and the Japanese not only built the famous Shinkansen Line but went beyond pioneering American research to construct a full-scale test track of electromagnetically levitated trains that have already reached test-run speeds in excess of 300 mph. The British, abandoning the Hovertrain, which had chalked up a splendid record at its Cambridge, England, test tract under the fine technical leadership of Tom Fellows, continued nonetheless with a well-funded program for an Advanced Passenger Train. With an energetic program of testing and development sponsored by Sir Peter Parker, chairman of the British Railways Board, the United Kingdom seems poised to join in the onward march of rail transport as soon as the two systems—British and Continental—are suitably linked by a channel tunnel (or bridge and tunnel?). Birmingham is to have a short MAGLEV next spring.

What will puzzle future historians is the nonchalance with

which Americans threw away what could have been a clear advantage: Dr. Henry Kolm at M.I.T.'s Francis Bitter National Magnet Laboratory had succeeded in producing a miniaturized electromagnetically levitated train that functioned perfectly on a test track several hundred feet long. This achievement, paid for by a consortium including the U.S. Department of Transportation, Avco Corp., and the Raytheon Company, exhibited at M.I.T., was not followed up by support for a full-scale prototype. The prototype was instead built by Dr. Yoshihiro Kyotani, director of the Technical Development Department of the Japanese National Railways. Having lost the opportunity to establish a new worldwide industry based upon magnetic levitation, there remains an opportunity for the United States to join with the Japanese in carrying their development one crucial step further. During a lunch that Professor Nakagawa kindly arranged in my honor at a downtown businessmen's club in Tokyo, I asked Dr. Kyotani whether he would like to see his experimental train tested in a tunnel from which air had been evacuated; he smiled his warm agreement to this proposition. Based on the calculations of Dr. Robert Salter, inventor of the "Planetran" concept,[7] a train levitated in this manner could proceed at supersonic speed through an evacuated tube. It is a less bold step today than was Governor Clinton's obstinate advocacy of an Erie Canal in the early days of the Republic, at a time, in fact, that preceded the organization by Stephen van Rensselaer of the first American institution—the Rensselaer Polytechnic Institute—qualified to grant a degree in civil engineering.

Of course, a supersonic subway will cost many billions of dollars, perhaps more than a hundred billion dollars if the project is conceived as a transcontinental link. But is it not imperative that a working prototype be constructed, and that the "teething problems" be ironed out while the necessary chores of traffic studies, environmental impact studies, and cost estimates are carried forward? The chief expense, of course, will be the boring of the tunnels through "competent rock," about fifteen hundred feet below ground level. Here again, it is time to support and coordinate an action-oriented research program: The Bechtel-sponsored studies of automated tunneling commissioned at the Carnegie-Mellon University, and the recent experiments in this direction carried out by private companies in Germany and Japan, need support and enhancement. What a boon to the environmental movement if it should prove to be feasible to replace aircraft—and a great deal of surface transport—with silent vehicles zooming underground without noise or air pollution. It may well turn out that the airplane is obsolete because it is too slow, and that its future will be mainly as an auxiliary carrier for local and intraregional transport!

The environmental movement is about to be faced with a grave challenge: Can it, in fact, become involved in the study and selection of new technologies that offer palpable advantages to human health and to environmental sanity; or will the leaders of environmental organizations persist in an exclusive preoccupation with obsolete—but continuing—engineering systems that threaten the environment and need replacement? I have never understood why passionate environmentalists gather at myriad conventions in gas-guzzling, polluting cars and buses: A firm contract to purchase fifty thousand electric cars would no doubt interest the most recalcitrant denizens of Detroit's decision-making complex! Environmentalists, together with sympathetic government agencies and university and research organizations, could constitute themselves as a commercially meaningful market; electric cars, even before the advent of the "miracle batteries" of which so much is expected, can offer safe and reasonable commuter transportation; electric trucks have been a commonplace in England ever since World War I. If well-understood available technologies are not used by groups that are publicly committed to their principles, how can we hope for rational action on technologies that have yet to be tested and perfected?

But there is hope. In 1978, Georgetown University's Center for Strategic and International Studies published, through Frederick Praeger's enterprising Westview Press of Boulder, Colorado, an impressive two-volume study entitled *Where We Agree: Report of the National Coal Policy Project*. For an entire year, the center had persuaded industry and environmental representatives to field joint task forces to examine the national policy issues involved in a major switch to coal. Not altogether surprisingly, a broad consensus emerged. Economists must breathe, and environmentalists must eat: There is no biological reason—and no theoretical reason—for the American political framework to be split between engineers and ecologists, between producers and consumers. Eugen Rosenstock-Huessy's 1949 pamphlet *The Multiformity of Man* suggests some theoretical underpinnings for the truism that individuals are greater than their labels, that each person plays many parts, and that our common interests, on grave public issues, must take precedence over our temporary, private situations.

The new wind of mutual comprehension was foreshadowed, I like to think, by the presence and remarks of Russell Peterson as principal speaker at the dinner that concluded the 1980 Macro-Engineering Symposium held in San Francisco in connection with the annual meeting of the American Association for the Advancement of Science. Dr. Peterson had been a chemical engineer with the Dupont Company, served as governor of the state of Delaware (our "first state"), and later administered the Environmental Protection Administration before finally accepting the presidency of the National Audubon Society. He and Dr. George Bugliarello later discussed the urgent need for informal meetings between environmentalists and engineers. In addressing the macro-engineering group gathered by the AAAS in San Francisco, Dr. Peterson was able to speak as an engineer to engineers: If all concerned do their homework, it is likely that we shall come up with the same answers. Some of the engineering systems to which the public objects were launched without a sufficiently thorough study of all the necessary ramifications; but to take an across-the-board stand against technology is to doom environmental concerns to a sterile and self-defeating romanticism.

Writing at a time of incipient recovery from a worldwide recession, is it "in the cards" to expect resources to be made available for projects and programs that dwarf all previous human efforts? Economists and historians may differ on detailed prognostications, but experience has convinced virtually all serious students that social life is subject to cyclical variations. The Soviet economist Kondratieff, who died under Stalin, presented convincing evidence for the existence of economic cycles lasting a half-century or more. Recently, the "Kondratieff long wave" has been confirmed by the painstaking researches of the System Dynamics National Model at M.I.T., and by the parallel investigations of Professor Walter W. Rostow at the University of Texas. Current research undertaken by Beverly Bugos and supported by Wallace O. Sellers, now a director of Merrill Lynch, Pierce, Fenner, and Smith, seems to indicate that macro-engineering investments tend to coincide with peaks in the economic long wave. If this finding should be verified, the world economy may be on the verge—perhaps as early as the 1990's—of a new spurt of investment in huge technical systems. In view of the complexity of such undertakings, ten years is none too short a time for the necessary preliminary studies, prototype tests, and above all the institutional preparation.

One characteristic of very large engineering projects is the long lead-time between conceptualization and realization. Alvarado, a cousin of Cortez, suggested a Panama Canal in the early days of the sixteenth century; it was about four centuries later that the Canal was finally opened to traffic (just before World War I). Jules Verne envisioned a manned mission to the moon—from Florida!—a full century before the Apollo Program. The Chinese began working on the Grand Canal, the longest man-made waterway on the planet, more than two thousand years ago, and today a vigorous program of modernization and expansion is under way.

Clearly, projects of this nature extend beyond the term of office of any individual in government or industry. But the public interest in basic infrastructure is so persistent that, through all the mutations of government, economic system, and preferred lifestyle, certain macroenterprises are rediscussed and relaunched again and again. If, despite widespread recognition that there are, indeed "limits to growth," we are to witness another doubling of the world's population within a century, then the international community must be prepared for a host of major construction projects, if only to take care of the housing, feeding, and education of these additional billions of people.

If such is, in fact, the task ahead, where are the institutions that are training the cadres that will be capable of performing the tasks of planning, analysis, design, construction, finance, and management? We shall certainly need all the existing skills of engineering, business management, public administration, accounting, environmental medicine, law, and so on. But for "top management," the challenges are so huge that no single profession can offer the requisite training. Moreover, the demands of the world's economy are now of such dimensions that heads of government are inevitably drawn into the decisions that will determine the macrosystems of the future. The day may not be far distant when leading universities will be called upon to draw up curricula for short courses in macro-engineering, for the benefit of heads of government.

We have already paid quite a price for political ignorance of this new feature in the arena of world affairs. The Soviet proposal of a gas pipeline to Western Europe caught American diplomacy off-base: There had not been, within the NATO alliance, a sufficient discussion of the energy needs of Western Europe during the remainder of the twentieth century. Although the North Sea is widely believed to hold gas reserves that would be more than sufficient for a decade or more ahead, coordinated inducements had not been offered to the Norwegians—or to the British—to assure the French, the West Germans, and our other NATO partners that their needs would be met. Nor had the option of a gas pipeline from Algeria been adequately explored. When Russia proposed using Siberian gas reserves to fill the gap, the U.S. government reacted angrily and hastily; fortunately, George Shultz had just joined the Cabinet, and a discreet withdrawal was made from what appeared, to our allies, as an unjustified position. We had not, alas, prepared a viable alternative to the Russian offer.

In 1933, the Fletcher School of Law and Diplomacy was established by a grant of Austin Barkley Fletcher, a prominent New York lawyer who had been chairman of the Board of Trustees of Tufts University. Harvard University was co-administrator during the opening year, and Harvard Law School professors participated in the program of instruction. Even today, there are cross-registration and other cooperative arrangements between the two schools. Generations of students have been better trained as diplomats because of this conscious effort to include international law—and the jurisprudence of individual states—as an integrated element of their training. Professor Leonard Unger, a distinguished former American Ambassador in the Far East, invited me to give a lecture on the channel tunnel project before his Fletcher School class, in which there were students from nearly all continents. My own experience forced me to take these young people very seriously. After all, I had studied law once with a relaxed young man who happens to have been foreign minister of Panama (before his recent promotion!). And I could not help wondering whether the time is now approaching for a further institutional invention: a School of Engineering and Diplomacy. If the very people who frame international agreements (and the business of diplomacy *is* agreement: Disagreement rapidly becomes the province of another, more copiously budgeted branch of government), then is it not imperative that diplomats be *professionally* equipped with the knowledge of what technology can accomplish on an international scale?

To enter the new era of macro-engineering, we shall have to train our leaders—and ourselves as individuals and as citizens—to take a "longer view." In no field is this readjustment more necessary than in the field of business. Business managers, following the prescriptions of their training, presided over the decline of America's major industries. By failing to reequip to meet the competition of less tradition-bound managements in Japan, West Germany, and other countries whose industries had to be rebuilt *from scratch* after the devastation of the Second World War, the United States abandoned a number of key bastions of the national economy. It would be poor strategy to limit reinvestment to a few "glamour industries" when opportunities are available virtually "across the board." Technology does not stand still. Does any sensible person imagine that it is not in the American interest to put together a major, supermodern industrial complex for the casting of steel? Are Americans less able to cooperate across sectoral lines than the inhabitants of Singapore or Korea?

I look forward to the establishment of a series of multisectoral, interprofessional study groups, each with a mission to outline the terms of a new industrial and social understanding, so that industry by industry we may regain lost ground and give vent, once more, to the genius for improvisation—and for production—that once characterized the Republic. By systematically renewing our infrastructure and our industrial base, we will be better partners for our Mexican and Canadian allies on this continent, and for our business and political associates overseas. And a wealthier America need not be a *polluting* society: Additional income will mean an environmental policy that is *affordable* and that will be less vulnerable, for that reason, to political attack and dismemberment. A sound and prosperous America will be able to support a permanent, professional Civilian Conservation Corps, and not a mere patchwork of temporary agencies put together for crisis situations that could have been averted or alleviated by foresight and devotion.

The word "infrastructure" may appear stern and forbidding, but it can be used, also, to cover a multitude of virtues. Earlier in this century, a United States Forest Service official, Benton Mackaye, decided that Americans should be able to walk, unimpeded and across attractive countryside, from Maine to Georgia. In 1922 his dream became the Appalachian Trail, now fully operational and supported generously by the gifts and labor of individuals, townships, counties, and state and federal agencies. The device of the "cooperative agreement" has been useful in promoting a host of useful public initiatives, and in a resurgent economy, other "internal improvements" are likely to attract sustained public support. In my early years at M.I.T., a group of Harvard Law School students led by John Cummins, now an attorney in Louisville, Kentucky, volunteered for some of the "legwork" and drafting chores essential to a transcontinental bikeway system; as an ardent cyclist, I have always hoped that it would be possible, one day, to cycle in safety from coast to coast. There is no contradiction between Appalachian Trails, transcontinental bikeways—and, let us add, interstate bridle paths—on the one hand, and supersonic subways underground on the other. By uncluttering the surface of the land, we can rededicate the countryside to environmentally benign activities. And the kind of space industrialization envisioned by Stewart Nozette, Peter Vajk (author of *Doomsday Has Been Cancelled*)[8], and Professor Gerard O'Neill of Princeton, will let us look forward to that distant day when the planet Earth may indeed be a park or garden, with unsightly activities banished to the edges of civilized habitation.

Meanwhile, we shall have to move incrementally, one step at a time. My own interest in large-scale engineering goes back to the 1930's, when as a teenager I was exposed to my father's concern, as Mayor Fiorello H. La Guardia's commissioner of Water Supply, Gas, and Electricity, with the infrastructure of New York City. My father signed the papers authorizing what remains, to this day, the world's longest true tunnel: the aqueduct that brings water to Manhattan from the Delaware water gap. That water supply is the most basic commodity of urban life has been reconfirmed by the very recent decision of New York to underwrite the largest investment in the history of the city—the $800 million water tunnel from the Hillview Reservoir in Yonkers to Central Park and across the East River to Queens; this section is but one portion of a four-phase project for a 60-mile aqueduct whose total cost—when completed in the next century—has been estimated at between $3.5 billion and $5 billion.

Tunneling is an ancient art—not only for water supply but, more extensively, in the mining industry. In the mid-sixties, I was traveling with the late Hollister Kent (the adventurous architect who headed the team that was entrusted with deciding upon the final site for Brasilia), in Pennsylvanian Appalachia. Both of us were attracted by a large sign at a small town called Brady's Bend, inviting tourists to drive through more than a hundred miles of tunnels in a single asbestos mine. We paid our dollar—and almost lost our way. I had been so fascinated by Dr. Kent's story of how, as a graduate student at Cornell, he had been sent by his ailing professor to take charge of an apparatus-laden caravan in the wild interior of Brazil, that I quite forgot to follow the vehicle in the dark passageway in front of us. We were only rescued by the lucky arrival of a dump truck whose driver cheerfully convoyed us to the exit!

Later, when the channel tunnel was briefly under construction in 1974 and 1975, I understood why the boring on the British side had been entrusted to a mining company (Conzinc Rio Tinto). The mining industry remains the great repository of skill and experience in the tunneling business, and as various world activities go underground—for both environmental and military reasons—it is clear that we shall have to do more homework on the methods and plans of this very special branch of human ingenuity and endurance.

There is no doubt that emotions play a part in the "decision process" that precedes authorization of large projects. That this should be so bothers some of my academic colleagues; but I think Woodrow Wilson came close to the heart of the matter when he said, in his Dartmouth Address on October 14, 1909, that "the world is governed in every generation by a great House of Commons made up of the passions; and we can only be careful to see to it that the handsome passions are in the majority." Surely the desire to create, to build, to develop, is a very basic and desirable attribute of human nature. Like the beaver, the human being is an engineering animal. The United States, as a nation that has drawn its substance and marrow from all over the earth, may yet find its higher vocation by leading the world to a new plateau of civilized building and development. This would be consistent with the American tradition of neighborhood barn-raising parties and with our twofold respect for self-reliance and unselfish service.

My own apprenticeship in large-scale engineering had much to do with emotion and with accident. In the summer of 1956, I had to proceed across the English Channel because of law business in London. It happens that my family and I ran into one of the worst storms ever recorded even for that windswept body of water. The trip from Boulogne to Folkestone, which ought to have taken only two hours and a half, lasted seven hours; and on the return trip, we experienced an even worse storm: Our car ferry was detoured from Boulogne to Dunkirk, and we were lucky to reach our destination in Normandy, after a nighttime drive of many hours, without harm. Recalling these adventures some weeks later, at Luchow's Restaurant,[9] with my college friend Professor Cyril C. Means, Jr., both of us remembered having read, as children, of the nineteenth-century attempt to build a channel tunnel. We asked a member of the *Life* magazine staff, Joan Reiter, to look up the project's history; and with her meticulous and moving account in hand, it was decided that I would write to the Suez Canal Company, to ask if that "maiden aunt" of investment companies would like to join some young Americans in reviving the channel tunnel project.

As luck would have it, the letter to the Suez Canal Company arrived during the period when President Nasser of Egypt decided to nationalize the Suez Canal. Monsieur Jacques-Georges Picot, the able and energetic chairman of the company, directed his New York representative, the urbane Claude Boillot, to contact my law office. Within a few weeks, Cyril Means and I, quickly joined by my brother Alfred (who was then employed as an executive by the Conzinc Rio Tinto group), and by a French brother-in-law who had won high honors at the Harvard Business School, M.I.T., and the Ecole Polytechnique, had organized a New York corporation, Technical Studies, Inc., to participate with the Suez Canal Company in the formation of a Channel Tunnel Study Group. Our timing seemed excellent, and within a few months the study group was enlarged to include French and British concessionary companies formed in Queen Victoria's time to build the tunnel. These companies included as shareholders the British and French railway systems and a group of the largest banks in England and France. To assure adequate representation to road interests, the International Road Federation (Paris Office) was represented on the group's governing board by its chairman, the respected Baron de Wouters of Belgium. Louis Armand, chairman of the French National Railways, joined the board not in his national capacity alone, but also as the elected secrétaire-général of the International Union of Railways. The Channel Tunnel Study Group was therefore adequately constituted on a *continental* basis, and gave fair representation to both public and private sectors in Europe.

To cap it off, we were fortunate in persuading the two men just retiring as permanent heads of the British Foreign Office and the Quai d'Orsay to serve as joint chairmen of the group. Ambassador René Massigli and Sir Ivone Augustine Kirkpatrick were not only loyal and intelligent members of the study group; they assured us of access to the "corridors of power" at various times when the survival of the project demanded prompt attention at the highest level.

In a later chapter, I shall recount in more detail the ups and downs of this project during the past quarter-century. What is interesting, at this point, is the degree to which both governmental and private authorities in the United States were ready to assist a macro-engineering venture that had as an evident objective the strengthening of social and economic ties among our European allies. President Eisenhower issued an executive finding that the project would "further the purposes of the Mutual Security Act and particularly the purpose of promoting trade and economic integration in Western Europe" (official determination of August, 1958). Dr. W. O. Smith, a senior officer of the United States Geological Survey, was permitted to assist his European confrères under this ruling, and one can honestly say that the Channel Tunnel Study Group had the benefit of the best governmental, industrial, financial, and legal talent that the United States could bring to the table.

The outcome of twenty-five years of effort is still in doubt as the present volume goes to press. What we do know is that President Mitterrand of France and Prime Minister Thatcher of Great Britain have launched a series of technical and financial studies with the intent of finding viable answers to the problems that remain. In the United States, we can learn from the device of a *"groupement d'études"*—or study group—which was the vehicle adopted for the early and critical research and development work. The study group had the advantages of cohesion, continuity, and commitment, but without the disadvantages of an inflexible corporate format. Essentially, it was a team formed by a cooperative agreement. The two essential officers were a secretary (Jacques de Vogüé) and a chief engineer (René Malcor, ably seconded by his British counterpart, Sir Harold J. B. Harding). The British and French governments entrusted the study group with a multimillion-dollar program of sea-borne exploration; and the study group, which itself had invested considerable sums in research and investigation, is to earn its compensation under arrangements negotiated with the two governments.

What I should like to emphasize is the precedent of an intersectoral, international, interprofessional group, formed voluntarily because of a common interest—a common passion, if you prefer—in a particular engineering project. Such study groups may be regarded as civilian counterparts to the "combined operations" staffs that Lord Louis Mountbatten popularized in the armed forces of the Allies in World War II. In general, government agencies cannot join incorporated bodies except under very restrictive conditions. But unincorporated study teams can reach out to government, industry, and the universities, so that the best advice can be brought to bear on recalcitrant problems that may have rational technical answers. Once an engineering direction is clarified, it is timely to devise whatever juridical entities are appropriate to see that the physical and other objectives are attained. If, on the other hand, it should be found that a program under review is impractical, undesirable, or premature, the members of the study group can step away without loss of reputation or money.

We are, in one sense, in the age of the committee: No single profession or sector has "the key to the door." But a distinction must be made between the promotional phase of a great project, when one individual champion can make a very great difference, and the phase of construction and operation, when more finely honed skills are needed. Looking back over the history of macroprojects (which is really a longer period of time than recorded history), what evidence we have seems to suggest the singular importance of individual imagination and commitment in the early stages. There is, after all, much truth in the insight of a primitive Brazilian tribe, as reported in the film *Fitzcarraldo*, that the essential reality consists of dreams. Without conceptualization, we cannot build a boat, or a sidewalk, or a space rocket. Macro-engineering does not, therefore, imply the exclusion of individual insights and preferences. And once a major goal has been settled upon, there is still much room—indeed, a major necessity—for individual initiative and versatility in carrying it out in a manner that meets the twin requirements of feasibility and desirability.

A. Lawrence Lowell, addressing a dinner meeting of *The Harvard Guardian* (America's first undergraduate magazine of the social sciences), said in 1938 that too much emphasis had been placed on college debating societies: In real life, according to this historian who became president of Harvard University, people spend most of their time trying to reach agreement! Mr. Lowell cited the case of congressional candidates who spend much effort arguing with opponents during an election campaign, only to find that as elected members of the Senate or House of Representatives they must practice the gentler art of compromise and persuasion.

It is patently nonsensical to think that Americans are less able than other, "more homogeneous" people in the business of consultation and agreement. What other nation has produced as glorious a consensus as that which resulted from the Constitutional Convention of 1787? The English, the French, the Germans, the Italians, and the Japanese have all experienced civil wars that lasted longer than ours. After World War II, it was the generous and effective initiative of the Marshall Plan that permitted Europe to recover and prosper. If the Japanese have astonished us with their industrial prowess, this is largely because we have aided and encouraged them to rebuild their damaged economy in the traumatic aftermath of defeat and desolation. Rather than complain because our policies of international reconstruction were successful, we should welcome a resurgent Japan and a vibrant Europe as partners in progress. The new wealth of our trading partners represents an opportunity for the United States: first of all, because they can afford to buy our goods if we can tailor our production to their markets; second, because they now have the capital to invest in major enterprises that will benefit all of us.

But we must make some choices. As David Fromkin has sternly reminded us in his unanswerable book *The Independence of Nations*,[10] this is still a world of nation states; and in pursuit of our own best interests, there are undoubtedly some sectors of technology that we will wish to develop "on our own." But where for practical reasons we do not intend to develop demonstrated technologies with domestic resources, we should be clear as to our desire for international partners, and we should be equally clear as to the precise terms on which we seek cooperation. And the pledged word of the Republic must be held as reliable beyond the term of office of a particular adminstration: In an era of macro-engineering, four years is simply too short a time-span for effective achievement.

This book will review the evidence and suggest some lines of inquiry and action that could help us as a nation to "get our act together" and yet preserve the cherished values of a liberal and diverse society. Congress had something of the sort in mind when it set up the Office of Technology Assessment. But the main impetus for this step came from fears that underevaluated technical developments might undermine environmental quality and hence the public health. To avoid harm is, as Hippocrates taught, a first rule of medicine; but progress is never entirely free of risks, and the assessment process, if it is to serve the nation's future needs, must accept the burden of reaching operational conclusions, in addition to warning us of the devils hidden under the rug. This is, one may hope, where a general theory of macro-engineering can eventually play a useful role, just as macroeconomics illuminated some of the dark corners neglected by microeconomic analysis.

The study of very large engineering projects and their impacts is inextricably linked to understanding the larger economic and political decisions facing our country. The physical underpinnings of even the ancient economies of Egypt, Rome, and Peru necessarily involved infrastructure—the communication, transport, and supply arteries without which no extensive group of human settlements can be held together, serviced, and coordinated. And infrastructure, whether we are considering the thirteen-hundred-mile-long Grand Canal that has been under intermittent construction in China for over two thousand years, or the Communication Satellite System, tends to be inherently large-scale. Moreover, engineering enterprises have tended to grow larger: A glance at the *Engineering News Record* over the past thirty years makes it evident that large-scale construction projects have grown both in number and size, despite the furor against them on several sides. Finally, the impacts of this "supertechnology" have become steadily more compelling, due to the addition of "high tech" attributes to large-scale organization. Engineering decisions are now more than merely technical or even economic events: They are deeply political, and touch the mainsprings of ecological, cultural, and religious tenets.

If we have implied that economics is too important a field to be left to the economists, it is only fair to add that engineering has outgrown the traditional competence of the engineering profession. A "feasibility study" of proposed new macrosystems can seldom be entrusted to engineers alone: Financial, legal, and political judgments are called for that demand the best advice of professionals in other fields. Nor is it helpful to inflate the scope of systems analysis to encompass areas of which the average systems analyst is completely ignorant. A generation ago, I was invited to a briefing by an aerospace company that sought a management position with the Channel Tunnel Study Group. When I asked how the company's management proposed dealing with the financial, legal, and political systems involved in a mixed-economy enterprise, I was assured that the same methods of "systems analysis" which won government contracts would be applied to the other systems involved in winning the approval of two parliaments, obtaining finance from an international consortium of private banks, and facing up to a whole congeries of social and environmental questions. Certainly, training in system dynamics could enhance the competence of lawyers, accountants, and bankers; but at the present time, the priesthood of systems analysis is not ready to assume the mantle of "supreme adviser" on "enterprises of great pith and moment."

We are all—editors, economists, engineers, lawyers, managers, analysts, and politicians—involved in the "seamless web" of an interdisciplinary mission; the engineer, in order to perform the highest functions of his calling, must be "recycled" for service in the ranks of management and decision-making. This is why, for more than a decade, the Massachusetts Institute of Technology has offered seminars in the new field of macroengineering. It is not, as some might infer, because of an infatuation with bigness or an aversion to smallness. On the contrary, smallness in organization is to be preferred, all other factors being equal. The choice is not between large engineering projects and little or no engineering at all, but between projects that can restore to humankind some measurable control over its destiny and projects that serve disruptive and unhealthy ends.

Reindustrialization, to use the current term for a process as old as history, requires behavioral adjustments, and not mere technical decisions to invest more dollars in this or that industry. The neat distinction between "sunrise" and "sunset" industries may not, however, be as sure a guide to the future as some commentators suppose. If shipbuilding and steel and textiles are "sunset" industries, does this mean that people will no longer use ships, or steel, or clothing? Or does this mean that, for the present, we have judged the markets saturated, our technology hopeless to cope with the perceived competition, and our institutions too inflexible to make the needed adjustments? By all means, let us retrain and retool for the "industries of tomorrow." But let us remember that a nation where no one can cook, sew, or drive a nail is not likely to be an enjoyable place to reside, even if we increase the numbers of engineering graduates so that we can compare more favorably with the statistics of the Far East and Europe. In short, we need a movement to emphasize excellence *at all levels*, including what we disparagingly call "low tech." Is there not a business opportunity in the United States for a chain of schools modeled on the écoles Ménagères of Belgium, Switzerland, and France? If we are to be a "service society," should we not learn the arts and traditions of personal service, as a balance wheel to higher mathematics and management science?

We must avoid slogans like the plague. Monsieur Emile Aubert, an honors graduate of M.I.T. who for years headed the famous French management consulting firm La Compagnie Française d'Organisation, has deliberately shied away from "high tech" industries; he has invested in yogurt and in Charolais cattle, with good effect. It is not the thesis of this book that everyone should go into macro-engineering or that *only* very large enterprises are worthwhile. There is a symmetry and a synergy between large, medium, and small, between high tech and low tech, between competition and cooperation. What we *are* saying is that as a matter of public policy, all elements of society must combine forces if we are to have an infrastructure worthy of our abilities and a basic industry that is reliable and resilient. If this means that certain assumptions of our antitrust tradition are no longer completely valid, then liberals will have to join in retailoring both laws and habits. It is one thing to oppose "combinations in restraint of trade." It is quite another thing to prevent combinations that are necessary to preserve our national economic strength. Whether the technology be advanced or traditional, American firms should not be hobbled in foreign markets by rules or taxes that place them at a decisive competitive disadvantage.

In the field of macro-engineering, close cooperation between government and industry is a necessity, not a luxury. A first provision will be the establishment of adequate data bases, so that all concerned will know "the state of play," that is, which large-scale systems are under discussion, where, and with what objectives; what are the likely costs, benefits, and unknowns; who are the players, what are the likely time-frames, and how do the probable impacts mesh with environmental, social, and economic policy? In the early days of the channel tunnel negotiations, I remember how much it meant to us to have David Bruce as American Ambassador in London. He understood large affairs, and did not hesitate to speak to prime ministers or others in authority when he had information he regarded as important and relevant. Far from being extraneous to the game of diplomacy, international technical arrangements are now core subjects. Diplomatic representatives at every level should receive periodic reports on large engineering projects in their assigned areas of concern. And a central data base should receive constantly updated information from both the public and the private sector.

Macro-engineering, as a glance back at the recent past will remind us, involves government at the very highest levels. Military engineering projects such as the Trident submarine or the MX missile are now commonplace topics of executive and legislative cognizance. Certain developments, like the Soviet gas pipeline to Western Europe, are headlined because of their obvious implications for allied and national security. What we must now do is to mesh macro-engineering plans with our wider interests and goals as a nation. A more comprehensive partnership with Canada and Mexico will be one constant theme of such an endeavor: In later chapters, reference will be made to transport, water supply, and energy projects that can strengthen the economies of North America, provided that they are jointly and sensitively broached and that they respond to the interests and perceptions of the three nations of this richly endowed continent.

In 15 B.C., the Roman Army under Drusus, a brother of the Emperor Tiberius, began a four-hundred-year occupation of the area now known as Holland. The local inhabitants, the Frisians, had built hundreds of mounds on which their villages would be safe from the ravages of the sea. It was thanks to the Romans that the lowlanders learned how to make dikes. Commencing in the Middle Ages, large works were undertaken. Andries Vierlingh, the first great engineer-scientist to specialize in waterworks, wrote in 1579, "Although the Dutch are a peaceful nation, diking against Neptune is like waging war and therefore we must be warlike." The invention of the efficient windmill in the same century had given the Dutch just the machine they needed to drain lakes and polders. The rapidity with which land was reclaimed from the sea gave rise to the saying, "God made the world, but the Dutchmen made Holland."

In 1754, the war against the sea was centralized under a permanent director general of the nation's River and Sea Works, now known as the *Waterstaat*. The minister of the *Waterstaat* is assisted by hydraulic engineers and scientists whose mission is to plan for centuries to come. As explained by Peter Spier in his charmingly illustrated book *Of Dikes and Windmills* (Doubleday, 1969), "The male population within the jurisdiction of a Waterschap is registered in the Dike Army and can be called up on the Dike Count's orders in time of danger. Whenever a man plans to be absent from his Waterschap for an extended period of time, he has to ask his dike council for permission to leave."

Here is William James's "moral equivalent of war" in full action: a true "army against nature," with a hierarchy, an enemy (the sea!), a glorious history of combat, and, eventually, victory. Sixty percent of Holland's population lives below sea-level. Without a permanent mobilization to defend the dikes, a beautiful and highly civilized country simply could not exist.

Now that congestion—and prices—on many of the world's land masses are reaching the limits of toleration, there is renewed talk of building artificial islands in the sea. The Dutch precedent and skill in reclamation are bound to lend impetus and conviction to this movement. We shall have to pay serious attention to Nigel Chattey's scheme (developed, by the way, with the aid of Dutch engineers) for a huge artificial island bordering New York Harbor, to be described in a later chapter as a major option in the provision of deepwater port facilities for the United States. The Japanese employed Buckminster Fuller to design a residential island considered for Tokyo Bay. Kuwait has commissioned the great Japanese architect Kiyonori Kikutake to draw plans for an offshore floating hotel. With an endemic problem of refugees, perhaps the United Nations should look into the possibility of an artificially contrived offshore territory that could be enlarged, in the Dutch fashion, to provide permanent homes for populations expelled from their native lands. This is, admittedly, an expensive procedure; it may be less expensive than a sterile irredentism and an endless succession of communal wars.

What is certain is that we shall be seeing strong pressures—if only as a result of exponentially growing population statistics—for new cities built either on the five continents, or on the seas, or "up there" in outer space.

Ever since American astronauts landed on the moon, the United States has followed what might be described as a "minimalist" policy. Without exaggerating in the direction of excessive flexing of technological muscle, it is time, however, to take stock of the macro-engineering capabilities we already possess—or could reasonably develop if we wished to. Landing astronauts on Mars is within our engineering reach; modernizing American steel and transport industries is feasible; we can even train many more scientists and engineers if the public can be persuaded that this is "the way to go." But a first task is to envision what macrotechnology might accomplish, and to assess the likely impacts. There is no doubt that the nation wishes to stay in business for a thousand years and more; if that is so, it will not hurt us as a community to do a little long-range planning. Armed with an up-to-date overview of the future, even the sky is no longer the limit.

Camp William James was reconstituted as a private effort on East Tunbridge Hill, Vermont, after the gathering clouds of World War II shifted attention from civilian to military priorities. Purchase of the "Rivers place" in 1941 was made possible by gifts from the Goodwill Fund and by Mr. and Mrs. Henry Copley Greene of Cambridge, Massachusetts.

Volunteers who formed Camp William James gathered in December 1940 at the Forest Service house in Sharon, Vermont. Front row, starting third from left: Alfred Eiseman, Arnold Childs, George Flowers. Back row from left: Frank Davidson, Enno Hobbing, Louis Schlivek, Page Smith, Jack Preiss, Roy B. Chamberlin, Jr., unidentified, William Uptegrove, Russell Greenlaw.

This terraced slope in Davis County, Utah, was restored by federal conservation efforts after being badly denuded and eroded. On May 11, 1934, Chicago was deluged by twelve million tons of topsoil from the dustbowl described in John Steinbeck's famous novel *The Grapes of Wrath*.

Gathering seeds—in the region of the Tennessee Valley—for reforestation work. Enrollees of the Civilian Conservation Corps worked under experienced foremen provided by the U. S. Forest Service, the Soil Conservation Service, and other specialized agencies.

A planting crew in action, in the Catahoula section of the Kisatchie National Forest (Louisiana). It has been said that more than half the trees planted since the establishment of the Republic were in fact planted by the Civilian Conservation Corps.

These three bear cubs were caught by CCC boys of the Laurel Fork Camp in the Monongahela National Forest in West Virginia. The photograph was taken by D. A. Oliver in May 1935.

William James (1842–1910), the American philosopher and psychologist who founded pragmatism, was described in the *Encyclopaedia Britannica* as "the most renowned and representative of the thinkers of America." Two of his sons attended the ceremonies dedicating Camp William James on December 14, 1940.

This young lady, engaged in trail building for the contemporary California Conservation Corps, illustrates one significant difference between the old Civilian Conservation Corps and present efforts and proposals: The original CCC recruited only young men; today's conservation camps include young women too, and on an equal basis.

Farming—viewed as the application of "know-how" to soil—is essentially an *engineering* type of activity. These slitted tunnels at Wilson Farms in Lexington, Massachusetts, are covered with plastic—a method of conserving water and energy and extending the growing season as well. Land-poor Japan, using such methods, has become a *net exporter* of rice! (American Vegetable Grower, *No. 2, February 1983*)

Top: An 1880's view of the Erie Canal's five-lock combine at Lockport, one of many new towns fostered by the advent of the canal. Bottom left: An 1825 sketch of the same locks. The entire Erie Canal was completed in 1825 in an unbelievable seven-year period. It covers 364 miles from Buffalo on Lake Erie to Albany on the Hudson River. Bottom right: A 1902 sketch, drawn for *Leslie's Weekly*, showing canal barges moored for the winter at New York City docks "about to start out for the Summer's work." The Canal Museum in Syracuse, New York, has a full documentary collection on the Erie Canal, whose tale is worth remembering at a time when "high tech"—and the need for cheap, reliable transportation—has led to a plethora of proposals for new canals.

This 1893 photo of the New York Central and Hudson River Railroad's *De Witt Clinton*—an engine built in 1831—pays ironic tribute to the promoter-statesman whose Erie Canal paved the way for railroad transport to the West.

The first locomotive to cross the Allegheny Mountains showed that cross-continental transportation, in an earlier age, could evoke the enthusiasm and hard work that William James might have recognized as another "moral equivalent of war."

Above: A west-bound Lehigh Valley passenger train in Sayre, Pennsylvania, after the turn of the century. Below: Reenactment (at a Chicago, Illinois, "Wheels a-Rolling" Pageant and Railroad Fair in 1948) of the "Driving of the Golden Spike" as rails from East and West joined at Promontory Point, Utah, on May 10, 1869.

Right: The "highest single piling trestle in the world," near Portland, Oregon. Below: An ore train rounding Dry Fork Bridge at Bingham, Utah. These photographs, taken just before the outbreak of World War I, indicate that American railroad technology has not changed in its essentials in the past seventy years.

These pictures of the Japanese National Railways' high-speed Shinkansen Line (up- .
per right and below) and of its computerized control room (lower right) indicate a
high-water mark of traditional railway technology. Shortly after World War II, the
Japanese officials were assisted in their planning by a technical aid mission of the
French National Railways—the famous SNCF whose TGV (*Trains de Grande Vitesse*)
service is now perhaps the most rapid in the world. What is not always well understood is the "creative ambivalence" which has fostered costly, long-range infrastructure developments within Japan itself alongside entrepreneurial responsiveness to
external markets for manufactured goods. Without basic transport, energy, communications, water supply, and educational networks supported centrally, it is questionable whether the private sector—consisting of a multitude of varied decision
centers—could have produced the "Japanese economic miracle." Thus far, few
commentators have examined the inevitable linkage between infrastructure and
industry—in Japan or elsewhere.

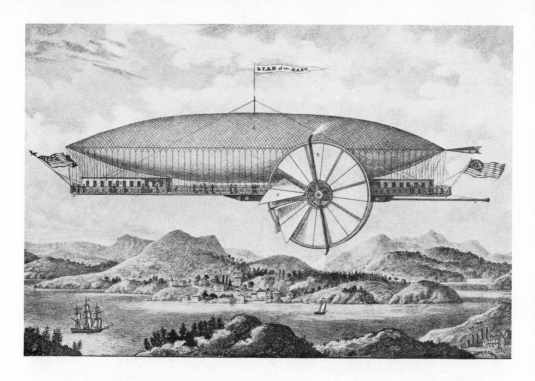

Above: Captioned PRINCE'S AERIAL SHIP, STAR OF THE EAST, this lithograph was published nearly a century ago by Norris's, located at the corner of Wall and Nassau streets in Manhattan. The Rube Goldberg–like invention never went farther than the drawing board. Below: View of the front gondola of a Zeppelin about to ascend, c. 1910 in Germany.

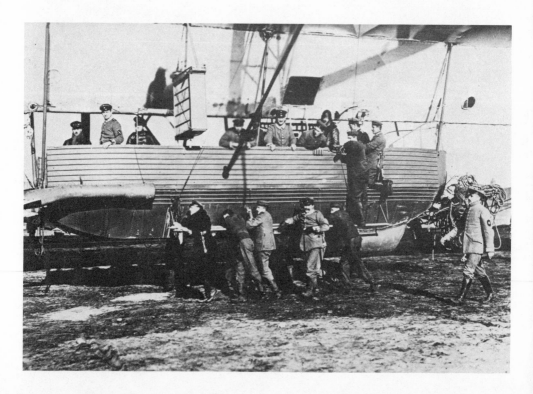

The *California Arrow* (Thomas S. Baldwin, captain) flying above the city and harbor of Norwich, Connecticut, July 5, 1909, in connection with the 250th anniversary celebration of the settlement of Norwich.

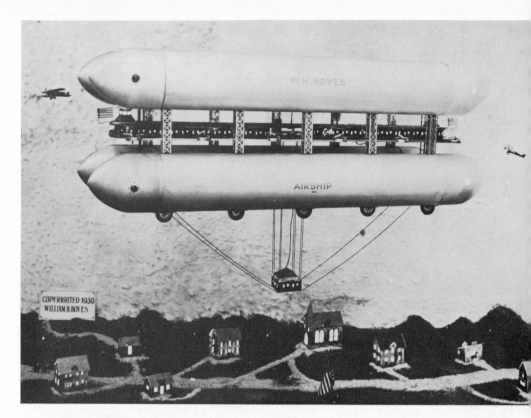

Above: Toy or scale-model airship of the Wm. H. Boyes Airship Co., 1930. Below: Grand salon of the dirigible R 100, commissioned as a result of a 1924 decision of the Imperial Defence Committee. The R 100 was built by a Vickers subsidiary at Howden, north of the River Humber.

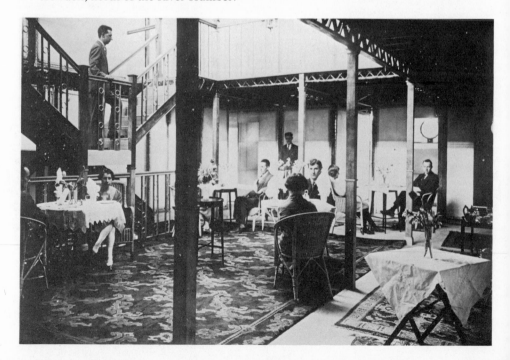

The R 100 moored to her mast at Cardington, England. This fine dirigible, designed by Barnes N. Wallis, was 709 feet long, 133 feet in diameter, and powered by
six Rolls-Royce aircraft engines. On July 29, 1930, the airship crossed the Atlantic
to Montreal in 78 hours, 31 minutes, returning to its base in Cardington a fortnight
later after a flight of 56 hours, 30 minutes. Apparently because of political considerations, the R 100 was never again authorized to take to the air.

Below: The ZR III (American code name given the LZ 126, a Zeppelin handed over to the United States as war reparations after World War I) approaching the U.S. Naval Air Station at Lakehurst, New Jersey, on October 15, 1924. Christened *Los Angeles*, this airship had crossed the Atlantic in 80 hours, 52 minutes, with Dr. Hugo Eckener supervising the delivery flight. The lower photograph shows the airship after its landing at Lakehurst. The U.S. Navy replaced the hydrogen in the fourteen gas bags with helium, and the *Los Angeles* had a distinguished and exceptionally long period of service with the navy, chalking up a world record of 4,320 flying hours. The *Los Angeles* successfully demonstrated, in 1929, a system for hooking up and releasing fighter and reconnaissance aircraft. Used both as a training ship and in fleet maneuvers, the *Los Angeles* was able to touch down on the deck of the aircraft carrier *Saratoga* without any special landing gear. In 1932 the airship was retired from the service because of the Depression. For an extended—and attractive—disquisition on the *Los Angeles* and its sister airships, the reader can consult *Airships Yesterday, Today and Tomorrow* published in 1976 by The Two Continents Publishing Group Ltd., New York, and written by Henry Beaubois with drawings by Carlo Demand.

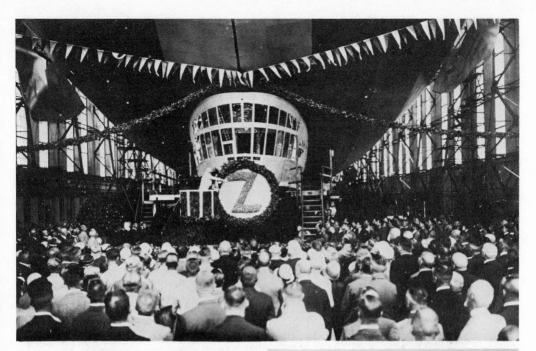

Above: The ceremony at Friedrichshafen, Germany, in 1928 as Countess Branden-stein, the daughter of Count Zeppelin, chris-tens the *Graf Zeppelin*, named after her father, the inventor and pioneer of lighter-than-air aircraft. Right: A photograph taken of the huge ship's final test flight over Berlin. In 1929, a spectacular round-the-world flight was accomplished. Commencing in 1931, regular commercial flights to Brazil were scheduled, with occasional return flights via the United States and the North Atlantic. When the *Graf Zeppelin* was with-drawn from service in June of 1937, it had carried out 144 transatlantic crossings, had flown more than a million miles, had carried 13,110 paying passengers without accident, and had shipped 116,790 pounds of mail. No effort had been spared in the effort to provide supremely luxurious accommoda-tions. Ten cabins had bedroom space for two passengers each, as well as two large wash-rooms and one toilet. There was an electri-cally equipped kitchen and an elegant dining saloon with bay windows that could be opened and closed at will. Cruises were un-dertaken to Palestine, Algeria, the Balkans and the North Pole. Charles Dollfuss, the well-known French aviator, and other celeb-rities were happy to take advantage of the *Graf Zeppelin*'s reliable service to South America and the United States.

This photograph (left) of Dr. Robert H. Goddard with a steel combustion chamber and rocket nozzle was taken in 1915. Often cited as the "Father of American Rocketry," Robert Hutchins Goddard was born in Worcester, Massachusetts, on October 5, 1882, and died in 1945, before extensive use had been made of the more than 200 patents issued to him. Below we see Dr. Goddard (second from right) and assistants placing the rocket used in a test (October 27, 1931) from a tower located on a prairie 10 miles northwest of Roswell, New Mexico. At right, we observe Dr. Goddard's rocket in flight, May 19, 1937, showing much-improved stabilization. This rocket reached an altitude of 3,250 feet. Dr. Goddard was both a theoretical scientist and a practical engineer. His dream was the conquest of the upper atmosphere—and ultimately space—through the use of rocket propulsion. According to the National Aeronautics and Space Administration, he was "probably as responsible for the dawning of the Space Age as the Wrights were for the beginning of the Air Age."

Top left: Dr. Wernher von Braun, director of the Marshall Space Flight Center, Huntsville, Alabama, relaxes after the successful launch of *Apollo 11* astronauts Neil A. Armstrong, Michael Collins, and Edwin Aldrin, Jr. Their historic lunar-landing mission began at 9:32 A.M. EDT, July 16, 1969. Center left: *Apollo 11* Commander Neil A. Armstrong. Lower left: *Apollo 11* command-module pilot Michael Collins watches technicians conduct spacesuit checks prior to his launch. Below is a view of the Apollo/Saturn V space vehicle carrying the *Apollo 11* astronauts on the nation's first lunar-landing mission.

Right: *Apollo 11* view of the moon: This outstanding view of a full moon was photographed from the *Apollo 11* spacecraft during its transearth journey homeward. When this picture was taken, the spacecraft was already 10,000 nautical miles away. Below: Astronaut John W. Young, commander of the *Apollo 16* lunar-landing mission, stands on the rim of Plum crater while collecting lunar samples at Station No. 1 during the first *Apollo 16* extravehicular activity (EVA-1) at the Descartes landing site.

At the Kennedy Space Center in Florida, 225 footcandles of light were prepared for the night launching of *Apollo 17* in 1972. This final lunar-landing mission in the Apollo program was manned by Eugene A. Cernan, commander; Ronald E. Evans, command-module pilot; and Harrison B. Schmitt, lunar-module pilot.

CHAPTER 2

Bricks and Mortar: Cases and Comments

WHAT IS MEANT BY THE TERM "MACRO-ENGINEERING"? Broadly speaking, it implies the study, preparation, and management of the largest technological undertakings of which human society is capable at any given time. Characteristically, macro-engineering involves "hardware"—the construction of pipelines, railroads, airports, dams, bridges, refineries, rocket bases, new cities. But it would be unwise to define "large-scale technology" too narrowly in terms of physical plant and equipment. Communication systems, for instance, while physically and financially impressive, connote highly developed elements of "software"—the research, plans, methods, regulations, and procedures that govern the design, building, and use of the installed network.

Nor would it be right to regard our own era as unique in its dependence on large-scale technology. There is already a vast historical experience—good, bad, and indifferent. Excavations have confirmed that the imposing and complex fortifications of Jericho are at least nine thousand years old—antedating by more than six thousand years the arrival of Joshua and his trumpet. It has been cogently argued that civilization only developed in the Tigris-Euphrates Valley, the Valley of the Nile, and elsewhere *after* the building of the great cities without which there could be no articulated division of labor, no leisure class, and none of the attributes that we like to think of as essential ingredients of culture and a diversified urban society. The claim has even been put forward that the existence of flourishing cities was a precondition to the establishment of agriculture: Settled farming requires safe areas for the sheltering of stock, the warehousing of seeds and utensils, the design and production of implements, and—not least—the provision of marketplaces and the assurance of a substantial nonfarming demand for agricultural goods.

No modern state has been able to match the record of Rome's 3rd (Augusta) Legion in halting the northward advance of the Sahara Desert, by placing in the Province of Africa, and maintaining for centuries, treebelts, aqueducts, and other effective public works on a scale worthy of a great civilization. E. W. Bovill, in a booklet published by the Oxford University Press in 1958 (and 1970) under the title *The Golden Trade of the Moors*, has demonstrated that there has been very little if any climatic change north of the Sahara in the past two millennia; the Romans simply assumed that water was a necessity for an urban civilization: They did not hesitate to build a ninety-mile aqueduct to bring water to Carthage. Bovill explains:

> The great aqueducts striding across the desolate plains and piercing mountain ranges remain as impressive monuments to the genius of the Roman water engineers, the *aquilegi*, under whose care came also the springs from which, far or near, the towns were supplied. But there were not always springs to tap. This was particularly so in Tripolitania where the water problem was, as today, much more acute than farther west. Here one method, which the Italians copied when establishing new settlements in the 1930's, was to collect rainwater from catchment areas and store it in cisterns. The catchment areas varied from rock faces to domestic roofs. Another method was to build dams across the river-beds behind which in the short wet season the flood water could be stored or led off into cisterns . . . In fairness to the Greeks, it should be added that farther east they did just as well as, if not better

than the Romans in still more difficult circumstances. They
so successfully developed the rock cistern method that they
had a chain of thriving towns and villages, surrounded by
fields and vineyards, extending all the way from Cyrene to
Alexandria.

The attempt to recapture the engineering knack of the Roman Republic and Empire was nowhere more pathetic than in
Charlemagne's ill-fated project to build a canal between the
Rhine and the Danube. The medieval genius was, architecturally, a *local* phenomenon: Castles, cathedrals, town houses, and
gardens were frequently stunning and complex, but it was only
with the arrival of the Elizabethan epoch and the Renaissance
that the arts of construction regained a wider horizon.

It was in France that a modern predilection first developed
for "les grands travaux." Louis XIV, coming to the throne after
the severe civil disorders of *La Fronde*, formed an alliance with
the rising middle classes and made the construction industry his
"right arm" in strengthening the royal power to a point where
the combative aristocracy would be unable to challenge the peace
of the realm. The Palace of Versailles became the model for all
the courts of Europe. The great minister Colbert granted to a
southern gentleman, Pierre-Paul Riquet de Bonrepos, a concession to build a canal linking the Mediterranean Sea with the
Atlantic Ocean. This feat was rightly described in Diderot's *Ency-
clopedia of the Sciences* as "*comparable à tout ce que les Romains ont
tenté de plus grand*" ("comparable to the very largest works attempted by the Romans"). Bonrepos proposed the project at a
moment when the royal coffers had been emptied by a series of
unsuccessful wars. Ingeniously, he proposed borrowing the necessary funds from Paris bankers, in exchange for the right to
charge tolls and collect salt taxes along the route. Colbert, doubt-
ing that water could be provided for the upper reaches of the
canal, required Bonrepos to build a miniature trial canal, a
ruisseau d'essai, along the entire designated route. This model canal, complete with working scale-model reservoirs and locks, was
finished within one summer. The canal itself was built in just
fourteen years after the early discussions with Colbert. Not surprisingly, a proposal for such a venture had been made during

the reign of François Ier. Henri IV named a review commission, headed by the bishop of Toulouse. The achievement of Bonrepos was so notable—a canal linking two oceans and built by private capital—that the entrepreneur was allowed to call himself the Baron de Bonrepos et du Canal de Navigation des Deux Mers.[1]

In 1747, the Ecole des Ponts et Chaussées was founded— the very first of France's "Grandes Ecoles." As Jean Lebel reminded the 1981 Macro-Engineering Seminar at M.I.T., the Revolution of 1789 suppressed the university, and established the Ecole Polytechnique. Today, although the university has been reinstituted, there are 150 engineering schools in France. In a total population of fifty million, there are about two hundred thousand engineers. The "Grandes Ecoles" provide France with perhaps two thirds of its top managers, higher civil servants, and research specialists. Graduates of the leading institutions know they are destined for broad responsibilities. I was not disappointed when the Channel Tunnel Study Group selected as its chief engineer an *ingénieur-en-chef des ponts-et-chaussées*, Monsieur René Malcor, now (in retirement) an *ingénieur-général des ponts-et-chaussées*. The quality of the roads, bridges, railways, and ports of France is a tribute to the high place accorded the engineering profession in that country ever since the days of Louis XIV.

What must strike even the most casual student of French history is the close correlation between achievements in public works and the establishment of engineering schools having high patronage and able to enlist the brightest minds in the country. The bifurcation in the United States and the United Kingdom between schools of management and schools of engineering presents an obstacle that must be frankly acknowledged if we are to deal honestly with our problem. What is needed is a new breed of engineer-managers, people who are professionally competent as engineers and who have the broader culture appropriate to management of very large enterprises. Adding a diversification requirement of a science course or two in liberal arts colleges, or launching seminars on technology management in business schools, while helpful as a palliative, hardly represents a credible attack on the underlying problem. We must move toward the establishment, with the fullest resources of the country, of graduate schools of engineer management; recruitment should be limited to the best students, there must be a strict but balanced curriculum in both engineering and management; and let us be sure to add a strong dose of American constitutional history and of behavioral science.

Macro-engineering is not necessarily identified with novelty and excitement. Very often, engineers are brought in to clean up a mess, or to rebuild a decaying system. Waste management is a growing business, an essential one for the survival of an industrial society that mass-produces new chemical products before environmental impacts can be known and provided for. One of the grave accusations against many large technical enterprises is that they have "suboptimized," that is, they have been too single-minded in pursuit of one goal such as short-term profitability, or economy of time in planning and construction, and they have drawn too heavily on those larger natural systems—such as pure water and air—on which all human livelihood ultimately depends. Love Canal in New York State has come to symbolize the detritus with which our society must now deal because of past neglect. But to clean up—and even to assess—such situations, we need trained scientists and engineers: The environment cannot be saved by environmentalists alone.

In the middle of the last century, Paris suffered from an urban blight more dramatic than the current woes of any of our major cities. The water supply was unreliable, many districts suffered from a lack of fresh air, and transport was difficult and dangerous. Napoleon III gave extraordinary powers to his prefect of the Seine, Baron Georges Haussmann; and between 1850 and 1870 the equivalent of over one hundred billion dollars was spent to transform the city from one of the unhealthiest in Europe—epidemics of cholera had been common—to the healthful and beautiful City of Boulevards we know today. "Only one house in five had water piped to it, and in all Paris fewer than 150 houses had running water above the first floor."[2] The achievement of Haussmann, in modernizing the sewage and water supply of Paris, in cutting broad avenues through districts where fresh air could not circulate, in designing parks and gardens—created a new *urbanisme* across Europe and had its in fluence in America—where Frederick Law Olmsted, Daniel Burnham, and others were inspired to emulate the parks and parkways of the City of Light. And in carrying out his task, Haussmann (a lawyer by profession) was able to call on two splendid aides from the Corps des Ponts et Chaussées, Adolphe Alphand and Eugène Belgrand.

The rebuilding of Paris, just before the Franco-Prussian War unseated Napoleon III, illustrates the truth of the axiom culled by Robert Seamans, Jr., from his unique experience as director of the Apollo Program: the sine qua non, the indispensable element for success in macro-engineering, is "sustained support." Can democratic government provide the kind of continuity that the emperor of the French was able to bestow on his prefect? That the answer need not be negative is attested to by the long career of Robert Moses,[3] who played such a key role in the rebuilding of New York City's infrastructure during the 1920's and the 1930's. By accumulating state, city and county appointive offices, Moses became a power in his own right. The public beaches, parks, and parkways stand as monuments to his imagination and determination. The bridges, tunnels, and roads that he instigated were an economic boon to a whole region; unfortunately, the massive housing projects that Moses sponsored lacked a sense of human scale, and to this day the United States has not found a valid and viable policy for the reurbanization of metropolitan areas.

The problem is not limited to the United States. Several years ago, the United Nations, sensing the need for a radically new approach, organized in Lima, Peru, a demonstration housing project—really a whole new town—with the participation of leading architects from more than a dozen nations. Peter Land, now a professor at the Illinois Institute of Technology, was put in charge; this remarkable Englishman, with a charming Peruvian wife, had already "earned his spurs" by rebuilding, at very low cost, a coastal fishing village destroyed by a hurricane. In the *Proyecto Experimental del Vivienda*, he accomplished, with the collaboration of other noted architects such as Japan's Kiyonori Kikutake, a miracle of economy, aesthetic and social harmony, and public delight. The basic principle was clustered housing; and in consonance with the fine Spanish traditions of Peru, each house was built around a central courtyard, with room for growth as families became larger. Most remarkably, Professor Land was able to accommodate, under the best conditions of light and air, a population equivalent to the residential capacity of a typical "high-rise" covering the same site. It remains an example for the whole world to examine and adapt, as population growth pushes major cities closer to the line of twenty and thirty million people per metropolitan area (there have been projections that Calcutta will reach a total of fifty million within the next century).

Chatting with Peter Land about his extraordinary accomplishment, I wondered why it is not better known; at a reception in Paris tendered by officials of the United Nations Educational, Scientific, and Cultural Organization (UNESCO), I had noticed that even United Nations personnel at a policy level knew little about PREVI, as the acronym for the project was denominated. Mr. Land, who had presented his findings to the first AAAS Symposium on Macro-Engineering, held in Washington, D.C., in 1978, came up with the wry—but accurate—explanation: There had been no scandals, and therefore no publicity! Since PREVI had been built within reasonable time-frames and costs, and provided a pleasant, traditional lifestyle for the families who elected to settle in the project, there had been general satisfaction with the result. About half the families had helped with their own labor, thus further reducing costs. Altogether, the high-density, low-rise concept so well demonstrated in Peru offers a strategy for urban redevelopment in industrialized as well as developing countries: The residents are happy with a healthful environment where walking is the main means of transportation—automobiles have been limited to the periphery—and the high density has meant that commercial and social centers are within easy walking distance. The close proximity of services and customers has brought about significant savings in energy. And the attractive diversity in architecture has provided an important lesson: Macro-engineering need not be monolithic. A great project can, by careful and considerate design, enhance individual and family privacy and foster the communal virtues of a free society.

The large city of today and the even larger city of tomorrow will require facilities and centers that can cater to masses of people: The model neighborhood alone will not "solve" the problem of planning. One obvious need will be for opportunities for sport and exercise: A purely passive society, however affluent, will not be healthy. Immediately after World War II, a Committee for a War and Peace Memorial in New York City considered a plan for a "Health Palace" that would occupy four square city blocks. Percy Corbett, chief architect of Radio City, had been introduced to the plan of a German refugee engineer, Isaac Goldmersteen, whose design envisioned a mammoth swimming pool as the centerpiece for a wide array of sport facilities; the waters of the world's great spas were to be duplicated by chemical engineering, and ultraviolet-ray sunlight would guarantee good interior weather, day in and day out. The medical departments of virtually all major industrial corporations and government agencies in the city endorsed the plan; Mr. Corbett had added a building to serve as a center for physical medicine and physiotherapy of all kinds. The federal, state, and city governments were ready to offer a total of twenty million dollars—an enormous sum in those days—to guarantee construction; but the committee (of which my father was chairman) could not agree: There was a split between those who wanted a "living memorial" and the sculptors and artists who wished a purely symbolic statue or painting as a public monument. Modern democracy has yet to come up with a contemporary equivalent of the Roman Baths that added so much to the cities of the ancient world!

The real point to bear in mind is the importance of balance: A city ought to afford opportunities for privacy, neighborhood character, and individual and group activity; but masses of people also want symbols and outlets for community feeling. This latter point was stressed by no less an individualist than D. H. Lawrence, who complained of England's "gingerbread façades" in neo-Elizabethan towns, and praised the American penchant for the "grand gesture" symbolized by our railroad stations. And should we not learn from Louis XIV's engineers, who showed us the beauty of very large water fountains—for which they often sought the collaboration of leading sculptors of the day? Can we not take fuller advantage of the talents of American sculptors such as Joseph Erhardy, whose works are beginning to adorn public squares in France? Dr. Jerome B. Wiesner, as president of the Massachusetts Institute of Technology, made a point of obtaining works of leading contemporary sculptors to decorate nooks and crannies of the campus in Cambridge. Houston, thanks to private philanthropy, boasts public fountains at many busy intersections. Erhardy, who recently won a commission for a bust of the economist John Kenneth Galbraith, will no doubt be appreciated—eventually—by more of his own countrymen. Macro-engineering not only offers new vistas for our technical and social future; it represents a challenge and an opportunity for the arts as well.

Good ideas are not self-executing. While the *coup d'oeil*—the vision of a feasible future artifact or project—must precede its realization, we must try to develop a new breed of professional, so that "the best intentions" are not trampled upon by lack of implementation. It is this spirit of accomplishment that was so well portrayed by the French sculptor Despiau in his fine statue of *Le Réalisateur* reproduced as the frontispiece of this book. In flesh and blood, history is fortunately bountiful with examples of men and women who could not only see possibilities where others saw nothing, but who could carry out their visions in a manner beneficial to the community. Florence Nightingale is not generally thought of as a macro-engineer, but the impetus her labors gave to the care of the sick led to the building of hospitals on a scale unprecedented in the whole previous history of humanity. One suspects that a further step in modern medicine will be the systematic construction of large-scale health and rehabilitation centers, where victims of accidents and people recovering from surgery may enjoy expert guidance—and thoroughly equipped recreational facilities—to regain their health as rapidly as possible.

That the phrase "the Great American Desert" had some basis in reality can be appreciated if we look at our country as it was prior to the developments following the Civil War. Two Canadians, the Chaffey brothers, played a major role, not only in opening the West, and in particular California, to agricultural prosperity; they played a similar and in some ways a more dominant part in the settlement and flowering of Australia's main agricultural region, the Murray River. According to the elegant *California Water Atlas* published by that state in 1979, George Chaffee "was probably the most successful example of the engineer as entrepreneur in his generation. Chaffee built the first hydroelectric plant in California and the first electrically lighted house west of the Rockies." But his greatest success, through the development of "mutual water companies," was to open large areas of California to settlement. It was Chaffee who had the idea of changing the name of the Colorado Desert to the Imperial Valley. In 1882, George and William Benjamin Chaffee built a model colony that they named after their native Canadian province, Ontario. Its beauty and prosperity launched the two brothers on the career that led to the establishment of two major agricultural areas: one in the United States and the other in Australia.

In 1884, the future prime minister Alfred Deakin, not yet in his thirtieth year, met the Chaffee brothers under an Australian gum tree in California. Deakin, at that time on a voyage of investigation for an Australian royal commission, was so impressed by what the Chaffees had accomplished in California that he and his staff encouraged them to visit Australia. In 1886, Deakin pushed a bill through the colonial parliament to encourage waterworks, and in that same year, on October 21, an agreement was signed "between the Government of the Colony and George Chaffee and William Benjamin Chaffee to secure the application of private capital to the construction of irrigation works . . ." This agreement is widely regarded as "the first step in scientific irrigation for intense culture in commonwealth history." Two hundred fifty thousand acres on the lower Murray River were granted to the Chaffees under rather stringent conditions. Today the production of fruits and vegetables from the Murray River Valley is as important in Australia's agronomy as the analogous production from the Imperial Valley is for the United States.

The true limits on Australian agricultural and pastoral production may be more political than technical. About twenty years ago, with friends in the Western Australia Land Use Study Group, I was able to negotiate the "reservation" of five million acres in the Nullarbor Desert. An earlier investment group from

the United States, including David Rockefeller and Art Linkletter, had succeeded in developing sandy soil near the port of
Esperance into profitable sheep stations and farms, mainly by
building earthen catchments for the area's scarce rainfall and by
adding trace elements to the soil. Our group brought in soil experts from Cornell University; there were useful technical contacts with the famous CSIRO (the Commonwealth Scientific and
Industrial Research Organization) and with the state government—principally with Charles Court, the minister for development (now Sir Charles Court, until recently the premier). The
limiting factor to expansion of the land devoted to farming
and ranching is really the willingness of the "backbenchers"
representing the landed interests of the state to see production
increased to a point where prices might be affected. But knowledge of how to bring "light land" under reliable cultivation
is now quite widespread. When one considers that Western
Australia alone is about one third as large as the continental
United States, it becomes evident that the potential acreage
for increased food production is almost beyond imagination.
I do not believe the world will fail to feed its growing population, although there are, of course, many sound reasons for
hoping that developing countries, where most of the increase
occurs, will eventually improve their own prospects by learning how to reduce the present exorbitant rates of population
increase.

Australia is justly proud of its Snowy Mountain Hydroelectric Project, one of the world's largest hydroelectric developments, which owed so much to the pioneering confidence of Sir
Robert Jackson. With Australia's strong tradition of civil service
guidance of ministerial judgment, it should not be anticipated
that Australians will indulge in imaginative macroprojects long
before a need or market has been demonstrated. The long saga
of the Sydney Opera House—where a devoted and amused public willingly subscribed to the completion of a project whose cost
turned out to be more than ten times the first estimate—may be
chalked up to genuine pride in a new civilization built in a distant
and difficult territory; but where conventional infrastructure is
concerned, the Australians are apt to be very conservative. A
proposal was bruited about, a generation ago, for the building of

a pipeline to carry the water of the Fly River in Papua-New Guinea across the Arafura Sea to northern Australia; but there is not yet substantial settlement in all of northern Australia, itself drenched by tropical rainfall. The idea of a north-south trans-Australian irrigation and barge canal may make sense in the long sweep of history; but there is no incentive in Australia, as there was in the United States, to open up and populate the vast interior desert. Moreover, the present landholders would understandably fear the competition of such a dramatic increase in the nation's food supply: reliable export markets on a commensurate scale simply do not exist. Nor has the United Nations adopted the old but interesting proposal for a central warehouse system for the planet's food. Perhaps one day Henry Wallace's idea of "an ever-normal granary" will be adopted internationally; but in an era of apparent agricultural surpluses, it is not realistic to expect such a prudent provision against drought and famine, which, although they are recurring phenomena, cannot be forecast with any degree of accuracy.

In the early sixties, I was invited to lecture at the Oak Ridge National Laboratory, partly because of my experiences in one of Australia's coastal deserts. The notion then given serious credence by the research staff was that coastal deserts all over the world could be developed very substantially through the device of a "NUPLEX," that is, a Nuclear-Powered Agro-Industrial Complex. It must be remembered that these were the early and optimistic days of nuclear power; predictions were lightly made that nuclear power costs would in a very few years be brought down to levels of one mill or less per kilowatt hour. Under these circumstances, the costs of desalinating seawater would be inconsequential, and projects that would make the Chaffeys look like small-time promoters could proliferate all over the earth, ending for centuries the threat of hunger and starvation. Having served, in the late 1960's, as founding president of an Institute for the Future, I know how difficult long-range forecasting can be; but a history of the NUPLEX proposal would have to stand alongside the West Virginia Turnpike and other such examples of statistical optimism run amok. Ramtanu Maitra, P.E., has reported (Special Report dated February 23, 1982, of EIR—Executive Intelligence Review, New York City) that the gov ernment of India "is constructing such a nuplex in the state of Uttar Pradesh, using the Oak Ridge ideas . . . The technology for such projects is proven." It will be interesting to learn more about this project, particularly with regard to power and other costs, as it evolves.

Settled agriculture has always had to contend against the competition of cattle and sheep ranchers, and a glance at early history will disclose a whole series of enormous walls erected, with brick and mortar, to keep nomadic pastoralists at bay. Egyptians of the Twelfth Dynasty built a wall from Heliopolis to Pelusium to halt pastoral tribes from unwelcome incursions. The Assyrians built a stone fence across the Euphrates to wall out the Medes, and the Persians a stone barrier against the Huns. The Great Wall of China, reputed to be visible with the naked eye from the moon, was intended as a defense against Mongol attack (although it had, too, the less publicized object of keeping settled subjects of the Chinese Empire within convenient boundaries for taxation and service). Hadrian's Wall in Scotland was not different. When I was a boy, the Maginot Line of France was regarded as a sufficient answer to the threat of German invasion; before dismissing it as obviously inadequate, the reader ought to look at some of the retrospective literature in its favor, including Vivian Rowe's *The Great Wall of France*.[4]

Today, with cruise missiles, atomic bombs, and the whole paraphernalia of modern warfare, it is unlikely that extensive fortifications will regain the importance they have held in earlier military history. But safety remains a paramount human interest, and in a quiet and realistic way, Europeans have begun to build underground shelters, on a very large scale, against the day when inadvertence or rapacity may loose the horrors of atomic warfare upon populations whose preservation will depend, not on the thickness of walls, but on the thickness and durability of roofs! The Swiss and the Swedes, for instance, have enacted sweeping legislation requiring dwellings and office buildings to have access to emergency areas underground where equipment, food, and personnel will be on hand to take care of "worst case" conditions. An America that has not known the devastation of war since the North overcame the South finds it hard to accept the new reality that all major powers are now vulnerable to instant and massive attack; in the dangerous world in which we are destined to live out our days, there is no doubt that the increase of underground construction of all kinds will represent an accelerating trend.

In a more pleasant vein, we may look forward to the establishment of new cities and towns as a flourishing field of activity for engineers, architects, and planners. In recent years, the newly wealthy developing countries have been the principal clients for purveyors of new settlements. But the new town movement remains alive and well in the United Kingdom; Milton Keynes, for instance, has attracted wide acclaim and even serves as home base for The Open University, which grants valid degrees to students who attend lectures given over TV and radio. Venezuela has made a success of its contrived industrial city, Valencia; in the United States itself, new incorporated real-estate developments such as Reston, Virginia, and Columbia, Maryland, have now become an accepted part of the landscape. It is well to remember that Washington D.C.; Canberra, Australia; Ottawa, Canada; and Brasilia, Brazil, were all towns that, like Alexandria in ancient times, were planned "from scratch." Peter Land has usefully reminded us that, with a high-density policy, we can preserve the clear distinction between town and country, and avoid the "suburban sprawl" that disfigures such extensive tracts in the developed countries.

Summer capitals may become increasingly attractive as the established seats of government are overwhelmed by haphazard incremental growth; even in the United States—which has been free of revolution for a longer period than any major power on earth—the time may come when the westward movement of population will lead to the suggestion that a summer capital be established in the West, perhaps at some point where three or four of the western states come together. There could be diplomatic, military, and administrative advantages to having a second seat of government, and with communications and transport optimally exploited, a bit of decentralization might find favor with both politicians and the public. Visitors from abroad ought to have a chance to see a more rural, relaxed America, even if they come here on official business. And stress-burdened bureaucrats, congressmen, and judges also need a break from the pressure-cooker atmosphere of our principal seat of government. But for whom should such a second capital be named? Jefferson? Grant? Kennedy? Ford? We are, palpably, in the realm of politics! But this is just where macro-engineering belongs: in the forefront of public and political consciousness, even if we are discussing such "unpolitical" questions as supersonic underground transport, or macrosystems for the delivery of solar power.

In the realm of diplomacy, one may legitimately ask whether engineering cannot provide new options in very complex situations. For instance, might not an investment in a transisthmian canal in Nicaragua constitute a constructive, unifying economic goal for that beleaguered country? And might not the Palestinians, with full Israeli cooperation, envisage a homeland built in international waters with funds that would otherwise be spent on warfare?

How can such complexities be approached? The identification and delineation of a logical engineering scheme is almost the simplest part of the chore of analysis and forethought. A basic first step may be no more than an unstructured discussion among persons with a professional or romantic interest in the subject. Such *ad hoc* groups have the advantage that they can include representatives from both public and private sectors: Consulting engineers can dine affably with contractors; geophysicists can consort with lawyers; and, at appropriate moments, bankers can contribute their cryptic but vital comments.

The present entrepreneurial impasse is sometimes discussed in terms of a supposed failure of the social sciences to keep pace with the physical sciences, but the problem may also be defined operationally: Can the costs and benefits of large-scale engineering "solutions" to social problems be assessed with sufficient accuracy to justify investment? If all concerned can be persuaded that a given project—or series of projects—will indeed have specific and desirable effects, the risks of decision are reduced and the likelihood of a favorable arrangement enhanced. Can the forecasts be trusted? For those whose political and financial necks are on the block, this is not a casual question. When Premier Bourassa of Quebec on April 30, 1971, decided to back a fifteen-billion-dollar hydroelectric development based on sites bordering James Bay, he could not have known that OPEC would drive up energy prices to the point where even the costly transmission lines to New England and New York would be included with ease in the program's budget. As G. K. Chesterton wrote in "The Ballad of the White Horse," "There is always a thing forgotten, there is always a thing downtrod." Certainty is rarely an element in the decisional process!

Having said this much, we can nonetheless take comfort from the circumstance that in many respects, engineering forecasts have now achieved a notable state of reliability and acceptance. Predictions as to the physical output of an oil refinery, the traffic on a toll road, or the demand for electric power in a given area are made by specialized organizations whose entire reputation and livelihood are based on a long history of expert and accurate prediction. Madigan & Hyland, a leading New York firm of traffic engineers, forecast traffic and tolls on the New York Thruway with remarkable exactitude. Each year, billions of dollars are invested on the strength of forecasts bearing the signatures of consulting engineers whose knowledge and integrity are bywords on Wall Street and in "the City" (London's financial district). Investment banking institutions, public and private, have come to place great faith in the judgment of such firms.

If, nevertheless, the complexities of forecasting in such an open-ended "system" as present-day society appear too disturbing to contemplate, uncertainties can often be reduced by the black and white of an enforceable contract: Where costs or revenues are in doubt, credit-worthy institutions can act as guarantors that necessary targets will be met. In the current negotiations for a rail tunnel under the English channel, a sticking point has been the United Kingdom's insistence that private finance guarantee all risks except a stoppage of the work due to government action. With traffic and toll revenues expected to be sufficient to pay all costs, this does not seem, on the surface, to be an unreasonable requirement. A guarantee might even be negotiated with the European Community, on the basis that the European Parliament has approved the project[5] and regards it as an essential part of a modern transport infrastructure for Europe.

Insurance companies, with their sophisticated array of purchasable safeguards (such as performance bonds), frequently play a helpful and even crucial part in project authorization. And where capital markets still sound an uncertain trumpet, consumers, in the form of private associations or governments, can agree to lease facilities or to purchase a "through-put" so that revenues can be calculated with an exactness based not on mere third-party forecasts but on the firm undertakings of an enforceable contract.

Improved forecasting, however, remains a tempting if elusive target. The recent interest in forecasting represents a healthy response to the evident unpreparedness of administrative cadres the world over to foresee in time many of our most glaring social problems. Within the past three decades, hundreds of research centers, often with impressive credentials, have been formed to seek answers to a variety of social problems; many of these "think tanks" are computer-oriented. But how can such diffuse intellectual resources be harnessed in order to optimize contributions to specific problem-solving tasks?

The joint venture among scientific institutions represents one hopeful approach. Another encouraging development is the growing sophistication of data processing. Plans are now afoot to design specialized computer banks so that projects and programs can be compared economically and rapidly, irrespective of the boundaries of space and time. Macro-engineering projects are becoming nonexceptional, yet information about them remains diffuse and dispersed. In view of the usual long lead-time for the implementation of major programs, it is essential for public policy makers to have ready access to plans that, while perhaps impractical when devised, may suddenly find that, with changed circumstances, "their time has come."

At least one major imponderable remains. Assuming that forecasts have been made in a responsible manner and that they have generated investor confidence, can finance be mobilized on the scale necessary to underpin the enormous construction projects of the future? More specifically, where can funds be found to build new cities, new space transport systems, new agro-industrial complexes with the same degree of confidence that attended the financing of, say, the Triborough Bridge or the New York Thruway? If the homework has been done correctly and projected revenues are sufficient and verified, there is a very good chance of obtaining finance even for such tremendous affairs. The problem is seldom lack of capital, but rather the negotiation of incentive and security arrangements that satisfy the legitimate interests of all concerned. Cordell W. Hull and Denis M. Slavitch have outlined the prerequisites of "macrofinance" in a brilliant paper, "The Engineer's Evolving Project Financial Role," published in 1980 by the Bechtel Group.

The world's capital markets, in short, are equal to the task. By some estimates, more than one trillion seven hundred billion dollars have been circulating in the Eurocurrency market; assuming that approximately half of that amount represents the wealth of countries seeking solid investments in overseas real estate and industrial developments—and that the world's monetary system remains stable—the capability surely exists to finance, over a period of years, selected projects costing five billion dollars and up. But a "Global Infrastructure Fund," as envisaged by the Mitsubishi Research Institute,[6] would doubtless improve present capabilities; it deserves the most respecful examination by the highest authorities of the world's leading industrial powers; and the acquiescence of developing nations lacking in financial resources should not be difficult to obtain.

These are complex matters requiring much forethought and patience, but the systems analysis of the future, if it is to be useful in the solution of social problems, must address itself conscientiously to these relatively unintellectual issues, or stand convicted of that most cardinal of social sins—irrelevance. In our pedestrian age, the banker is a necessary partner of the social technologist: A precondition to the successful use of macro-engineering in the campaign to improve humanity's lot may well be the lowering of semantic barriers between them. Fortunately, the two groups share a familiarity with mathematics! And experience suggests that the future macroentrepreneur will be well advised to bring in potential investors early in the game. For when all is said and done, it is the investing group (public and/or private) that has to decide whether the picture of the future produced by feasibility studies is believable.

But the feasibility of new technology-based macroprojects goes far beyond the narrow question of the relation of costs to revenues. The public is increasingly an *educated* public: It is widely known that not all experience with novel technologies has been favorable. Few now doubt the power of modern engineering to restructure the environment—it is, rather, a matter for searching inquiry as to whether a given program will in fact deliver the scintillating benefits promised by its advocates. The R.M.S. *Titanic* set out without enough lifeboats to carry more than half the persons aboard. Engineers, scientists, and managers must not be shocked when the public demands "environmental impact statements" or other prudential documents! And a wise "public relations" policy will treat the concerns and values of society with very great respect: Macro-engineering in particular must operate under the self-imposed motto of Frederick the Great: *Ich Dien.**

I remember, a generation ago, visiting the charming province of Prince Edward Island to advise on the finance of a bridge scheme to connect the island with Canada's mainland. Together with Ernest Tracy, a bright young investment banker, and Norman Wuestefeld, a senior traffic engineer, our group was able to address the twin problems of finance and traffic. But as the studies proceeded, it became doubtful that the island's population really wished to forego its insular isolation: The prospect of motorcycle gangs roaring across the bridge from New Brunswick did not appeal to an aging rural populace. And despite projected benefits to the island's economy, the scheme has not moved forward. One upshot of our visit, however, was crystallization of support for an "Institute on Man and Resources," an idea developed by Premier Alexander Campbell and his astute advisers David Morison and Andrew Wells. The discussion of a macroproject for Canada's smallest province thus led, indirectly, to a miniproject that has brought a number of "low" and "intermediate" technologies to the attention of the islanders. In order to provide a varied menu of ideas for institute activities, Premier Campbell visited a number of *small* research institutes in New England, New York, and elsewhere, and also organized a structured conference in Charlottetown to consider possible programs. At this fascinating series of meetings, I recall meeting the secretary and deputy secretary of agriculture of Pennsylvania

---

*I serve

(James McHale and Jane Alexander); the chief project engineer of the Electric Boat Division of General Dynamics Corporation (J. Vincent Harrington), John Evans of the innovative Institute for Educational Services of Massachusetts, C. Lawrence Meador, who had carried out a special study on aquaculture, and Major Jacques Istel, the famous founder of Sport Parachuting, who arrived in his own airplane, piloted by his vivacious wife.

If Prince Edward Island should eventually decide on a mainland connection, perhaps a good solution would be a tunnel or tube that, quite unobtrusively, could ferry passengers and vehicles across the nine-mile-wide Northumberland Strait even when that body of water is obscured by autumn fog or obstructed by the winter ice. What is amusing in this whole story is that when the island (where, in 1864, there was a much-celebrated meeting of "the fathers of confederation") finally decided to join the Canadian Confederation, the PEI delegation insisted on an iron-clad guarantee of reliable transport to the mainland.

Like the case of the Prince Edward Island Causeway—but against a larger backdrop—the history of the controversy over the supersonic transport—the SST—highlights the changes that have taken place, within one generation, in attitudes toward big technology. Professor Mel Horwitch, who recently taught a course with me at the Alfred P. Sloan School of Management at M.I.T., has written a lively book, *Clipped Wings*, which reviews this instructive episode (or, more accurately, series of episodes). Horwitch rightly concludes:

> When the conflict began, technological decisions as a rule were not considered appropriate matters for debate in the public arena. These decisions tended to be made by experts in government agencies, research organizations and industry. It was implicitly accepted that the general public had neither the competence, the right, nor the interest to question seriously the actions resulting in a major technological advance . . . But during the 1960s . . . a new mindset emerged. Gradually disciplines and professions that had hitherto been absent from technological decision making entered the various technological debates.

Whether the defeat of the United States SST—(*Concorde*, of

course, is alive if not well)—was inevitable and justified will long serve as a thesis subject or debating topic for budding historians of technology—and of politics. From my limited vantage point, I did notice one or two missed opportunities. When Alan Boyd was President Johnson's Secretary of Transportation, he telephoned my (small) New York law office, urging me to "take the next plane" to Washington. Apparently, Rear Admiral R. K. ("Jimmy") James had suggested to the secretary that my experience of building a billion-dollar syndicate for the English Channel Tunnel might be duplicated for the SST. I was in the office of the administrator of the Federal Aviation Agency, General J. C. Maxwell, the next morning.

The general asked whether I would take on a consulting assignment to see if private finance was a viable option for the SST. I demurred, on the grounds that I did not personally possess or control the three-quarters of a billion dollars then thought necessary for the program, and that it seemed to me that the government should not be satisfied with "third party" opinions as to what other people—in this case, bankers—might do. However, we compromised by writing into the contract a stipulation that my report had to be endorsed by an investment bank capable of underwriting the necessary sum.

Within two weeks, I was able to present to the government a solid alternative to government finance. John F. Fowler, Jr., an authority on investment banking who had recently retired from a leading Wall Street house, collaborated on the report, which was duly endorsed by the famous firm with which he had been associated. Government guarantees would have been required, in view of the immense sums at risk for a government-initiated program; but this was long before the Lockheed and Chrysler guarantees had soured public and congressional opinion on the use of the guarantee power. The program managers continued to be so confident of congressional willingness to provide funding for the SST that the option of private finance was not seriously considered. This turned out to be a misreading of the political firmament. Had the government turned the whole venture over to a private or mixed-economy corporation, much mischief might have been averted.

After the event—and especially after a failure—it is a hazardous enterprise to define "what might have been." I have been fascinated for many years by the failure of Ferdinand de Lesseps, after his stunning success at Suez, to complete a canal in Panama. All sorts of reasons are given: the inadequacy of French engineering or equipment, the ravages of disease, the route selected, and so on. It is conceivable, however, that all these difficulties might have been overcome if the Vicomte de Lesseps had followed the advice to raise twice as much capital as he thought necessary![7] The old man, in his pride, was too confident that the "French peasants" would always provide whatever funds were needed. When the well ran dry, the coffers were empty, and Lesseps's reputation went down the drain also! *Sic transit gloria mundi.* The example demonstrates, too, that even in the last century, public confidence and support was a sine qua non for macro-engineering success.

Public dismay at supertechnology's "darker side" has been particularly poignant in the case of nuclear power. I served, in the sixties, on a Commission on Nuclear Power Plant Location appointed by Governor Dempsey of Connecticut. The experience drove home to me the depth of public feeling on this issue. I believe that nuclear power, for carefully defined purposes and in appropriate circumstances, must remain a technology that the United States can master and apply. We need more, not fewer, engineers versed in this intricate technology. But nuclear-power plants should probably be clustered in remote locations, despite the fact that their safety record appears to compare so favorably with the record of coal-fired and oil-burning plants. Dr. Arthur Parthé, a former senior staff member of the Charles Stark Draper Laboratory, has shown in a magnificent series of lectures that the costs of such nuclear power plants as the Seabrook, New Hampshire, project have literally "gone through the roof." But it is not sufficient to blame the public for the endless delays and the lengthy approvals now required: An engineer-management team that launches such large and costly affairs must stand or fall on the confidence of the public—*caveat vendor.*

Perhaps no project better illustrates the dependence of macro-engineering on public and private sentiment than the many proposals for a fixed link between England and France.[8] A tunnel through the "lower chalk" was first proposed by the young French geologist Demarets in 1751. Napoleon, during the brief Peace of Amiens in 1802, spoke enthusiastically of the project to the visiting English statesman John Fox. With the coming of age of railway technology in Queen Victoria's time, it is not astonishing that railway promoters, in the United Kingdom and in France, were able to obtain concessions and lobby a treaty through the two parliaments. In 1881, construction was started from both coasts. The work was halted after about a mile of progress, because of the strident opposition of Sir Garnet Wolseley, Adjutant-General of the British Army, who forced Prime Minister Gladstone to recant his support of the scheme. Wolseley, still a national hero because he snuffed out the Louis Riel Rebellion at Fort Garry in western Canada (in 1870), later was to lead the ill-fated attempt to rescue General "Chinese" Gordon from Khartoum in the Sudan.

After World War I, General Foch declared that the war could have been won in 1916 instead of 1918 if the Entente had been supplied through a channel tunnel. Winston Churchill argued for the project in a long, copiously illustrated article for the February 12, 1936, *Daily Mail*. But except for some skirmishing in the House of Commons in 1936, there was little significant activity on the project until its accidental revival, in 1956, by a group of friends who listened sympathetically when I recounted my tale of woe. Cyril Means and I were aware of the question put to Harold Macmillan, then Minister of Defense (in 1956), as to whether there were still military objections to a channel tunnel, and of Mr. Macmillan's succinct reply, "Scarcely any." The stormy crossings of the channel during that summer led me to contact one of the leaders of the American engineering profession, George R. Brown, to see if anything practical could be done. Mr. Brown, who had been a leading member of the Houston Chamber of Commerce Military Affairs Committee when I worked in Houston after graduation from law school (the committee was one of my responsibilities as a staff member) asked just one question: the distance from shore to shore. When I said "twenty-one miles, maybe a little more," Mr. Brown looked pensive. "Well," he drawled, "Brown and Root has just about completed the Roberts Tunnel, which brings water to Denver across the Great Divide; it's almost as long!"

Mr. Brown, with his brother, Herman, had built up one of the nation's great construction companies. He invited me to lunch at the Pinnacle Club atop New York's Mobil Tower on Forty-second Street and Lexington Avenue, and asked if I knew any bankers. I had to confess that I could not remember ever having met an important banker. Shortly, on Mr. Brown's introduction, and in my best gray suit, I appeared before the desk of Mr. Thomas S. Lamont at the 23 Wall Street headquarters of what was still known as J. P. Morgan & Company, now the Morgan Guaranty Trust Company of New York. After explaining the channel tunnel idea, I was slightly taken aback when Mr. Lamont peered over his bifocals and quietly asked a younger man, at an adjacent rolltop desk, whether he thought the bank should help build a channel tunnel. Mr. Henry Alexander, then president of the bank, lowered the paper at which he had been glancing, looked me over quizzically from head to toe, and replied, "Why not?"

On this slender basis, I was propelled into a round of enthralling meetings with people who were accustomed to getting things done. Mr. Lamont showed up, unannounced, at my law office a few days later, to inquire if I knew any engineers besides George R. Brown. When I admitted that I did not, he suggested that I invite Mr. Brown, Mr. Stephen D. Bechtel, and Mr. Jack Bonney (then chairman of Morrison Knudsen Company, Inc., now of Standard Oil), to lunch with us. To make sure they would come, Mr. Lamont put in personal calls to each of them. And at the resulting lunch, these three heads of firms agreed to furnish, without any cost whatsoever, a careful report on the channel tunnel project. To this very day, their recommendation of twin rail tunnels, with a service tunnel between, has been "par for the course."

Cyril Means and I, joined by a brother of mine, a brother-in-law, and a few others, organized a corporation, Technical Studies, Inc., in New York City in March, 1957. This seemed necessary because a casual letter to the chairman of the Suez Canal Company had evoked a prompt and interested response: President Nasser had just deprived the company of its canal, and this most elegant of European investment companies was looking for a large engineering project to replace it. The New York representative, Monsieur Claude Boillot, with a very keen sense of humor behind his bland Oxford accent (although French, Monsieur Boillot had been raised in Oxford, where his father was a well-known don) sent one of his staff to "look things over." Within weeks, Technical Studies, Inc., and the Suez Canal Company (its name now changing to Suez Financial Company) had met in Paris with representatives of the two firms that had started to build the tunnel in 1881. Because the old railways had been nationalized, we found that the successor companies had, respectively, the government railways as leading shareholders. When the four companies, joining with the International Road Federation (Paris Office) formed the international Channel Tunnel Study Group, we found that Monsieur Louis Armand, chairman of the French National Railways, and Sir Alex B. B. Valentine, chairman of London Transport, were among the conferees!

The study group was formed by the ancient device of a "cooperative agreement"; there was a common budget, and a director was appointed to propose and manage a thorough planning and research program. To make a long story short, the group's plans were the basis of the construction undertaken in 1974 and 1975 after signature of a Franco-British Treaty.

My brother Alfred, who had known Mr. Harold Wilson in Washington during World War II, accompanied me on a visit to Mr. Wilson's parliamentary party office, just before he moved into Number 10 Downing Street as prime minister. Mr. Wilson told us the old story of the problem of starting from both coasts and finding that the tunnels did not meet in the middle: "Two for the price of one," he concluded. And there was truly no partisan problem about the project: An all-party parliamentary committee maintained good relations with Tories, Laborites, and Liberals. The project fell apart when, just before the third (and usually perfunctory) reading of the bill to ratify the treaty, a late-night Cabinet meeting was held—this was during Britain's worst postwar economic crisis—and apparently the problem of funds for modernizing the railway line from the Coast to London was raised. I was not present at the meeting, and am not privy to a full report of what was said; but the upshot was a decision to abandon the project. The French were furious at this second (1975) *volte-face* by "perfidious Albion" (the first having been brought about almost a century before, by General Wolseley).

This was, of course, a great blow. The only solution seemed to be to meet British financial fears by proposing what became known as "the mousehole": a lone single-track tunnel. Our traffic advisers, De Leuw Cather & Company, of Chicago, studied the matter and decided that, surprisingly, the single-track tunnel could pay its way. British Rail adopted the suggestion, and the French National Railways (the SNCF) in a generous gesture to keep the project alive, agreed to a number of conditions that would reduce the expense and the impacts for Britain. Because one fear was the effect of increased "lorry" or truck traffic on the roadways of Kent, the engineering design was modified to reduce this contingency. But where was the willing client?

Unexpectedly, when Prime Minister Margaret Thatcher held her initial luncheon meeting with President Mitterrand of France, in London, in September of 1981, the two heads of government formed a close and sympathetic personal understanding. To celebrate their goodwill, an announcement was made that both countries would send representatives to early meetings of a Joint Technical Commission. When the commission reported favorably, a second group was appointed to look into financial aspects. It is therefore not impossible that this shaggy-dog story will have a happy ending, perhaps shortly after the general election in the United Kingdom! Having been cast in the role of "promoter," I must confess to intermittent feelings of optimism, even after twenty-five years of effort! However, I take some consolation from the thought that my father labored for at least as long a period as one of Senator George Norris's early group of advocates of the St. Lawrence Seaway and Power Project. In 1955, one week before my father's death, he attended the opening ceremonies for the power portion (the most costly part) of this project. It is not exactly the sort of effort that would win high marks at the Harvard Business School. But I must take my hat off to the international platoon of diplomats, bankers, engineers, and lawyers who labored—quite unselfishly—for a result that they knew might take a long time a-coming. The European Parliament has, several times, pronounced itself in favor of a fixed link across the English Channel, as a vital part of a modern infrastructure for Europe. It is admittedly an old idea. But if it is out of date, that will be because the conception is not broad enough: With even the speeds already attained by Mr. Kyotani's test train at Miyazaki, it is evident that an electromagnetically levitated system could provide one-hour service between the city centers of London and Paris. In the next century, we may confidently expect proposals for a tunnel that is continuous between London and Paris, to accommodate trains flying at supersonic speed. The inhabitants of such a "new London" (or "new" Paris) will be blessed by the absence of aircraft-noise pollution once high-speed transport goes underground, as it now should!

It may be asked how an American could become involved in a project that seemed to assume that nineteenth-century military theories no longer were valid for Britain. Well, having served for five years in "the king's uniform" (although I never swore allegiance to the king, and maintained American citizenship throughout the war), I decided to approach the principal military authorities directly. Through Ward B. Chamberlin, Jr., of the American Field Service, I obtained an introduction to Admiral Lord Louis Mountbatten, then serving as first sea lord at Admiralty House. I had performed some legal services, and AFS had kindly entrusted me with a copy of their recently published account of the American Field Service in World War II, to present to Lord Mountbatten. He was a "quick study." At once accepting the book, and very graciously, he then stepped in front of his desk and said directly, "Now I am sure you have some other question for me!" I asked, as directly, whether there was any naval or military objection to the construction of a channel tunnel. Mountbatten replied, "That is entirely a *commercial* question. And good luck!"

A few days later, with the benefit of an introduction from my late and much-lamented friend and classmate Philip H. Bagby, Cyril Means and I called on the Earl Alexander of Tunis, who had been minister of defense in the last Churchill government. Philip had received the U.S. State Department's highest decoration, for carrying a message through both American and French lines, shortly after the landings in North Africa, to the

French high command. This exploit brought about a rapid cessation of hostilities; the French troops rallied to the Allied cause.

Cyril Means and I were kindly offered a sumptuous tea at the Alexanders' home in Windsor Great Forest. When we explained the reason for our visit, Field Marshal Alexander slowly "refought" the battle of Dunkirk, on the assumption that a channel tunnel had then existed and that the British forces would have retreated to a perimeter defense around the tunnel mouth in France. I was so worried about the outcome of the simulation that I found it hard to swallow the delicious tea and crumpets. But the battle came out right, and Alexander finally told us, smiling, that had the tunnel existed, he would not only have got the whole army safely home to Britain, but its heavy guns and equipment as well!

The Channel Tunnel Study Group had a strong team of leading Britons to champion the project's case. Lord Harcourt, a managing partner of Morgan Grenfell and Company, Ltd., succeeded as the group's cochairman after the death of Sir Ivone Augustine Kirkpatrick. Leo d'Erlanger, a banker who inherited his great-uncle's shares in the English Channel Tunnel Company, Ltd., was a passionate advocate. William Merton, originally an aide to Mr. d'Erlanger, later became head of Fleming's, the Scottish bank that invented the investment trust; he was a good choice to become head of British Channel Tunnel Investments, Ltd., the reorganized British company that included British Railways as a leading shareholder. For the 1974–75 effort, a consortium of the leading British banks joined the French group headed by the Banque Rothschild and the American group headed by Morgan Stanley & Company.

The present position of the project is somewhat confused: On the British side, consortia have been formed to propose both finance and construction, with each consortium consisting of a group of contractors together with a merchant bank. The British Steel Corporation, headed by the dynamic Ian MacGregor before Mr. MacGregor took over the (even larger) Coal Board, has proposed a "brunnel," with causeways on the coasts leading down to tubes that would be laid across the middle section of the channel where there is the heaviest shipping activity. To provide a further option to all concerned, I have proposed a somewhat

novel arrangement, designed with the help of the experienced
J. Vincent Harrington: With a submerged caisson in the mid-
channel area, it would be possible for a bored tunnel to be dug
from the center *toward* the coasts as well as from the coasts
toward the center! The idea might reduce the time of construction by as much as two years or more, thus saving the sums that
would otherwise have to be paid out as interest during this period; and revenues would begin flowing into the project's coffers
about two years earlier.[9] Whether such an idea will ultimately
prove attractive, despite the risks always implicit in a new technology, will have to await further data on interest rates, costs,
and other vital details.

On the French side, there have been very few political problems. We have even had some good luck from time to time. I
remember calling on Monsieur Georges Pompidou when he was
still a managing director at the rue Laffitte offices of Rothschild
Frères; my mission was to ask him to see General de Gaulle, the
president of France. Monsieur Pompidou said he could not take
the initiative—he would have to wait for the general's call; it
came, almost the next day, and the reason for the summons was
that Pompidou was asked to become prime minister! (In due
course, he, too, became President of France.)

The European press has been almost uniformly friendly to
the project. We had a bad moment or two when the French
members of the group contrived an important ceremony in
order to open an exhibit, atop one of the major French department stores, of a working model of the French terminal area. To
everyone's dismay, the model failed to function when the button
was pressed! But so great was the enthusiasm for the general
scheme as represented by the model, that the malfunction was
not mentioned. When the subcontractors repaired the switch on
the following day, crowds of people were able to watch miniature
cars load on to the railway flatwagons and disappear into the
small tunnel marked *Angleterre.*

The British Railways Board had had a highly detailed scale
model made of the terminal area on the British side; and this
model was exhibited at Charing Cross Station in London and at
key points throughout the island of Britain. It was even the subject of an excellent short documentary film shown on the BBC. I

am not sure of the exact origin of this model, which helped appreciably in interesting public opinion in the project. One version is that the British Railways people were shocked by the inaccuracy of a model contributed to Technical Studies, Inc., by a model-train company. Put together hastily and displayed on the main banking floor of the Morgan Guaranty Trust Company at 23 Wall Street, this model was photographed by—and subsequently displayed in—*The New York Times*. What seems to have bothered our British friends the most was not the miniature rolling stock, which was American, but the fact that the trees on the model could not have withstood the harsh conditions on the south coast of England! Of course we were all most grateful that the British Railways Board had commissioned such a beautiful, accurate working scale model.

Every effort was made to bring only first-class American representation to the table. Mr. Thomas S. Lamont and the Hon. Lewis W. Douglas (former United States Ambassador to the Court of St. James's), represented us on the governing board of the study group, as did our onetime counsel, George W. Ball, Esq., before he became Undersecretary of State of the United States. The Technical Studies board of directors has included the Hon. Paul Nitze, now United States Arms Negotiator in Geneva, and several former ambassadors. The study group deliberately excluded contractors and consulting engineers from its board, and this policy has been followed by Technical Studies, Inc., so that objective judgment can be used in selecting only the most qualified people for the various jobs to be done. I think the Channel Tunnel Study Group, as a mixed-economy enterprise, fulfilled its mission of relaunching the project and did so with remarkable harmony and good effect. Now, with "new actors" on the political scene, and so much basic groundwork already accomplished, it will be interesting to watch the framework to be set by further Anglo-French agreements if, as seems not altogether unlikely, 1984 should be the year of decision for the channel tunnel.

In a way, I suppose macro-engineering could be recommended as a "hobby" to people who have reached a position in life where their "bread and butter" is taken care of, and who would like to make some major contribution to human progress.

Large projects, like small ones, need champions and sponsors. I believe we must be very grateful to the handful of serious entrepreneurs who have given our era new major projects to think about, to improve, and perhaps to build. Without Governor Clinton's long advocacy, one doubts whether America would have had an Erie Canal. No one denies that Brunel was essential to the *Great Eastern*, the very large nineteenth-century steamship that ultimately laid the Atlantic Cable. In further chapters, I shall discuss some contemporary projects that, in the nature of things, were the creations of gifted individuals. Nor are such people necessarily lacking in the finer arts of analysis and criticism; what I am saying is that the conceptualization and advocacy of a new large design is almost a métier of its own. Without the late Benton Mackaye, it is unlikely that we would today have an Appalachian Trail, with an unobstructed walkway from Maine to Georgia. Even old projects ultimately need renewal or recasting in a new form: Thus, de Lesseps took the basic idea of the Pharaoh Sesostris and gave it a new location, and Judah Benjamin saw that the railroads slowly extending to the western territories could, by a bold and articulate effort, unite the American continent from coast to coast.

After VE-Day in 1945, I was stationed with the Fort Garry Horse, a Canadian armored regiment to which I had been posted for most of the campaign in northwest Europe. The regiment was settled in the lovely but partly destroyed village of Doetinchem, in Holland's province of Gelderland. Due to the shortage of shipping, we knew it would be many months before we could embark for demobilization in Canada. Our colonel, E. M. Wilson, DSO, decided to prepare the troops actively for re-entry into private life. As a civilian, he had been advertising manager of the *Montreal Star*; he certainly knew the arts of persuasion and publicity. As one of his aides, I watched with admiration as the regimental carpenters built huge chess sets, and noticed that for weeks virtually the only topic of conversation among all ranks was the intricate game of chess. A club was opened for officers, noncommissioned officers, and enlisted men; once within its doors, anyone who addressed a comrade by his military rank was subject to humiliation and temporary banishment! When I described to my colonel the brief article written by Eugen Rosenstock-Huessy entitled "A Peace Within," which proposed that a unit of the German Army be delegated for civilian construction (in the tradition of the Roman Army), Colonel Wilson instantly expressed his admiration, and ordered me to join him in half an hour, dressed properly for a ceremonial visit to the old burgomaster in charge of the town. The burgomaster received us most courteously, and listened with patience and a flicker of a smile around his heavily bearded lips as the colonel proposed that the regiment use heavy equipment from Canadian Army Headquarters to clean up the rubble caused when the German SS Frundsberg Division and ourselves were debating control of the area.

With unusual care and deliberation, the burgomaster poured us glasses of Bols, the famous high-quality "Geneva gin" made in Holland. Then he explained to us some of the facts of local political life: Under funds provided by the Dutch government, the town was on the verge of employing more than a hundred unemployed heads of family to utilize their two-wheeled horse-drawn carts to take away the rubble that disfigured the town and impeded rebuilding. If we insisted on doing this job in a few days with machinery from headquarters, Doetinchem would lose its qualification for relief work and many families would go hungry! At this point, the burgomaster had an inspiration: The regiment *might*, he suggested, concentrate on an open area not far from the center of town, and build a park to be named after our colonel; thus the troops would have the experience of useful accomplishment, the town would have a lovely rebuilt park, and no one would be thrown out of work! Colonel Wilson, for whom the park was in fact named, promptly acceded; and Army Headquarters, where our previous colonel, Ronald E. A. Morton, DSO, now served as a major-general, was instantly cooperative. Thus, at least in a small way, the idea bruited by William James in 1910 and reinforced in 1912 by Rosenstock-Huessy in Germany, was fully implemented by a western Canadian regiment fighting homesickness in a delightful but somewhat desolated town of Holland!

When I was an undergraduate at Harvard, several of us had met Rosenstock-Huessy, who had taught in five different departments of the university and ultimately received a permanent appointment as professor of social philosophy at Dartmouth. My roommate, George Phillips (who recently retired after a splendid but self-effacing career in the State Department); Philip Haxall Bagby of Virginia (whom I mentioned earlier as the American who nonchalantly drove across the combatant lines in Morocco to deliver a message that halted the fighting between two old allies); Enno Reimar Hobbing of Pennsylvania, whose adventurous life has included the editorship, immediately after VE-Day, of *Die Neue Deutsche Zeitung* in Berlin and authorship of one of the first articles (for *Fortune* magazine) on the technology of building artificial islands for airport and industrial uses—the four of us decided *not* to rush off to graduate school, but to spend a full year as hired hands on backhill Vermont farms. Then, with Rosenstock-Huessy's advice, we obtained permission from President Roosevelt to enter the Civilian Conservation Corps as volunteer enrollees; we were joined in these efforts by a group of Dartmouth students, including Charles Page Smith of Baltimore (now a noted American historian); Robert O'Brien (one of several members of the group who became farmers in Vermont—Bob has also been the state's commissioner of higher education), and several others. This was the true genesis of Camp William James, described in detail by our campmate Professor Jack Preiss of Duke University, in his 1978 book published by Clinton Gardner's Argo Press in Norwich, Vermont.

As a senior in college, I had begun preparing, with the benign aid of the eminent historian Dumas Malone (best known as author of a series of comprehensive books on the life of Jefferson), a volume coedited with Thacher Winslow, and entitled *American Youth: an Enforced Reconnaissance*. Published in 1940 by the Harvard University Press, this slender book, which reprinted both the William James 1910 essay "The Moral Equivalent of War" and the 1912 memorandum "A Peace Within," intended by Rosenstock-Huessy for the German Army, was destined to play a larger role than any of us foresaw. Sargent Shriver, in an article on the origins of the Peace Corps written for the 1962 edition of *The American People's Encyclopaedia* (pp. 499–500)—Grolier—cited both Camp William James and the volume *American Youth* in his careful listing of events and precedents that led to President Kennedy's 1961 executive order setting up the

Peace Corps. When, six months after the March 1 executive order, Congress made the Peace Corps permanent, those of us who were veterans of so many early initiatives were pleased that many others, in oncoming generations, would be able to experience some of the benefits that we felt we had derived from a period of outdoor service; the Peace Corps, interestingly, was often touted under the rubric of "technical assistance." In today's much-vaunted "information society," I wonder whether we should not also be *collecting* information from technical practices in developing nations, which really have much to teach *us*! Sheila Kitzinger, the English anthropologist who systematically observed birthing technologies in primitive tribes in Africa and elsewhere, has enriched Western society by her reports—and by the simple artifacts she has had copied for the benefit of many thousands of women in our somewhat oversophisticated urban environments in Europe and North America! [10]

Ours is a twofold task. On the one hand, we must become a more consistent, better educated, technically competent nation. On the other hand, we must reach beyond the realms of technology and management, or we will be unable to make the readjustments so necessary for success. The Japanese are profoundly right in realizing that excellence in technology demands rigorous teamwork and a voluntary submission to standards of performance. Americans, while more individualistic, are quite able to form disciplined groups when objectives are clear; and this book is an appeal to leadership, at all levels, to form the necessary groups so that, sector by sector, we may upgrade our industry and our communities.

The combination of individual enterprise and collective, voluntary action constitutes an unbeatable recipe for national success. Nor need this formula be seen as a threat to our trading partners: The world economy is not a zero-sum game; a more prosperous America will be a better trading partner for the international community. And by learning to work with each other to better effect, we shall be equipped to enter into those international joint ventures that supertechnology has brought within the range of achievement. It goes without saying that a mature technological society will be a healthier place in which to live and work; and we shall be more secure as a nation when more of our young people have experienced the processes of outdoor and indoor teamwork and when engineering, far from being regarded as a specialized activity for a minority of the population, is placed "front and center" as a key ingredient in education and management.

Where is the leadership to come from? A generation of managers that presided over the deterioration of America's basic industries can nonetheless provide needed detailed guidance; but the incentive for those larger groupings that now appear indispensable must come from the wellsprings of patriotism and love of community that have always saved the Republic in its hour of need. While I am very respectful of cost accounting, it is not through cost accounting alone that we shall win through to a resurgence of technological preeminence. We need not only be dedicated champions for specific macro-engineering feats, but patient study groups, drawn from the best talent in all relevant fields, to examine problems and alternatives, and to shape the guidelines within which our various macro-engineering initiatives can emerge. A model for this pattern was, I think, largely established by the numerous public seminars organized by the late Carroll L. Wilson.

Carroll L. Wilson had been general manager of the Manhattan Project. He was a lawyer and mining engineer who spent his last years as a professor at M.I.T.'s Sloan School of Management. It was he who organized much of the preparatory work for the 1972 Stockholm conference on the World Environment: During the summer of 1970, in Williams, Massachusetts, he gathered leading experts on each of the main areas of environmental concern. Young law students were attached as *rapporteurs* to each committee, and the resulting "SCEP" report[11] (published by the M.I.T. Press) has been the "law of the case" ever since. When energy concerns began to be preeminent, Professor Wilson held seminars that included leaders of business, industry, and government; the seminars met in Tokyo, Buenos Aires, and elsewhere. And when the importance of coal evolved as a practical "bridging fuel," WOCO emerged: the World Coal Study.[12]

Professor Harold D. Lasswell, who served with Dean James M. Landis of the Harvard Law School on the advisory committee for the CCC, invented the idea of the "decision seminar." On the national and continental scale, this is a direction in which we must strive to move. Those with the knowledge and the power to influence high policy must now come together to seek, "with all deliberate speed," the answers we need for a restructuring of our industry so that the knowledge undoubtedly possessed by American experts on steel, transportation, shipbuilding, and other vital sectors is not needlessly ignored at home, while other societies avidly utilize this information for competitive purposes. The free and unrestricted flow of nonmilitary technical knowledge will be enhanced, not impeded, by the kind of effort recommended in these pages. Entropy—the tendency to disintegration highlighted by the laws of thermodynamics—is an ever-present danger to human communities. As George von Lengerke Meyer proclaimed a century ago, "Things alter for the worse spontaneously, unless altered for the better designedly."*

---

* George von Lengerke Meyer received his A.B. from Harvard in 1879. He was Postmaster General under President Theodore Roosevelt, and was appointed ambassador to Rome by President McKinley. He served as president of the Board of Overseers of Harvard University from 1914 to 1917.

This version of the biblical Tower of Babel was painted by Pieter Brueghel; the original is in the Kunsthistorischesmuseum in Vienna. Tradition links a zigurrat in Iraq, excavated in 1854 by Sir Henry Rawlinson, with the legendary tower; the site, a hill 100 feet high surmounted by a 40-foot "mass of vitrified brick," lies about 15 miles southwest of Babylon.

The Colossus of Rhodes was a bronze statue, 70 cubits high, built by Chares of Lindus, and representing the sun god Helios. It was thrown down by an earthquake about 224 B.C., but the broken pieces remained visible for 1,000 years.

This view of the hand and torch of the Statue of Liberty shows that colossal scale has had its millennial appeal, even in modern times. The total height of the statue and pedestal comes to 305 feet, 6 inches. The French people contributed $450,000 for the statue, erected between 1884 and 1886. The sculptor was Frédéric Auguste Bartholdi.

The Philae Temple at Aswan, shown above, was partially drowned by the original Aswan Dam in 1902. When it was submerged entirely by the new Aswan High Dam, a wit remarked, "It's a case of one macro-project destroying another." The Philae Temple was built by the Ptolemies on the site of an earlier Egyptian temple to Isis.

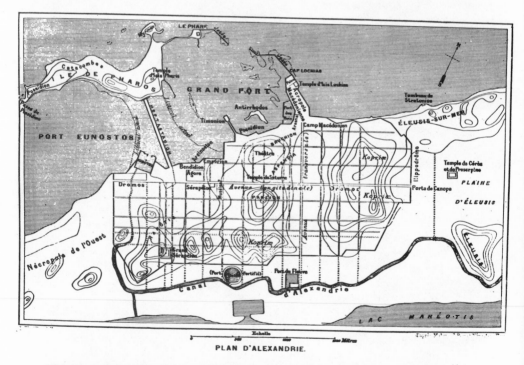

PLAN D'ALEXANDRIE.

This Plan of the City of Alexandria in Antiquity was drawn up by the French historian Duruy. The city was founded by Alexander the Great in 331 B.C. after he was crowned Pharaoh. (*H. Roger Viollet, Paris*)

The Lighthouse—or Pharos—of Alexandria is often listed as one of the seven wonders of the ancient world. Although frequently damaged by earthquakes, it endured until the fourteenth century of our era. Precise dating of its construction has not been feasible; the impulse for the project is generally ascribed to Ptolemy Soter, about 280–270 B.C. This ruler also played a large role in the foundation of the library which became a leading center of Hellenistic culture for nearly a thousand years. P. M. Fraser, in his authoritative three-volume work *Ptolemaic Alexandria* (Oxford University Press, 1972), concludes that "the Pharos was polygonal in shape, and built of three stages, tapering towards the top, and that near the summit there burnt a fire which shone far out to sea." Fraser also surmises that "the Pharos . . . was probably the earliest architecturally developed lighthouse, and was the direct or indirect model of many others throughout the Greco-Roman world." (See pp. 17–20.)

The Via Appia was originally built to join Rome and Capua but was later extended to the port city of Brindisi. Commenced by Appius Claudius in 312 B.C., the "oldest" road of Rome was found to be in excellent condition eight centuries later by Procopius, the Greek-speaking secretary of Belisarius during the sixth-century reconquest of Rome. Victor W. Von Hagen cites, in his monumental *The Roads That Led to Rome* (London: George Weidenfeld and Nicolson, Ltd., 1967), a Byzantine historian who followed Belisarius to Rome and "marvelled at the preciseness of the stone paving of the Via Appia: 'The Consul Appius caused all the paving-stones to be polished and cut so as to form angles and had them jointed together without any kind of cement. They adhered so strongly that to look at them they do not seem to be jointed at all but to form one whole mosaic of stone. . . .'"

Vitellius Aulus, who ruled as Roman emperor from January 2 to December 22 in A.D. 69, was generally regarded as an incompetent, weak emperor; but his reputation as proconsul of Africa remains untarnished. In the province of Africa, road building in particular had been revived after the Punic Wars, and good communications formed the basis of the only successful onslaught known to history on the encroaching Sahara Desert. With the 3rd (Augusta) Legion providing both military and civil engineering, a system of aqueducts, cisterns, pipelines, and tree breaks made it possible for new towns to flourish in the teeth of the desert. In the end, the old Roman system survived in Africa for more than a century after it had been vanquished on the Italian peninsula.

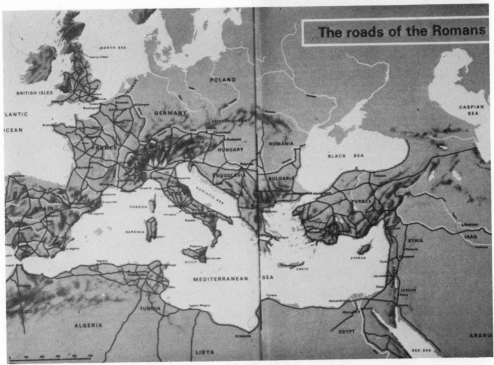

The roads of the Romans

Von Hagen generalizes that "Roman roads brought unification to all peoples. . . . There was a single coinage and a single law. There were no frontiers and no major customs barriers. Travel was open and free. On the Roman roads, police guarded against highwaymen; inns, taverns, and halting stations were open to all."

Public works were the hallmark of the Roman system. These photographs identify three aspects of Roman macro-engineering: the aqueducts (top left), which sometimes extended for more than 100 miles; the monuments (such as Hadrian's tomb [below lower left] which is still in use as the Castel San Angelo); and the Baths of Caracalla, right. From the time of Tiberius, Rome had 267 miles of conduits. Gale Young of the Oak Ridge National Laboratory has reported (in a November 1966 paper presented to The Engineers' Society of Western Pennsylvania) that "in the heyday of the Roman Empire, there flowed into the Imperial City a half-billion gallons of water per day via many aqueducts, of which the largest brought 90 million gallons per day from a distance of 150 miles. The per capita consumption was high (450 gallons per day), presumably due to the popularity of Roman baths." Infrastructure development was the basis of Roman power and prosperity. Not surprisingly, it was the Emperor Augustus who institutionalized many of the administrative arrangements. For example, he established a stable supervisory system for roads and bridges, appointing special *curatores operum publicorum tuendorum*. Costs of upkeep and of new construction were the responsibility of the treasury, but with the assistance of toll charges, municipal participation, and contributions (in the nature of taxes) from abutting landowners. The Pax Romana having extended throughout most of the known civilized world, the Roman legions—each with its own *architectus* and its tradesmen—were available for public works on the grand scale. Admirable though it was in theory, in fact there was a series of revolts by soldiers who resented the "hard labor" of unremitting peacetime toil. Vitellius Aulus was both beneficiary and victim of the military revolts that eventually shook the empire to its foundations.

Above: A view from the north of Chichén Itzá, the great Mayan metropolis which prospered from A.D. 300 to the fifteenth century. Located west of Mérida in Yucatán, it was eventually the principal base of the Itzá dynasty. These ruins include, in addition to spacious temples and a pyramid, a tennis court! Below is an artist's reconstruction of the "Acropolis" of Copán, another great center of Mayan civilization. Copán, located in Honduras near the Guatemalan frontier, contains sculptures of much interest as well as altars in the form of a turtle and stelae inscribed with hieroglyphs. Its ruins include large-scale public halls, temples, and pyramids. Much interest now attaches to the question of precisely which groups were the creators of the classic cultures, now widely admired, of Central America and southern Mexico. Archaic cultures disappeared during the early centuries of our era, and it has been customary to ascribe the development of sophisticated art, mathematics, and astronomy to the Maya alone. But as knowledge of archaeology and anthropology increases, a more complex picture is beginning to emerge. Miguel Covarrubias has an extensive discussion of this issue in *Mexico South: The Isthmus of Tehuantepec* (Alfred A. Knopf, 1954). Important ancient centers have been unveiled farther north: One may cite the pioneering work of Dr. Manuel Gamio in restoring the city of Teotihuacán, with its awe-inspiring pyramids of the sun and the moon. Clearly, large-scale engineering was a feature of indigenous civilizations in the New World as well as of the better-known civilizations of Europe and Asia.

Aigues-Mortes (above) is still surrounded by stern ramparts. Founded by Louis IX and completed by Philip the Bold in the thirteenth century, the town was a a major port of embarcation for crusaders setting out for the Holy Land. The town is situated in southeastern France, at the western edge of the Rhone delta and only two and a half miles from the Gulf of Lyon. Until the reign of Louis XIV, every ship navigating within sight of Aigue-Mortes's lights had to put in there. . . . Opposite are two views of Carcassonne, possibly the best-preserved fortified town in all Europe. Capital of the Department of Aude, the town's prosperity was enhanced during the reign of Louis XIV when it became a port on the new Canal des Deux Mers which linked the Atlantic Ocean (near Bordeaux) and the Mediterranean Sea (near Toulouse). The fortifications were restored in the period 1850–1880 by Viollet-le-Duc. Carcassonne is separated by the river Aude into two towns, the Cité, on the summit of an isolated hill—where tourists flock to visit the fortifications—and the "new town," formed in 1262 when the principal inhabitants, who had revolted against the royal authority, were permitted to relocate on the other side of the river. It is curious that the evident talent for large-scale construction exhibited in the Middle Ages in countless castles and cathedrals was essentially a *local* emanation. Despite the theoretical unity of the Holy Roman Empire and the church, there was no pan-continental institutional base for public works on the grand scale. Sieges were so costly and difficult to mount that for many centuries the engineering skills evident on these pages tended to reinforce local rather than central authority. It was perhaps not entirely an accident that the centralizing force that followed the French Revolution was incarnated in an artillery officer, Napoleon Bonaparte.

Above: A remaining section of the bridge of Avignon, built during the twelfth century and still bearing the chapel of Saint-Bénézet. Only four of the original piles are still standing. Below: Mont Saint-Michel, the fortress-abbey in western France whose Benedictine monastery was founded in 966 by Richard I, duke of Normandy.

Left and below: The Cathedral of Chartres, celebrated in Henry Adams's famous book *Mont St. Michel and Chartres.* The two towers were completed in the eleventh and sixteenth centuries, respectively. The stained-glass windows—extending over more than 3,000 square yards—represent the largest single collection extant. These superb windows illustrate the Bible, the lives of the saints, and even the everyday occupations of old France.

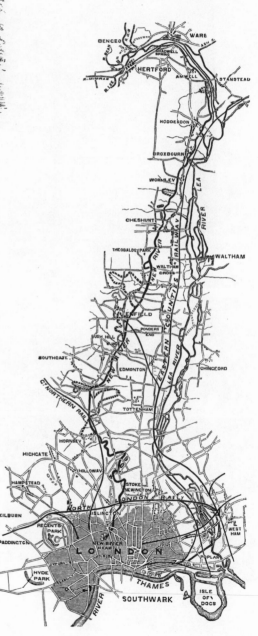

Although minuscule by Roman standards, the "New River" which brought fresh water 40 miles to London was by far the greatest construction project accomplished in England since the end of the Roman occupation. The work owed so much to the promotional efforts of one Hugh Myddelton (warden of the Company of Goldsmiths) that King James I conferred a knighthood upon him in 1622. Considerable accuracy in surveying was necessary, because along the whole course of the aqueduct from Ware to London, the total drop is a mere 18 feet, or about 5 inches per mile. The above drawing, from the *Gentleman's Magazine* (Vol. LIV), shows a "Brick Arch under The New River Formerly Near Bush Hill." The map at the right, supplied by W. C. Mylne, Esq., engineer of the New River Company, appeared in Samuel Smiles's nineteenth-century work *Lives of the Engineers.*

King James I of England was a consistent supporter of the project. Not only did he grant the New River a right to traverse royal property along the optimal route, but he invested half the money needed to bring the work to completion. In 1616, in a Privy Council letter to the lord mayor and aldermen, the latter worthies were reminded that "unless his Majesty had been graciously pleased to favoure and supporte his undertakinge, he had suncke under the waight of that burthen." (J. W. Gough, *Sir Hugh Myddelton, Entrepreneur and Engineer*, Oxford University Press, 1964, p. 68.) Historians have perhaps been slow to acknowledge that King James had an essentially modern appreciation of the role of engineering in the business of government. It was he who helped bring the Dutch engineer Cornelius Vermuyden to England to help with drainage problems in the fens of Lincolnshire. Myddelton is pictured below.

References

1 St Pauls	7 St Sepulchres
2 St Dunstans	8 Bow Church
3 Temple	9 Guild-hall
4 St Brides	10 St Michaels
5 St Andrews	11 St Laurence Poultney
6 Baynards Castle	12 Old Swan

A View of LONDON *as it was*
before the dreadful-Fire

Above: This sketch of the City of London, made in 1615 by Visscher, shows Old London Bridge as it stood until the Great Fire of 1666 destroyed the wooden buildings on it. The first stone bridge seems to have been commenced under the impetus of Peter de Colechurch, a priest-architect who had been responsible for the last of the timber bridges on the same site. Started in 1176 and completed by 1209, the work had gone so slowly that King John had replaced Peter with Isenbert, "our faithful, learned and worthy Clerk . . . Master of the Schools of Xainctes." With a degree of foresight that might be envied by many of today's practitioners of "management science," the king provided "that the rents and profits of the several houses which the said Master of Schools shall cause to be erected on the Bridge aforesaid, be forever appropriated to repair, maintain and uphold the same." More than six centuries later, the antique bridge, with its twenty stone arches (the center arch being 72 feet wide) was found to be a nuisance to navigation and an unwarranted expense, and in 1823 George IV gave the royal assent to "An Act for the Rebuilding of London Bridge." In 1825 the foundation stone was laid for a new bridge designed by John Rennie, having only five arches; the celebration of the opening of the new bridge was held on August 1, 1831, and is depicted on the opposite page. William IV and Queen Adelaide led the waterborne procession in the State Barge, and afterward there was a banquet for 2,000 guests, including the lord mayor, on an awning-covered portion of the bridge itself. It is this "new" London Bridge that ended as a gift to Lake Havasu, Arizona, from the McCulloch Oil Corporation. The purchase price was $2,460,000.

Louis XIV—whose portrait (far right) was painted in 1667 during the Establishment of the Academy of Science and the Foundation of the Observatory—was a builder on the grand scale. After the disorders of *La Fronde* (the civil wars which almost cost the king his life when he was a child), Louis required the contentious aristocracy to take up residence in Versailles. The palace became the effective seat of government and a model for all the courts of Europe. Neoclassical statuary, like the aging deity at the left, embellished ponds and fountains. The general feeling conveyed by the ensemble (below) was one of order, beauty, and power. Orange trees set in movable boxes were sheltered during winter time in the Orangerie (bottom right). The Orangerie can also be glimpsed in the view directly to the right, at a lower level in the distance.

In the cartoon at right (taken from the March 13, 1869, issue of the Paris magazine *L'Illustration*), Cholera protests to Haussmann that demolition of old houses in Paris has left him homeless—a jibe at critics of Haussmann who complained that public works had created a housing shortage. Below: The Boulevard Haussmann, a typical broad thoroughfare created by Napoleon III's efficacious prefect. Before Haussmann's tenure of office, the city's water supply depended on the Seine river—in effect, the main sewer of Paris. Haussmann rebuilt the entire infrastructure of the city, holding office as prefect of the Seine from 1853 to 1870. Cholera was wiped out and the death rate appreciably lowered. As David H. Pinkney summed it up, "Napoleon's and Haussmann's revival of classical city planning . . . demonstrated that a big city can be beautiful, even magnificent. . . ." (From *Napoleon III and the Rebuilding of Paris*, Princeton University Press, 1958.) The cost? At current values, close to $100 billion.

Above: The Rue de Rivoli at night. Napoleon began this major east-west artery at the Place de la Concorde and constructed it as far as the Palais Royal. His nephew, the future Napoleon III, made the street's extension a first order of business, even before the reestablishment of the empire in October 1852. (The other major project launched by Louis Napoleon as "prince-president" was the building of a large and easily accessible central market.) Right: This view of the Bois de Boulogne also owes its origin to Louis Napoleon who as an exile in London had admired the Serpentine in Hyde Park and announced, "We must have a river here, as in Hyde Park, to give life to this arid promenade." Today, the Bois de Boulogne has lakes, cascades, ponds, flower gardens, lawns, two racecourses, and cafés and restaurants to permit a pleasant halt.

Two views of the George Washington Bridge over the Hudson River. Completed in 1931, this road link between New Jersey and New York attracted so much traffic that in 1955 the decision was made to build a second "deck." Foreseen in the original plans as a useful option, the double-decked bridge continues to play a vital role.

The Goethals Bridge was built as a result of a cooperative agreement between the Port of New York Authority and the Triborough Bridge Authority. It was named after General George W. Goethals, builder of the Panama Canal.

The Triborough Bridge links the three New York City boroughs of Manhattan, Queens, and the Bronx. The bridge, for which toll charges are still levied, has paid for itself several times over. The Triborough Bridge Authority remains, with the Port of New York Authority, a center of power in the nation's largest city.

The Aswan High Dam was built in the 1960's with Soviet support, after Secretary of State John Foster Dulles withdrew American financial aid in a dramatic announcement on July 19, 1956. An earlier dam had been completed, at the head of the first cataract above Aswan, under British auspices in 1902.

The High Dam at Aswan has had adverse as well as favorable impacts. Lake Nasser provides the environment needed by the snails (no longer washed out to sea) that serve as hosts to the slow-killing disease called schistosomiasis. And the interference with silt deposits in the Nile Delta seems to have reduced the sardine catch. There have also been problems with soil salinity on irrigated farms.

Thinking Big: Bloopers or Bonanzas?

IT WOULD BE PRESUMPTUOUS AND INSENSITIVE TO REGARD BIG technology as a "surefire" answer to all our problems: Inappropriate applications of technology on the grand scale have on occasion proved ludicrous and even tragic. Barely a year after the conclusion of World War II, the British Parliament, facing food shortages at home and wishing to provide a "shot in the arm" for colonial development, plumped for a gigantic "groundnuts scheme" in East Africa, to make up for acute shortages of fats and oils. The Labor government under Clement Attlee set up two specially contrived public corporations, an Overseas Food Corporation and a Colonial Development Corporation;[1] they botched the job, and a reading of Hansard's parliamentary reports of the period reveals general fury at a scheme marked by mismanagement and ineptitude. Curiously, an even greater blunder was made by the Russians when, in 1954, Khrushchev broadcast an announcement of his "virgin lands" program: In that year, a hundred million acres of marginal land in Kazakhstan and Siberia were plowed up for grain production. After two years of lucky rainfall, the program fell apart. Many thousands of animals died for lack of fodder; machinery rotted;

production statistics zoomed downward. Khrushchev's fall from the highest office in the Soviet Union is often ascribed to the failure of his grandiose schemes for Russian agriculture.

Ecclesiastes, however, reminds us that "to everything there is a season, and a time to every purpose under heaven." Timing is of the utmost importance in human affairs: That some large schemes have failed is hardly a reason to condemn all large enterprises. Statistics indicate that the vast majority of *small* businesses fail; yet one does not hear it argued that this is a reason against ever starting a small business! Apart from inherent difficulties of feasibility and management, "there is a tide in the affairs of men," and time must, indeed, be "seized by the fetlock." This is especially true for "enterprises of great pith and moment"; for this reason, those who wish a deeper understanding of the vicissitudes of large engineering schemes must take seriously the cyclical nature of many societal phenomena.

Polybius, the Achaean Greek historian who became the protégé and friend of Scipio—the conqueror of Carthage—has publicized the cyclical nature of forms of government: the observable progression from democracy through aristocracy to monarchy and back again. Pitirim Sorokin, who had been secretary to Kerenski on the eve of the October Revolution in Russia, later wrote a four-volume work, *Social and Cultural Dynamics,* to describe what he regarded as the inevitable fluctuation between "sensate" and "ideational" poles in history. In our own time, we have been preoccupied with economic cycles, and there is much current interest in the "long wave" that affects the timing of investment trends for very large projects.

Last December, I learned through Peter Güller, on the eve of his departure for Kathmandu to assume the directorship of a new international center for mountain research, that a group of Swiss scholars has detected evidence of the existence of mass "emotional cycles," somewhat along the lines of Sorokin's assumptions. System-dynamics analysis has long demonstrated that the public welfare is not necessarily served by the sheer tendency of individuals, however brilliant, to pursue their own self-interest! Such proclivities lead, willy-nilly, to the "tragedy of the commons" outlined in the sociologist Garret Hardin's landmark article in *Science* [162 (1968): 1243]. Clearly, if all peasants of a village have a legal right to graze unlimited numbers of cattle on the village common, there is little incentive to avoid overgrazing: Each peasant will feel that "just one more cow" could not affect the productivity of the commons as a whole. But at some point, the whole system succumbs to the danger of collapse.

In the United States, we have reached a point where virtually the entire population has become aware of the need for a more cooperative approach to public affairs. Although not every individual exemplifies the "change of consciousness" that has taken place, postwar American society has, on the whole, experienced some quite fundamental shifts in attitude. First in time came a much greater acceptance of the principle of racial equality; this was followed by a general desire to equalize the treatment of women in workaday life; now, we are beginning to see a general impatience with sanctimonious distinctions between the roles of the government and of the private sectors. Americans feel, rightly I would say, that semantic and operational barriers to teamwork must be drastically lowered, so that the best minds in the nation may be free to provide leadership and guidance for a more effective employment of our "know how" in all the domains of industry and commerce.

If I am correct in this feeling, then there is a "perception gap" that has caught many of our politicians and business leaders several steps behind the ranks of voters, employees, and consumers. At a moment of a far more dramatic change of public consciousness, when France had overthrown its traditional monarchy, the National Convention suppressed the university founded by Philippe Auguste and established an Ecole Centrale des Travaux Publics, or Central School for Public Works, whose name was later changed to the famous Ecole Polytechnique. In today's United States, on the basis of a very wide consensus, I think it is timely to think in terms of interdisciplinary education that will give science and engineering a genuinely equal place with the liberal arts, and I believe the nation expects a concerted effort, by all sectors, to plan and carry through a program that will make our infrastructure and our industry "second to none." Perhaps we, too, need a high-quality graduate school where "the best and the brightest" are thoroughly grounded in the essentials of engineer management.

As every lawyer knows, the term "private property" is a result of law: Without the public enactment of safeguards, limitations, and guidelines, the individual "owner" could not have publicly defined rights that are protected, when threatened, by the police and adjudicatory power of the community. The "private" corporation is, likewise, a creature of the law, and subject to the changing rules legislated by our constitutionally appointed authorities. There is, therefore, no logical reason why laws and regulations should stand in the way of consortia formed, in the public interest and subject to reasonable constraints, to advance the nation's stake in an optimized series of technological enterprises. And just as the public wealth was made available in the form of land grants for railway development and for colleges, there is no basis in our traditions for excluding public support for funds designed, on a prudent basis, to modernize today's aging networks of transport and other services "affected with a public interest."

Meanwhile, much of the "action" in terms of large-scale engineering has occurred abroad. Less than a decade ago, King Ibn-Saud, after a historic meeting with Stephen D. Bechtel, authorized construction of a vast urban-industrial complex based on the sleepy fishing village of Jubail. Thus was set in motion a process that could eventually cost more than the Apollo Program that sent American astronauts to the moon. In a gesture of comparable scope, the Republic of Nigeria has begun construction of its new federal capital, Abuja, which is now the largest civil engineering site in Africa. Not only new cities, but new transportation networks, energy projects, water-supply schemes, and the whole arsenal of industrial modernity can be seen spreading like the tentacles of a gargantuan crab across the remaining empty spaces of the earth.

The industrialized nations that have been invited to participate in such developments have little choice but to follow the wishes of the powers-that-be in each of the countries striving for "modernization." But there *are* on occasion opportunities for avoiding projects that are excessively and inappropriately expensive. I recall a UNESCO exercise that can still serve as a useful guide to *African* priorities: In 1974, a Delphi survey on "Technologically Feasible Futures for Africa" asked panels of international and local African experts to identify those technologies most needed for African development. The results, published in 1974,[2] showed that the African engineers and scientists overwhelmingly favored the use of airships as a primary means of opening up the interior! A second priority was the development of all-terrain vehicles capable of operating in countrysides devoid of roads. For those who see a "business opportunity" in the survey conclusions, one next step would be to read the excellent, concise article "Airships in the Future," which Christoph-Friedrich von Braun, a Sloan School alumnus, wrote for the December 1975 issue of the English journal *Futures;* in this summary of the present capabilities and problems of dirigible construction, Von Braun proposes a sensible design strategy based on very careful analysis of both market requirements and general support capabilities.

Although cyclical problems will remain—they are, to an extent, endemic in human affairs—nonetheless, we have seen a number of developing nations make a remarkably happy association with modern technology. Any remaining sense of "innate superiority" that may linger can be quickly dispelled by travel: In all continents, there is irrefutable evidence of a worldwide trend toward the effective absorption of the technological message. For better or for worse, we are witnessing a massive urbanization of the planet as the growing world population finds civilization's first artifact—the city itself—a better bet than the "overcrowded" countryside! Supertechnology has brought about the age of what I would call "the pervasive society": Even the remote kingdoms of the Himalayas find themselves inexorably drawn into the net of modernity.

During a trip to Nepal nearly two years ago, I was accosted by several people involved in the conference I was attending (on the subject of management of "renewable resources"), not to discuss the matter under review but to press upon me the importance of a subject I knew nothing about: the need for a direct transport artery to the Indian Ocean. The point is a logical one: Nepal is landlocked, and for the present all merchandise must travel on the Indian Railways whether the purpose is import or export. Some effort had been made to broach the subject of a canal from the low-lying Terrai district of Nepal to the port of Calcutta; but there are alternatives. One alternative might be a product pipeline along the lines investigated by M.I.T.'s Macro-Engineering Research Group! Without coming to definitive conclusions, a series of meetings in Cambridge, Massachusetts, had indicated that there are existing prototypes for pipelines that can transport solid merchandise with reliability and safety. Professor David Gordon Wilson of M.I.T.'s Department of Mechanical Engineering has patented one device; and a New Jersey shipping magnate, Mr. William Vandersteel, has taken an interest in a system developed by one of the principal gas-pipeline companies of the United States.

There are those who will deplore the "linking up" of Nepal with the outer world. It may indeed be too late for such regrets. Tourism has occurred on a scale that has already damaged many fragile mountain areas. The detritus left by trekking expeditions is unsightly and unhealthy: It is a situation not different in kind, only in degree, from that experienced by New Hampshire's Mt. Monadnock, a too-popular tourist site analyzed in a brilliant system-dynamics model by George Richardson, who has demonstrated to the hilt that there *is* a conflict between the interests of conservation and recreation. It is partly, however, a matter of improving public habits: If every climber and camper would assume *personal* responsibility for waste disposal, the despoliation of favorite natural sites could be halted, to everyone's benefit.

For Nepal, it is time to think in terms of a new and more benign type of tourism. Today's trekkers and sightseers may patronize inns and restaurants, but they contribute very little to the infrastructure the country needs. A century ago, Switzerland faced very similar problems of poverty, deforestation, and soil erosion. One solution available to the Swiss, with their disciplined population, was to pass a law making it illegal to cut down a tree, even on private land, without the permission of the Forest Service. But the Swiss were helped also by the arrival of a new breed of tourists: families who wished to rent or buy chalets. Thus "tourist villages" developed, where British and other vacationers employed the local peasantry as guides, ski instructors, barbers, governesses, and so on; and the newcomers insisted on—and were ready to pay for—pipelines for purified water and other amenities that the natives were only too happy to benefit from!

Of course, not *all* such tourists were British; but perhaps they "set the tone," as indeed they have in Nepal. When our group trekked in the foothills of Annapurna, I was grieved to be told that the local villagers had no water with which to feed their yaks; the yaks had to graze on the limited, lovingly cut terraces that could otherwise have been used to grow needed vegetables and fruits. Yet not too far away were the waterfalls, from which vast tonnages of the purest water tumbled down, virtually untouched, to the river valleys below. This is the problem: The villagers are not really in a cash economy; they cannot afford the water pipes, reservoirs, and ancillary equipment that could bring them water. Nor could they, unassisted, afford hydroelectric power if it were developed. But a deliberate and careful policy of tourist villages on the Swiss model might represent at least a practical beginning on an enormous problem.

For one whose twin interests have been resource conservation and macro-engineering, the 1981 experience in Nepal was both reassuring and appalling. Reassuring, because the American team with which I traveled, as well as our Nepalese hosts, were all civilized, well trained, and good communicators. Appalling, because the problem of deforestation in a region of explosive population growth demands efforts on a scale not yet even imagined.

Chaired by Roland J. Fuchs, head of the geography department at the University of Hawaii, our National Academy of Sciences group included the dean of the Colorado State College of Forestry; a biogeographer specializing in mountain grasslands; a University System of Georgia specialist in rural technology, and a qualified environmental engineer. We also had the good company of two ex-Peace Corps volunteers: Charles Bailey of Cornell and Donald A. Messerschmidt of the University of Oregon; both these men spoke several of the hill dialects, and through the courtesy of Professor Messerschmidt we were all invited to meet the remainder of our party at one of the most unusual and rewarding restaurants on earth: "K.C.'s," in the heart of Kathmandu. There I came to know and appreciate Eckhart Dersch, a water-management expert at the University of Michigan; and Tom Dunne, a distinguished young geologist from the University of Washington who specializes in hillslope erosion and hydrology. Three extraordinarily valuable people from Washington were with us, too: Mrs. Rose Bannigan of the National Research Council central office, Dr. Dennis M. Wood, who put our expedition together, and Miss Ming Ivory of AID.

My hat is off to this fine group—and to their counterparts on other missions to remote parts of the world—for the breadth with which they approached the very real problems faced by our interlocutors, who, it must be admitted, face a plenitude of foreign advice. We had the occasion to meet with impressive representatives of the Swiss, German, and other foreign-aid missions in the country. I think it is fair to say that most of the European and North American advisers would genuinely like to see more rapid solutions to a host of problems. But considering that it is barely more than a quarter-century since the kingdom opened its doors to foreign visitors at all, we should learn the virtue of patience. Bhutan, observing the trouble caused in Nepal by so many tourists and advisers, has decided upon a very strict limitation of the tourist traffic. And in Ladakh, where the redoubtable Helena Norberg-Hodge has introduced solar housing on a substantial scale, there is a real danger that a valuable local culture will be overrun by the curiosity of outsiders looking for one of the few remaining "exotic" corners in a homogenized world.

I was introduced to the whole network of specialists interested in the ecology and social traditions of mountain communities by a remarkable American public servant, Dr. John E. Fobes. For a whole generation, while storms gathered around the rarefied halls of UNESCO in Paris, "Jack" had calmly served as assistant director general for administration and later as deputy director-general of this unusual intergovernmental agency. Acting promptly when Joseph Allen Stein, the distinguished American architect resident in New Delhi, had pointed out the extent of deforestation in the Himalayan region, it was Jack Fobes who secured the loyal and indispensable cooperation of Dr. Klaus Lampe, who helped persuade the government of Western Germany to serve as host and cosponsor with UNESCO of the first international Conference on Mountain Environments, held in Munich in 1974. Mr. Aspie Moddie of the Himalayan Mountain Club, a retired UNILEVER executive, seconded Joe Stein's efforts; and the eventual outcome has been the formation, in 1981, of the International Mountain Society headquartered in Boulder, Colorado.

More than 15 percent of the world's population lives in upland regions; there is now a worldwide crisis in the mountains: Population pressure has led to overcutting of the forests, overgrazing of upland pastures, and the steady erosion of the thin layer of soil that alone can sustain life in mountainous regions. And downstream there are the effects of siltation, flooding (the most notable example being the overflowing of the Ganges and the recurrent tragedies of death and homelessness for millions in India's Gangetic Plain), and the migration of hill people to already crowded regions such as the Nepalese Terrai. India has an evident interest in reducing erosion in the Himalayan uplands; a long-range regional pact, as recommended by the eminent Dr. John Cool, could offer China, India, and the border kingdoms substantial hope for the future. The United States is fortunate in having a larger cadre than one might expect of people who have lived in the Himalayas for years, are acquainted with local languages and customs, and can offer realistic assessments on alternative programs. Together with our friends in Canada, Western Europe, and Japan who have likewise contributed to aid and understanding, there is every opportunity to play a constructive and valued role. It is not at all unlikely that careful hydroelectric development will prove to be a long-term viable alternative to the present disastrous cutting-down of trees for firewood. As a third-party amicus curiae, perhaps through the acceptable channels of the World Bank, United States diplomacy has a major option: Big technology, after all, has something to offer to both the small and the large powers in a region of vital interest to the peace of the world.

It is interesting to note that the Global Infrastructure Fund (GIF) overall plan has proposed "damming of the Sanpo River on the upper reaches of the Brahmaputra in the frontier area between China and the Indian province of Assam to make it flow into India through a tunnel across the Himalayas." GIF estimates a hydroelectric generating capacity of about three hundred billion kilowatt-hours per year. In time, if this and other projects should be expanded to include extensive irrigation works, India might become a net exporter of food! Maitra has indicated that Indian officials have recently developed a Himalayan Rivers Development Plan to interlink the Brahmaputra with the Ganges. This macroconcept would not only bring more than ten million acres under irrigation, but would generate over thirty gigawatts of hydroelectricity per year. The GIF says, "It would also considerably assist flood control in the Ganges-Brahmaputra basin, and could no doubt benefit Nepal and Bangladesh as well as Northeast India."

In India itself, we would be unrealistic to assume that there has not been substantial progress, both in improved living standards and in the more sophisticated evolution of high policy. There has been desultory interest in a "Garland Canal" that would unite the main river systems, impound their floodwaters, and serve as a reliable source for irrigation waters throughout the subcontinent. The astute Mr. B. B. Vohra, former joint secretary of the ministry of agriculture, has pointed out that with hundreds of thousands of small, efficient pumps, the scattered villages of India can find what they need from groundwater reserves: The time has not yet arrived for Captain Dastur's megaproject. But if solar-power satellites move to the "active list" for international development, India and no doubt other rapidly developing countries will wish "a piece of the action": They are not short of qualified engineers, many of them trained in the United States, Europe, and Japan, who have both the wit and the specialized knowledge to be good team-members. Carefully researched megacanal schemes and realistically assessed projects for transmitting solar power from space will play their due part in Indian affairs.

While millions of Americans have been mesmerized by films such as *Star Wars*, and by books offering fictionized tableaux of potential developments in outer space, we may be on the verge of a dramatic evolution toward expanded human habitation on contrived islands built in the ocean. A few pioneers such as John Craven, Kiyonori Kikutake, and Ernest Frankel have sensed the imminence and the high importance of such a step. But are

those who fashion industrial and governmental policy aware of
the capability that now exists—and of its ramifications?

We are not really speaking of the future, but of the present.
For several decades, the oil and gas industry has been operating
offshore: fixed platforms are now feasible and almost commonplace in water depths greater than six hundred feet. Since 1967,
Italy has operated a complex offshore installation, the San
Marco Launching Facility, off the East African coast not far
from Kenya: This facility, with its own independent generators
and consisting of a control platform and launching pad, has
been used for the launching of satellites into equatorial orbit. In
Europe, the French have completed (in 1970) an artificial island-
harbor that can accommodate tankers of up to 500,000 d.w.t.,
seventeen miles from Le Havre, outside French territorial waters. Brazil has constructed an artificial island eleven miles from
Rio Grande do Norte for ships up to one hundred thousand
tons; the island will also be used for stockpiling salt.

Floating docks of considerable size are currently in use at
Hong Kong, at Yokohama, Japan—and the Soviet Navy has a
four-hundred-foot floating dock able to accommodate two nuclear submarines at the same time, thus saving the long weeks
they would have to spend "off station" for repairs.

The subject of ocean habitations and industrial development was held to be so vital that in 1974 the United States National Academy of Sciences sponsored a Conference on Seaward
Advancement of Industrial Societies. Although much of the relevant technology is available in the United States, most of the
"action" has been taking place elsewhere. With the United Nations predicting a doubling of the present world population in
forty to fifty years, there will be pressures of all kinds to intensify
the use of ocean space. Sea cities—or lesser installations—could
easily be built in the shoal waters that constitute at least 10 percent of the surface area of the ocean. There is ample scope for
industrial activities of all kinds. And new sovereign states could
be built in international waters.

At Kobe (Japan), several artificial islands are already in use,
at forty-meter water depths, to provide easy access to offshore
coal mines. It is only a matter of time before offshore islands will

be built to mine submarine mineral reserves in water depths at least as great as those found at the outer limits of the continental shelf. There have been proposals to group nuclear power stations on floating platforms—quite a feasible idea. In the United Kingdom, public interest was aroused by a proposal of the Pilkington Glass Age Development Committee to build a "Sea City" for thirty thousand people fifteen miles from Great Yarmouth off the coast of Norfolk. It has been stated that for many localities the "extra construction cost of building at sea has proved no more than the cost of purchasing dry land."[3]

One fascinating prospect is the building of cities—or whole new states or nations—on the numerous submerged underwater mountains known as seamounts. A result of former volcanic activity, there are seventy identified seamounts within two hundred meters of the surface in the Pacific Ocean alone, and located outside the territorial waters of any existing state. While jurisdiction over artificial islands is a somewhat technical matter in international law, the legal niceties are not too hard to grasp and have been summed up in a well-referenced, authoritative book by N. Papadakis, *The International Legal Regime of Artificial Islands,* published (in the English language) by Sijthoff, Leyden, the Netherlands, in 1977. That most of Holland could be considered as a series of linked artificial islands makes the Netherlands a most logical venue for the publication of such a treatise.

I remember attending, last year, a seminar given by Professor Frankel on the technology of movable seaports; floating airports have also been suggested, and of course D. K. Ludwig's macroventure in Brazil involved the towing across the Pacific from Japan of a power plant and a pulp-and-paper mill on oceangoing barges. There is currently an immense amount of offshore-construction activity, and it is not limited to the oil and gas industry. While Nigel Chattey's 1977 proposal of an offshore island—or series of islands—near the entrance to New York Harbor struck the press as somewhat grandiose and outlandish, this is only because the United States has grown seemingly weary of industrial prowess. Nor is the updating of the Erie Canal either unprecedented or unreasonable in principle: What *is* shocking is the long delay that has occurred in initiating detailed cost and revenue estimates.

Water transportation remains one of the most economical methods of moving bulk commodities. Yet there are only nine ports in the whole world that can handle ships of more than two hundred thousand tons. That the East Coast of the United States should have at least one such port seems beyond reasonable dispute, unless we are to assume a gradual, complacent decline of America's industrial position in a world that, whether we like it or not, clings to economic expansion as a preferred policy.

The upgrading of canals to cope with new conditions of traffic and technology is a process that has been going on quite literally for more than two thousand years. The Grand Canal of China is now the subject of a major rehabilitation scheme; the Erie Canal has already been modernized several times: Between 1835 and 1862, the canal was widened and deepened and equipped with double locks to speed traffic; and just before the First World War, a further expansion of capacity occurred, as the old canal route was melded into the substantial New York Barge Canal, which still provides for a great deal of freight traffic from the Great Lakes, through the Hudson River and to New York Harbor.

In testimony before the Merchant Marine and Fisheries Committee of the United States House of Representatives on June 22, 1979, Mr. Chattey pointed out that "New York has the highest receiving, storage, and transshipment costs of any major industrial port city of the world." He went on to show how poorly the port of New York compares with Rotterdam and Yokohama. But does anyone imagine that the Dutch and the Japanese enlarge their ports "by private enterprise alone"?

Nigel Chattey's "ICONN-ERIE" Project includes *both* the modernization of the Erie Canal and the construction of an industrial-port energy complex on an artificial offshore island. The Northeast and the Midwest would be equal beneficiaries with the New York Metropolitan Region, as they were when the Erie Canal was first built in Governor Clinton's era. To fund the costly but necessary detailed feasibility studies, perhaps a special intersectoral study group, sponsored by leading authorities in government, industry, and the professions, should be assembled and put to work. Far from damaging other sections of the country, such a study group could serve as a model for similar groups on the West Coast, to explore aggressively the improvement of waterway transportation at our principal maritime gateways.

Imagination is helpful; but so is experience. I recall the days of my early youth when, living on Riverside Drive, my father would arrive home on Friday afternoons and promptly bundle his wife and five sons—and sometimes my grandparents as well, into the speedboat that he kept anchored in the Hudson River: Without traffic jams or a sense of urban pollution, we would proceed joyfully up the Hudson, across Spuyten Duyvil Creek and the Hell Gate, and finally onto the broad waters of Long Island Sound. We felt that we were truly on holiday the moment our feet touched the dock in Manhattan. But the waterways around New York are now virtually deserted. Where is the "infrastructure" that might encourage yachting and pleasure-boating of all kinds? Has no one visited Venice?

Americans who live on rivers or harbors owe it to themselves and to their future to visit, at least once, the "Pearl of the Mediterranean." I had this precious opportunity in 1977, when my brother Alfred and I were invited to a series of meetings held on the island of San Giorgio at the fine conference center operated by the Cini Foundation. Fortunately, our fellow conferees shared a taste for epicurean delights, and this gave us ample scope to walk around Venice and to ride on the large, attractive motorized gondolas that serve as "buses." What struck me was the cleanliness and efficiency of the equipment, the competence and courtesy of the staff, and the clockwork regularity of the service. Waterway transportation can add much zest and pleasure to urban life: The economics deserve a very close look—and I doubt that a financial projection would show anything approaching the gloomy "balance sheet" (if one can call it that) of the New York subway system!

That we are, to a great extent, creatures of habit is nowhere better illustrated than by the deadliness with which urban subway systems repeat each other. Although Max Beerbohm quipped, "History repeats itself; historians repeat each other," I suspect that engineers are as prone to this malady as the other professions. At least in Paris, the *métro* is linked with that splendid regional rail system the R.U.R. (Réseau Urbain Régional). One would think that if subway tracks have standard gauge, regular trains might be allowed on them where this arrangement could facilitate service to passengers. I recall discussing such questions with two gentlemen in their eighties who, about twenty-five years ago, visited my law office in New York. Alas, I have no record of their names. But I do remember that they had come over from England in the early years of the century to help with the building of the Holland Tunnel, and they had stayed on ever since as consulting engineers. Their own views on subway design were innovative and interesting: They envisaged a "piggy-back" undercarriage that would be fitted to transport suburban buses: once the bus was "locked in," the bus driver would become the subway engineer, and the vehicle could continue to the end of the line as part and parcel of the underground system. My visitors also mentioned that by giving the subway a piggy-back capacity for garbage trucks, delivery wagons, and private cars, surface congestion and noise would be vastly reduced, and subway revenues proportionately increased. Inasmuch as most subway systems are only used to capacity during morning and late-afternoon rush hours, I think the idea of my visitors is well worth exploring!

Subways, like all new transport mechanisms, inevitably improve downtown real-estate values. I know that the private railroad companies of an earlier era were careful to "cash in" on the increased value of the land in and adjacent to terminal areas. Kennedy Airport, I was told, earns nearly half its fees from the rentals and royalties derived from shops in the various terminal areas. Could not new subway systems likewise benefit from the dramatically increased value of the properties above and near stations? Transport and settlement are interdependent variables: By considering them together, we ought to come up with more sensible answers to vexing financial questions: *ars celere artem.*

Within Japan itself, there has been much debate and soul-searching about one of the most remarkable achievements of modern civil engineering: the completion of the undersea portion of the Seikan Tunnel. It was to cheers of *Banzai!* that Prime Minister Yasuhiro Nakasone pressed a button at his Tokyo residence late in January 1983, setting off explosions four hundred miles to the north that ripped open a one-yard thick wall, the last barrier beneath the Tsugaru Strait separating the two main islands of Japan.

When the landward approaches are complete, this will be the longest railway tunnel on earth: 33.46 miles from portal to portal. The first train may run through the double-track tunnel as early as 1986.

The total cost of the project will be equivalent to nearly three billion dollars. According to press reports, some critics have called the tunnel "the most expensive hole of the century." Apparently, the Japanese Imperial Army suggested a series of tunnels in the 1920's, not only to link Japan's main islands, but also to provide a connection to Korea, then a Japanese colony. A tunnel between Honshu, the island on which Tokyo is situated, and Kyushu to the south was completed in 1942—over a distance of 2.5 miles. The Seikan project was given its first real impetus by a tragic ferry accident in 1954, when 1,155 people were killed. Although as many as twenty workmen may have lost their lives in construction accidents, this is regarded as a lesser evil than the fatalities that have occurred so often when ferryboats were buffeted by the region's typhoons. Yutaka Mochida, manager of the project, wisely commented, "It is silly to talk in terms of immediate return."

When I visited the tunnel with Uwe Kitzinger, CBE, chairman of the Major Projects Association of the United Kingdom, and C. Lawrence Meador, my fellow coordinator of M.I.T.'s Macro-Engineering Research Group, in 1981, the devotion and efficiency of the staff and the workmen were very evident. Asked to comment, for a nationally televised program broadcast from Sapporo, I could not help complimenting the Japanese Railway Construction Public Corporation on a magnificent accomplishment having worldwide implications. The digging took nineteen years; but the Tsugaru Strait is more than four hundred feet deep, and the tunnel has been excavated nearly another four hundred feet below the seabed, through extraordinarily difficult and tricky ground. A novel system of automated grouting was devised, so that a wide arc ahead of the blasting would be sealed against the infiltration of seawater. Horizontal probes were pressed ahead of the construction, and both a pilot tunnel and a service tunnel have been provided as part of the scheme, with regular crossways between the main two-track tunnel and the service tunnel, which can be used to evacuate passengers and crew in the event of an emergency.

It is hard to avoid the reflection that the Japanese have succeeded in a very challenging and dangerous location, while the comparable tunnel between England and France, in the ideal excavation conditions provided by a virtually continuous bed of the "lower chalk," remains largely on paper. Macro-engineering cannot proceed from blueprints and plans alone, however elegant, but must develop from a determination to overcome obstacles and render the services for which particular projects have been designed. Of course, the Japanese have the advantage of operating within the territory of a single nation. Moreover, the "decision environment" is favorable to continuity. And I could not miss noticing the great pride in this project evidenced by the city fathers of Sapporo, the town in Hokkaido that still displays on a promontory overlooking the city a larger-than-life statue of an American teacher of the nineteenth century who encouraged his students with the words, engraved in gold at the statue's base, "Boys, be ambitious."

On February 18, 1983, Messrs. Steven Hofman and Matthew Cook wrote to the editor of The New York Times, "As incredible as it may seem, the Federal Government allocates billions of dollars for public-works investments each year without an inventory of the nation's public facilities." One reform that these staff members of a congressional group recommend is the adoption of federal capital budgeting. It seems to make sense to identify and separate "expenditures that represent investments in public capital, such as roads, highways, dams and water systems, and those that represent current operating outlays, such as salaries and interest payments."

The idea of a federal capital budget needs to be supplemented by a process of consultation that will permit explicit priorities and public capital-investment plans to go forward with a wide measure of informed support. But mere conferring, while an advance over isolation of the various sectors from one another, will not be sufficient by itself: There must be "decision support systems" comprehensive, accurate, and up-to-date enough to provide a reliable basis for discussion and choice. A data base on public works and on large "private" projects that directly affect the public interest seems indispensable in this age of computers and telecommunications. A great deal of information already exists in the offices of journals, associations, and companies in the construction industry; but financial institutions are also involved, and government agencies as well as independent research institutions maintain voluminous files and other types of data-storage facilities. In the establishment of a central data base, the advice of organizations such as the Conference Board and the U.S. Chamber of Commerce should also be sought. The research staff of an intersectoral conference institution would doubtless wish to have access to a variety of data sources: There may even be competing "central" data banks.

It is fashionable nowadays to deplore the "proliferation" of journals and other data sources; but much depends on the *focus* of such activities, and I must confess that in my own experience I have been surprised to find a shortage of *certain types* of quarterly journals, conferences, and even guided travel tours! For instance, it is my view that as Americans we must develop more of an awareness of our place as *North Americans,* and that Canadians and Mexicans, too, need to feel that they are part not only of a nation but of an exciting and rewarding *continent.* The new macro-engineering systems can only bring their greatest benefits if they are considered as susceptible to continent-wide deployment. But the intracontinental agreements needed as a basis for implementing infrastructure plans will be facilitated if there is a deliberate effort, on the part of specialists and opinion-leaders, to educate the public in all three countries as to the issues and merits of a continental "systems approach." What complicates this task is the rather overwhelming preponderance of the United States in terms of population, wealth, and other indicia of power. For citizens of the United States, especially, efforts to build confederal arrangements on this continent must involve great patience and sensitivity.

But it is clearly in the general interest of all three countries to work for their mutual enrichment and to share infrastructure improvements where these are demonstrably very beneficial to all concerned. The St. Lawrence Seaway stands as a symbol of Canadian-American friendship. With Mexico, there are a host of possibilities for engineering partnership, particularly in such fields as transportation, water management, and energy development. I remember my father's delight with his frequent business trips south of the border; he had many good friends in Mexico, and was not surprised when Sumner Welles, the Undersecretary of State in the administration of President Franklin D. Roosevelt, asked him to come along with the mission that negotiated the agreement under which the United States Navy was authorized to use Mexican port facilities during the difficult days of World War II. My two older brothers, who served in the navy, were careful to explain to me the usefulness of these arrangements.

In early 1941, Camp William James dispatched a group to Mexico after one of its Dartmouth members (Arthur Root, now a psychiatrist) reported that he needed reinforcements for his attempt, with the help of local high school students, to rebuild part of Colima, a town recently destroyed by an earthquake. Arthur had made the trip south essentially for his health; and when disaster struck the Colima area where he had been traveling, he felt he had to pitch in. Back at Camp William James, which had returned to the private sector after President Roosevelt's energies were concentrated on preparations for war itself rather than on "moral equivalents," three young men volunteered: Robert O'Brien, James Tierney, and Paul Keefe. They traveled from Vermont to the state of Colima in a secondhand jeep donated by Mrs. Henry Copley Greene of Longfellow Park in Cambridge, Massachusetts, who as a young girl had been a frequent visitor at William James's home.

The expedition was a sociological success but a tragedy for two of the boys: First, O'Brien contracted a severe case of amoebic dysentery and had to be repatriated; and then, on the way back north, Tierney lost his leg while trying to hitch a ride on a railway train. But Ramón Beteta, Mexico's undersecretary of state for external relations, was so impressed by the Colima reconstruction project that he said he would be delighted if fifty or more such volunteers would catalyze similar projects all over Mexico.

But this was now wartime. Arthur Root returned to Vermont to found the Volunteer Land Corps, which, throughout

World War II, enlisted high school students by the hundreds to help plant and harvest crops on the undermanned farms of New England.

Learning, as my friends and I did in connection with Camp William James and its offshoots in Mexico—and Alaska—that *small* projects can be enjoyable and even significant, I have never understood why larger affairs must be conducted without a sense of humor and with an attitude of dull and solemn obeisance to routine. In my experience, part of the appeal of appropriate macro-engineering ventures lies in the opportunities they afford for a sense of adventure and achievement too often lacking in mundane affairs. I believe such emotions are *legitimate* reinforcements to public purposes. Groups that are essentially happy with the objectives and methods of their labor—whether that labor be physical or intellectual—will probably be better able to enjoy and appreciate their leisure. That country dancing has experienced such a remarkable renaissance in the Boston area may be due in part to the general feeling that the economy of the New England heartland is on a healthy upswing and that there is, indeed, much to be happy about after decades of deterioration and decadence.

After graduating from the Harvard Law School in 1948, I traveled to Texas on the thoughtful invitation of my college friend Malcolm R. Wilkey (now a distinguished federal judge). In Houston, where my duties with the Chamber of Commerce included the secretaryship of the Committee on Military Affairs, I was struck by the amount of time—and the quality of the intellectual effort—that busy businessmen devoted, as volunteers, to the welfare of their community. Colonel Robert Ives of our Military Affairs Committee was quite ready to listen to a much younger man, recently returned from Canadian service, who thought that reserve training for the army, navy, and National Guard should be carried out in contiguous locations. One of the great lessons of the war had been the absolute necessity for the various branches of the service to learn how to work together, but cooperation under fire is not a mere matter of goodwill: There are technical imperatives, and these must be learned and absorbed. Serving as "order-of-battle" captain for the 22nd (Texas) Armored Division, I asked my colonel (Malcolm Wilkey—also my roommate) for help, and with the encouragement of Malcolm and General Gainer Jones and Mr. George Brown of our committee, I was able to develop plans for a combined Houston Armed Forces Center. Private interests favorable to the project helped assemble the necessary land; I was sent off to the Pentagon wearing a Texas hat to raise the necessary federal funds, and within months construction was under way.

A decade or so ago, I had the opportunity to return to our second largest state when Dr. George Kozmetsky, the brilliant entrepreneur who became dean of the Graduate School of Business at the University of Texas in Austin, invited me down to deliver a guest lecture. Dr. Kozmetsky became interested in the field of macro-engineering and made a noteworthy contribution to its terminology and structure when he addressed, in 1979, the Macro-Engineering Symposium held in connection with the annual meeting of the American Association for the Advancement of Science, in Houston.[4] Dr. Kozmetsky urged senior executives to become personally involved with, and to institutionalize their consultations on, macrosystems "to meet the demands of society that involve large-scale needs." Mr. George R. Brown, surely one of the great Americans of his generation, had come to the symposium, and so set an example along the lines recommended by the speaker. I could not help recalling one occasion when, sitting in Mr. Brown's modest office in Brown & Root, he answered a telephone call from Lyndon Johnson, then President of the United States, who owed so much of his rise to power to the astute advice and support of Mr. Brown.

In effect, George Kozmetsky was calling for the kind of regular, high-level consultation that has taken place at the "policy centers" of Japan or in the various meetings of "Le Plan" in France. One obvious reason for involving the topmost levels of business and government in such "palavers" is that society now has the ability to build macrosystems that are enormously expensive, and whose impacts inevitably affect the livelihoods—and the lifestyles—of many millions of people. It is *beyond the power* of a single decision-maker to marshal the resources needed for many of the new systems whose utility will form the subject of political—and expert—debate during the coming decades. Where new systems are continental or intercontinental in scope, multinational discussion groups will have to include, on a structured basis, executives with a power to influence decisions at both the governmental and the industrial level in their respective countries.

Happily, there are useful precedents in the American experience. During World War I, President Wilson encouraged the formation of the National Industrial Conference Board (now known simply as "the Conference Board") in order to maximize the industrial mobilization effort. The Conference Board can still be a vital link with industry, finance, and commerce. It is essential, too, that Organized Labor be part of the consultative process on new macrosystems, not only because so many employees are affected by decisions in this field, but also because, as economists have reminded us, labor unions, through their pension funds and other instrumentalities, actually control a growing portion of American industry. One could argue that labor has the *greatest* stake in the modernization and competitive success of industry; in time, we may even see the financial power of labor unions devoted deliberately to the inauguration of more effective, more modern industrial units. In the steel industry, for instance, labor has recently had to accept contracts that actually *reduce* wages, because of management's failure, in earlier years, to build modern, competitive facilities. And it was labor that bargained for plant modernization!

With machines doing more, must people do less? The question is hardly novel. Valéry Giscard d'Estaing, in a book written just before he left office,[5] pointed out that the process of progressive automation is a very old one, and that new methods had in general created not only new wealth but new opportunities for work. IBM, in a grant of five million dollars to Harvard University two decades ago, established a program on "Technology and Society" to investigate precisely this question. Under the leadership of Dr. Emmanuel Mesthene, a series of comprehensive monographs[6] led to the generalized conclusion that although dislocations were severe as new techniques replaced older, more cumbersome methods of work, there has been no demonstrable net loss to society; on the contrary, new machines such as the computer have added to human wealth and capabilities.

Part of the confusion on this matter comes from a dichotomy in society, which I suspect is not limited to the privileged position of the United States: Each of us must earn a living, develop some sort of career and compete for monetary and psychic rewards. But beyond the world of competition, there is a world of cooperation and service. It is better to look at facts than at slogans: No one is suggesting that the United States Army be "privatized"; but there *was* a time when armies were in fact "private" affairs: The feudal levies that were mowed down by English crossbowmen at Crécy and Agincourt were in effect private armies mobilized by the owners of the great properties of the realm. During the later Middle Ages, Swiss mercenary armies were hired out much in the same manner as a modern capitalist might hire out a football team. And just as the modern army is, if we use exact terminology, a "socialist" institution, that is, an institution wholly owned and controlled by the state, so are many other services state-owned or, in fact, "socialist." We in America therefore live in a "mixed economy," part capitalist and part socialist. Now that negotiations with "socialist" states in the Eastern bloc are made inevitable by the greater range and impact of modern weapons, we can point out that a large part of our own population is in public service (of course with the paramount distinction that ours is truly a government of law, and that the individual, whether in the public or the private sector, has the full protection of the laws and the Constitution).

It is a sign of the times that the one project that has commanded the enthusiastic assent of both Giscard d'Estaing, the conservative former president of France, and Mitterrand, his socialist successor, is the new Museum of Science now under construction in the old section of "Les Halles," the market and stock-exchange area where tourists can still find unsurpassable onion soup after midnight. This edifice, when completed, will apparently be the largest museum in the whole world. Mitterrand has gone "all out" for technology and technology training; as president, Giscard d'Estaing sponsored and personally opened a huge conference on "*l'Informatique*." Mitterrand has placed billions of francs from the government budget in "high tech" programs. And megaprojects are to be among the subjects featured in the celebrations whose planning has already commenced, for the commemoration in 1989 of the two-hundredth anniversary of the French Revolution.

For the United States, a question that politicians and the public must answer is whether we do or do not wish to continue our leadership role in "high tech" applications, on a macroscale, in outer space. When "Buzz" Aldrin reported "a small step for a man, a giant step for humanity," the impact was so dramatic that it appears to have exhausted our imagination and energy. We have maintained a high NASA overhead, but with little "action" beyond the intermittent flights of the space shuttle. If we are to avoid the creeping paralysis of indecision that overtook the Northeast Corridor studies in the sixties and seventies, then priorities must be set, and some decisions must be made. The options are now becoming less unclear.

Space technology has not stood still, and the shuttle, while admirable, should not mesmerize us simply because it is the world's leading example of "spacemanship." New, improved engine designs could doubtless give us a more cost-effective space-transportation system for the future; one possibility is the "dual-fuel" engine, utilizing both solid and liquid propellants, designed and patented by Dr. Rudolf Beichel of Aerojet General Corporation and by Robert Salkeld, a director of the American Institute of Aeronautics and Astronautics. With an optimized space-transportation system, it would be feasible not only to mine the asteroid belt, as suggested in an earlier chapter, but to install prototypes for solar-power production from orbiting satellites or, perhaps more economically, from the moon itself. General Benjamin Schriever, a veteran leader of air force research and development, has followed such proposals closely, as have Dr. George Mueller, head of Systems Development Corporation, and several other, very competent authorities. If we as a nation do *not* intend to make the necessary investment of money and people in outer space, then we should at least specify the areas where we are "opting out," so that our trained personnel may serve as advisers and abettors of entrepreneurs in countries associated with us. But it should not be beyond the wit of the American polity to come up with an adequately funded and reasonably designed program to maintain our leadership in outer space, and specifically to engage in programs that may bring us tangible benefits in terms of our economy and our security.

Inasmuch as the kind of effort we are challenged to mount will involve equal psychic energy and moral and material support from both the public sector and the private sector, a story from the early 1600's may offer us both precedent and hope. Samuel Smiles, in his 1861 *Lives of the Engineers,*[7] has given us a concise and charming account of how, when "fever and plague . . . decimated the population," a Welsh goldsmith resident in London, Hugh Myddelton, stepped forward and offered to bring fresh water twenty-four miles from Hertfordshire to London. "The practical knowledge which he acquired . . . cultivated in him that power of grappling with difficulties, which emboldened him to undertake this great work, more like that of a Roman emperor than of a private London citizen." Opposition came chiefly from the landowners and occupiers along the route, and such were the difficulties placed in the way of construction that Myddelton had recourse to the king himself. But King James, whatever his faults, had been a consistent champion of large-scale engineering works of public benefit: He had employed the Dutch engineer Vermuyden for extensive drainage and reclamation works, and had himself, although monarch, assumed the entrepreneurial risks of the improvement of the Great Level marshes of the fens in Lincolnshire. In 1612, the king made an agreement with Myddelton, granting "the new river" a right-of-way through the royal domains and promising to pay "a moiety" of all expenses for bringing the water within one mile of the city. For its time and circumstances, this was "macro-engineering" on a grand scale. Samuel Smiles, in a footnote, remarks: "The fact that so large a sum as 17,000 pounds sterling was expended on the construction of a public work at the beginning of the 17th century is quite strong enough, and stands in no need of exaggeration. It was a very large sum to be expended at that time, when London was comparatively small, and England comparatively poor. . . . It appears from the 'pageant' which took place on the day of opening that as many as 600 labourers were employed upon the works at one time."

Smiles also comments, "It was the greatest enterprise of the kind that had yet been attempted in this country." King James expressed his satisfaction with the accomplishment of the project "by conferring on Hugh Myddelton the honour of knighthood." Several million gallons of fresh water a day were thus delivered to London, and in the city itself more than four hundred miles of wooden pipes were laid to distribute the water. After 1640, the proprietary company became one of the most prosperous in England. In modern terms, we might say that this was a splendid model for a mixed-economy corporation, devoted to a project of evident public benefit, and able to "stand on its own bottom" financially.

Part of the difficulty of lining up support for a modern macroproject lies in the incremental nature of our institutional history. We make laws in response to perceived emergencies or needs of the current scene, and create agencies and government departments to administer those laws. In view of the fact that the statute books still reflect much legislation that has not been revised or restated for long periods of time, it is hardly to be wondered at that different agencies of the same government have quite separate and not always concordant legislative histories.

I bumped into this situation, quite by accident, when I called on a college acquaintance, Douglass Cater, then serving as an administrative assistant to President Johnson. It happened that I met Cater just before Madame Indira Gandhi's first official visit to the United States as prime minister of India; Cater had been interested in my experiences in Australia, and asked if I would like to get together an informal group to draw up a proposed "position paper" on the food policy of the United States. Dr. James Killian, then president of M.I.T., and several other experienced people agreed to help; our conclusion was expressed in a single sentence, to the effect that different federal agencies seemed to pursue independently mandated policies, and that it would be in the public interest to mount a general review of our food policy, perhaps through an advisory group of public-spirited citizens, so that the State Department, the Department of Agriculture, and the many other agencies with responsibilities bordering on the problem could speak with one voice.

The fact that our report was expressed in one sentence created a problem, for the reason that in the whole history of the

Republic, no advisory group had been known to express itself so succinctly! (I remember the Vice-President, the widely admired Hubert H. Humphrey, arriving out of breath at our conference in one of the basement rooms.) We did expand the one sentence to two or three pages, but by that time Madame Gandhi's visit was virtually over; and to this day, it is not clear that we have "optimized" our food policy. Selling vast amounts of grain abroad is perhaps a good short-term notion; but if it is at the expense of the precious topsoil of marginal lands, then it's time to do a bit more thinking.

The plea for top-level consultations does not mean, and should never lead to, a monolithic decision structure. When Admiral R. K. ("Jimmy") James took over the Bureau of Ships of the United States Navy, he introduced "design work study," a procedure that involved naming two competing teams to design a projected new-type vessel. This introduction of a competitive element in the administrative decision process made for more and better thinking, and for more innovative and often less expensive ships and other naval artifacts. In macro-engineering, too, there is no reason to suppress disagreements, criticisms, and alternative solutions to problems. Quite the contrary. We have *far too little* interest in alternative systems. Macro-engineering, partly perhaps because of its inherent and inevitable "entertainment value," has been equated with science fiction. But quite aside from the fact that science fiction has often enough proven a more accurate guide to the future than conventional forecasting, we have now reached a point in history where much of the "far out" hardware can be designed, tested, built, and operated. This is why I have insisted on the importance of an orderly, systematic approach to the subject. While too many cooks may indeed spoil the broth, if there are no cooks at all there will be no broth to spoil. This is why we must set out, as a society bent on improvement and excellence, to take a number of specific steps to keep ourselves aware of what can be achieved and to train the people with the right skills and perspectives so that achievement will more nearly match ambition.

Concept and organization must be commensurate with the task in hand. This is, I suspect, why the Roman legions that conquered Carthage were also able, for long centuries, to contain and even push back the Sahara Desert, while constructing a regional civilization that outlasted the Roman Empire itself. Both space and time are ingredients of large-scale endeavors; the Romans were not too proud to be practical. What volumes are suggested by the remark of Sextus Julius Frontinus, who headed Rome's Department of Water Supply at the time of Pliny: "Who will venture to compare with these mighty conduits the idle Pyramids, or the famous but useless works of the Greeks?"[8]

In our own time, Professor Joseph Debanné of the University of Ottawa has designed a submarine aqueduct to carry the water of the Rhône River under the Mediterranean Sea and over the Atlas Mountains; the plastic duct could be laid on the sea-bottom itself or suspended below the surface at depths that avoid shipping.[9] It has been estimated that such a project would have the capability of doubling the irrigated acreage of North Africa; it could facilitate the maintenance of protective tree belts and would make possible the establishment, in the Roman fashion, of entire new garden communities. The cost? Perhaps thirty billion dollars! But such is the disarray of our world of nation-states that this careful proposal has been put aside as unrealistic, as more fit for the humorous sallies of "worldly" politicians than for the close analysis of competent engineers and economists. Only the irrefutable pollution of the Mediterranean Sea has brought about a treaty accepted by all the riparian states.

That this pollution is unavoidable and excessive became apparent to me several summers ago when my brother Alfred and I were invited by a descendant of the Monsieur Eiffel who built the Eiffel Tower to bathe from the palatial villa that he had erected near Cap Ferrat: We were able literally to walk out the back door and into the Mediterranean. But what a disappointment! Globules of oil and tar disfigured the water, and on returning to the villa we needed showers before dressing. With waste products so rapidly overrunning what Cleveland Amory has aptly called "the last resorts," can we wonder that the experienced and practical Dutch have proposed an island based largely on garbage, to be built under up-to-date hygienic conditions in the North Sea? Or is it to be wondered at, now that Thor Heyderdahl has eloquently reported on the pollution he witnessed while crossing the Atlantic Ocean on a raft, that sensible people both in the Americas and in Europe are beginning to ask themselves whether shipping is really a long-run answer to ocean transportation?

The Eiffel Tower was assembled in a matter of months, and it is not altogether astonishing that the French, in order to celebrate the two-hundredth anniversary of the French Republic, are thinking in terms of "megatowers" as symbols of French interest in a technological future. Probably Frank Lloyd Wright was the world's first professional architect to design a "mile-high tower." I think it was in 1964 that Monsieur Louis Armand, chairman of the French Railways and at that time possibly the most highly decorated citizen in Europe, suggested that I visit his younger friend, the French engineer Gabriel Bouladon. Monsieur Bouladon served at that time as chief of the Mechanical Engineering Division of the Battelle Memorial Institute in Geneva, Switzerland. At the end of a long and wide-ranging meeting, Monsieur Bouladon and I talked about Frank Lloyd Wright's idea. "My architect friends," I remarked, "say the building would not fall down but that it would consist almost entirely of elevators!" Monsieur Bouladon smiled enigmatically: "Let me give this matter some thought."

Half a year later, back in my New York law office on upper Fifth Avenue, a large package arrived in the mail: Monsieur Bouladon had not only solved the elevator problem, he had patented his solution! [10] With John L. Gray, who was my companion on many trips to Australia and who served as general counsel of the Battelle Memorial Institute at its Columbus, Ohio, headquarters, I showed the drawings to Mr. John M. Kyle, Jr., then chief engineer of the Port of New York Authority. Jack Kyle, who had been a sound and resilient adviser on channel tunnel matters, liked the Bouladon solution: Instead of large elevators, the system began as an escalator; each step, as it rose upward, became an enclosed box holding just two passengers, and with the boxes piled one on top of another in the fashion of the German "Paternoster" system used at the turn of the century, the whole system turned continuously, without interrupting the smooth flow of traffic. This had been true, too, of the Paternoster elevator, but Bouladon, by adding "high tech" gadgetry, was able to make his design both "fail-safe" and more rapid. The continuous flow of passengers into and out of the system meant that the halls adjacent to the elevator entrances could be much reduced in size, and inasmuch as the shafts themselves were miniscule, more "rentable" space was left for the landlord to let to tenants. Mr. Kyle explained to us that he would very likely have recommended the system for use in the World Trade Towers, for whose design and construction he was responsible (these highest buildings in New York were a project of the Port of New York Authority), but, alas, there had not been time or money to build a prototype, and it was impossible to obtain authorization for such a radically novel system when it was still untried even in a "low-rise" building.

Despite risks of all kinds, "megatowers" are now under discussion, not only in Europe but in land-short Japan. An alternative proposal to deal with population pressures was proposed by Mr. Tanaka before he became prime minister of Japan: He outlined a "Tanaka Plan" for a series of entirely new coastal cities, to be linked together by high-speed rail lines. This scheme is no longer considered "practical politics," since Mr. Tanaka has withdrawn from the political spotlight in the wake of charges that he was involved in payoffs by large American corporations seeking business advantages in Japan. If "high-rise," despite its questionable sociological rationale, is to tempt investors, however, it is likely that elevator systems will be devised that can move horizontally as well as vertically. And in an effort to provide an environment more suited to sociability and an antidote to the "alienation" experienced in mass housing and office projects, I suppose consideration will be given to "common rooms" of all sorts, for dining, reading, playing indoor games, or listening to music. The traditional urban apartment house is surely one of the dreariest artifacts accepted by urban populations. Just as the house plan that President Lowell introduced at Harvard, in imitation of the Oxford and Cambridge colleges in England, constituted an epochal improvement over dormitory life, just so a diversification of social opportunities in the large urban dwelling house would be a boon to all of urban humanity. "Big" need not be "stupid" or "monolithic"; on the contrary, larger structures, with their more ample space, should challenge the architectural and planning community to think more deeply of the social and cultural needs of urbanized humanity.

Having come this far, it is timely to ask how "practical" planners are to obtain finance for projects and programs that are more costly, often by an order of magnitude, than previously known construction ventures. When the elder J. P. Morgan decided that a larger company was needed to take advantage of new opportunities for the steel industry, he simply called a meeting in his office; this was, I have been told, the origin of the United States Steel Corporation. Today, although the "numbers" of dollars controlled by professional financiers are larger, it cannot be said that any individual occupies the commanding position once held by a J. P. Morgan or a Commodore Vanderbilt. Nonetheless, I think that the most knowledgeable and experienced people connected with macrofinance are still to be found in the ranks of the investment bankers (in the City of London, one would say "merchant bankers"). It is to investment firms that we must look for many of the devices and combinations that have made many difficult large-scale enterprises feasible. And of course there are the indispensable legal advisers, many of whom have worked so closely with banking consortia that they are trusted with the leading role in delicate negotiations involving governments, business corporations, and financial institutions. Lloyd Cutler is believed to have played a key part in the arrangements for the Alaska Pipeline, a fifteen-billion-dollar project that has been as important in the Northwest of the American continent as the equally costly James Bay Hydroelectric Project has been in the Northeast. That President Carter, faced with a plethora of complex problems halfway through his term of office, called on Lloyd Cutler to be his counsel and "right arm", came as good news to Democrats and Republicans alike. The same kind of high competence combined with unimpeachable integrity characterized the public and private career of George Wildman Ball, who was the Undersecretary of State when I was invited to lead a "private enterprise" delegation to Panama. Such individuals have never been of greater value to our country than in today's troubled and portentous times, when in order to seize major new opportunities we shall have to structure new *ad hoc* agreements among major institutions.

Whether new opportunities in space, on the high seas, and on our own continent are to be developed primarily by government or by private enterprise is hardly the essence of the issue: We need the best efforts of both private and public sectors, or we shall be left behind by history. The question is rather one of precedence and style. If government agencies take the lead, then the role of the private sector will be that of subcontractor and consultant. Another approach would be to authorize private groups of various sorts to carry out defined tasks with the protection of government participation either through guarantees, promises to purchase output and services, or partnership arrangements. Philomena Grodzka, addressing this issue in a presentation before an AAAS Macro-Engineering Symposium in 1978,[11] put forward the idea of "a TVA for Space." She would call it a "Space Utilization Authority," and points out that the 1967 Outer Space Treaty mandates governmental agencies for space activities. Two other considerations are the difficulty that private entities have found in raising funds for long-term research and development, and the greater ease that a government agency would have in dealing with other sovereign states concerned with developments "out there."

The public authority idea has also been proposed for ocean developments. As we can all remember, the public-authority concept has been used successfully in the United States for toll roads, dams, bridges, and ports; this approach still permits private financing of structures and operations, and facilitates the kind of flexible cooperation between the private and public sectors that most of us regard as desirable in large affairs. My father served on the Power Authority of the state of New York, and found that this instrumentality was ideal both for raising large sums through the investment banking community and also for negotiating with a homologous institution, the Ontario Hydroelectric Authority, which has been a loyal partner in the complex, highly successful arrangements for the electric power aspects of the St. Lawrence Seaway and Power Program.

Dr. Julius A. Stratton, president emeritus of the Massachusetts Institute of Technology, served as chairman of the Commission on Marine Science, Engineering, and Resources whose 1969 report led to establishment of the National Oceanographic and Atmospheric Administration. I wonder whether the time has not come for equally prestigious and influential commissions to be appointed, so that our governmental structure can move forward to take advantage of the nation's opportunities both in outer space and in the equally neglected area of ocean development. Such commissions ought to be bipartisan: Where the use of large-scale technological capabilities is envisaged, programs are bound to last longer and result in impacts that stretch out far beyond the term of office of either Republican or Democratic administrations of today or tomorrow. Admittedly, presidential advisory commissions have a mixed record: Thomas R. Wolanin, in a 1975 book on the subject describes a number of such commissions and provides a checklist of those that led to legislation and those that led nowhere. I am assuming that we shall have a President and a Congress desirous of having the nation put its best foot forward, and that advice from a group of people of untarnished integrity, judgment, and experience will be solicited to frame recommendations for a more effective, long-term thrust by the United States into ocean and space engineering.

In a sense, the whole commentary set forth in this book could be regarded as an essay on the subject of institutional assessment: Every institution, whether governmental or private, needs to take stock of its performance from time to time, and although the recent and impending rapid growth in technology may seem to call for especially prompt readjustments and responses, in fact the whole history of government and enterprise has been characterized by periodic reevaluations and changes of course. As a young Wall Street lawyer, I remember having my shoes shined by a man who kept saying, as he very ably brought my worn but dignified shoes to a high polish, "You've got to know what to do with what you've got." This wisdom is especially applicable to our present predicament, in which we seem to have *too much* technology and too little idea what to do with it. One solution, of course, is to turn our educated technologists into a race of consultants, so that the actual "industry"—that is, the realization of ideas developed in American laboratories—is carried out elsewhere. Perhaps this notion lies at the root of much of the present interest in a "post-industrial society." Such a society would run the risk of becoming, also, "post-agricultural," "post-intellectual," and even *post-mortem*.

There is a large and growing literature on the subject of managing large-scale technical projects and programs. In the United States, the National Science Foundation at first took a rather gloomy approach to the whole subject, sponsoring extensive and expert reports by the Stanford Research Institute on the *difficulties* of such enterprises. Currently, a constructive review is taking place and ought to be ready for publication in three or four years. In England, the Institution of Civil Engineers published, in 1978, a report on the special problems of managing large-scale capital projects. In 1979, an attractive volume entitled *A Multi-Disciplined Study of Problems of and Solutions to Successfully Accomplishing Giant Projects* was published in the wake of an international conference organized in London during the previous year by OYEZ-IBC. The foreword seems worth quoting:

> For many reasons the size and complexity of capital projects have increased to the point where giant projects are becoming much more common. Such projects pose problems which are different not only in size but in nature from more moderately sized projects. The number of people with experience of giant projects is small: the number with experience of *successful* giant projects is even smaller. It is from this latter group that the authors of this collection of papers come.

In an eloquent introduction to this volume, Allen Sykes begins by saying:

> I believe I speak for most experienced people who have ever worked seriously on giant projects when I say that few would ever choose to develop a resource on a gigantic scale if there was any choice. The need to gain the simultaneous approval, co-ordination, and enthusiasm of so many people, firms and governments, which alone makes giant projects possible, requires the greatest possible dedication of the project sponsors over many years. To work on giant projects is always exhausting and often demoralising for repeated postponement and

change of plans is normal, and the ultimate failure rate of actually launching such projects is almost unbelievably high.

In one of the outstanding contributions to this volume, the manager of the $4.3 billion pipeline portion of the Trans-Alaska Pipeline Project, Mr. Frank P. Moolin, Jr., of Anchorage, argues for a small management élite: "If I had to sum up in one brief sentence my observation of the effectiveness of various project management organizations, it would have to be 'Small is Beautiful.'"

One illusion, implicit and thus more insidious than an examined misapprehension, is the belief that scientific knowledge, if widely enough diffused, will solve society's outstanding problems. That science can be helpful is not in doubt. But the implementation of knowledge is far from automatic: It must be mediated by human beings with their fallibilities, eccentricities, and penchant for cantankerous behavior. The liberal confidence in inevitable progress has not really survived the jolt of two World Wars, a Great Depression, the ravages of an adolescent drug culture, and the increasing threat of nuclear and other forms of scientific holocaust. Expert knowledge of the *management* of large-scale enterprises is not, therefore, a sufficient approach to the general problem that, if we are honest with ourselves, is how to *choose* those giant enterprises that we wish to have managed. Competent management is of course very necessary and important. But if we may speak for a moment of management in its broadest sense, we are going far beyond the bounds even of "management theory"; what we are confronting is society's need to get a better "fix" on its own future and the problem of choosing wisely and prudently among alternatives that are—each one—so costly that there is no way of escaping the primary task of assessment and decision.

To limit ourselves, for the moment, to the case of energy, we are at once confronted with two important facts: Energy supply and demand are cyclical (and therefore policies that seem wise in times of shortage seem foolish in times of abundance, and vice versa); and second, there are so many vast programs that have been proposed that even a nation as wealthy as the United States cannot go "all out" for every single one of them at one and the same time. Are we to maximize hydroelectric power, as recommended by the late Ralph M. Parsons and by Professor T. W. Kierans? Is Ocean Thermal Energy Conversion (OTEC) so promising in the light of recent improvements that we should give it a "green light"? What of all the hullabaloo about new systems for synthetic oil and gas? Are we to abandon a program already on the books? Is it worth building a prototype of a solar-power satellite, or should we think in terms of a primary solar-power station built of lunar materials and constructed on the moon itself? Should we really proceed with the Clinch River Breeder Reactor? How about tapping those seemingly illimitable pressurized gas reserves under the Gulf of Mexico? In 1897, according to the Fall 1977 issue of the journal *Co-Evolution,* 30 percent of Pasadena's homes had solar water heaters! Should we not invest heavily in such a demonstrably useful technology? What about shale oil and the tar sands of the West and Canada?

If the public seems confused, it is not yet clear that the "scientific establishment" is less so. People with experience of life's uncertainties will not wish the United States to adopt an energy strategy that puts all its eggs in one basket (or even in two baskets). But clear decisions must not only be taken, they must be adhered to with reasonable consistency over a period of years. "Gut reactions" must be mistrusted: It is precisely when there is an "oil glut" that it is most economical to purchase petroleum products for the nation's strategic reserve, but the popular impression, in such times, is that the "energy shortage" is over and will not recur.

The country wishes to go back to work. The world's wealthiest nation can afford to invest in a selected series of programs and projects that will restore the nation's pride, self-confidence, and competitive position. If this means that leaders of government, industry, and engineering science must meet, pencil in hand, to launch the necessary detailed estimates so that wise decisions can be made, so be it: The country expects nothing less.

Aerial view of Nigeria's new capital city, Abuja, now under construction. The central axis of the city traverses four rounded hills, interspersed with minor stream valleys. Important public buildings will be erected where the axis crosses the high point of each hill. The Federal Capital City has been planned to grow to a population of 1.6 million people by the year 2000.

MASTER PLAN FOR THE CAPITAL CITY

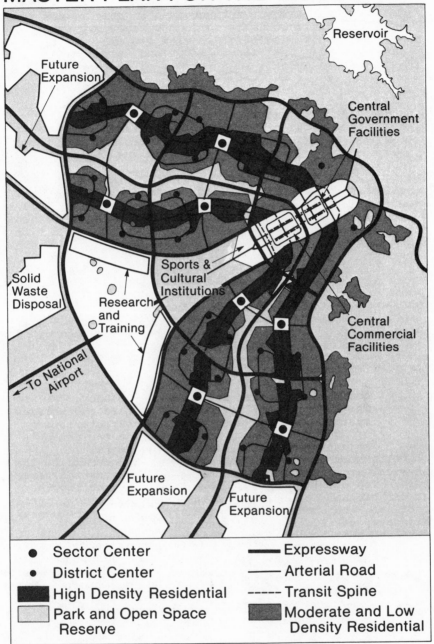

Reservoir

Future Expansion

Central Government Facilities

Solid Waste Disposal

Sports & Cultural Institutions

Research and Training

Central Commercial Facilities

To National Airport

Future Expansion

Future Expansion

● Sector Center
● District Center
■ High Density Residential
□ Park and Open Space Reserve

━━━ Expressway
─── Arterial Road
----- Transit Spine
■ Moderate and Low Density Residential

The Master Plan for Abuja was the result of a worldwide competition won by International Planning Associates, a consortium of Archisystems, Inc. (a division of the Summa Corp.), Planning Research Corporation, and Wallace, McHarg, Roberts and Todd. Upper left is one of the "inselbergs" that provide a distinctive setting for the new city. The two views of actual construction show (center left) a major highway entering the city (with Aso Hill in the background) and (lower left) the National Legislative Building. The rate of construction has been somewhat curtailed by the current economic depression.

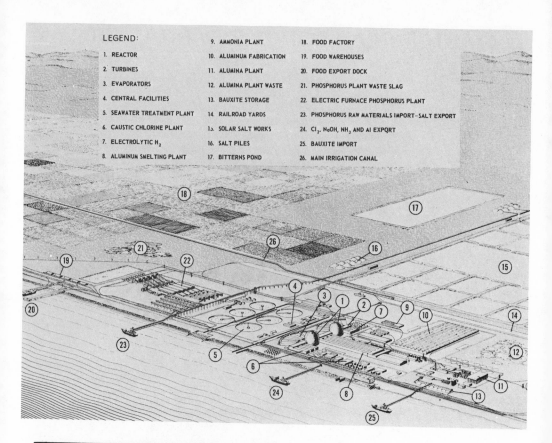

The NUPLEX (Nuclear-Powered Agro-Industrial Complex), diagrammed above, was conceived by staff members at the Oak Ridge National Laboratory in the early 1960's, when there were still widespread expectations that nuclear power would be highly economical. The general idea was to use cheap power to desalinate seawater near coastal deserts; then immense tracts of irrigated land could provide food for the world's hungry populations. At left is a scheme developed by Robert Panero and publicized by the late Herman Kahn for a chain of artificial "Great Lakes" in South America. A large dam across the Amazon at Monte Alegre would form a lake the size of Montana. The hydroelectric and transportation development, proposed in the mid-1960's, did not meet with a favorable response.

Case study for an artificial island in Osaka Harbor, Japan, showing the configuration of a coal-fired thermal power plant (floating type).

Alternative case study for an artificial island in Osaka Harbor, Japan, showing the configuration of a coal-fired thermal power plant (reclamation type).

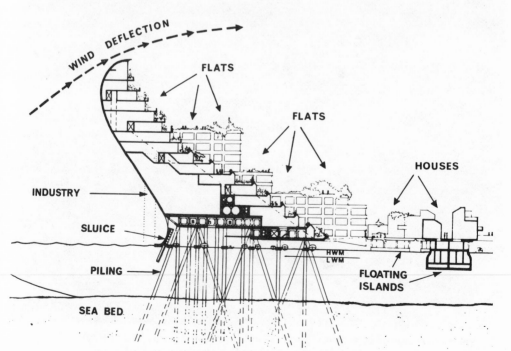

WIND DEFLECTION

FLATS

FLATS

HOUSES

INDUSTRY

SLUICE

PILING

HWM
LWM

FLOATING
ISLANDS

SEA BED

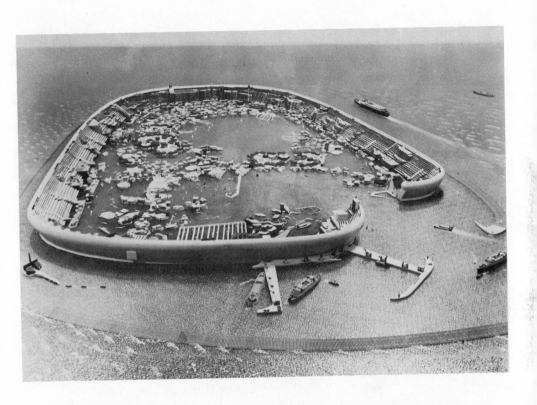

Sea City, designed by leading British architects and engineers as a possible successor to the present mainland city, was announced at a February 28, 1968, press conference by the then Minister of Technology, Anthony Wedgwood Benn. The imaginative concept, produced by the Pilkington Glass Age Development Committee and designed by architect Hal Moggridge and engineers John Martin and Ken Anthony, envisages a self-sufficient community of 30,000 "living in comfort and safety many miles out to sea." The cross section of the city wall (top left) indicates how power, heat, and refrigeration requirements for residents and industry could be provided from a central power complex. In the center can be seen high-speed gas turbines using natural gas pumped from nearby gas fields to provide electricity. The diagram (lower left) shows how important the outer wall is to Sea City. Resting on the completed base and starting 30 feet above sea level at its highest point, the superstructure is made up of concrete cells joined together at the corners. Each cell, prefabricated on the mainland and brought to the site, forms either a small flat or part of a large one. The picture directly above shows how Sea City would look from the air. Built on concrete stilts and protected by a floating breakwater (seen in the foreground) and by a curved 180-foot-high city wall, it could be built in any of the shoal waters that exist over 10 percent of the surface of the ocean. Outside the walls (right foreground) special articulated container ships berth in the "moat" of calm water to unload stores, while a hovercraft heads for the harbor entrance to discharge passengers.

The proposed artificial island depicted by the dotted hexagonal line on the photograph above suggests the ambitious scope of the planned expansion of Japan's Port
of Osaka. The Greater Osaka Region may be said to include Japan's largest production and consuming center with a population of more than 15 million. Reclamation
work now being contemplated will recover more than 1,500 acres from the sea.
Waste materials from the city will constitute an important segment of the 71 million
cubic meters of landfill needed by the project. In the light of what Osaka is actually
achieving, it is curious that programs for artificial islands to improve port facilities
in the United States are looked upon as "science fiction" or "unrealistic." The sketch
(above right) of one portion of the ICONN-ERIE project put forward by Nigel

Chattey is not in principle very different from current accomplishments in Japan, Holland, and elsewhere. An "Island Complex Offshore New York and New Jersey" has been welcomed by Governor Mario Cuomo of New York and by other political leaders, but will require the energetic adhesion of industry, labor, and professional groups if it is to achieve the sustained support needed for effective long-range implementation. The model of the Pilkington Glass Sea City, shown with illumination at night (lower right), suggests interesting possibilities for a diplomacy ready to use technology as an active ingredient: Artificial islands could be built in international waters to house intergovernmental agencies and to provide new sovereignties for landless populations.

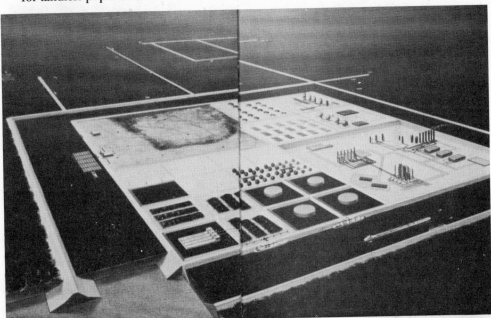

This photograph of "the highest lift lock in America" was taken at Little Falls, New York, on the Erie Canal in 1941. It suggests that further modernization of inland waterways is an option worth looking into, as costs of competing systems soar. Where rights-of-way exist, they should be regarded as a solid asset.

The last lock on the Erie Canal before ships and barges enter Lake Ontario. Nigel Chattey, who has proposed widening and deepening the Erie Canal system, points out that transportation costs account for more than 75 percent of the delivered cost of coal. Canals or pipelines? An issue for tomorrow.

Water pouring into Lock 11 in Amsterdam, New York. Fascination with "high tech" has led otherwise well-informed people to dismiss, perhaps too soon, the contribution to prosperity that can be made by the appropriate use, on a large scale, of familiar "intermediate" technologies such as canal building.

Another view of Lock 11 on the Erie Canal in the vicinity of Amsterdam, New York. If transportation industries as a whole account for approximately 20 percent of the gross national product, does the country not need a central research and training institute encompassing *all* forms of transportation, new and old alike?

SUBMERGED CAISSON SYSTEM WOULD MAKE IT POSSIBLE
TO BUILD THE CHANNEL TUNNEL IN MUCH LESS TIME
THAN WOULD BE REQUIRED IF EXCAVATIONS WERE POSSIBLE
ONLY FROM EACH SHORELINE.

Patent Pending

Above: A submerged caisson system developed
by J. Vincent Harrington that could facilitate
the construction of intercoastal tunnels such as
the railway tunnel long discussed as an arterial
link between the United Kingdom and France.
By providing one or more additional work faces
for crews and boring machines, such a system
may appreciably reduce both the time and the
cost of building intercoastal tunnels. Left:
C. Lawrence Meador, Uwe Kitzinger, CBE, and
Frank P. Davidson prepare to go below (1981)
to inspect the Seikan Tunnel whose undersea
portion—more than 13 miles—has now been
completed. At right are various views of this
longest existing undersea tunnel, which links
the main islands of Honshu and Hokkaido in
Japan. Thus far the Japanese have spent more
than eleven years building it. They chose a single large bore that will accommodate two three-
rail tracks; that is, both narrow-gauge trains
and the high-speed Shinkansen Line will be
able to traverse the tunnel. Ferries take four
and a half hours to cross the dangerous waters
of the Tsugaru Strait; the train trip will be accomplished in 50 minutes. The motivation? In
1954, five ferryboats of the Japan National Railways sank in a September typhoon, and 1,414
people were drowned. This was the third worst
shipwreck in history.

Engineering for Tomorrow: Broader Concepts—and New, More Extensive Transport Linkages

IN THE FILM *FITZCARRALDO*, INDIANS OF THE AMAZON JUNGLE are said to fear a neighboring tribe that clings to the belief that reality consists essentially of dreams, and that what most people call reality is only the slow working out of plans and insights that have come to us in dreams. If instead of "dreams" we substitute the word "concepts" or "plans," the feeling behind the strange tribe's belief becomes at least partly accessible to us: Unless a person has the *idea* of a sidewalk, the sidewalk literally cannot be built. This is why, much as we may dislike and distrust people who call themselves "planners" or "forecasters," we cannot operate our society without the kind of activity in which they are engaged.

Most of the reality by which we are surrounded is a contrived or constructed reality: To experience "nature in the raw" we must take a trip to quite remote regions, and even there we may be disappointed to find that civilization has already left its heavy footprint. People who shun "planning" and "futurism" have, of course, a perfect right to abhor change, to prefer continuity within the changes already brought about by others, and to say to "enthusiasts" that we should "put on the brakes" and avoid "future shock" by limiting the dislocations and inconveniences that can be brought about by a rampant technology.

The genius of the British lay, perhaps, in this instinctual preference for tradition, incremental growth, and loyal continuity with the past. But the Industrial Revolution, in its day every bit as disruptive as contemporary and prospective societal changes, was a home-grown British product! This revolution reached outward, and still persists, with gathering momentum, on a worldwide basis. It would be hypocritical to deny that today's relatively comfortable standard of living in the industrialized countries owes much to the infrastructures designed and built generations ago. The people of Boston enjoy California artichokes and Texas grapefruit because of transcontinental railways and airways, and while an organic, smaller-scale agriculture has a valid and essential role in the scheme of things, there is little or no public disposition to dismantle the infrastructure that makes interregional exchanges possible. We think of ourselves as a peace-loving nation, but the hard fact remains that California and the West were won not by settlement alone, but also by warfare; yet few pacifists among us have wished to propose the rendition to Mexico of the conquests won by Sam Houston and John Tyler.

Past innovations remain on, often for thousands of years. Because mobility has always been a matter not just of utility and comfort, but often of survival, old systems of proven worth (such as messenger systems, which function very much the same whether at the court of Darius the Great or in the antechambers of a Wall Street investment bank), continue to coexist with such relatively recent accretions as the pneumatic tube and the jet aircraft. In the same American or European city, one finds streets that could have been built by the ancient Egyptians or Greeks, canals that are less complex than the canal that Drusus built to connect the Rhine with the North Sea, and railway stations that hark back to Victorian times.

Any fundamental improvement in the technologies affecting mobility is bound to change the patterns of human settlement. Because of the railway and the automobile, commuting has become a way of life from Mexico City to Tokyo; subways, once the pride of London and New York, are proliferating on a global basis. I know at least one married couple where the husband teaches at M.I.T. and the wife in California: They commute across three thousand miles to maintain a lively—and harmonious—household! We are rapidly becoming, the arms race notwithstanding, a single planetary society, with a lingua franca understood from Seoul to South Bend, and that is the language of technology, the "software" that programs our machines and facilitates the cooperation of people from different cultures and jurisdictions. The jet airplane and the ballistic missile have given us a taste of both the positive and negative aspects of this evolution. What are we to make of it all? Can some sense of "system," of order and purpose, be projected onto such a swiftly changing landscape where apparently nobody is in charge? Is the pace of technology too fast? Too slow? Can guideposts be erected and respected?

To this series of questions, macro-engineering can make at least a modest contribution. It is now clear that mobility and stability must be studied together, that the conditions of one variable have dynamic effects on the constraints and opportunities of the other. Human settlements have always been selected with a view of access to resources—that is, from the standpoint of transportation. This is why Alexandria, St. Petersburg, London, New Amsterdam, Montreal, Sydney—and Paris—were situated on reliable waterways. It is also why for more than two thousand years China has been expanding the Grand Canal network south from Peking, and why ports on all continents are endeavoring to modernize in order to service new markets. Macro-engineering must to an extent counter the parochial intellectual compartments that have been labeled "aircraft," "ships," "railways," "automobiles," and so on. Each of these categories has had a (deceptive?) technical validity for distinct periods of time, but in fact each mode of transportation must now be seen as a congeries of elements that, together with the human beings who designed and built and used them, has constituted a purposive "man-machine system" that satisfies perceived needs under certain (not necessarily permanent) conditions. Today we have a new situation brought about by the advanced technologies of ballistics, computer science, telecommunications, and their mutually reinforcing cousins in the biological and materials sciences. And that new situation is bound to produce new combinations of component technologies. We had a foretaste of things to come with the "Flying Boat" that carried Pan American passengers across the Pacific after World War I, and with the amphibious jeeps and tanks of World War II. As a young lieutenant in the Fort Garry Horse (the famous 10th Canadian Armored Regiment), I remember the thrill of climbing aboard our amphibious fleet of tanks for maneuvers in the English Channel during the weeks and months before D-Day. If automotive vehicles can learn to swim, why should we be astonished at a railway train that can "fly"? But such is the force of habit, that attachment to a particular technological tradition can almost acquire the force of a cult. The Duke of Wellington had a passionate aversion to the railway and a stated preference for horse transportation: to this day in Europe, the separate "religions" of rail and canal transportation compete not only for funds, but also for loyalty and group adherence.

At the April 1982 annual meeting in Baltimore of the American Institute of Aeronautics and Astronautics, I suggested that the airplane may now become obsolete on long-distance routes because it is too slow. The next conceptual leap forward for rail transportation will not be the mere electromagnetic levitation so conclusively demonstrated by Mr. Kyotani's team on Kyushu— the test runs have demonstrated a capability of slightly better than 300 mph—but the placing of such a wheelless train in a tube from which the air has been partially pumped out! This was the idea put forward by Dr. Robert Salter of the RAND Corporation, at the very first Macro-Engineering Symposium in 1978.

I should amplify my characterization of the electromagnetically levitated train as "wheelless": Although the rail vehicles will "fly" above the track—an inch or even several inches above it, depending on the various adjustments and tradeoffs—the Japanese Railways have sensibly provided wheels as well, so that there will be a smooth transition when the train "takes off" or "lands." In my own office. I have a small working model which demonstrates that a train of this type can successfully set itself down on a standard gauge track. The significance of this feature is that it will permit the transcontinental trains of the future to use the existing infrastructure of tunnels and rails at the entrance to major cities. Tunneling costs in the city of New York have now, in the case of the new subway line being built crosstown, reached and passed the hundred-million-dollar per mile mark! Some thought must be given, therefore, to interconnection with the traditional system, or the promising new technology will go the way of the famous broad-gauged Great Western Railway that Brunel built in Queen Victoria's time: It was the most stable and therefore the fastest railway of its era, but inasmuch as it could not be interconnected with the existing system of standard gauge track, the new line suffered bankruptcy and closure despite its conceded technical superiority!

The technical feasibility of levitated tube transport can probably be demonstrated, even at supersonic speeds, within the present decade. Whether it can be introduced commercially amid the mundane constraints of budgets, insurance, and competing claims for scarce capital funds must await the verdict of the future. Macro-engineering investments are apt to be preclusive: They amount to major choices that prevent whole communities from realizing alternative options. Moreover, any radically new system such as supersonic ground transport will arouse a certain amount of opposition from people who regard their interests or loyalties as inextricably intertwined with the perpetuation of existing transport systems.

But there are solid reasons to bet on long-distance underground transport, and hence there is a good case for investing in the research *and development* needed to transform Salter's concept from blueprint to reality. First of all, the congestion of airways, shipping lanes, and surface arteries has led to inconvenience and pollution. On the count of inconvenience, anyone who has made a jet trip across the ocean or across the country, only to be held up for one hour by highway traffic on the way home, can testify that rapid transit from city center to city center would be a preferable alternative. As for pollution, above-ground automotive traffic and airplanes have posed grave problems of both air and noise pollution; and the destruction of landscapes for airports, parking areas, highways, railways, and shipping terminals has been detrimental not only from a visual point of view, but also from the standpoint of removing productive acreage from agricultural, industrial, and residential use.

Second, although some may regard it as bad form to allow "military" considerations to affect what is usually viewed (wrongly, I think) as a purely civilian matter, nonetheless it is inescapably true that societies that value their survival will now look carefully at the option of underground transport systems. As such systems may be built in "competent rock" about fifteen hundred feet below the surface, they can assure—through increased stability—definite technical advantages for levitated vehicles flying through carefully calibrated tunnels. Third, as a counterbalance to the use of more energy than a conventional electric train would require, the increased speed would mean a proportional increase in capacity and therefore in overall system revenues: The fuel costs per passenger or per ton would be dramatically lower than for either a supersonic or subsonic jet airplane, although higher than for conventional rail traffic.

Dr. Salter has taught us that there is no *scientific* barrier to the design of a tunnel or tube transit system that would make it possible to travel from coast to coast in twenty-one minutes. As a leading physicist who has been personally responsible for the coordination of hundreds of engineers in major system programs of the United States Air Force, he is respected as a prudent planner and administrator; when he came to M.I.T. two or three years ago for a working lunch with engineering specialists from a variety of departments, he graciously agreed that as a matter of *engineering*, it may be preferable to build the initial systems with average speeds in the range of 1200 to 1500 mph. And a speed that does not exceed the experience of the *Concorde*, in which I have traveled in remarkable comfort at speeds greater than MACH I, will be more marketable than an advertised speed that would appear to imply astronaut training as a "condition precedent" to boarding the bus.

Two major cost elements are involved in Dr. Salter's scheme: building the tunnel or tube, and building the guideway-vehicle combination to be placed inside. By far the major cost element would be the tunneling. And despite steady improvements in tunneling technology, tunnel costs have been increasing. For deep tunnels of a thousand miles or more, a cost-effective approach will be mandatory. We may hope that some far-seeing group will eventually establish a research and test center for new tunneling techniques; meanwhile, several useful initiatives have been taken.

As early as 1975, the National Science Foundation published a rather favorable assessment of the Subterrene digging method developed at the federal government's Los Alamos Scientific Laboratory in New Mexico. This method involves a tunneling machine that heats whatever material it comes into contact with to so high a temperature that the material is glazed and becomes the initial lining. The Subterrene was designed to operate with either conventional or nuclear power; the safety advantage, in this case, may well lie with a miniaturized nuclear engine attached directly to the Subterrene.

The second initiative is the program for fully automated mining that has been carried on at Carnegie-Mellon University (CMU). Automation has already reduced the manpower needed to mine coal, limestone, and other valuable materials deep beneath the earth's surface: what is proposed, therefore, is somewhat less dramatic than might otherwise appear. CMU's Robotics Institute, however, has set itself the objective of building "an unmanned boring and tunnel-lining machine that will also handle muck and debris."[1]

Recently, from Japan has come the announcement that a Tokyo firm, Japan Aviation Electronics Industries, Ltd., has worked on a shield tunnel monitoring and control system that will eventually be capable of fully automated tunneling operations, although complete success in this program may be several years away.[2]

Meanwhile, the Japanese test facility on Kyushu has continued with its methodical and adequately funded (about ten million dollars per year) experiments with its full-scale levitated train. This is the year that Yoshihiro Kyotani, chief engineer of the Research and Development Department of the Japanese National Railways, will integrate the test engines into a three-car set providing for passengers, so that actual tests can be made of passenger comfort and other market factors. Within a decade, we may expect to see some of the high speed *Shinkansen* lines converted to magnetic levitation.

To Americans, the step-by-step, intelligent, coordinated Japanese test of a new transport technology should serve as a stimulus and a model. We cannot forever complain of "unfair" Japanese competition because we have not had the wit and the wisdom to cooperate with each other in building a new engineering system *originally demonstrated in the United States*. The fashionable shouting match in this country between "Big Government" and "Big Industry" has in fact jeopardized the future of "Big Technology": We have not yet outlined a reasoned series of investment programs looking to the future welfare of American society.

An interesting feature of the Japanese magnetically levitated train is the curious fact that Japan itself is almost too small to take maximum advantage of the new system. High-speed ground transport will be of greatest utility over the large continental expanses of the United States, Canada, Australia, Europe, Africa, Asia, and South America. The United States does have a chance to recover its lost leadership in this field, but only by building a determined and adequately funded long-range program; such a program could take the next conceptual leap by working with the Japanese to develop a levitated train capable of operating subsonically and supersonically in a partially evacuated tube, as briefly suggested in the first chapter of this book. But how are we to learn if this admittedly expensive program is "worth the candle"?

Dr. Julian Gresser, an American lawyer resident in Tokyo who has been a professor both at M.I.T. and the Harvard Law School, has proposed drawing up a list of "strategic industries," those in whose future the nation has a vital stake. He would then have the White House sponsor intersectoral meetings so that a process might be initiated that would lead to agreements for joint commitment by government, industry, the labor unions, and indeed all relevant sectors of society. This seems to me a reasonable and timely approach. Part of America's apparent helplessness has been due to excessive fascination with general economic theories. We have argued about "supply-side economics" and "monetarist theory" and other perfectly respectable topics, but in the meantime we have neglected to focus on the unavoidable planning and engineering steps without which major new techno-economic enterprises cannot be launched at all. It doesn't matter whether one's point of view is "capitalist" or "socialist"—or whether one is Democratic or Republican: For a new transport system to exist at all, someone has to design it, build prototypes, make market analyses, carry out safety tests, and obtain the resources for construction, operation, and maintenance. The American economy, regardless of the political fashions of the day, will require an efficient infrastructure in transport, energy, water supply, and other basic services, or it will cease to function satisfactorily. While arguing passionately about economic and political *trivia,* have we perhaps failed to do what is *necessary?* Surely the histrionics of the Northeast Corridor Program illustrate the perils of substituting rhetoric and sterile research for a coherent and sustained program of design and construction. And without a functioning infrastructure, what is to be the future of "strategic industries"? Just as the reconstruction of Europe with Marshall Plan aid, and the reconstruction of Japan that began under the "proconsulship" of General Douglas MacArthur, started with infrastructure rebuilding, so must the United States, by an effort of will, commence its own reindustrialization with a thorough examination of the requirements and the opportunities of our principal infrastructure networks.

Will American citizens wish to make such an effort? Clearly, the nation can rise to crisis situations. But with the apparent return of a more hopeful economic climate, will there be the public will and insistence necessary for the kind of initiatives proposed herein? I think that the American public knows very well that the economy is cyclical, and that it is foolish to "whomp up" and then dismantle major programs, just because temporary circumstances have or have not produced a panic reaction. When oil is cheap, we ought to be *building up* the strategic petroleum reserve, not dismantling it! And if fear is not to be the great engine of state, then a long-term assessment of the public interest can serve as a sure and reliable guide. The building of major technological systems—either new infrastructural networks or new industrial complexes—cannot be completed within a single phase of a short-term business cycle. While the *magnitude* of a program may properly vary somewhat in accordance with changing economic conditions, it remains true that our grand-children—politics and economics aside—will need fresh water to drink and good schools in which to be educated. There is a growing constituency for the longer view. The very term "strategic planning" implies a preference for a longer time-frame and a wider "overview" of the country's needs. This is the year in which Americans celebrate the two hundredth anniversary of the Battle of Yorktown. An essential ingredient of that victory was the sound strategic sense of both General Washington and the commander of the French expeditionary force, le Général Comte de Rochambeau, who had kept his forces intact, despite pleas that he detach a battalion here and a regiment there, for the final decisive stroke against Cornwallis.

Just as it makes sense to plan now for an eventual network of high-speed transport tunnels in the United States, so will our children be led to speculate on "the ultimate tunnel system," which could provide high-capacity transport links with our trading partners around the world. It has always been characteristic of macro-engineering enterprises that they require long lead-time, that they entail political as well as technological and financial decisions, and that the early conceptualizations may seem closer to fantasy than to tomorrow's reality. But what a sad place the world would be if there were no "impractical plans" for human achievement! And at the present rate of engineering progress, it is not unrealistic to look forward to the day when automation will reduce the perils and costs of tunneling and when guidance and control systems will be competent to handle supersonic trains in a safe and routine manner.

The July 23, 1981, *Engineering News Record* carried a report that the Bechtel Corporation had been employed to examine the feasibility of laying a natural-gas pipeline in water depths of up to eight thousand feet across the Mediterranean Sea. "If built, the new line between Algeria and Spain would be up to four times deeper than the previous record holder, a pipe from Tunisia to Sicily. . . . the proposed crossing is estimated at $5.67 billion and would stretch about one hundred fifty-five miles." Rounding off these figures, one arrives at a per-mile cost of about thirty-three million dollars. Curious as to the multiplier that would have to be applied if one speculated about a tube or

tunnel for rail-type transport at even greater water depths—
across the North Atlantic—I asked J. Vincent Harrington, one
of America's most experienced authorities on submarine construction, how he would view such an enterprise.

Harrington estimated the average cost per nautical mile
(6,080 feet) at approximately $200 million, exclusive of support
services and work from the surface. "Each depth region," Harrington explained, "has an optimum configuration of structure
where safety is maximized and cost is minimized; therefore,
structural design along the length of the tunnel will vary to best
satisfy the depth considerations of a given location." To reduce
costs, some combination of tunnel and immersed tube may be
advisable. And because of the much shorter distances involved in
the northern routes, they will be likely to be preferred: After all,
the laying of the North Atlantic cable more than a century ago by
Brunel's macrosteamship, the S.S. *Great Eastern,* followed a
northerly route—between County Kerry in Ireland and Cape
Ray, Newfoundland.

A North Atlantic tube (or tunnel, or tube-tunnel) will doubtless be an assignment in ocean engineering classes of the next
century. The advantages of such a system are already discernible. First, the dramatic reduction in trans-Atlantic shipping
would significantly reduce ocean pollution. Second, the virtual
elimination of long-distance air flights between Europe and
North America would reduce toxic emissions in the atmosphere
and the stratosphere and would abate noise pollution near airports in the vicinity of established communities. Third, there
would be economies of raw material resources because it would
no longer be necessary to replace so many ships and airplanes
every twenty or thirty years. Fourth, as is the case with all fixed
links, a North Atlantic tube or tunnel would be less vulnerable
than ships or aircraft to inflationary pressures and could thus
offer transport at steadier prices.

Students would quickly realize that the pipeline or tube section of the work must involve reinforcement to withstand the full
external pressure of the water: Submerged oil and gas pipelines
have the advantage, which a rail tube does not, of providing an
internal pressure force to help counteract the external force of
the water. The best guidance may indeed come from the already

considerable experience garnered from the configuration of the cylindrical pressure hulls of submarines. The submarine *Aluminaut,* for instance, built for the Woods Hole Oceanographic Institution, has demonstrated the feasibility of structures that can be inhabited by human beings at very great depths.

An interesting obstacle to an eventual North Atlantic Tunnel will be successful and safe penetration of the volatile area of the Mid-Atlantic Ridge. I once discussed this hazard with Dr. Herman Sheets, a very senior submarine designer; according to my best recollection, he felt that there are enough alternative routes so that a solution can be found. But it seems to me that the first ultra-long tunnels will be built *across* continents, when satisfactory automated tunneling machines are built and tested; only as a subsequent step will tunnels be attempted *between* continental land masses (unless the narrow Bering Strait is singled out for a joint USA-USSR megaproject).

Two decades ago, a leading Canadian consulting firm, Acres Ltd., published a dramatic proposal for a "Mid-Canada Development Corridor."* The concept was based on the perceived "anomaly" of a "highly developed two-hundred-mile southern band" as contrasted with "vast areas of potentially rich northern resources and undeveloped space." Calling attention to the fact that mid-Canada's corridor could be very productive agriculturally and that the climate is quite suitable for settlement, a key element in the Acres scheme was the provision of both rail and highway service on an east-west basis to the north of the present transcontinental transport arteries. Although the project has not become a focal point for either popular enthusiasm or official planning, it is much too soon, in macro-engineering terms, to pronounce it "dead." Human settlement has tended to grow into new areas as soon as viable transportation has been arranged; the availability of very rapid ground transportation—whether on or beneath the surface of the land—will surely have repercussions in Canada. If the Canadians are reluctant to industrialize and settle their wilderness areas, this is a state of mind with which many of us must sympathize; meanwhile, there are bound to be schemes for linking the populous eastern cities such as

---

*Acres Research & Planning, Ltd., Toronto, Ontario, 1967 (3rd edition).

Montreal and Toronto with major centers in the United States and Mexico in an effort to close the "transportation gap," so noticeable between Europe, with its rapid, integrated rail service, and North America, where not even the indispensable preliminary meetings and studies have taken place.

Canada has first-class research facilities of its own, not least the railway research center established by the Hon. Gerald Stoner during his long and constructive tenure as permanent head (deputy minister) of Canada's Ministry of Transport. A gallant officer in the 1st Canadian Hussars, Stoner served in the Canadian Embassy in Paris at a time when I found myself apprenticing on the staff of the late, beloved Horace G. Reed, counselor of the United States Embassy in the French capital. Now serving as head of the Restrictive Trade Practices Commission in Ottawa, Gerald Stoner was for many years—perhaps ten—the secretary of the Canadian Cabinet, and as such the only nonpolitician to have access to the highest level of policy discussion and design in Canada. He has been a member of the Royal Commission on Administrative Management, which has published some of the most *readable* government reports ever written in the English language. It is experienced Canadians of his caliber to whom Americans should turn, as we balance former preoccupations with Europe and the Far East by an overdue return to the problems and prospects of our own not uninteresting continent.

The Russians have long had an interest in large-scale engineering, particularly because they have not been blessed with as much easily tilled land as other large countries such as the United States or Canada. Every day, the Ob and Yenisei rivers discharge hundreds of *billions* of gallons of fresh water into the Arctic Ocean. Reversing such north-flowing rivers could create a lake almost the size of Italy. A canal has been projected to link the two rivers, with the damsite on the Ob. A consequence could be that 12.5 percent of the waters now flowing into the Arctic would be freed for irrigating the central Soviet steppes. However, according to one scientist on the staff of the United States Geological Survey, such projects could shift so much weight toward the equator that the planet would begin to wobble.

Another much-talked-about Russian idea is to dam the Bering Strait between Alaska and Siberia. Here, it is thought, there could be traumatic climatic consequences: Whether a melting of the polar ice cap results or not, there would be many international problems and recriminations. Although these two examples may not be typical, they do underline the condition in which the world increasingly finds itself: Macro-engineering within one country or between two countries may have planetary impacts and implications. At some point, the United Nations may be deputized to establish a data bank to keep up-to-date on plans and developments, with a view to exercising foresight by pointing out hazards before they reach the stage of needlessly creating international tension. As a sequel to the highly useful Stockholm Conference on the Global Environment, the United Nations could consider a Conference on Macro-Engineering and the Global Future: Although certain projects should be discarded and others will need more study, it is not impossible that even ideological opponents will agree upon a basic list of large-scale engineering schemes that could vastly benefit the world standard of living. An exchange of views on this matter would not interfere with "business as usual" or with the political or ideological views of participants. Understandably, the two "superpowers" will wish to be assured that a conference on large-scale engineering will not degenerate into an exercise in chauvinistic debate. But if the entire world applauded a meeting on environmental problems, there seems every reason to hope that, correctly managed, a conference on "Macro-Engineering for the Benefit of Mankind" (to paraphrase a symposium held in 1970 by the United States National Academy of Engineering, and entitled simply "Engineering for the Benefit of Mankind") will meet with equally unanimous approval.

For the United States, such a conference could go far toward correcting the impression of inadequacy that flowed from our indignant reaction to the Soviet gas pipeline to Western Europe at a time when we had not done our homework in providing an alternative source of supply. "The bar of world opinion" is more than an abstract expression: World public opinion *does* count. If it did not, why do we expend so much effort in international broadcasts, missions, aid programs, and informational broadsides? I am assuming that "next time round" we will not be caught napping, that the physical needs of our trading partners and allies will have been assessed by expert and experienced advisers, and that a "forward" policy will have placed a number of projects on the table for international consideration.

One program already studied by the United States not only does not jeopardize our national security posture; it can be viewed as one of a group of initiatives that, as the wealthiest nation on earth, we have undertaken as surrogate for humankind. I refer to Project Cyclops, carried out under the very competent and professional leadership of Bernard M. Oliver of Hewlett Packard. The Cyclops study was prepared as a joint venture of Stanford University and the NASA/Ames Research Center. Released in 1973, the engineering systems-design study on the search for intelligent life in outer space was conceived by Dr. Hans Mark, then director of Ames Research Center, and Dr. John Billingham, chief of its Biotechnology Division. Quoting Martin Rees's aphorism that "Absence of evidence is not evidence of absence," the study guides the reader through recent developments in interdisciplinary science to the emergence of exobiology, in essence "a synthesis of discoveries in astronomy, atmospheric physics, geophysics, geochemistry, chemical evolution and biochemistry."

The report states the underlying philosophy of the quest for intelligent extraterrestrial life:

> Looking far ahead, suppose we are successful in controlling our fecundity, in recycling our wastes, and in developing new energy sources. Will we then accept forever the ceiling on our growth imposed by the finite size of Earth? Will we be content to know forever only one advanced life form—ourselves? Or will such stasis sap us of our lust? In other words, after ecology, what?

The distinguished panel that produced this report informs the public that "establishing contact with intelligent life on another world is a major undertaking involving expenditures comparable to those of the Apollo program." It does not seem to me very likely that the American public or Congress will wish to undertake such an expense unilaterally; perhaps this is an instance where a very large program can be offered as an exercise in international cooperation. It should not be beyond the capabilities of our scientists to tailor such cooperation in a manner consistent with national security interests. While there is a strong case for the existence of advanced civilizations somewhere "out there," they may really be quite "far out"; the program to find them could last for years, perhaps for centuries. I wonder whether, sooner rather than later, the United Nations itself should not be given a coordinating role.

In contradistinction to Project Cyclops, a wholly *earthbound* scheme has aroused international interest on an intermittent basis, but for the moment the "champions" have been somewhat silent. A decade ago, the idea of transporting icebergs from Antarctica won headlines in the world press when a Saudi prince attended a seminar on the subject in the American Midwest. A well-conducted "Iceberg Transport Seminar" was held February 1–3, 1974, at the Institute on Man and Science in Rensselaerville, New York. After looking at the practicalities involved: water depths at delivery points, markets able to pay for the water, legal complications, etc., the idea seems to have died a quiet death. But it could be an excellent seminar topic for graduate students and, if the United Nations had its own budget with which to fund tests of novel engineering ideas, it could be worthwhile to capture, tow, and deliver an iceberg, somewhere on earth, to see if this might not be at least a partial answer to the irrigation of coastal deserts. Uncaught, the icebergs simply melt away. That there *could* be environmental damage by cooling seawater in fishing areas is more than possible; but it has been suggested that the use of icy water for cooling nuclear reactors might actually *reduce* ecological impacts by lowering the temperature of the water released into streams and harbors after the cooling process.

John L. Gray, Esq., the highly experienced former general counsel of the Battelle Memorial Institute, was induced to visit the Los Angeles Department of Water Supply about a decade ago, to discuss iceberg transportation to this large and thirsty city. My own best recollection of the episode is that the city fathers found it difficult to make an offer, partly because there is (quite understandably) a legal requirement that the city have in prospect an assured water supply for a certain number of years in the future. To contract for *additional* water now might seem unnecessary; and to contract for it in the far future would be complex, especially in view of the nonexistence of a supplier, an agreed method of transport, or any trustworthy assurances that a supply contract could be fulfilled!

Very different in spirit, intent, and organization was the World Coal Study organized in 1978 by the late Carroll L. Wilson, Mitsui Professor Emeritus in Problems of Contemporary Technology at the Massachusetts Institute of Technology. Industrial and government leaders and experts from more than fifteen countries gathered at Aspen to outline a year-and-a-half program of "hardnosed" studies. It seems clear that this effort justified the high expectations of the late Professor Harold D. Lasswell of Yale University when he coined the term "the policy sciences." Carroll Wilson's group took a realistic look at the detailed problems posed by a major shift from oil to coal on a worldwide basis; there is little doubt in my mind that the meetings and reports of "WOCO" (the World Coal Study) have had a tangible effect on governmental and industrial policy on all continents.

Conferences have been much derided, and I suppose that I have attended my share of meetings where the results appeared trivial at best. The most scathing attack on this form of academic pursuit came out in a novel by Arthur Koestler, *The Call Girls,* published by Random House in 1973. The title refers to professors who will run off to almost any conference, anywhere, on any subject, in return for travel expenses and a small fee. But the conference is, even if overworked, our best artifact in reshaping the world scene. Translated literally from its Latin roots, the word means "make together"; the conference that is merely a disguised vacation, a form of escapism for weary routineers, should not be allowed to interfere with humankind's talent for new associations with a constructive end in view. Without the redirection that can come from a focused meeting, the world would continue without those changes of direction that are occasionally necessary both to health and to survival.

One of the "showcases" for macro-engineering is the Churchill Falls project in Labrador. It was developed in a series of meetings, most notably the promotional meeting in which

"Joey" Smallwood, the underestimated premier of Newfoundland, interested N. M. Rothschild & Sons, the London merchant bankers, in backing the project. In the early 1970's, over one-half *billion* dollars of bonds were sold, in a single issue, on Wall Street. To tame the Churchill River, engineers built a huge reservoir almost half the size of Lake Ontario and containing twelve hundred billion cubic feet of water. When completed, it was by far the largest hydroelectric development at a single site in the Western Hemisphere. Leadership was provided by a series of remarkable men, including William Mulholland (now president of the Bank of Montreal), who described some of the management episodes quite vividly before the 1981 Macro-Engineering Seminar held at M.I.T.[3] The Province of Newfoundland was not required to invest a single penny in this immense project, which brings it an automatic revenue of fifteen million dollars per year, *grosso modo*, through royalty payments, taxes passed on by Ottawa, shares in the company, provincial taxes, etc. Quebec has had the benefit of "low-cost, inflation-proof power"—and of providing 70 percent of the workforce (over six thousand at its 1970 peak).

That Joey Smallwood had been a "disc jockey" before running for office should not blind us to his qualities of prescience, dogged determination, and negotiating ability. I had one occasion to visit him at his sprawling ranch house on a windswept, rather barren acreage, when with two or three friends I had flown to Newfoundland to look into the prospects of Mortier Bay, one of the remaining deepwater harbors near the Great Circle shipping route. I was told that if a German submarine had interrupted "the Atlantic Conference" between Churchill and Roosevelt, both the Royal Navy and the U.S. North Atlantic Fleet would have retired to Mortier Bay, which had ample anchorages for both fleets! The steep slopes of the bay constitute a challenge to developers; but perhaps in the future there will be a surge of interest in transshipment ports correctly located.

Canadians are nervous about the size of American investment in their country. As the present prime minister has put it, Canada's situation is a bit "like that of a flea sleeping with an elephant." In other words, even if the elephant only sneezes, it can be very disturbing. But Canada is itself growing into elephantine proportions, and the partnership between Canada and the United States is an enduring one based on history, common interest, and a common set of institutions and beliefs. Just as Americans have played a role in Canadian development—Karl Landegger, an Austrian-born Connecticut Yankee brought Saskatchewan a needed and appreciated pulp-and-paper mill—so Canadians have played vital roles in American development: We have already noted the role of the Chaffey brothers in the settlement (and naming!) of the Imperial Valley; and in our own time, the economist John Kenneth Galbraith has enriched American economic thought while bringing a sense of wit to politics and diplomacy.

Having, through the force of circumstances, found myself several times in the position of being "out front" and therefore in a more or less "promotional" role, I have sometimes been asked the question "How do you do it?" At this moment in our national affairs, when new and untried groupings *must* be formed, I think it important to demystify the process and to strip it of obfuscatory academic verbiage. Whether it is to start a new school or to build a new bridge or to form a group to develop a new space transport system, the sine qua non is to get people together—and hopefully to assemble a team that will have both the power and the knowledge to accomplish the end in view. In my experience, there are three or four "methodologies" to choose from; I doubt if they will vary very much with the passage of time. The first and often the most productive route is lunch; where a less formal approach seems better, *interlocuteurs valables* may be invited for tea or a drink; a third possibility, but only in certain carefully considered cases, is dinner; finally, and not to be neglected where people have busy and intransigent schedules, is breakfast. Joseph Gies, in his excellent little book *Adventure Underground*, devotes a chapter to "Lunch at Luchow's," where he accurately describes the genesis of the Channel Tunnel Study Group. (In this case, as the project progressed, the lunches tended to move uptown, from the private dining rooms of Wall Street investment banks, ultimately to the Harvard Club and other "Establishment" emporia midtown.)

Despite the attractiveness, in the long perspective of history, of undersea tunnels for long-distance rapid transit of goods and passengers, bulk commodities will be shipped, for generations to come, in large ocean-going vessels. As the world economy grows—with population increases and technology improvements interacting—there will be increasing demand for adequate port facilities and for a shortening of maritime routes. I think we may confidently predict, therefore, a steady market for those "watering places" and gourmet havens where people tend to gather to discuss such matters. The conversation may turn, often enough, to "old chestnuts" rather than entirely novel schemes, but there can always be "new wrinkles" to the "old chestnuts."

One scheme, proposed a century ago by no less a geographer than the Vicomte Ferdinand de Lesseps, keeps bobbing up: the Kra Canal. The United Kingdom, when it set the terms of peace with Siam in 1945, insisted upon a clause that "no canal linking the Indian Ocean and the Gulf of Siam shall be cut across Siamese territory without the prior concurrence of the Government of the United Kingdom." Apparently Ernest Bevin, then foreign secretary, was apprehensive that the Thais would—in the words of an *Economist* article dated December 9, 1978, "collude with the French to do in Singapore." The British abandoned their veto power in 1960, but political rather than technical or even financial obstacles have been persistent and paramount. First of all, there has been unending violence in Southeast Asia; until there is a genuine peace in the region, it will be difficult to obtain political agreement authorizing a project of vast dimensions across the thinnest part of Thailand.

The cost estimates have ranged from five billion dollars to upwards of ten billion dollars; my brother Alfred was very courteously received, about two decades ago, by the plan's champion, Mr. K. Y. Chow, a former professor at Peking University who made a fortune in oil and has since become a noted philanthropist and geostatesman. Mr. Chow points out that the canal would save more than six hundred miles of steaming time from the Gulf to Japan. Singapore, however, is not opposing the plan: It is—again according to the *Economist*—"now intent on becoming a manufacturing, financial and tourist centre on tropical isle, rather than a highway station for polluting supertankers." Premier Lee Kuan Yew's "sensible message to Mr. Chow has apparently been 'you form your consortium and we can buy shares in it.'"

But the project has not been authorized: A canal would divide Thailand's minority Muslim population from the Buddhist majority (although one must assume that bridges could overcome this difficulty); more pertinently, the canal would run through an area where Communist insurgents from Malaysia have had the habit of camping—but, as the *Economist* observes, "that seems an opportunity to kill several birds with one bulldozer." Perhaps the real fly in the ointment has been the fear of invasion from Vietnam. If peace broke out definitively, a prosperous Southeast Asia might very well pump for the Kra Canal—despite the opposition of Indonesia, which would expect to suffer from the improved competitivity of oil from the Gulf delivered to Japan.

We may in fact be on the verge of a new worldwide surge of investment in canals. If this seems disappointingly "low tech," we must nonetheless concede that underlying cost factors have not changed so much in two thousand years: Bulk commodities still move most economically in large ships and barges. Thanks to the extensive improvements designed by the United States Army Corps of Engineers, the Mississippi and other large American rivers have been "canalized." Despite stormy congressional opposition, the highly controversial Tennessee-Tombigbee Canal is being extended. China, as we have noted, is expanding the Grand Canal and connecting waterways. The Common Market is trying to complete the half-built Rhine-Danube connection that so baffled Charlemagne and whose current budget difficulties have created a new wave of sympathy for the obstacles facing the first Holy Roman Emperor. (He did actually begin work on a canal between the Altmühl and the Rednitz, hoping thereby to connect the Danube and the Rhine.) A new Panama Canal has become the subject of official consultations involving the United States, Japan, and Panama.

Considerable as the above-listed undertakings may be, they are dwarfed by several new proposals for building macrocanals. We have already mentioned Nigel Chattey's bold scheme to build a new, modern Erie Canal, largely to provide economical transport of coal from the Great Lakes to a new deepwater port to be built offshore New York. In another chapter, we shall have occasion to describe T. W. Kierans's concept of a canal to bring water from the region of Hudson Bay to the Great Lakes. When Chaban-Delmas, the mayor of Bordeaux who was an accomplished rugby player, served as prime minister of France, there was speculation that he might revive the scheme, much mooted at the time of Napoleon III, to widen and deepen the canal built during the reign of Louis XIV that still connects the Atlantic Ocean with the Mediterranean Sea. In India, Captain Dastur's proposal of a Garland Canal, to link the Ganges with the other great rivers of the subcontinent, has yet to be taken seriously; but such ideas, unlike rolling stones, do gather moss: A megacanal system may not be in the cards for India, but the mere discussion of it may catalyze other projects, such as the canal from Nepal to Calcutta.

The Himalayan Rivers Development Plan, calling for the establishment of storage basins on the Ganges and the Brahmaputra "and its principal Indian and Nepalese tributaries," and providing also for a canal linking the two rivers, results at least in part from the wider interest among experienced professional engineers in the capabilities of large canal schemes with a variety of mutually reinforcing objectives.

It would be shortsighted to be so mesmerized by "advanced technology" that we neglect the basic industry and infrastructure developments that are the permanent underpinnings of prosperity and national achievement. Nor is it altogether correct to relegate such areas of concern to the domain of "low tech." There are, in fact, some fascinating "new wrinkles." In canal building, for instance, Dr. Ernest Frankel, now with the World Bank (more accurately, the "International Bank for Reconstruction and Development"), has resurrected a canal-building technology that seems to have originated with the Venetians in the late Middle Ages: Instead of excavating canals—very difficult in any case in the soggy Venetian soil—walls were prefabricated in sections and then placed in shipyards so that partially constructed or even completed vessels could be moved around conveniently within the shipyard by means of these movable, temporary canals. In Jubail, prefabricated wall sections were similarly utilized to "wall in" new canalizations. For larger applications, the walls might consist of linked boxes with lids that can be opened so that whatever suitable material is at hand—slag, sand, rock, even water—can be poured in to stabilize the boxes, which might have a Teflon seal underneath to minimize leakage.

In canal building as in tunneling, the major cost is excavation. The idea of building a canal on the surface and walling it in could, especially in cases where a very wide ditch is wanted, result in appreciable savings in money and time. This is, as in so many macro-engineering matters, a very old debate. Confucian and Taoist theorists disputed for centuries the values of excavation versus the advantages of dikes in canal building. Joseph Needham, in Volume 3 of his monumental series *Science and Civilisation in China* refers to this ongoing argument, and incidentally informs us that extensive encyclopedias on waterway construction were published as early as the eighth century A.D.

For crossing narrow strips of land, technology is not limited to the obvious penchant for canalization: Ships can be moved by other means. When the ancient Greeks wished to move their ships across the Isthmus of Corinth, they cut a road suitable for enormous ox-drawn wagons; the ships were then loaded on the wagons and drawn overland on wheels! Gustav Schlumberger, the nineteenth-century Byzantinist, has written a vivid description of a siege of Constantinople, where the invading fleet, in 1453, won the upper hand by suddenly switching itself *overland* to another body of water from which they could deliver the coup de grâce. Ship railways have been used to transfer barges across short distances from one canal to another in the Netherlands. In 1881, *Scientific American* published a lavishly illustrated cover story describing a scheme for a ship railway across Mexico's Isthmus of Tehuantepec. The concept involved placing steamships in a huge cradle mounted on several parallel railway wagons; a team of locomotives on parallel tracks provided the motive power.

Recent technology has suggested several variants. The development of large car-carrying hovercraft for the cross-channel service between England and France led to the idea of supporting a ship-cradle on an air cushion; the whole apparatus could then be towed overland by a macrotractor, or several of them. Admiral R. K. James (U.S. Navy, retired) has reminded us that "water cushions" work as well as air cushions, and that large ships have in fact been transported within shipyards by means of a water cushion constantly replenished when water leaks out underneath the "skirts" of the supporting cradle. Dr. Frankel has put forward the idea of a "movable lock," in effect a huge bathtub in which ships can ride in their accustomed element while being towed across an isthmus. The Cape Canaveral precedent of an ultra-heavy-duty wheeled vehicle for transporting rockets to the launching pad suggests that even a wheel-supported system could do the job: The real variable to watch out for is the cost and availability of power!

In our own "backyard," there may be an opportunity to test ship transport systems if Canadian entrepreneurs or partners should be interested: The eleven-mile-wide Chignecto Isthmus separates the Bay of Fundy from the Northumberland Strait—what an ideal site for a novel "Isthmian Transport Study Group" to test alternative methods! With the maritime wisdom of Nova Scotians, such a group—or institute—could render a distinctive service to the world community.

I sometimes think that my countrymen, who retain a passion for organization and accomplishment despite the veneer of worldliness resulting in part from what George N. Kates might have called "the years that were fat,"[4] have a tendency to formalize organizations too early. Whether the object is to build a novel ship transport system or a mile-high tower, it is best, I think, to let groups grow by organic accretion, and only to formalize them when everyone is clear as to purposes and membership. This is the great strength of the idea of a "study group," a "preorganization" format called, under the flexible French commercial code, *une association en participation*. As I remember it, the French *groupement d'études* has few formal requirements: There must be regular meetings and therefore a secretary to call them and to record minutes, and a person delegated to spend the group's money within prescribed limitations. That's about it. Under Anglo-Saxon legal traditions, a similar result can be reached through the simple device of a letter agreement. The nice thing about the terminology of a "study group" is that it's formal enough so that individuals and institutions from all sectors can usually join; there is no feeling of engaging one's reputation or pocketbook in an excessive commitment; and the "study group" can always progressively formalize itself, dissolve, or fade away without embarrassment.

For many accomplishments in this modern world, I would recommend this "minimal" format to begin with. In the first place, without a commitment to meet again, "the best-laid schemes o' mice and men/Gang aft a-gley," as the poet reminds us. Even if two enthusiasts meet for tea, they should, if they are serious about continuing their structured discussion, appoint one of them as a sort of "secretary," both to write up the main points adumbrated, and to be responsible for making sure that a second meeting is held. Once a project is seriously intended, it is likely that funds will be required; and someone should be delegated to have the right to spend those funds, under agreed limitations as to amount.

A brief agreement—I think it was just about two or three pages—constituted the Channel Tunnel Study Group, more than twenty-five years ago. Before going to Panama in 1965 with a group that wished to explore the possibility of private finance for a second Panama Canal, the participants formed an Isthmian Canal Study Group. I suppose I have been connected with a half-dozen or more such groups, some of which have ripened into corporations and some of which have lingered on or faded away. I retain my preference for this type of "entry point" into large affairs, because of its flexibility and general acceptability. Once there is a substantial income or outgo, the lawyers and accountants can be brought in to formalize relationships—and to put the group in a posture to receive funds from third parties. In developing study groups, we have not been short of legal advice: Some very distinguished lawyers on several continents have participated in the early work of such groups. Perhaps it is the "laymen," the "nonlawyers," for whom the mysteries of incorporation hold the greatest appeal and temptation.

Transportation, viewed generically, can make a varied contribution to a better quality of life. In suburban America, for instance, there is a need for the revival of the footpath or sidewalk and for other facilities for self-propelled locomotion. It is within our means to build skateways (for ice skates in winter, roller skates and skateboards in summer), cross-country ski routes that can double in summer as bridle paths, and bicycle and tricycle paths modeled on the excellent facilities publicly provided in the Low Countries and on the Japanese resort island of Kyushu, near Myazaki and other towns.

In terms of building a habitat conducive to health and pleasure, few societies can compete with the practice of North Germany's Hansa cities, where it has been traditional for nearly a century to construct alongside suburban streets three lanes, each separated from the next by a strip of grass interspersed with attractively planted trees and bushes: a sidewalk for pedestrians, a bicycle path, and a bridle path. Happily, in the United States there are stirrings of widespread support for extensions of the Appalachian Trail, for other extensive foot-trails, and for interstate bridle paths and bikeways.

Because of the serious risk of accidents due to commingling of bicycle and automotive traffic, some enterprising M.I.T. students, led by Vincent Darago, established a very popular nationwide "Urban Bikeway Design Competition," in which students from many institutions participated, in 1973 and 1974. The promoters announced that "transportation is responsible for 25 percent of the nation's total energy budget, largely as a result of automobile usage . . . An empirical study in Philadelphia reveals that modest provision for bicycle lanes and bike parking would result in a 10 percent conversion rate of auto commuters to bicycles . . . A 10 percent conversion rate would mean a 0.6 percent savings of the present annual rate of energy consumption in this country, or *roughly 30 percent of the current energy crisis*" (italics mine). This estimate was substantiated in Richard A. Rice's landmark article "System Energy and Future Transportation," in the January 1972 *Technology Review.*

On March 19, 1973, the House of Representatives of the Congress of the United States published a statement submitted by John Cummins of the *Harvard Journal on Legislation,* published at the Harvard Law School. The statement, in the form of a letter addressed to the chairman of the Committee on Public Works, proposed a National Bikeway Act, drafted by Cummins and his fellow students at the Legislative Research Bureau of

Harvard University. The Cummins initiative must be viewed as one in a series of developments that led to a turnabout in the attitude of the American Association of State Highway and Transportation Officials (AASHTO), previously regarded by some bikeway advocates as "a bastion for automobile and highway interests." But in June 1981, *Pro Bike News,* published monthly in Washington, D.C., by the Bicycle Federation, reported favorably on the efforts of AASHTO's executive director, Frank François, to win support from the states for a nationwide bikeroute project.

Significantly, bicycle ownership in "high tech" Japan has grown in the past decade from twenty-nine million to more than fifty million: When half the population rides a bicycle, it would seem that we need not accept the false dichotomy that "advanced technology" must mean the demise of "low tech" industries such as bicycle manufacture! The basic point is to strive for excellence in all domains—including health. We could be on the verge of a new and hopeful coalition to lobby for such outdoor improvements as a national bikeway system: Health enthusiasts can join with environmentalists; military advocates of a "fitness" campaign can break bread with "low tech" partisans; and the construction industry can join the bicycle industry in supporting a concerted scheme for a series of interstate bikeways based on cooperative agreements that encompass federal and state agencies, private property owners, and volunteer organizations of all kinds. If this does not sound like macro-engineering, it is because we are looking at the trees, not at the forest: A transcontinental bikeway system is true macro-engineering of the very best kind. Even the pyramids were built block by block!

The energy crisis has had the useful consequence of instructing us on the many alternatives available when one source of supply is cut off or reduced. Automobile traffic has *not* become obsolete, and current studies on "the future of the automobile," carried out under the aegis of M.I.T.'s Professor Alan Altschuler, and a group of distinguished colleagues from other institutions, reassure us that the automobile, in one form or another, is "here to stay." If that is so, I think we ought to take a hard look at accident statistics. An entire nation was indignant because of the loss of life incurred by the war in Vietnam. But highway deaths have exceeded the total of deaths caused in America's wars, yet there is no mass indignation; this is why many mature people sympathize with the late Alan Chadwick's stern view that driving is "immoral." But driving could be virtually "fail-safe," if we were willing to make investments in safety that would amount to only a small fraction of national expenditures in Vietnam.

When I first arrived at M.I.T. in 1970, I was intrigued by Professor David G. Wilson's desk-top working model of a "palletized transport system" for cars and trucks: the idea was to set aside one lane (in each direction) on heavily traveled throughways and tollroads, for an automated guideway; once on its pallet, a car would be propelled to its chosen exit and gently eased off the system; meanwhile, the driver would have had a complete rest, and could resume control of his car for the drive on secondary roads to his destination. Depending on design, location, and the cost of fuel, such a system might or might not result in substantial overall fuel economies; but it would *undoubtedly* save many lives: Once our population becomes more technologically literate, I think there will be a strong constituency demanding that such a system be advanced at least to the prototype stage, so that it may be given a market test on a highway where traffic accidents have been endemic. Driving on Hokkaido, I was impressed by the speed limit on principal roads of 25 mph! Lacking such discipline and restraint, our best bet is to retain high speed, but on a guideway where safety has been assured by the best mechanical engineering of which the country is capable.

These pages have referred from time to time to the use of troops for what we now consider "civilian" work. The twelve thousand men of the 3rd Augusta Legion left a legacy of public accomplishment scarcely matched by any other organization, military or civilian. At some point, when political leaders are ready for massive international public works, would it not be wise to consider the option of nominating army units—or naval or air force units—to join in strategically chosen large-scale works? At the moment, it is not thinkable, in terms of politics or economics, that armed forces be disbanded or even significantly reduced. But in a proper case, the engineering troops, with auxiliaries from other arms, might perfectly well engage in worth-while work, especially in troubled areas where there has been internecine strife—or to repel the encroachment of a desert. "Strategic planning" has become a catchword of business and government "management theory"; but where is the "strategic plan" for rolling back the Sahara? Would not even the discussion of such a plan tend to reduce tensions in the area? Are modern countries incapable of water engineering on the scale of the antique Romans? Is our "management theory" bankrupt when it comes to the major questions facing what Jay Forrester has called the "closely coupled" international community? Where do we begin? And how?

I think the Mitsubishi Research Institute is to be congratulated upon its "first cut" at the problem of drawing up a list of twelve projects "which exemplify the massive infrastructural approach." Perhaps a near-term possibility would be a series of well-structured conferences on a foreshortened list of such enterprises, with outstanding international authorities in attendance. There is ample historical precedent: The Congrès International d'Etudes du Canal Interocéanique, which opened on Thursday afternoon, May 15, 1879, proved to be a decisive event in the realization of the Panama Canal. Despite the ubiquity of telecommunications, the personal and more intimate atmosphere of a conference would, I submit, have more of a human impact than even the most expertly contrived "teleconference," which might however be a useful subsidiary technique. Transport and telecommunications are, after all, not "substitute goods": They are, correctly understood, mutually reinforcing.

I suggest that the first necessity is the designation of a group charged with listing problems amenable to major technological solutions; once the problem areas are agreed on, alternative strategic initiatives can be proposed, discussed, and redesigned. The end result would be a listing of major projects and programs believed to be: a) in the national interest, b) feasible within stated time-frames, and c) practical from a fiscal and financial viewpoint. After prioritizing the list—a task that must be redone periodically in the light of changed conditions—study groups can be formed to establish realistic parameters. But such groups need not be an exclusive responsibility of the White House. In a free, pluralist society such as ours, appropriate groups can be formed on an *ad hoc* basis. For instance, although it would be very desirable to have White House support for a study group on a national bikeway system, from the viewpoint of the inhabitants of the White House it would be preferable if responsible, self-financing groups would pre-study the question and then seek "high level" backing once there is something more definite to "back"! It is always important to have a sincere conviction that something "ought" to be done; but to come to the seats of power and influence with "demands" for action, rather than with mature projects that can be evaluated and ranked, may in the end be a waste of everyone's time. And in preparing blueprints for intersectoral approval, it is essential to seek the best advice in *all* relevant fields: engineering, law, accounting, investment banking, environmental medicine, public relations, and any other professions appropriate to the particular question at issue.

I have included "public relations" in the list; some eyebrows may be raised, but it is a sober fact that people who are good at their profession can offer useful advice to amateurs, even in a field previously regarded as nebulous and almost as a subset of advertising or journalism. In today's society, major projects *do* involve public opinion, and therefore relations with the media. In my own experience, public relations people have proven every whit as professional as lawyers, doctors, and management experts. Whether Edward L. Bernays founded the profession during World War I when press support was systematically sought in the United States on behalf of the British war effort, I cannot say with certainty; surely a history of the profession would have to cover its seminal years. But I can attest that my friends in this field have demonstrated a high type of professionalism; and their ethical standards compare favorably with those of other professions. That Sydney A. Morrell was decorated with the C.B.E. by Queen Elizabeth II is evidence that the "métier" may be said to have "arrived," at least in the United Kingdom. Viewed more broadly, the whole career of leaders such as Winston Churchill and John Buchan shows the high importance attached to skills of writing and public speaking in an age that depends heavily on telecommunications and the press for the dynamic interaction of politicians and the public. The

Hon. William Buchan's excellent (recent) biography of his father makes this point crystal-clear. That the younger Buchan, as a public relations professional, was willing to espouse the cause of the channel tunnel long before it became popular showed, I trust, not only courage but discernment.

If we are to bring about the kind of interprofessional teamwork that is now called for by most of the organs of public opinion, we shall still need a cadre of leaders who are not only advocates but exemplars of interdisciplinary training. But before entering on a discussion of the basic elements of a "new model" for engineer-management, it will be well to evaluate some basic terms. "Cooperation" has been a shocking term to economists fixated on the virtues of competition as the sole legitimate engine of business activity. What appears to be especially distasteful to some is the fact that cooperation is not a complex intellectual artifact, an exercise in Newtonian reductionism, or a Spencerian analogy. The absence of complexity, in some university circles, automatically deprives an idea of its authority, or so it sometimes seems. But surely it is time to recall some home truths. Prosperity has always depended on the twin pillars of individual enterprise and an acceptable form of co-operative, or corporate, activity.

The category of "necessity," if it could be invoked, would override even the most entrenched of academic disciplines. In a peacetime era of demiprosperity, it takes an added effort of will and imagination to perceive what is necessary to get from A to B: in this sense, it was less difficult for Lord Mountbatten to "sell" his idea of "combined operations" after a series of dreary setbacks had convinced even the most ardent service traditionalists that the artillery should learn how to cooperate with the infantry and that the air force should at least learn how not to bomb its own side's tank units and naval vessels.

Today's necessity is more elusive, but the lesson is still the same: A dogged insistence on sectoral integrity is leading us toward defeat. We have been too respectful of an outdated economics that, regarding itself as a discrete science, promises miracle cures from some vague mechanism called "the market," which in turn is supposed to respond in predictable and therefore controllable ways to manipulations called "fiscal and monetary policy." But economics remains, as its best practitioners have admitted, a half-science: It treats primarily surface manifestations of processes whose dynamics have not always been adequately embedded in its theory.

Broadly speaking, the top management of American business—*and government*—has been drawn from cadres with no engineering training. While American top management ranks include fewer than one professionally trained engineer out of five, in Japan and France engineering provides the *typical* route to advancement into management. Thus, the severe limitations of conventional economic indoctrination have been exacerbated by a system of management training—whether at schools of business or of public administration—which fosters a cast of mind that "assumes" the existence of science and technology without bothering to inquire into the "messy details."

In this way, our schools of management have brought about a trained incapacity to deal with the major issues on which the future of the American economy depends. This in no way implies that all would be well if the managements of Chrysler, Lockheed, and U.S. Steel were turned over to the summa cum laude graduates of our leading engineering schools. Just as schools of management have been too narrowly concentrated on commerce, accounting, economics, and systems analysis, the engineering institutions have had too restrictive a focus on technology. What is wanted is a creative fusion, *plus* some acculturation not adequately present either in our schools of management *or* our schools of engineering. The fear of a disembodied management science is precisely what led Alfred P. Sloan to establish the school that bears his name in an institution broadly devoted to technology.

The present response to the situation has been a series of agreements that pragmatically inaugurate programs of "technology and management" or, more simply, "technology management." This could be a first step in the right direction; more cynical observers will regard it as a bureaucratic Band-Aid that preserves the independent fiefdoms of both the engineering schools and the schools of management without, in fact, requiring any awkward readjustments in either camp.

The difficulty of the realignment proposed herein is magnified by the presence of powerful national associations that tend to reinforce the self-esteem—and also the expansionist aims—of the disciplines they represent. However, there is a growing feeling that the national interest may require a new kind of management training, based squarely on professional competence in engineering. Dare we hope for a new consensus reflecting a creative collaboration of the American Management Association, the American Society for Engineering Education, and the numerous other professional institutions whose full participation would be both appropriate and desirable?

This is not a hypothetical or remote issue. The demise of Detroit, the decline of the American steel and shipbuilding industries, and the inefficiencies of American public transport are due in part to the incapacity and unrealistic orientation of too many top managers. Furthermore, it is impossible to deal with this subject adequately without bringing into the open an element most of us have been reluctant to admit, let alone confront: In our society, with its lingering aristocratic pretensions, the career of engineering has been regarded as less prestigious than management, law, or medicine. Management has been regarded as a profession apart, with its own arcane rituals and formulas. It is now increasingly realized that the rituals are not altogether appropriate and that many of the formulas and prescriptions have led us fearfully close to "the tragedy of the commons" discussed earlier. Narrow "self-interest," expertly pursued, is not a sufficient ethos for the development of responsible leaders of *teams*. It is becoming a truism to observe that managers—and also, let us be fair, the shareholders who employ them—have paid too much attention to the short-term "bottom line"; this has been true of attitudes in government as well. Now we find that we have neglected both the long-term health of the nation's physical infrastructure and the capacity of the nation's basic industries to survive and compete. Structural reform is now what the legal profession would call "a necessary condition precedent" to the national resurgence to which lip-service is paid on every hand.

Once it is widely perceived that the performance of the economy is inescapably linked to the quality of engineered goods and services, we shall be equipped to deal honestly and forthrightly with other insistent concerns, such as the altogether reasonable requirement for a healthy environment and for a better record in protecting vulnerable groups from the vicissitudes of unemployment and discrimination. Ours is a "technomic" society: We live in a "built environment," and the building of it has been done by the minority of engineers and technologists in our midst. In this sense, the macro-engineer's multidimensional vision can provide a pragmatic basis for dealing with social and environmental issues.

On the social side, the Japanese are slowly teaching us that a more responsible attitude toward the work force actually pays dividends: When employees know that they will not be displaced by automation, they will welcome automatic machinery as a means of reducing drudgery, instead of opposing it as a threat to economic security. On the environmental side, who can doubt the importance of high technical competence in the management and inspection of nuclear-power plants? American society can no longer afford the luxury of confining decision-making on matters "affected with a public interest" to people whose training does not permit them to understand the components of the systems they are supposed to regulate.

Faced with the *immediate* need to provide management services for such projects as the Churchill Falls Hydroelectric Program in Labrador, the Alaska Pipeline, or the construction of cities such as Jubail and Yanbu in Saudi Arabia, American engineering companies have developed an informal corps of engineer-managers who have proved their merit in one large-scale job after another. The result has been the maturing of a pool of senior talent on which future enterprises can draw. But the universities and institutes of technology have been a full generation behind developments "in the field." There is now almost an oversupply of seminars in project management. But the universities and industry have not yet reached a meeting of minds on the subject of training future engineer-managers.

Part of the problem, no doubt, is the difficulty of knowing, when cadets are at West Point, which ones will be the successful generals of the future. A merely academic approach to such a problem is not very useful. No solution is completely "waterproof," but it is worth looking closely at the French approach. It has been a Gallic tradition since before Napoleon to select exceptional young people for the arduous training of the Ecole Polytechnique and its sister academies. The best graduates are appointed to special corps, like the Corps des Mines or the Corps des Ponts et Chaussées or the Inspection des Finances. After specialized training in these prestigious corps, the young people are placed on a "fast track": They are given accelerated promotion and responsibilities, both in government and in the (shrinking!) private sector. I remember learning with astonishment, when the French representation was assembled for the governing board of the Channel Tunnel Study Group, that each of the men delegated had been to a "*Grande Ecole*," and two had been *inspecteurs des finances*! These men were, to everyone's delight, both highly competent and successful professionals; they were also people of broad culture and experience, obviously trained for a "great career."

Although the French system may smack of *élitisme*, we should remember that admission to the leading schools is exclusively through very demanding competitive examinations; the rigidity of the system is due to the circumstance that families tend to "pass on" the attitudes and habits conducive to success in examinations.

In the United States, the rigorous training provided by Rear Admiral Hyman Rickover (USN, ret.) for future commanders of the nuclear fleet is a shining example of the thoroughness and expertise in preparation that should be standard in all high-technology endeavors, whether military or civilian. Macro-engineering education should have equally high standards, so that its graduates will command respect and earn advancement because of their unique combination of professional competence and breadth of comprehension of the complexities of modern life.

When Valéry Giscard d'Estaing was president of the French Republic, he established an entirely new school, the Institut Auguste Comte, on the hallowed ground of the old Ecole Polytechnique, which had been moved to a spacious site in the rural environs of Paris. The purpose of the new institut was to train selected middle managers—those expected to be promoted to the highest positions—in the skills and attitudes appropriate for *les grands programmes d'équipement*—roughly what we call "macro-engineering." The succeeding (socialist) president, François Mitterrand, has replaced this initiative with a "think tank" dedicated to a "quantum leap" in informatics; but the ideal (to some) and anathema (to others) of an élite corps of managers, most of them trained first in engineering, remains a powerful feature of the French scene.

In England, concern for the competitive stature of British industry led to the appointment in July 1977, by the secretary of state for industry, of a Committee of Inquiry into the Engineering Profession. The chairman, Sir Montague Finniston, FRS, was widely respected as the last engineer-manager who had been able to report a profit as head of the British Steel Corporation. In January 1980, the report *Engineering Our Future* was printed and submitted to Parliament.[5] It was based on an exhaustive survey of the education and employment of engineers not only in the United Kingdom, but in the United States, Japan, France, and other countries. Recommendations covered government policy, education at all levels, the role of professional institutions, and the attitudes and procedures of industry.

I had the privilege of meeting "Monty" Finniston in the relaxed ambience of a London club. Fit, erect, and with penetrating, humorous eyes, he answered my inquiry about the "readiness" of British industry by suggesting that I visit the Research and Development Corporation, of which he had been a director, in Newcastle-on-Tyne. This "think tank," I quickly learned, was far ahead of the stream; they had, for instance, developed submarine welding and inspection technologies for the North Sea oil industry, clearly in advance of general practice. And the "Finniston Report," which has recommended sweeping changes in the training, classification, and employment of engineers, is now a part of history—a very useful part, in my view.

The restructuring and improvement of opportunities both for the training of engineers and for the preparation of that special breed of engineer-manager required for large affairs must become central questions for public decision in the United States. It would not be amiss to name a panel of eminent authorities to look into this matter and report to the President and the Congress.

When Fiorello H. La Guardia (the short man at the left, under the large black hat) was elected mayor of New York in the depths of the Depression, he appointed a nonpartisan team to rebuild the infrastructure of the city. Just as Brasilia was placed where it is—by the team led by the late Hollister Kent of Cornell—because of the primordial need of human settlements for water, so established cities must deal with their future water supply as a first order of serious business. The photograph above, taken on January 6, 1936, shows the mayor with his commissioner of water supply (Maurice P. Davidson, center rear, with glasses) and other officials inspecting the recently completed Tunnel #2 Catskill—a vital link because at that time more than two thirds of the city's daily consumption of water (941.4 million gallons) came from the Catskill watershed. (With average New York per capita consumption at 128.9 gallons per day, it is interesting to note that the per capita consumption per day in ancient Rome was 450 gallons.) In a letter to the mayor dated January 23, 1936, the commissioner recommended a start on an immense project to bring water into Manhattan from the Delaware Water Gap. The resulting 80-mile tunnel is still the longest true tunnel on the planet. Meanwhile, enough water empties into the sea from the heavily polluted Hudson River to supply the needs of twelve New Yorks—if only it were sufficiently clean.

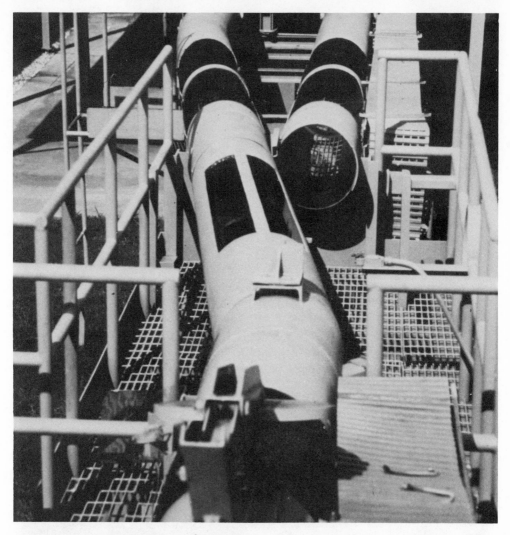

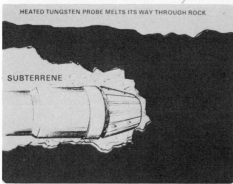

HEATED TUNGSTEN PROBE MELTS ITS WAY THROUGH ROCK

SUBTERRENE

The above view of the "Tubexpress" system shows a prototype originally developed by the TRANSCO companies and recently taken over by the New Jersey shipping entrepreneur William Vandersteel and AM-POWER Corporation. The idea is to ship goods in an ordinary gas pipeline (but without gas in it!) so that every household and office can receive supplies directly from stores and warehouses. David G. Wilson and his colleagues have designed an analogous system. If a dry-solids pipeline can be successfully equipped to carry coal and phosphates, there would be tantalizing economic and environmental benefits because the need for water—an essential component of slurry pipelines—would be eliminated. The diagram at left illustrates a novel tunneling system designed at the Los Alamos Scientific Laboratory: the "Subterrene," which proceeds by melting the rock or other material through which it is desired to bore.

This rather futuristic concept actually demonstrates a technological opportunity that may well be within the grasp of engineers in the next century. Dr. Robert Salter of the Rand Corporation has outstanding credentials as a physical scientist. His concept of an underground planetran system functioning at supersonic speed depends, for practical realization, more on advances in the art of tunneling, so that expenses can be brought down, than on the needed but feasible improvements in the transport system to be installed in the tunnels or tubes designed for transcontinental and intercontinental service. A very preliminary survey by Wilbur Smith & Associates (an old-line traffic-engineering firm) indicates that even with present methods, a coast-to-coast planetran service might earn more than 10 percent of the revenues needed to finance a total system. Considering that the U.S. government subsidized 90 percent of the Interstate Highway System, it could be argued that an eventual planetran service need not be considered "out of this world," especially if population and affluence increase and the costs of tunneling are brought down by "high tech."

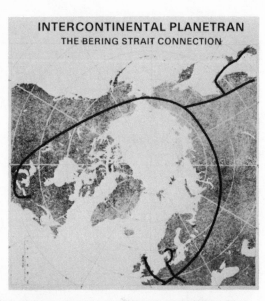

INTERCONTINENTAL PLANETRAN
THE BERING STRAIT CONNECTION

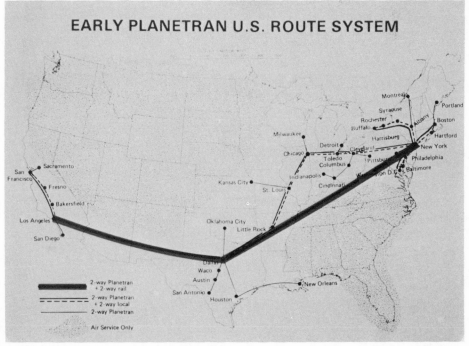

EARLY PLANETRAN U.S. ROUTE SYSTEM

2-way Planetran + 2-way rail
2-way Planetran + 2-way local
2-way Planetran
Air Service Only

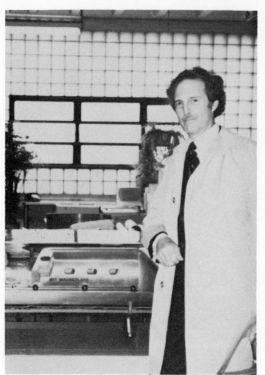

Frank P. Davidson stands next to the Magneplane model displayed at the M.I.T. Museum and developed a generation ago by Dr. Henry Kolm and a talented team at the Francis Bitter National Magnet Laboratory. Financed by the U.S. D.O.T., Avco Corporation, and the Raytheon Corporation, this model levitated train functioned impeccably and may embody features still necessary if electromagnetically levitated transport is to play its optimal role. That the Japanese and Germans have built full-scale prototypes is due more to institutional than to technological advantages. The diagram below simply illustrates the basic principles involved. The United States now has an opportunity to regain its leadership in this technology by demonstrating that such a vehicle system can function at speeds that exceed current aircraft performance; what is needed for such a demonstration is the functioning of a Magneplane or similar system in a tube or tunnel from which vacuum pumps have evacuated air.

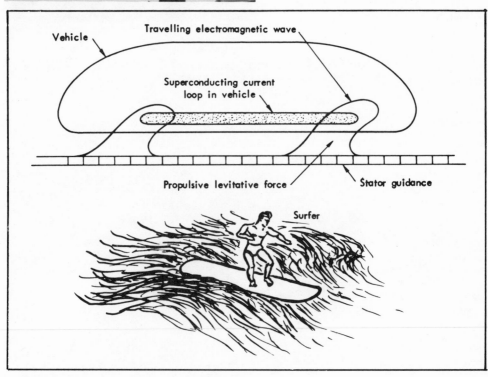

Above and to the right are photographs taken in 1982 of the Linear Motor Car, that is, the test vehicle and test track developed by Dr. Yoshihiro Kyotani and his able group at the Myazaki Test Facility of the Japan National Railways on the southern island of Kyushu. The vehicle has already achieved a record run of 517 kilometers per hour. This year, passenger vehicles are being added to the train set and live passengers are trying out the characteristics of the novel system. Although the United States and the United Kingdom have not provided government financing for a similar effort, there is some possibility that a leading American university will initiate intersectoral meetings to bring about a cooperative technical effort in North America. Ultra-high-speed underground levitated train service could, paradoxically enough, serve both environmental and national security interests. Economic use will depend heavily on the rate of advance in tunnel and tube technology, an elusive variable which might, however, be influenced by a sustained program of national support. There is, moreover, the potential option of a cooperative international research effort, with U.S. and European markets offering the most lucrative future outlets.

The three snapshots on this page were taken in the spring of 1982 at Guilford, Connecticut, by John Stuart Cox. These views of a passenger train—approaching, rumbling through, and departing—illustrate both the vulnerable state of the roadbed and the *déjà vu* condition of the rolling stock. Amtrak has endeavored to upgrade the line and the timetable, but passengers with recent experience in the United Kingdom and Europe note the utter absence of any linkage with local subway systems and the generally inferior level of restaurant facilities and catering.

One option worth exploring may be a "rent-a-train" service tailored to the special needs of schools, travel agencies, professional groups, and businesses. With computerized controls and long-distance telecommunications, it is now feasible from a technical standpoint to have flexible scheduling; it is a matter of management initiative and competence, not a problem of hardware.

These sketches from the December 27, 1884, edition of *Scientific American* depict a proposed "Interoceanic Ship Railway" across the Isthmus of Tehuantepec in Mexico. The upper drawing shows "The Lifting Pontoon and Railway Cradle," while the lower sketch is a "Sectional Elevation of Pontoon and Railway Cradle." In fact, "ship railways" have long been used in the Low Countries to transfer barges between canals. A number of alternatives to conventional canal construction, which avoid the heavy costs of excavation, are now worthy of the most serious attention.

Top: A June 1913 photograph of the famous Gaillard Cut, the deepest excavation section of the Panama Canal, between Gold Hill (*Cerro de Oro*) and Contractor's Hill (*Cerro del Contratista*). The lower picture shows the opening of the canal to maritime traffic, with the S.S. *Ancon* passing Cucaracha Slide on August 15, 1914. Eleven days earlier, German troops had crossed the Belgian frontier, and World War I's orgy of destruction was already under way. The Panama Canal became an instant asset to a two-ocean U.S. Navy.

Above: A "water slope" has replaced five locks on a canal in southwestern France. The water is shoved uphill by a blade pushed by two locomotives. Below: This model by Joseph Hodnick of Boston illustrates a method, developed by Dr. Ernest Frankel from early Venetian precedents, for building canals above the surface of the land by means of prefabricated, automatically emplaced wall sections. First displayed at the Macro-Engineering Seminar held at the Massachusetts Institute of Technology in June 1981, attended by executives from five continents, the model is now situated on the desk of Frank P. Davidson in Building E40 at M.I.T. (*Photograph by Lilian Kemp.*)

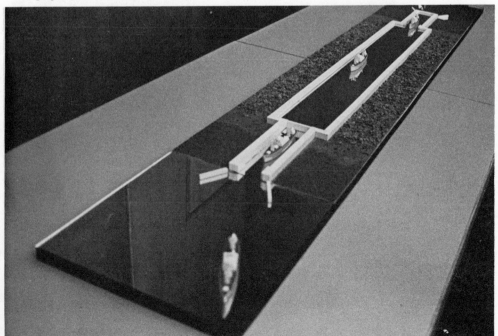

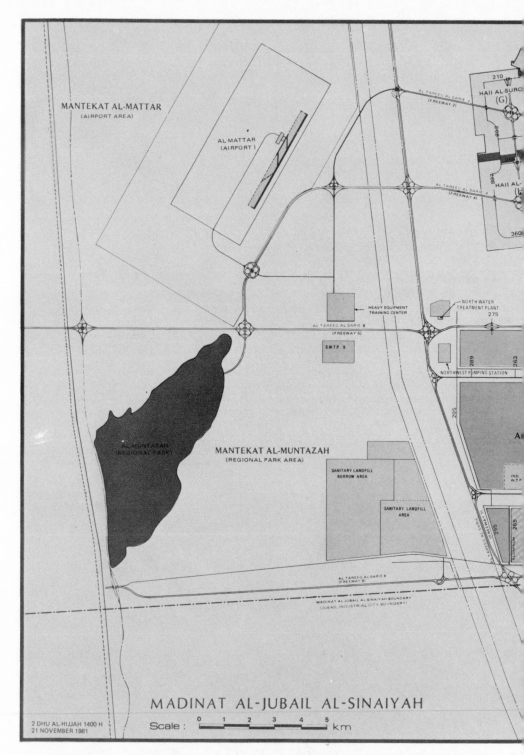

MADINAT AL-JUBAIL AL-SINAIYAH

2 DHU AL-HIJJAH 1400 H
21 NOVEMBER 1981

Scale : 0 1 2 3 4 5 km

This plan of the new industrial city of Jubail depicts what may well be the largest construction project currently under way on the planet. Designed at the outset as a conservation measure to utilize natural gas previously flared off into the atmosphere, the project now includes a highly diversified industrial development. The

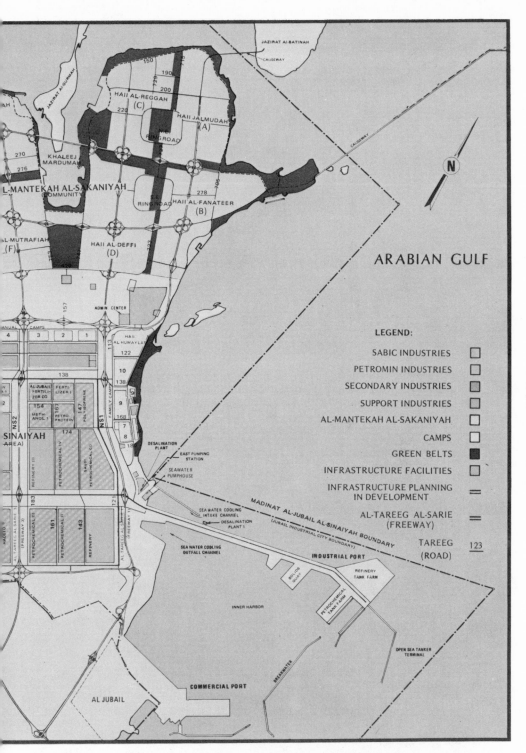

Jubail's seawater cooling canals are of interest to technologists because they appear to have been built by means of prefabricated retaining walls. It has been suggested that a similar approach could reduce excavation costs in new trans-Isthmian canals.

The Hadeed Steel Mill, seen under construction, will take full advantage of Jubail's location on the Arabian Gulf. A maritime site offers the advantages of economical transportation costs for imported raw materials and for exported finished products.

Coastline development at Jubail has taken into account the physical characteristics of the site as well as the need for recreational opportunities for a population that may reach 200,000 or more. Ample drinking water has been assured by desalination plants.

Residential subdivisions reveal an interesting blend of modern technology and traditional social preferences. Although high tech has not been neglected, it is noteworthy that the economy of Jubail will be based largely on heavy industry.

As tunneling technology is automated on earth, it may become increasingly feasible to build underground complexes on the moon, with roofs of sufficient thickness and strength to provide protection against occasional bombardment from objects in space. A lunar university and research institute might have its own laboratory for lunar mining and for the manufacture of needed artifacts from lunar materials. The moon itself is an extensive "space station," and could capture solar power and beam it to rectennae on the earth. Because of the moon's lower gravity, the launching of materials for the construction of communication or solar-power satellites, or for building small colonies in space as envisaged by Professor Gerard O'Neill and Dr. Brian O'Leary, may be less costly and difficult from a moon base than from the earth itself. The United States is the nation with the most experience for assuming leadership in the development of a permanent settlement on the moon.

Possible experimental model of a robotic rover to search for life on the surface of Mars, designed at the Charles Stark Draper Laboratory under the direction of Louis Sutro, 1968. (*Copyright © by Charles Stark Draper Laboratory, Inc.*)

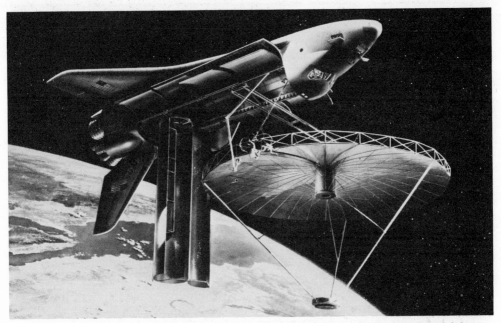

This drawing shows how a space shuttle might place a large microwave antenna into orbit.

A (future) space platform supports multiple antennas for various communications functions.

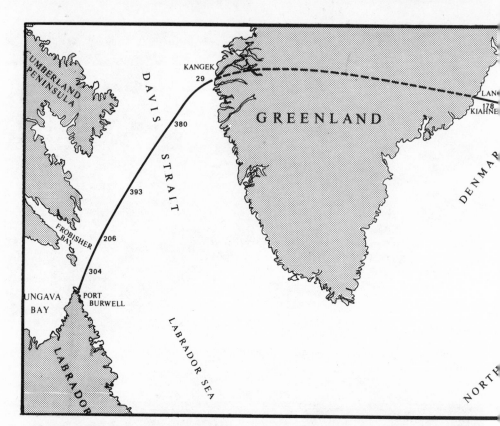

The above map of a practical route for a tunnel or tube across the North Atlantic represents a "best case" version, prepared by the submarine engineer J. V. Harrington—challenged by Jules Verne's short story about an Atlantic tunnel. Below is the map for a less difficult macroproject: a transcontinental bikeway as envisioned by the artist and cycling enthusiast Joan Joos. If congestion and land costs continue to escalate, the movement for an interstate bikeway system may itself gather momentum; a completely separate right-of-way would enhance cycling safety.

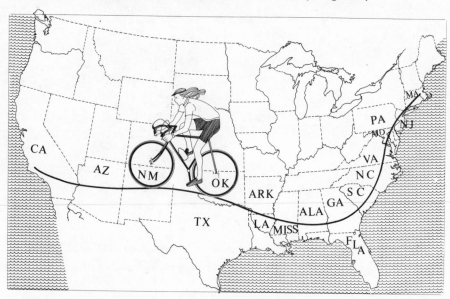

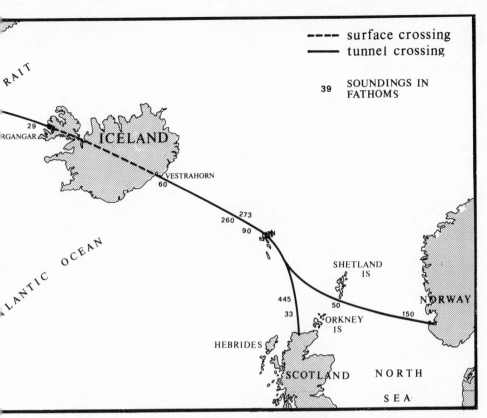

STRAIT

RGANGAR

29

ICELAND

VESTRAHORN
60

ATLANTIC OCEAN

273
260
90

SHETLAND
IS

445
33

50

ORKNEY
IS

NORWAY

150

HEBRIDES

SCOTLAND

NORTH

SEA

A precedent for the east-west bikeway scheme is provided by the stunningly useful Appalachian Trail, conceived by the late Benton Mackaye, a friend of Camp William James who suggested that Americans would welcome the opportunity to hike "from Maine to Georgia." Below right is a conceptual map of one element of what could become, in the next millennium, a trans-Australian canal system. A group led by Art Linkletter and David Rockefeller proved, in the 1960's, that the desert soil of Western Australia could be transformed into very satisfactory pasture and cropland by the addition of trace elements, water, and intelligent, hard work.

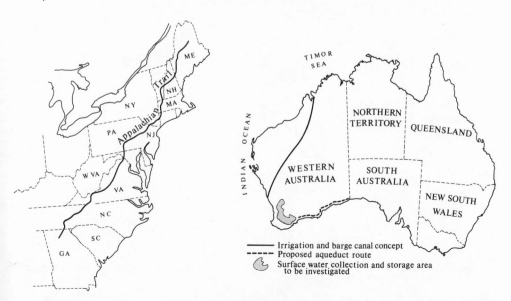

—— Irrigation and barge canal concept
---- Proposed aqueduct route
Surface water collection and storage area
to be investigated

Strategic Planning in an Interlinked but Disunited World

NEARLY A HALF-CENTURY AGO, A. LAWRENCE LOWELL, IN AN essay that deserves to be resurrected in the light of subsequent history, pleaded for "Foresight in Foreign Affairs."[1] After listing dire events that took the State Department by surprise, he contrasted this insouciant approach to public matters with the meticulous attention to future contingencies exemplified by war games. "There have been probably no conditions suggested in which our fleets might be placed that have not been played out on the table of the Naval College at Newport," Mr. Lowell admonished. He went on to cite the story related of Prussian Field Marshal von Moltke who, in 1870, when wakened to be informed of the French declaration of war, "told the officer to find the portfolio of orders in the third drawer and went to sleep again."

Since World War II, the State Department has endeavored to set its house in order. For several years before becoming Secretary of the Navy and Deputy Secretary of Defense, Paul Nitze devoted his not inconsiderable talents to directing a State Department policy planning staff. But in the realm of *domestic* affairs, the government has preferred the "pragmatic" course of dealing with issues *seriatim* as they arise. The brief—but impressively serviceable—experiment with a National Resources Planning Board set up by President Franklin D. Roosevelt has not been repeated. The present "high tech" push for computerized "decision support systems" may smuggle some strategic-planning concepts in by the "side door." But the basic problem was well aired in a 1940 volume coedited by Enno R. Hobbing and Laurence I. Radway with Professor Fritz Morstein Marx of Queens College: As David Cushman Coyle summarized it in his chapter, "Theoretically, the one man who sits in the President's or governor's chair should have in his own head both the field of technical knowledge and the political sense to make every decision fit into the pattern of policy that will lead his administration to success. In practice, no such man has ever been born. The technical advisory body is therefore required to be an attachment to the executive's brain, and the nearer it can come to instant communication the better."

We cannot sensibly discuss the place of macro-engineering in the general field of government without at least alluding to the structure of advice touching this subject. We are fortunate indeed that the President has a "science adviser" who can serve as a channel for the transmission of the best *scientific* opinion when such opinion is sought. But it is not at all disrespectful of science to insist on the useful and essential distinction between "science" and the *applications* of science known as engineering. When President Lyndon Johnson was faced with political turmoil in Panama and there were insistent pressures for a new canal to be built on the "Plowshare" model—that is, with nuclear explosives—he turned to his longtime friend and supporter George R. Brown, who *happened* to be one of the most experienced engineers and engineer-managers of his generation. It was Mr. Brown's eminently sensible suggestion of a survey of alternative routes that provided necessary "breathing time" for a reassessment, by all concerned, of the situation in Panama. It was, time and again, Mr. Brown's experience that was sought. Not being more than mortal, Mr. Brown may have made some errors; but in the absence of an institutionalized engineering adviser, the President was, in my view, absolutely correct in turning for advice on large new engineering propositions to a professional engineer in whom he had confidence.

Peter Drucker has wisely said, "Whereas objectives are 'strategy,' the concentration decision is 'policy.'[2] It is, so to speak, the decision in what theater to fight a war. Without such a policy decision, there can be . . . no strategy, that is, no purposeful action." In today's world, where infrastructure involves government participation on the grand scale—and government authorization and assistance are indispensably involved even where ownership and management are considered "private"—the President of the United States needs direct access to men who have "hands-on" experience in the formation and execution of very large engineering enterprises. Such experience is usually not to be found among the academic scientists who (correctly, I think) are chosen to be science adviser to the President. The President needs, in addition, an engineering adviser, or if there is not such an official appointment, then it should be understood that the chairman of some recognized body such as the National Academy of Engineering will be consulted on general matters of engineering strategy and policy.

If strategy indeed connotes purposive action, then the subordinate policy decisions must comprise innovative steps that will set the stage for long-range consultation and planning on a number of projects, programs, and systems deemed valuable or—some might say—essential for the American future. Ever since Pitirim Sorokin (in 1959)[3] popularized the notion of the fifty-to-sixty year business cycle first perceived by Professor Kondratieff, economists and systems thinkers have known that there may be long-term as well as short-term fluctuations in the business cycle. But we must try to cut through surplus verbiage and look to the realities that lie beneath such misunderstood terms as "economics" and "the economy." We must ask the fundamental but rarely posed question, "Of what does the economy consist?" The answer may provide a key to our dilemma. For the "raw material" of economic activity can only be the goods and services that are the result of an activity best described generically as "engineering," that is, the deliberate application of knowledge and skill to the design and manufacture of utilities—"goods," if you will—that the public wishes to buy.

Without engineering, there can be no economics. And without a conception of how engineering fits into the larger picture of trade, livelihood, human settlement, and politics, the isolated study of economics is destined to remain disembodied. Economists have legitimate and vital functions in studying the mechanisms of trade and investment and the interplay of market and other factors in our complex, monetarized economy; historians of the economy such as William N. Parker have contributed important insights into the development of agriculture and industry. But the point remains that economists without an engineering background may not be the best judges of the relative efficiencies of alternative techniques or even of their long-run economic impacts. And these, as it turns out, are very important considerations. Engineers such as Jay W. Forrester have fully understood the value of basic insights such as those of the economists Kondratieff and Keynes; the choice of macro-systems for investment over long periods of years is not a decision for economists alone: It is one of the main *political* decisions to be taken in an age of burgeoning technology, and it must be taken with the best advice from *all* the relevant professions: science, economics, *and* engineering.

There are technical constraints that inevitably govern the course and timing of engineering investments; this is one reason why we cannot treat the provision of fresh water as a subproblem of short-term business cycles. It takes a generation or more of *sustained effort* to build the infrastructure of a regional water supply system. Accordingly, seven-year business cycles are as useless as four-year political cycles in providing realistic policy guidance for a nation that expects to remain in business for the next century or more. To yield basic decisions over the nation's fate to economists, regardless of their "school" or persuasion, is to neglect the permanent needs of a human community for defense, supply, and cohesion.

Intersectoral groups united by common concern can often span the gap between research and implementation. Did not the Mohole Project commence with informal gatherings of a group that called itself AMSOC, "The American Miscellaneous Society"? And although cost overruns eventually halted this historic effort to drill from an ocean platform through the "Mohorovic discontinuity" in the earth's mantle, should we not be encouraged by such an episode, which at least underlined the opportunity for small groups to initiate large ventures in our complex techno-political environment?

With respect to many of the great projects needed in the coming decade, it is difficult to see how they can move forward at all unless leaders in all sectors of society are willing to meet informally and to develop viable procedures for concerted research and action.

Intersectoral study groups are needed to define, market, and develop a whole range of programs. Even the most sketchy list will indicate an impressive scope for "inventing the future," to use Dennis Gabor's prescient phrase. New communities on seamount-supported artificial islands; high-speed underground transport systems to replace obsolete rail-passenger services; new shipways and deepwater ports; automated industrial installations; new towns and agro-industrial areas linked to older centers by efficient, nonpolluting transport systems; new centers of learning benefiting fully from emerging telecommunication technologies; innovative arrangements for waste disposal; the beginnings of mining and power production from outer space— all of these are within the range of technical and financial feasibility if people of goodwill who possess the necessary knowledge and self-discipline can evolve adequate methods of cooperation.

It would be wrong to omit the need for a new approach to basic engineering research and development. There has been a tendency that has cost us very heavily already, to ignore basic *engineering* research as somehow having less importance and validity than basic research in "pure science." But if we are unwilling to fund this type of activity, how are we to accomplish the *technical* breakthroughs essential to an America that intends to remain internationally competitive in a whole range of engineering products and services?

We need new and reformed institutions. Having a large internal market, Americans have not perceived the need for any structural readjustment as dramatic as that undertaken by the nations of Western Europe when, in the aftermath of World

War II, the Common Market was constituted. Nor have we experimented with any confederal, intersectoral arrangement as extensive as the European Coal and Steel Community. But our fifty states, with the present lumbering machinery of regional cooperation, find it difficult to take advantage of the new, wider opportunities implicit in macrosystem development. The "regional commissions" intermittently funded by Congress were able to emit some interesting reports, but their contribution to regional infrastructure has been at best quite modest. A series of public authorities along the lines of the Tennessee Valley Authority may offer a better route for interstate and state-federal cooperation in areas such as water supply, energy, transportation, and even education and health services.

If as a nation we are to have a "go" at strategic planning, we shall have to develop new capabilities for implementing the plans that are made. Merely employing well-dressed staffs of "strategic planners" cannot help either government or industry if mechanisms do not exist for carrying out approved recommendations. Lester Thurow, the economist, has put forward the idea of a national finance committee that would function very much in the manner of a corporate finance committee, "a committee that would not seek to plan the economy but to direct investment funds into new growth areas."[4]

Thurow cites the example of the semiconductor industry, which is now "in the process of shifting to much larger and more capital-intensive production techniques." He points out that the shift to the new manufacturing processes occurs in the United States at a pace limited by current profits, whereas the Japanese have the advantage of "massive debt capital lent by the Bank of Japan. Their aim is to jump directly into large-scale, capital-intensive production techniques, sell at prices lower than those of the rest of the world, and capture most, if not all, of the market."

Rather than semantic outrage, I think the sensible American riposte to the kind of trade competition identified by Thurow is to create the necessary public-private instrumentality for investment banking so that the promising new industries, many of them "invented here," can compete on equal terms in the world marketplace. If such decisions are made by a politicized body, however, it seems to me that we will run the risk of bailing out major *old* corporations (the Chrysler-Lockheed syndrome?) rather than encouraging our "best bets." To assure professionalism and a measure of objectivity in the selection of investments, I think that the kind of national finance committee or investment bank suggested by Thurow should be set up somewhat independently. After all, our highest judicial appointments are for life! While terms of office might be less lengthy for a "court of investment decision," insulation from lobbying would appear to be a prerequisite to efficacy in this case.

I very much doubt if "indicative planning" arrived at by consultation with all the broad sectors of American life will really raise the hackles of an educated electorate. Nor will Americans of either political party object if steps are taken to equalize the conditions under which American engineering firms must compete for business abroad.

Dr. Kathleen Murphy, in a recent book,[5] has catalogued the various ways that OECD governments use to win lucrative construction contracts abroad for their nationals. A goodly share of the consortia examined by Dr. Murphy are "composed of companies of a single nationality who had come together at the behest, and with the support, of their own government." She cites Technip in France, and Italimpianti and Snamprogetti in Italy as examples of "permanent national consortia that reorient and regroup to meet the changing conditions of various projects." Far from assisting Americans who are qualified to contract for major engineering responsibilities in other countries, our laws and regulations often impose burdens and restrictions that are counterproductive. While the antitrust tradition is a vigorous and valid part of the American legal heritage, the new situation in which American companies now find themselves should cause some fundamental soul-searching among liberals and conservatives alike: Where the old rules have become counterproductive, it is time to have a "restatement" and realignment that can release, once more, the cooperative energies of American technological enterprise. And Americans who are willing to work in inhospitable, remote areas should be offered the kind of tax and other incentives awarded their competitors.

Strategic planning should not be confused with long-range forecasting. Having served as president of the first "think tank" exclusively devoted to comprehensive studies of the long-range future, I have developed some impressions of this activity, which dovetails with humankind's innate curiosity about whatever may be coming down the road "later on." Rather than deride all forecasting as mere delusion and speculation, I think we can identify a number of organizations that have good "track records" in their specialized fields. Traffic forecasting, for instance, as practiced by leading engineering consultants such as Wilbur Smith & Company, or the De Leuw Cather organization, have an enviable reputation for reliability and balance. Dixon Spees in the field of air traffic, and the Arthur D. Little Company in maritime traffic, have likewise performed most admirably, as have several other leading firms in their specialized areas. Forecasts of electric power demand have been made by other types of consulting firms (e.g., Ebasco Services), and of course real-estate developers employ highly skilled and specialized forecasters before investing in new supermarkets or residential developments.

I think that critics of forecasting have tended to ignore the great mass of forecasting that takes place every year—on the basis of which billions of dollars have been invested annually, usually with satisfying results. What has been much more difficult is to forecast major discontinuities in public life: The "exogenous variable" has a way of cropping up at unexpected moments, upsetting the most careful prognostications. But a wise strategic plan will not depend on the minutiae of a long-range forecast. Mature individuals have learned to expect the unexpected, and to the extent that circumstances permit, a good plan will be good "for all seasons"; nowhere is this stricture more necessary than in the planning of macro-engineering developments. Such enterprises take a long time to prepare, to build, and their outcomes may be with us for scores or hundreds or even thousands of years. The decision to enter upon such an undertaking is *necessarily* a *strategic* decision: It asserts priority interest and must accept the fact that it is preclusive in nature and will preempt other options. No major investment is made without some sort of effort to discern its likely implications and impacts. For those who enjoy reading about mistakes in forecasting, I recommend Peter Hall's 1980 book *Great Planning Disas-*

ters.[6] But history is replete also with examples of successful strategic planning and implementation.

Man is quintessentially an engineering animal. The progress of civilization has been marked by successive stages of agglomeration and construction. The first states were literally "city-states"; gradually, requirements of water and food for growing populations, and the widening arc of commerce and communications, led to larger territories and a consequent regionalization of engineering and control. As regional empires collided and coalesced, the range of engineering projects was extended once more: Roman and Chinese infrastructure were continental in scope.

Where whole societies were so palpably dependent on the maintenance and improvement of aqueducts and other public works, governments naturally regarded macro-engineering as one of their primary responsibilities. A lengthy—and delightful—account of *Les Travaux Publics aux Temps des Romains* (*Public Works in Roman Times*) was published in 1979, in Paris, by a French engineer, Alfred Leger. He explains the manner in which Augustus took public works as his personal function when he became the first of the Roman emperors. And in China, for many centuries it was the director of the Grand Canal works who was the second highest official under the emperor. Alexander the Great was an innovator in many ways, but his most lasting monuments were the new cities and towns he ordered built. He had much broader objectives than the satisfaction of the physical and security needs of the inhabitants: He was the first leader of a great civilization to embrace the idea of a common humanity, without the former invidious distinction between "native" and "barbarian." The Macedonian conqueror sponsored mixed marriages on a macroscale; the cities he built were intended as centers and examples of a new enlightenment. The great city of Alexandria in Egypt, with its famous library and lighthouse, stood out as a symbol of free trade in goods, services, and ideas for the whole of the civilized world.

To preserve their independence, the Chinese long ago realized that they must maintain large armies in a state of readiness in the north. A north-south waterway (which nature failed to provide: The main Chinese rivers flow from west to east) would at once assure the supply of the armies and the government bureaucracies in the north, and facilitate the collection of the grain tax in the center and south. In the whole history of humanity, there are few examples of engineering works so bold in conception, of such immense magnitude, and with consequences so beneficent. That China has remained a unitary state is due in no small measure to her sustained and single-minded devotion to a strategic engineering concept despite upheavals in religion, politics, ideology, and the economic and social system. The Grand Canal has always been multipurpose: It serves at one and the same time the interests of defense, commerce, irrigation, flood control, fisheries, water supply, and recreation.

China's need to regulate its water supplies may be gleaned from a brief glance at climate and geography: Eighty percent of the annual rainfall comes during the three months of summer. Moreover, there are substantial fluctuations in rates of precipitation, producing alternate threats of flood and drought. The Yangtze River, flowing 3,450 miles from Tibet to the ocean, is the source of irrigation waters that produce 70 percent of China's rice. The Yellow River, flowing 2,890 miles from Central Asia to the Pacific, has extreme variations of seasonal flow. The mouth of the river changes its configuration continually. But the seasonal floods that spread immense tonnages of silt over the land have had the virtue of revitalizing the soil and making possible a variety of dry crops such as wheat, millet, and maize.

The mountain ranges (two north-south parallel ranges and three chains running west-east) have created natural provinces that have been recurrent barriers to national unity. But central government has been essential, both to deal with periodic incursions from the Mongolian plains in the north and to provide the labor and supervision needed for long-term water control in the general interest.

From time to time, there have been conflicting views as to the principal goals to be served by the canal. A too-exclusive priority for irrigation interests would deplete the canal to the point where transport functions would be placed in jeopardy. In times of scarcity, military and transport objectives threatened to monopolize the water supply to the point of provoking peasant revolt. There have been persistent, well-researched debates between Taoist and Confucian hydraulic theories: The Confucian penchant for confining and repressing nature led to a preference for high dikes. The Taoists, with their reverence for nature and their devotion to observation and scientific inquiry, argued for deep channels, low dikes, and a considerable latitude for waterways.

The first section of what is now the Grand Canal was begun in the sixth century B.C.—the "Canal of the Wild Geese." By 200 B.C., some 1,250 miles of waterway made navigation possible between Changan and Canton. But the first official section of the Grand Canal (a Y-shaped system from Peking in the north to Changan in the west and Hangchow in the south) was completed only in the Sui Dynasty in the early seventh century A.D. Over five million laborers were said to be enrolled in the corvée at one time. The present Grand Canal is really the work of Kublai Khan, who straightened the route to run from Peking directly to Hangchow. In 1327 A.D., the canal was eleven hundred miles long, flanked by paved highways and tree plantings, and with imperial resting places at regular intervals.

The system disposed of a considerable arsenal of dredges, ice-breakers, and towing equipment. Until the nineteenth century, the West did not begin to approach the magnitude or sophistication of the Grand Canal in water-control works. Today, with the Soviet Russians replacing the Mongol hordes as a potential danger from the north, the government of China has resumed a major program for the rehabilitation and enlargement of the Grand Canal system. That poetry and art have celebrated this masterpiece of millennial technology can hardly be astonishing. As an example of strategic, multi-objective planning, based on a very long time-horizon, the Grand Canal of China stands in a class of its own.

Wherever strong governments have established their dominion over a wide territory, macro-engineering has been a major element of their strategy. Admittedly, in the simpler—and less populated—world of the eighteenth century and before, it could almost be assumed that new engineering enterprises would have a large margin of utility. Today many more factors must be taken into account, including the desire of a highly urbanized society to preserve remaining natural landscapes—and even landscapes that have been developed for agriculture and stock-raising and forestry. That is, everyone today believes that limits must be set to the engineering thrust, lest the whole planet be industrialized and polluted. The perceptive planner and engineer must acknowledge that he or she shares this feeling, and that the full panoply of engineering knowledge must now be placed in the service of environmental protection and public health.

Considerations of health and amenity will propel many of the "grand designs" of the next decades: the recycling of wastes, the reorganization of production to emphasize quality and longevity, the building of artificial islands—at sea and in outer space—for certain types of industrial activities; and perhaps massive interbasin water transfers on the basis of an informed allocation of benefits and costs.

In large affairs as in small ones, we must watch out for the "N.I.H." (Not Invented Here) syndrome. When the late Ralph M. Parsons announced his concept of NAWAPA—the North American Water and Power Alliance—from his Pasadena office, I happened to be closeted with an official of "B.C. Hydro" in Vancouver. My host made it clear that no Canadian official could condone the proposal by an American to build a five-hundred-mile-long reservoir in British Columbia. That this water was to serve not only the United States and Northern Mexico but would also be used to facilitate a trans-Canadian canal to the Great Lakes, and that literally billions of dollars would accrue to the Canadian treasury, seemed almost irrelevant. And to this very day, an increasingly nationalistic Canada will not discuss the project, to which a special subcommittee of the United States Senate had devoted respectful attention. Similarly, when the redoubtable Herman Kahn proposed, through the pages of *Fortune* magazine, to dam the Amazon River to produce a vast amount of low-head electricity, there was a furor in Brazil. Only slightly more remarkable was the proposal by the imaginative German engineer Herman Sörgel to create a vast "Congo Lake," which would have had the effect of obliterating areas that today include several independent and sovereign states!

Shortly after the late Ralph M. Parsons announced the

NAWAPA plan, a distinguished Canadian mining engineer, T. W. Kierans, proposed a Great Recycling and Northern Development (GRAND) Canal project. The essence of the scheme is to store the runoff of rivers emptying into James Bay (at the base of Hudson Bay) by converting James Bay into a freshwater lake; this water would be transferred, largely by canalizing the Ottawa River, to the Great Lakes, which would then become a distribution reservoir for major water requirements of Canada and the United States.

Professor Kierans, a former director of the Alexander Graham Bell Institute near Sydney, Nova Scotia, now teaches at the University of Newfoundland, where he has catalyzed a major harbor-development scheme for St. John's. I had the pleasure of inviting him to explain his proposal to the third Macro-Engineering Symposium held in connection with an annual meeting of the American Association for the Advancement of Science.[7] In San Francisco, before an enthralled assembly, Professor Kierans explained why his project would benefit North America. He emphasized that there are two generally agreed problems that the GRAND Canal scheme would address. First is the need to stabilize and regulate both the level and the outflow of The Great Lakes-St. Lawrence system by means of new inflows balanced by additional outflows—a much better stabilization system than the present one, which penalizes flows in order to maintain levels or vice versa. (Presently the Great Lakes region suffers soil erosion in years of plentiful rain and interrupted ship traffic in years of drought.) The other major requirement is to halt and reverse the present trend toward desertification in the Middle West and Far West of both Canada and the United States. Much of the Great Plains—the main source of the continent's wheat crop—is included in the U.S. Geological Survey's area of "high risk," the survey having shown, among other things, that ground-water levels in parts of Kansas have declined more than sixty-two feet since 1950, largely because of pumping for irrigation. If the trend continues, many experts believe the damage will be irreversible.

Professor Kierans's basic premise is that a macroproblem of such proportions demands a continent-wide solution, one that takes into responsible consideration the present and anticipated needs of Canada, Mexico, and the United States. What has been suggested is nothing short of a continental program for hydrology improvement.

The focus of the Kierans scheme, James Bay, is thirty thousand square miles in extent, not quite one-third the surface area of the Great Lakes. The James Bay watershed, which is subarctic and sparsely populated, covers an additional three hundred thousand square miles, from which an average of four hundred thousand cubic feet of runoff per second is drained—the equivalent of two Niagara rivers. At present, rivers that empty into the bay are being harnessed by development of the La Grande Complex of Quebec Hydro: It is the largest hydroelectric project ever undertaken on the North American continent, and in a few years will make a major contribution to the energy supply of eastern Canada, New England, and New York. In June 1982, when Professor Mel Horwitch and I visited the La Grande worksite at dam Number 4, in the company of two M.I.T. students, we were impressed by the beautiful but barren landscape: The soil is so thin atop the Canadian shield that tree growth is stunted and only the lovingly tilled gardens around the construction site itself revealed the possibility of raising crops in this difficult environment. We were told that we were one thousand miles from the nearest settlement.

The proposed source of new water for the GRAND Canal scheme would be the bay itself, which by means of construction of three staged dikes would be progressively converted into a freshwater lake for the storage of runoff that thereby could be recycled for eventual transfer through a network of rivers, canals, and lakes between James Bay and the Great Lakes. As shown in the photos in Chapter 6, this mammoth water management scheme would then be used for flood control, navigation between the Great Lakes and the Atlantic ocean, and water distribution to the entire North American continent.

The potential advantages of such a system are manifold. By utilizing the existing Great Lakes, there would be no need (as in the NAWAPA proposal) to flood extensive land areas to create new storage space for water. The La Grande Complex, during the intervals between periods of peak demand, would provide the electric power to pump James Bay water from sea level over the system's highest divide (920 feet) and into Lakes Michigan and Huron (520 feet). The new configuration would improve the Great Lakes by increasing the flow of water through them, thereby reducing pollution. The project would indeed provide a new and reliable water service of continental scope.

Rough cost estimates run to one hundred billion dollars, approximately ten times the cost in constant dollars of California's Central Valley Project, which recycles the waters of the Sacramento River just before they reach San Francisco Bay and pumps them up the San Joaquin Valley to Los Angeles. If benefits were to match those reported for the California project, they would total an estimated hundred billion dollars annually.

Professor Kierans has urged that more detailed cost-benefit analyses be undertaken, particularly with regard to environmental impacts and the social and financial implications for Canada; it does seem likely that this recycled water, which will augment rather than reduce available supplies, could bring in many billions of dollars to the Canadian federal treasury during the project's long lifetime. The project is evidently comparable to—but less grandiose than—the oft-discussed projects in the Soviet Union for interrupting northward-flowing Siberian rivers that now empty into the Arctic Ocean so that their waters can be diverted into the oversalinizing Black and Caspian seas.

The Kierans proposal could be viewed as a challenge to Canadian and American diplomacy: This is an instance where technology policy and foreign policy commingle. If "strategic planning" is to become a feature of our national policy, then the State Department and the departments and agencies concerned with water supply, irrigation, agriculture, and finance will have to develop, under suitable executive direction, a mechanism for the development and exchange of information and for the preparation of policy advice to the President. The case illustrates the importance of having a person in a post such as that of engineering adviser, so that the necessary information flow can be guided laterally and vertically through the machinery of government. Macro-engineering projects are, by definition, of such overriding dimensions that they are beyond the management or financial capabilities of any single government agency; if the machinery for coordination is not established, we shall be unable to take advantage of the new potentials offered by large-scale applications of technology, regardless of how many excellent reports may be emitted by individual government bureaus.

Macro-engineering now constitutes, for better or for worse, a major portion of domestic and international politics. Looking at almost any daily newspaper, anywhere on earth, we notice that official bodies are continually occupied with pipelines, dams, bridges, highways, airports, housing projects, ports, industrial complexes, and other physical structures typical of a technology-based society. Domestic and foreign affairs are increasingly intertwined. That there is a need for an articulate national strategy on large-scale engineering becomes more evident day by day. In no field is this more true than in the field we used to call, with polite deference, "diplomacy."

The recent "flap" about the Soviet gas pipeline to Western Europe is a case in point. In an earlier chapter I referred to this (successful) use by the Russians of a macro-engineering enterprise as an instrument of national policy. What was unpleasant about the situation was the increasing dependence that France and her neighbors will have, because of the pipeline, on energy supplies directly controlled by Soviet Russia. Although the announcement in February 1982 of this scheme appeared to take "Foggy Bottom" by surprise, must one conclude that the United States government had not taken the trouble to calculate the energy needs of our NATO allies during the coming decades, or, if we did, there was no strategy for an alternative source of supply? The lack of a policy on this matter left a power vacuum at a critical point, and as everyone knows, "nature abhors a vacuum." Meanwhile, the immense gas reserves in the North Sea, controlled by Norway and Britain, were not fully exploited.

Although Secretary of State Shultz skillfully extracted the United States from an embarrassing diplomatic "limb," the fact remains that there should have been a negotiating effort, many years earlier, to develop an agreement with Britain and Norway in order to provide for substantial gas exports to France and any of her neighbors who wished to participate. There is always the lurking suspicion that leaving the gas unexhausted in the North Sea may, in the *very* long run (if there is one) better serve the needs of the Alliance: in this view, the pipeline deal can be made to look like a Machiavellian scheme to deplete Soviet supplies! But the whole episode does point up two lessons: the need for more attention to the underlying realities of technology and energy, and specifically the requirement that the United States develop a policy and a believable posture on international technological questions.

The United States does not suffer from any genetic incapacity to use macro-engineering as an instrument of its own national policy when there is one: President Theodore Roosevelt was quite willing to help Panama set up shop as a nation independent of its parent, Colombia, in order to facilitate arrangements for a Panama Canal to be built by the United States. And when President Kennedy decided to concentrate NASA's resources on a series of trips to the moon, this dramatic use of engineering capabilities fully restored America's standing in what has been widely perceived as a "space race" with the Russians.

But it is one thing to sponsor occasional projects of very high visibility, and another thing altogether to develop a consistent, long-range policy on the use of engineering abilities as an enduring element of American foreign policy. Anyone who has tried to promote a project abroad, even a substantial one fully endorsed by the highest level of government authority in Washington, D.C., will have tales to tell on the varying degree of assistance received—or not received—from the diplomatic establishment of the United States. It was to improve government support for British businessmen seeking foreign business (I suppose) that Lord Harcourt, the senior partner of Morgan Grenfell & Company, was despatched on a survey mission by the British government several years before his death, to strengthen the ties between British diplomacy and British industry.

We cannot wait for an ideal reorientation of American education that would greatly increase the dose of science and engineering administered to oncoming generations of schoolchildren and college students. For at least a score of years or more, management of the nation's affairs will probably remain in the hands of people having only the vaguest idea of what large-scale technology can accomplish. What *can* be done, however, is to initiate a *policy* and above all an *attitude* that will favor the systematic acquisition and dissemination of information about large technological enterprises under construction, in the planning stage, or believed to be entering the sphere of feasibility. The construction industry already has data banks tailored to its needs; but a modern superpower should not conduct its foreign—or domestic—policy as if it were operating from the corner garage: Solutions to problems such as Western Europe's energy deficit should be studied years before the crisis point is reached. And the judgment about programs to be studied in depth should be made by persons with practical experience in the field of engineer-management.

Some comfort may be taken from the view expressed by Sir Charles Carter in his September 6, 1982, presidential address before the British Association for the Advancement of Science: "The successful use of science," he said, "depends on the overall quality of management rather than specifically on its degree of scientific knowledge." Sir Charles was not, I think, arguing *against* the idea of giving future managers some background in technology and science!

The vastly increased range, speed, and pervasiveness that "high technology" has conferred on large-scale engineering makes it logical to recognize the close interconnection between technology policy and foreign policy. Only by placing the former "front and center" will the State Department be able to avoid the trivialization of American diplomacy in an era when choices among major technical systems are bound to constitute one of the key subjects of national and international politics. The present need is to see that appropriate machinery, guidelines, and people are set in place. The fiasco over the Siberia-Paris gas pipeline illustrates to the hilt the folly of a foreign policy *optique* that treats large-scale technical affairs as extraneous to the game of diplomacy. If indeed it was a vital American interest to minimize Western European dependence on Soviet gas supplies, why was there no sustained U.S. initiative to organize alternative supplies from the reserves held by Norway and Britain in the North Sea? A purely negative approach provided Russia with a diplomatic opening; U.S. inaction set the stage.

It would be a misrepresentation, however, to see the "real world" only in terms of competition and rivalry. Even the escalated rhetorical and arms competition with Soviet Russia has not interfered with what cynical observers might describe as an "unwritten understanding": The United States government continues to facilitate huge grain shipments to the Warsaw Pact, and the Russians have been cautious enough to avoid exacerbating Western sensibilities beyond a certain point. As the folly of a nuclear exchange becomes apparent even to "diehards," it is "thinkable" that both blocs will opt, eventually, for joint programs of development in areas where neither side sees its vital interests threatened. The treaty that neutralized Antarctica and in which the United States and the Soviet Union participate with other nations, seems to indicate that even Russian-American relationships are subject to cyclical alterations.

With respect to United States relations with Japan, it is important to function not only on the problem of United States competitive ability; there is also the dimension of cooperation. Japan, having become successful in "microtechnology," has accumulated enough capital—and confidence—to be a worthwhile partner in joint technological ventures on the grand scale. I have already referred to the Japanese interest in a joint development, possibly with European partners, of a second trans-isthmian canal (probably although not necessarily at Panama). Here is one of many instances where the commercial and strategic interests of Japan and the United States coincide. Having participated, in May 1965, in discussions with the then president of Panama, Marco A. Robles, and his foreign minister, the bright and urbane Fernando Eleta, I know a bit about the complexity of the issues of finance and authorization for a second canal. It is fortunate for the project that the Japanese are seriously supportive, and that the United States has a Secretary of State who thoroughly understands such matters, as a result of his own recent experience as senior executive of a leading firm of engineer-managers. "It is a consummation devoutly to be wished," if Shakespeare may be cited—albeit without his knowledge or consent.

More difficult to set in motion will be appropriate large-scale teamwork with Japan in the arena of outer space. The problem is the lack of a clear definition of NASA's mission, budget, and guidelines during the decade to come. Public attention has been riveted on the space shuttle; but admirable though this "space transportation system" may be, it is susceptible of improvement, and it is not the *only* system or project to which the United States should be devoting its attention in outer space.

As allies and trading partners of Japan, Americans must appreciate the extraordinary vulnerability of that island-nation to interruptions of its energy supplies, most of which must be imported. Despite all the unknowns, Japan might be willing to share the costs of a solar-power satellite experiment so that the technology, costs, benefits, and environmental and social impacts can be evaluated on the basis of experience and not merely through simulations. At an April 1982 Macro-Engineering Symposium that I chaired in Baltimore, in connection with an annual meeting of the American Institute of Aeronautics and Astronautics, John W. Freeman gave an excellent "Status Report on the Solar Power Satellite Concept." Dr. Freeman reviewed the $19.5 million report on the concept by a joint team from NASA and the Department of Energy (DOE) led by DOE's Fred Koomanoff. The opinion of the National Academy of Sciences was sought; that appraisal was conducted by a Committee on Satellite Power Systems of the National Research Council and appeared as an NRC report in 1981, entitled "Electric Power from Orbit: A Critique of a Satellite Power System." After recommending that no further funds be expended on the project for the next decade, the committee remarked, "The worldwide ramifications are so extensive that a multilateral approach with the participation of other countries would probably be the only viable one if an SPS were ever to be established."

Dr. Freeman also cited and reviewed the report carried on at about the same time by the Office of Technology Assessment (OTA) for the Congress. "The OTA report," Freeman concluded, "was generally more optimistic about the chances for technical success of an SPS type concept." He cited as an intermediate step the innovative proposal by E. C. Okress and R. K. Soberman to build and mount a passive microwave reflector for point-to-point power transmission on a balloonlike platform that would hover in the stratosphere. The Okress-Soberman proposal, emanating from the well-regarded Franklin Research Center in Philadelphia, involves essentially a "solar thermal aerostat research station," and had been described by Dr. Okress at an AAAS-AIAA seminar held in 1980 in San Francisco. At that meeting, Dr. Peter Vajk, author of the notable essay *Doomsday Has Been Cancelled*,[8] set forth the rationale, from the standpoint of India, for a system of solar-power satellites that would be used for the "synthesis of readily transportable liquid fuels (such as methanol), made from water and carbon dioxide extracted from the air." It was suggested that a system of two hundred ground rectennas might produce enough power to help solve the subcontinent's grave problem of deforestation.

So rapid is the march of technological thinking that even since the above-cited reports were published, opinion has been moving in the direction of a solar collector on the moon itself; orbiting reflectors could then transmit the energy collected from the sun to desired locations on earth.

Robert Salkeld has been looking into the lunar option for solar power; he is becoming widely known for his invention, with Dr. Rudolf Beichel, of the "dual-fuel" rocket engine, which many believe would substantially reduce the costs of space transportation. If such a development were to be funded, it could have the effect of accelerating not only the use of the moon for a multitude of purposes, but also the testing of prototypes for the SPS and for the mining of asteroids. A "new generation" rocket engine would also assist the United States in its necessary development of a space platform.

Salkeld represents a unique combination of attributes: He holds an MBA from the Harvard Graduate School of Business Administration; he is a professional engineer; and he is also a science writer of distinction. A director of the AIAA, he has collaborated with me on a series of books reflecting papers on macro-engineering at the various symposia held under the joint auspices of the AAAS and the AIAA since 1978. He has successfully bridged the two cultures of management and engineering, is highly articulate, and will no doubt help guide professional and public opinion as the United States, however hesitantly, enters the new era of space exploitation.

This new era will be a challenge also to the resilience of American diplomacy. The financial and marketing success of communication satellites has already made the negotiation of airwave channels a feature of the day-to-day international scene. A host of legal and diplomatic problems are involved in the industrialization of space, and I suspect that lawyers accustomed to large ventures will be cajoled, along with investment bankers, insurance specialists, and accountants into the various enterprises that are already looming on the horizon. We are, thanks to the pioneer educational work of Professor O'Neil of Princeton and of the astronaut Brian O'Leary[9] and others, just sufficiently educated to be ready for the more detailed debates on "next step" questions. I take it as a significant event that the editor of M.I.T.'s *Technology Review* regarded discussion of a manned landing on Mars as sufficiently cogent to deserve a commentary that he signed with his own initials.[10]

Much as it is to be regretted, potentially dangerous rivalry exists between our country and the USSR in the field of weaponry and deployment. Space is rapidly becoming an arena for military as well as civilian activity. With expensive new systems proposed for both military and civilian uses, the United States cannot "go it alone" in space, on the oceans, and on land. To be successful in our space endeavors, there are two steps that must be taken. First, those programs that are not to be carried out by the United States on a "sole source" basis should be internationalized, with our trading partners and allies invited to participate on a businesslike basis in a manner fully consonant with the security and economic interests of all concerned. Second, the private sector must be brought in by the government as a partner in the nonmilitary aspects of space development. Money can be made "out there," and a public conscious of the limits to growth of the national budget will wish private finance fully deployed to the extent that this can be justified.

Strategic planning is a very good concept, not only for private institutions of all kinds, but for government as well. But in laying out ideas for present and future implementation, one question is unavoidable: planning for what? Without a purpose, methodologies are "missiles on the loose"; systems theory itself brings us back to this essential question, for the man-machine systems with which this book is concerned are only "systems" if they serve some discernible purpose. Russell L. Ackoff has popularized the term "nonsystem," and anyone with practical experience of what is called, euphemistically, "the school system" or "the military system" or "the medical system" will wish to question whether these institutions, which result from slow accretions of inputs from many sources and with diverse objectives, can properly be called systems at all. James Grier Miller, who was a graduate student when I was an undergraduate, has published the most comprehensive book I have seen on *Living Systems*. Now president of the University of Louisville (Kentucky), Dr. Miller has provided those with curiosity about systems science an encyclopedic handbook that is unexpectedly readable and enjoyable. Ever since C. K. Ogden and I. A. Richards published *The Meaning of Meaning* in 1945, pundits have been on notice that they must look behind the superficial connotation of even our most accepted words, and the word "purpose" is, I realize, no exception. Miller has cautioned, ". . . if purpose is defined not in terms of the observer but in terms of specific values of internal variables which systems maintain . . . by taking corrective actions, then the concept is scientifically useful."[11]

Strategic planning, then, cannot take place in a vacuum; it must serve some larger, coherent purpose—or set of purposes. Sensing this semantic truth, Presidents Eisenhower and Nixon tried to integrate high policy by establishing a National Goals Commission. The problem with this exercise was that it was, if anything, on too lofty a plain: Platitudes of almost religious import cannot be translated into the black and white of laws and regulations and plans unless they are expressed in operationally useful language. And there is another requirement: There must be the kind of persuasive leadership that "percolates" down through the creaky machinery of government; we have already had the experience of a splendid statement of "national goals," some few months before the nation was thunderstruck by the tragedy of Watergate.

The question of leadership cannot be sidestepped; and leadership brings us back, willy-nilly, to the question: "leadership for what?" The charisma and appeal of "great leaders" has always been linked to the causes that they espoused. Especially in a society that vaunts its complexity, it is the function of leadership to select key leverage points, to articulate a path of action into the future—however murky and unpleasant that future may appear—and to release the energies of free men and women so that our constitutionally established society may move forward along the lines so brilliantly traced by the founders of the Republic.

This is a point that has not escaped the attention of perceptive analysts and advisers. Dr. J. F. Music, whose small but high-grade consulting business is named Strategic Management, Inc., now specializes in problems of leadership within business organizations. Professor Peter Senge of M.I.T.'s System Dynamics Group has written eloquently on this subject—and co-teaches seminars on "Leadership and Mastery" offered by the Framingham concern Innovation Associates. And leadership problems are very much in the mind of Dr. Nancy Wardell, the former Harvard Business School Professor who directs the Institute for Corporate and Government Strategy, Inc., in Boston.

The perceived need for leadership is so compelling that consultants on the subject have flourished; the country still awaits an opportunity for the objective-setting, clarifying "clarion call" to bring out the best in each of us, and make of our diversified society a coherent, coordinated team. In the meanwhile, we continue to react in the most immature fashion to conditions that are clearly cyclical: With what appears to be an "oil glut" pushing OPEC itself into a "crisis mode," the United States has cut back drastically on investment in synthetic fuels and in the Strategic Petroleum Reserve. (I take it as fairly obvious that when oil prices are low, this is precisely the time to make bulk purchases so that the nation is not caught short in a future moment of scarcity.) It is the precise syndrome noticed by Jay Forrester when he found, as reported in his fundamental text *Industrial Dynamics*,[12] that many corporations respond to cyclical market downturns by such drastic reductions of inventory that when an upswing occurs, they may lose market share because they simply cannot fill orders! True leadership would rise above momentary considerations, and summon the public to shoulder temporary disadvantages for the sake of the long-term safety and well-being of the Republic.

Similarly, the nation *must* invest in the production of prototypes of new engineering systems that have a reasonable chance of serving as the basis of entire new industrial markets.

In a thoughtful September 1981 article in *Technology Review,* "Reindustrialization: Aiming at the Right Targets," Nathaniel J. Mass and Peter M. Senge expressed the view that "effective policies must focus on the next long-wave expansion, which may not begin for a decade . . . ill-timed choices may appear to be appropriate and can be politically popular. For example, quotas on imports of Japanese cars might bolster the production of less efficient cars in the United States in the short run, but would ultimately reduce the pressure on domestic automakers to meet competitive standards, thus diminishing choices and reducing U.S. energy efficiency. Similarly, schemes that set minimum prices for imported steel subsidize domestic inefficiency and outmoded production processes . . . On the other hand, a reduction in the capital gains tax for investment in new or small enterprises could be very beneficial, increasing the supply of equity capital to these businesses."

In a multiconstituency electorate, there is great temptation for candidates to blur choices and to stay on the politically safer "high plane" of moral maxims and generalizations. Here, a more perceptive leadership will "level" with the voters and at the least state what the more basic choices really are. By ignoring what macro-engineering, enhanced by the demonstrated capabilities of high technology, can accomplish for the American future, candidates for high office are in effect foreclosing important future additions to the prosperity, the quality of life, and the security of the American people. A decision *not* to regard a vital potential choice as an "issue" is tantamount to downgrading it in public esteem; this is not the appropriate posture for the world's leading technological power. This is why we must hope that groups will be assembled to advise candidates—and the administration now in office—on those major engineering programs that can offer significant advantages to the broader goals espoused across the whole political spectrum. It will not do to regard all "public works" as mere emanations of "pork barrel" politics and "log rolling": If *certain* large programs are needed in the public interest, let them be organized honorably and efficiently. If the Department of the Interior is too cumbersome an instrumentality, perhaps we shall have reason to suggest a major new government Department of Macro-Engineering with across-the-board responsibility for the coordination of large-scale technological programs on land, at sea, and in the new realm of aerospace.

We like to think of ourselves as an "advanced" or "developed" country. My international travels have given me a perspective that has a few nuances: We are, once more, a comparatively *undeveloped* nation in fields such as public transport, maritime affairs, and water supply. In other areas, we are subject to severe competition. And where we retain the leadership, as in computers and telecommunications and aerospace, have we really designed the integrated programs to assure the continuation of our leadership in the generations to come?

The small island nation of Sri Lanka (formerly Ceylon) is now building one of the world's largest networks of dams, hydroelectric stations, reservoirs, and irrigation canals. Sandra Nichols, who has visited this project in order to explain it to the American television audience, emphasizes that this vast hydraulic undertaking is no mere dream of a modern technocrat: Its origins are indeed Sri Lankan—its ancient engineers constructed massive earth dams to hem in artificially created inland seas; water was delivered all over the island by an intricate network of canals. By the fifteenth century, the splendid ancient system had decayed, and the population moved from the dry lands to the humid southwest; now, with a rapidly growing population, food shortages, and high unemployment, the Sri Lankans have decided, with foreign aid, to rebuild their ancient, exemplary hydraulic civilization. The Mahaweli Ganga Project is, Sandra Nichols explains, "a huge social engineering project as well." When it is completed, Sri Lanka expects to have a revived agriculture, new towns and settlements in the arid areas, and many key opportunities for employment. The project consumes half of the country's annual capital budget.

Such macro-engineering on the grand scale will radically transform the environment and society of an entire nation. Americans, aware of the risks and costs of large projects, often feel that our country needs a "breathing spell," that new industrial investments are misguided unless they are in "clean" and problem-free industries, and that after all it is better to be in a "service society" with a touch of "high tech." But"service" is not limited to *garçons de table:* In my many years as a rail commuter to a Manhattan law office from a Connecticut suburb, I learned that second-rate railway service can play havoc with one's disposition. Service in a modern "service society" *ought* to include reliable, clean, courteous commuter services on a par with European, Japanese, or Australian standards. But railway improvement involves the building of equipment, the supervision and maintenance of the right-of-way, the meshing of rail terminals with other transport modes; all of this involves "industry" and engineering *and* leadership. We are too complex and varied a nation to look to any single project or any single field of activity to rescue and restore us in the manner to which we would like to become accustomed. But work—and in modern times this means engineering and organization at both the microlevel and the macrolevel—can, if wisely planned and conducted, bring us quite far in the direction we wish to go.

The word "work," however, covers a multitude of meanings. It is possible to have everyone "working" and yet not have a productive or even a contented society. Without belaboring the point, it must be reiterated that the variety of intellectual work called "research," while often very valuable and occasionally indispensable, may also prove to be a trap for the unwary. I have mentioned that the millions of dollars spent on "research" for a modern Northeast Corridor rail service were in fact wasted, for the reason that there was *no decision to develop such a service.* Politically speaking, a research program can be used as an alternative and obstacle to action: The long history of presidential and royal commissions is not devoid of examples. But if the task of leadership is to lead, the end result must somehow go beyond mere words and reach that stage "devoutly to be wished": action. There are other actions besides the steel and concrete of an engineering project; but in a technological age, a fair proportion of governmental—and private—decisions do concern the design and building of physical structures.

Lest we become mesmerized by organizational and methodological clichés, we should clear our minds by looking at an actual "case," an example of life that has been lived. In courses and seminars on macro-engineering, it has always seemed to me that the much-derided "case method" should be retained, even in "high tech" management schools: "Models" and "cases" can be mutually instructive and symbiotic. To ignore what has been accomplished by people of flesh and blood is to miss the savor and complexity of life itself. Even "models" have their champions, and a "model" *could* be considered as just one case (or one model, if you prefer) among many: Comparison is a good teacher.

History boasts few episodes surpassing in human interest the persistent and ultimately successful promotion of the Suez Canal by the diplomat Ferdinand de Lesseps. Lesseps's involvement with the Canal began with Napoleon Bonaparte, but the story of the Canal itself begins much earlier. Charles Beatty has summarized the long background:

> Almost two millennia before Christ, Sesosteris I, Pharaoh, Lord of the Two Lands, connected the Nile with the Red Sea, though the first record implying such a waterway dates from five hundred years later, in the reign of Queen Hatshepsut. . . . It was not heard of again until about 600 B.C. when Necho, that King of Egypt whom Nebuchadnezzar chased out of Palestine, re-excavated most of it, at a cost, according to Herodotus, of a hundred thousand lives. When he occupied Egypt in 521 B.C., Darius the Persian worked on the project which was still unfinished in the time of Xerxes, fifty years later. It was probably finished by the Emperor Trajan in the first century A.D. . . . Even Roman engineering skill was not able to maintain the waterway and, like its forerunners, it merged into the sands. It is said that in A.D. 788 Harun Al-Raschid, Caliph of Baghdad, conceived the idea . . . at the end of the fifteenth century a plan was put forward by the Republic of Venice whose supremacy was threatened by the discovery of the Cape route to the East. . . . The next step was taken by Prosper Enfantin in 1847 when he formed a Survey Committee.[13]

Actually, Napoleon had had the route surveyed during his abortive campaign in Egypt. Lesseps, whose father had represented Napoleon as French consul in Cairo, decided to obtain the concession and build the canal himself; he made this decision after his first wife died and he was already in his mid-fifties.

The canal was built on the basis of risk capital, most of it subscribed in France, and with the intermittent but generous subsidies and advances provided by the viceroy of Egypt. Lesseps spurned the offer of Baron de Rothschild to raise the money for what was then considered the normal commission (5 percent) and, despite the opposition of the British government of the day and the time-consuming intrigues that any large project affecting the world balance of power involves, Lesseps carried the matter through to a brilliant conclusion. In 1869, fourteen years after the concession had been granted to him by the pasha of Egypt, the Empress Eugénie (a cousin of Lesseps) led a flotilla representing the world's leading powers on a triumphant parade through the hundred-mile waterway connecting the Mediterranean and the Red Sea.

Meanwhile, back in Queen Victoria's England, joint stock companies competed in obtaining concessions for railway lines whose ubiquity still causes headaches for the (nationalized) British Railways Board. Strong-minded individuals, Isambard Kingdom Brunel foremost among them, left their stamp on the landscape in no uncertain terms. Brunel and his father, who had been the first chief engineer of the Port of New York after the family fled France in the aftermath of the Revolution of 1789, completed the first underwater bored tunnel in the history of the world—under the Thames. This tunnel is still in service with the London "underground." Brunel went on to build the experimental broad-gauge line from London to Bristol, the famous Great Western Railway; and he designed and built the S.S. *Great Eastern,* for many decades by far the world's largest ship. All these enterprises were accomplished on the basis of risk capital. And the risks were real. The Great Western Railway went bankrupt and had to cease business: Technically brilliant, its trains—built for a seven-foot gauge—could not transfer to the standard-gauge lines that had been built elsewhere. The S.S. *Great Eastern* went through several bankruptcies before finally—and gloriously—laying the Transatlantic Cable.

In today's more institutionalized world, the individual promoter, unless like D. K. Ludwig he personally commands billions of dollars, cannot usually go off "on a frolic of his own": He is constrained by the peculiar requirements of regulatory commissions, the various requirements of financial firms, the specialized fine print of the insurance industry, and the exigencies of consultants and contractors of all kinds. The interprofessional team typically assembled for a large project, even one that is privately financed, is apt to operate as a committee. Despite the odds, there are individuals not only with enough intestinal fortitude to propose new macroprojects, but also with the persistence and clarity of mind necessary to do the preliminary detailed research, often with very little or no assistance from others, and to bring to the attention of the professional and general public a serious new option. Of such a mettle were the Chaffee brothers from Ontario; and in our own day, T. J. Kierans, now in Newfoundland, and Nigel Chattey—the New Yorker from England—deserve to rank with those pioneering spirits who, while equally courageous and farseeing, have operated from a "firm base" with the advantage of established institutional support backing them up. There is just as much major promotional activity going on now as ever; but where it is of *high quality,* it may take a unique kind of sensitivity or training or experience to recognize it.

Rebecca McCann expressed it well in her *Complete Cheerful Cherub,*[14] which has already gone through at least twenty printings:

> Progress comes from adventurers,
> Explorers of land and thought.
> The absolute conservative
> Gives civilization naught.

However, there is no conflict between enlightened conservatism and the kind of prudent, value-enhancing and environment-protecting technology that the whole world now desires and seeks. Is there some magic in authoritarian institutions that enables them to choose macroprojects more wisely or to make better decisions as to when to modify or abandon them? The March 5, 1983, London *Economist* comments:

> Grandiose civil engineering schemes have long held a fascination for Soviet planners. The much-publicized project to divert southwards, to water the arid steppe, the great rivers

which now discharge uselessly into the Arctic dates back to the 1920s—when atheist campaigners cited the rivers as proof of the non-existence of God (since any Omniscient Being worth His salt would have known how to design Russia better). Yet last week, in an article in Pravda, the Russians admitted that one pet project, the Kara Bogaz dam, has proved something of a disaster.

The dam had been proposed ten years ago as one way to help save the shrinking waters of the Caspian Sea. Not only has the Caspian been gradually drying up for more than a century and a half, but more recently the same fate has overtaken irrigation projects along its principal feeder river, the Volga.

According to the *Economist,* it had been calculated that the Kara Bogaz Gulf on the Caspian's east side was responsible for "five cubic kilometres a year" of the water loss: "Broad and shallow, it acted as a giant evaporation pan." It was thought that if the gulf were dammed, this loss would be terminated. Construction was started in 1979 and completed in 1980.

The Kara Bogaz is already down to a third of its earlier eighteen thousand square kilometers and is a mere half-yard or so in depth. But a whole Pandora's box of unforeseen problems has resulted. Farmers have been concerned by the seepage inland of salt from the dried out parts of the gulf. Ecologists are alarmed by the effect on the Caspian's sturgeon of "the possible long-term build-up of salinity in a Caspian deprived of the Kara Bogaz gulf as its natural desalinator." And a huge sodium sulphate plant that depended on the underground brine lake under the gulf reported an alarming drop in the brines' sulphate content and a corresponding increase in counterproductive chlorides: the Karabogazsulfat engineers demanded sluice gates to reintroduce Caspian water as might be needed in the gulf from time to time. Meanwhile, Turkmenian scientists set up a Commission for the Kara Bogaz Problem. "Now, everyone is passing the rouble," the *Economist* reported.

Bloopers, clearly, are not the special property of East or West, capitalism or communism. In fact, one of the most glaring examples of miscalculation on a grandiose scheme comes from Australia: The Sydney Opera House designed by the Danish architect Jørn Utzon was estimated in 1957 to cost not much more than seven million Australian dollars; it was completed in 1973 at a cost of one hundred two million Australian dollars. But it is a beautiful, striking monument, one that has come to symbolize Sydney even more than its famous Harbor Bridge. The Australians "gambled" on the architect's novel design, and now that the dust has settled, probably most residents of Sydney would say that the game was "worth the candle."

The Opera House is dramatically situated on Bennelong Point, regarded as "Australia's Plymouth Rock" because it helps enclose Sydney Cove, where Captain Phillip landed in 1788. It appealed to many leading citizens as a perfect place for a cultural showcase. From 1947, Eugene Goossens, conductor of the Sydney Symphony Orchestra and director of the New South Wales Conservatorium of Music, joined the campaign for a great opera house and concert hall. The labor prime minister of the State of New South Wales perceived political mileage in "a great imaginative gesture," as Peter Hall has described the episode in his well-researched and amusing book *Great Planning Disasters*.[15]

Quite appropriately, most of the money for the Opera House was raised from lotteries.

While the Opera House was under construction, I remember passing through Sydney on trips to Western Australia in connection with our group's study of the Nullarbor Desert. On one occasion, we were privileged to visit Art Linkletter's model sheep station near the coast at Esperance. Noticing the sleek, healthy-looking sheep grazing on lush pastures (across the road from unimproved desert), we asked the young scientist in charge how he had succeeded. After recounting the water-conservation measures necessary in a territory with less than seven inches of rainfall per year, and having explained the need to add trace elements to the depleted soil, he said that a crucial element had been the selection of ewes: The sheep "mothers" from research stations had not looked after their lambs carefully enough during times of poor weather. The solution had been found by importing ewes from the dry pastures in the north, where the survival of the young depended on constant maternal care and affection.

Stopping in Melbourne for a dinner of the Australian-

American Association, our chairman, the late and greatly beloved Floyd Blair, asked me to address a few remarks to the thousand people gathered, with great ceremony—many guests wearing their decorations over formal attire, because the occasion was graced by the presence of Sir Robert Menzies, the wartime prime minister of Australia. I had to explain to those present that my comments would be brief and diffident because Sir Robert was, in a sense, my landlord! As lord warden of the Cinque Ports (a post that Sir Winston Churchill held in the years before his death), Sir Robert was an overseer of Dover Castle; and the Channel Tunnel Study Group had arranged to store core borings extracted from the seabed during our 1964–65 core boring program in some of the castle's least-frequented rooms!

In *his* introductory talk, Sir Robert "kidded" his old and dear friend, Floyd Blair, about spending time in the "barren desert" of the Nullarbor. But Mr. Blair completely captivated the audience, including Sir Robert and Lady Menzies, by his knowledgeable and humorous insistence that Australian history was "just beginning," and that in future generations land now regarded as without value would be cultivated and settled through the steadily increasing knowledge conferred by agricultural science and technology.

The close and cordial ties between America and Australia make it a delight for Americans to travel "down under." I was privileged to be able to visit several parts of the country with perceptive companions such as John L. Gray, then the Battelle Institute's general counsel, and the late Hollister Kent, the architect who was commissioned to choose the site for Brasilia. But we made one huge mistake: After an official visit to the Australian capital, Canberra (itself a notable macro-engineering project—designed by a Chicago architect after an international competition), we made the mistake of staying over for Saturday and Sunday. The city was utterly devoid of life, its denizens having retreated by air to Sydney and Melbourne for a sportive Australian weekend, while in Canberra both movie houses and other places of entertainment were deserted or closed.

Strategic planning, I think, takes place outside the four walls of "offices of strategic planning." The dreams, perceptions, hopes, and fears of the public—and of individuals who influence the public—are the true arena where long-range schemes arise or are nurtured. Because of the inescapable need for "macrofinance" and sustained support over a long period of time, a plan that is a disembodied brainchild of a technical staff may have difficulty, in the rough-and-ready politics of the Western world, in achieving that solidity of acceptance that seems to be a prerequisite to actual accomplishment.

One idea, which at first blush seems logical enough, has never attracted support in Europe: The idea of an entirely new capital city for the institutions of the Common Market and the other confederal bodies set up since World War II.

In 1961, on September 8, Professor J. Marshall Miller went so far as to participate in a "prededication ceremony" at a site near the junction of Luxembourg, France, and Germany. An ambitious, lavishly illustrated brochure was published in 1963 by Books International and entitled *Lake Europa: A New Capital for a United Europe.* But the Europeans have preferred to parcel out offices of the new confederal institutions in established centers such as Strasbourg and Brussels! If the Valley of the Mosel is to be developed as a host territory for a European headquarters, I suspect that it will be done, if at all, by private enterprise.

To plan strategically, I take it that one needs something like Napoleon's *coup d'oeil,* the rapid glance over a whole field that can pick out the main features and, almost in the twinkling of an eye, devise a plan that is feasible and perhaps unexpected. To Dr. Robert Salter I think we shall owe much: A rather conservative physicist and engineer, he had the courage to set down, with detailed logic, what modern technology *can* accomplish in the domain of rapid long-distance transport. Even if the world decides against building a "planetran"—that is, a tunnel linking Asia, America, and Europe—the consciousness is dawning that the feat *could* be accomplished, and that in another century or less improvements in the methods of tunneling may bring the cost of such a project within the range of serious consideration. Once three-hour travel to any point on earth is available at reasonable cost, there will be almost surely a resurgence of interest in *inter*planetary travel: Such is humankind's curiosity and thirst for novelty that, once this planet becomes too accessible to every tourist, the further planets, and the spaces beyond, will tempt even our more sober statesmen and financiers to underwrite a macroprogram for space exploration and development.

Of course, we have already been alerted, by such books as Peter Vajk's *Doomsday Has Been Cancelled*,[16] to the fact that "single stage to orbit" vehicles could already, if funded and built for the purpose, provide *two*-hour transportation from New York to Tokyo!

It is becoming clear that "high tech" plus macro-engineering means that the range of technological projects will be increasingly continent-wide in scope and even *inter*continental. This statement carries an implication not yet mentioned in these pages, but one that should surely be considered in any national "strategic planning" for our technological future: languages. If we are to cooperate with our Spanish-speaking neighbors in Mexico and Central America, our French-speaking neighbors to the north in Quebec, and with our trading partners in Japan, China, and elsewhere, we must cease to be parochial in our approach to foreign languages. Like the Dutch and the Swedes, we shall have to develop "the gift of tongues," if only for workaday reasons of "market penetration." But of course there are other, even more compelling reasons for Americans to improve their capacity for understanding different languages, cultures, and traditions. That learning a foreign language can become "the thing to do" has been amply demonstrated by the success of such popular institutions as the Bibliothèque Française de Boston (the French Library of Boston), where throngs of people, encouraged by General Georges F. Doriot, enjoy vintage movies, music from the age of the Sun King (Louis XIV), lectures by visiting scholars and statesmen, and champagne-tasting accompanied by appropriate dissertations.

One interesting but little-noticed aspect of recent American history has been the extension of Corps of Engineers responsibilities to very distant locations on the planet. In addition to its statutory duties to plan and supervise river and harbor development within the United States, the Corps has been employed to assist countries such as Saudi Arabia in supervising and monitoring development and engineering contracts. For the Roman legions, foreign service was a perfectly normal duty; and each legion—about six thousand men—included in its ranks not only engineers but also plumbers, bricklayers, toolmakers, and all the other trades and professions needed to build and maintain a camp or community. Perhaps our Congress and executive branch should study the precedent established by the 3rd Augusta Legion, which maintained a whole civilization in the teeth of the Sahara Desert. In the right circumstances, might not units of the United States Army be designated, under the guidance of the Corps of Engineers, to cooperate with units of other armies on construction tasks that serve the purposes of mutual security and benefit? To reduce the number of people serving in military forces may be either imprudent or difficult to attain, depending on the state of world affairs. But the Romans taught us that the army itself, in certain circumstances, can build the infrastructure of peace. "Strategic planning" along these lines could offer one more string to the bow of American diplomacy.

The Great Wall of China is reputed to be the largest single construction carried out on the earth. Emperor Shih Huang Ti implemented the idea in 214 B.C. by connecting a number of existing defensive walls. The Great Wall has a length of 2,150 miles, plus 1,780 miles of branches. Average height: 30 feet.

Sacsahuaman is by far the most formidable fortress ever built by the Incas. Begun by the Inca Pachacuti (c. 1438), it employed more than 30,000 Indians in the seventy years of its construction. Erected to defend the capital city of Cuzco, it enclosed great water reservoirs for the city. The combined parapets rise to a height of 60 feet.

Regarded by many *cognoscenti* as the civil-engineering work of most enduring utility, the Grand Canal of China has been under intermittent construction for more than two thousand years. It extends 1,300 miles from Peking to Hangchow. The main rivers of China run from west to east, so the Grand Canal serves as the major watercourse for internal travel and transport between north and south. In times of crisis, it has made it easier for the government in the north to send soldiers south to collect the grain tax, and for the grain to be shipped to the army and bureaucracy in the north. But the canal has always been multipurpose. It has provided a reservoir for floodwaters of the rampaging rivers, and has been a dependable source of irrigation water and of fisheries. The canal has facilitated peaceful commerce and has actually saved many lives by offering a secure inland route as an alternative to the stormy, pirate-infested waters of the ocean. Upper left is a view near the city of Lin-Tsin on the banks of the Grand Canal. Below left is a scene of junks passing an inclined plane on the canal. Above is a recent snapshot, taken by Jacquie L. Kay, of one of the wider sections of the Grand Canal. . . . The oldest section, dating from the fourth century B.C. or earlier, connected the Yellow River with the Huai Valley. The Sui dynasty (A.D. 581-618) linked the capital at Loyang with the key bread-basket area of the lower Yangtze Valley. Kublai Khan and the Mongol emperors straightened the canal to bring it to Peking. Joseph Needham, author of the authoritative *Science and Civilisation in China* (Cambridge University Press, 1971), has commented, in a footnote on page 319 of Volume IV, 3: "It is much more impressive than anything in Europe," and, on the following page, "It serves the twentieth century better than it did the thirteenth." A Sui report tells of five and a half million people assembled to work on the canal—which would stretch from Maine to Florida.

Two views of Shasta Dam under construction in 1942. The dam is the centerpiece of California's Central Valley Project. Covering most of the Sacramento and San Joaquin valleys—an area 50 miles wide and 450 miles long—the plan transfers water from the Sacramento basin to the San Joaquin basin, which suffered from dramatic shortages of irrigation water. The multipurpose project also aids flood control, navigation, and hydroelectric power in the region. Its design enables it to repel salt water encroaching upon channels that irrigate upwards of 400,000 acres of valuable delta land. In addition, supplies of fresh drinking water and of industrial water have been made available to a number of towns and cities, including Antioch, Pittsburg, and Martinez. Work on the dam was completed by the U.S. Bureau of Reclamation in 1949. The project was of notable use during the severe drought of September 1977. For a remarkable description and analysis of the most extensive state water-supply system in the United States, consult the *California Water Atlas*, 1979.

Imperial Dam, shown in a 1939 photograph, is an essential element in the All-American Canal Project. Situated at the southern border of California and serving parts of Arizona as well, the Imperial Irrigation District lies in an area with barely 5.84 inches of annual precipitation, a rainfall comparable to that of Western Australia's undeveloped Nullabor Desert. Indeed, the entire western third of the United States (with the exception of the mountainous areas and a strip along the northern Pacific Coast) is correctly described as arid or semiarid. But thanks to extensive irrigation, the Imperial Valley is one of the world's most productive agricultural areas. Passage of the Federal Reclamation Act on June 17, 1902, increased dramatically resources available for irrigated agriculture. . . . That irrigated agricultures need not be transitory is proved by a number of farms on the Rio Grande, near El Paso, that have been continuously cultivated under irrigation since the early days of the Spanish Conquest. . . . The view below is taken facing upstream along channels 2, 3, and 4. One remarkable feature of the project is the large-diameter twin welded-steel pressure pipes carrying the All-American Canal across the New River near Calexico.

The St. Lambert Lock, most easterly lock on the St. Lawrence Seaway, begins to take form under the Victoria Bridge, one of four connecting Montreal and the South Shore. This 1958 photograph shows bridge modifications to provide 120-foot overhead ship clearance.

The first ship of the 1982 season goes through the St. Lambert lock on April 5, the latest date on which the seaway had reopened since the April 12 reopening in 1972 after severe late-winter conditions. The Liberia-registered *Stolt Castle* is headed toward Sarnia and Detroit with a cargo of metal products.

An aerial picture, taken in 1956 during construction of the St. Lawrence Power Project, looks almost due east toward Cornwall. To the right a ship moves along the old canal. The abutments of the closure structure, on the course of the diversion canal, can be seen in the center of the picture. The start of the temporary tunnels below the canal are at top center. They emerge at top right, the site of the generating station. The St. Lawrence Seaway was opened to traffic on June 26, 1959. The 27-foot channel linked Montreal and Lake Erie, thus permitting the passage of many seagoing vessels between the Atlantic Ocean and the Great Lakes. Canadian-American coordination had not been easy to achieve. Neither a 1932 treaty nor a 1941 executive agreement received the requisite legislative approval. In 1954, however, a complex arrangement was negotiated, under which the seaway is operated by two national agencies: the St. Lawrence Seaway Development Corporation for the United States, and the St. Lawrence Seaway Authority for Canada. In practice, the Canadian agency collects the tolls, which are apportioned between the two public authorities. For the relevant U.S. legislation, see the St. Lawrence Seaway Act, 68 Stat 92, as amended, 33 USC secns. 981–90.

Currently under construction in the north of the province of Quebec is one of the world's major hydroelectric developments. By building a series of reservoirs and power plants, the hydroelectric potential of La Grande Rivière, principal tributary of James Bay (located at the base of Hudson Bay) will be exploited for the benefit not only of Quebec but of communities in New England and New York. Above is the scene at the official commissioning of the first of twelve generating units of the La Grande 3 powerhouse. To the left are two views of the uninhabited territory in which the James Bay hydroelectric development is taking place. The few existing townships are spread along the James Bay coastline. The project was launched in 1972, when Premier Bourassa correctly gauged the impending expansion of the market for electric power. The La Grande river is 500 miles long and drains a territory larger than Switzerland. The 6 major reservoirs of the project will involve building 9 dams and 170 dikes requiring 150 million cubic meters of fill.

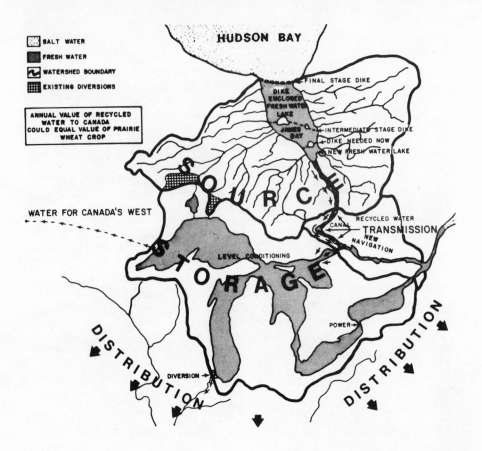

SALT WATER
FRESH WATER
WATERSHED BOUNDARY
EXISTING DIVERSIONS

ANNUAL VALUE OF RECYCLED
WATER TO CANADA
COULD EQUAL VALUE OF PRAIRIE
WHEAT CROP

HUDSON BAY

FINAL STAGE DIKE

DIKE
ENCLOSED
FRESH WATER
LAKE

JAMES BAY

INTERMEDIATE STAGE DIKE
DIKE NEEDED NOW
NEW FRESH WATER LAKE

S   O   U   R   C   E

WATER FOR CANADA'S WEST

S   T   O   R   A   G   E

LEVEL CONDITIONING

CANAL

RECYCLED WATER
TRANSMISSION
NEW
NAVIGATION

POWER

DIVERSION

DISTRIBUTION

DISTRIBUTION

RECYCLE STEPS
EXISTING MAJOR DIVERSIONS
PROPOSED TRANSFER CANALS

The Great Recycling and Northern Development (GRAND) Canal Concept, outlined on these diagrams, was originated by the Canadian mining engineer T. W. Kierans. Professor Kierans has calculated that the annual value of recycled water could be equal to that of the prairie wheat crop. Improving on the NAWAPA (North American Water and Power Alliance) proposal by the late Ralph M. Parsons a generation ago, the Kierans plan would not require the flooding of valuable existing land to create a storage reservoir; the 100,000-square-mile water surface of the Great Lakes would be used for this purpose. Transmission from the James Bay source to the Great Lakes storage would include the Harricanaw River valley and other James Bay rivers combined with the Ottawa and other regional streams. Kierans stresses that from the centrally located, elevated Great Lakes storage, recycled water would be available to Canada's water-short West and to other North American areas with water deficits. Because of excessive pumping for irrigation, groundwater levels have declined alarmingly since 1950.

This overflowing river streaming past an on-ion-domed church in northern Russia illustrates the dilemma that the Soviets share with their neighbors across the North Pole in North America. Vast quantities of water that flow into the ocean might, if rechanneled, help reclaim arid areas and replenish jeopardized bodies of water such as the Caspian Sea. The map shows diversion projects that have been discussed for more than a century. A 900-mile canal has been proposed to an immense new storage reservoir at Tobolsk, whence a canal of equal distance would carry water to the region of the Caspian Sea. Projects of this magnitude could cause major environmental upheavals; deprivation of water coolants could affect the Arctic ice cap. (*New York Times News Service*)

The "Power Tower" is located at Barstow, California. A large number of heliostats direct the sun's rays to a boiler on top of the tower; the boiler produces steam which drives a conventional steam turbine. A similar system was pioneered by Dr. Vladimir Baum in the 1950's in the USSR, at the Solar Energy Laboratory in Tashkent.

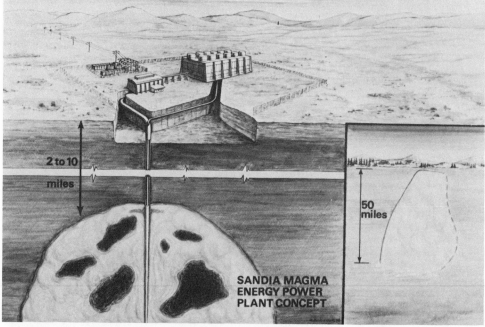

2 to 10 miles

50 miles

SANDIA MAGMA ENERGY POWER PLANT CONCEPT

The U.S. government laboratories at Sandia, New Mexico, publicized a daring concept of obtaining energy directly from the magma or molten core of the earth itself. Fifty miles below the earth's surface the temperature is high enough to produce steam that can turn turbines; the problem is to discover or develop practical heat-resistant materials.

In 1966 the French government constructed the first commercially utilized tidal-power facility. Situated on the Rance River in Brittany, the Saint-Malo plant has a capacity of 240 megawatts. Wilson Clark has explained in *Energy for Survival* (Anchor Press, 1974), "To harness the 44-foot tidal range required the design of a completely new kind of turbine generator unit whose blades have adjustable pitch and are reversible. This permits the turbine to not only adjust to the tide's varying flow speeds, but also to continue to generate electricity no matter which direction the tide is moving." The Soviet Union has also operated an innovative tidal-power plant in a narrow inlet connecting the White Sea with Ura-Guba Bay. Numerous studies have indicated a tidal-power potential in Canada's Bay of Fundy, and in the adjacent Passamaquoddy Bay where the United States has useful proprietary rights. Northern Australia possesses attractive sites but the demand for power is not yet commensurate. The Severn Estuary in England has potential; Argentina has a site too.

At left is a solar-power satellite in geosynchronous orbit 22,300 miles above the equator, directing a microwave beam back to earth. At right is a receiving antenna on earth, converting microwaves directly into electricity.

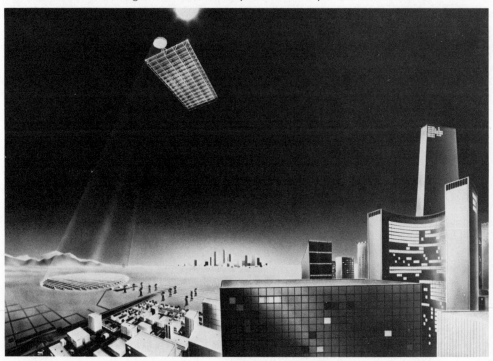

An artist's conception of a solar-power satellite producing power continuously to supply the electricity needs of a major metropolitan area.

Implementation: The New Entrepreneurship

THREE YEARS AGO, VISITING JERRY KOMES—ONE OF THE SEA-soned engineer-managers developed by the Bechtel Group—I asked him how well he was satisfied with the training of young graduates of technical institutes hired by his firm. He paused a moment, smiled his quizzical, crinkled smile, and said, "The trouble is, they always look for logical answers to problems. But the world is not a logical place!" For the benefit of the more brilliant students not yet "wet behind the ears" but with the ambition of participating in large projects, the Bechtel organization—and no doubt other similarly situated firms—decided to inaugurate three-month "internships" for students. An institute of technology would not be worth its salt if it taught less than the "optimal" answers to questions; but experience, too, is a necessary teacher: What *can* be done in a world where there are numerous and at times innumerable "in-putters" to the "decision pie" may be less desirable than what is theoretically "best." What is "feasible" needs as much attention and study as what seems "desirable."

To cope with this issue, engineering firms developed the "feasibility study," which is now an accepted staple of industrial and governmental affairs. When an engineering program is under review, surely the first question to ask is whether it can be built. If the answer is positive, then the next question is one of cost. And if the costs do not seem wholly preposterous, a follow-on problem is the calculation of the cost-revenue ratio or, more broadly, the relationship of costs to benefits. Although our modern terminology had not yet been invented and refined, a feasibility report is essentially what King Henry IV of France asked for when he appointed the bishop of Toulouse as head of a commission specially appointed to look into the idea of building a canal between the Atlantic Ocean and the Mediterranean Sea.

A second device for testing the practicality of an engineering proposal is to demand a working model. This was the requirement stipulated by the wary Colbert, when Riquet de Bonrepos made the trip to Versailles in order to request a concession to build the project studied and approved by a previous monarch's royal commission. The *ruisseau d'essai* built along the entire length of the contemplated Canal des Deux Mers proved, as no stack of papers and blueprints could have, that enough water could indeed be pumped uphill to assure all reservoirs and channels of an adequate supply.

Today's feasibility inquiry is likely to be much broader: Engineering practicality and costs may be calculated to the penny, but the decision as to financial viability often requires professional judgment by people trained in the intricacies of investment banking. Even where costs and revenues are adjudged to be in a satisfactory relationship, there is the hurdle of authorization: Are there legal or regulatory obstacles, and if so, how can they be defined and surmounted? Beyond the legal problems may lurk questions of environmental impacts and public health: In a democratic country particularly, the mere authorization to proceed by a group of officials can be overturned if there is cogent evidence that the project is contrary to the public interest, convenience, or necessity. Experts on ecological matters may be indispensable; and no stigma attaches to the employment of reputable public relations counsel, who can often anticipate difficulties that other specialists fail to foresee.

Because of all these considerations, I have taken the position that for major projects the judgment as to feasibility must be made by an interdisciplinary and interprofessional team, not merely by engineering consultants, however expert and reputable they may be. The larger team is not necessarily more negative! The contrary may be true: I know of cases where engineers have pooh-poohed a project as being "too expensive"; but a professional banker is apt to be more flexible, for the reason that the critical factor in finance is usually not the absolute cost of a project, but the *relationship* of costs to ascertainable revenues. The whole theory of "costs" has, as we know, undergone a definitional inflation during the past decades: We now look not only at the narrow, easily calculable monetary costs, but also at those "external" costs that fall on the public at large—a new dump for hazardous wastes may be a very profitable operation until we calculate, in addition, the risks to the public and the further precautions that government at different levels will mandate. There is, moreover, the phrase "opportunity costs": If project A is authorized, will we have to forego projects B, C, and perhaps D as well?

As a maverick in the world of finance, I have been agreeably surprised by the receptiveness of investment bankers to new ideas and projects. From the viewpoint of a "promoter"—and I think we must all accord the word a measure of respectability if we really believe in innovation and flexibility—then it is better to speak to the underwriters early in the game, before mountains of reports have been written and the plans and schedules are "cast in concrete." For one thing, the choice of engineers is itself a matter for judgment: Not all engineers or engineering firms are equally trusted by investors. If a project is to be underwritten by the financial community, it is simply courtesy and common sense to check out *in advance* the standing of the engineers to be entrusted with critical estimates of costs or revenues. It is a waste of time to bring in a "feasibility study" to a hoped-for "backer" who may distrust the firm signing the report or, almost equally hazardous, may simply not have had confidence-building *experience* with that firm.

There is also a psychological side: Even bankers are human. Imagine the dilemma of a busy executive, especially at the end of a long, hard day, if a bright young person comes in with a bulging briefcase and presents a three-thousand-page report purporting to outline why a certain tollroad or pipeline or industrial plant ought to be financed. How much better and easier the situation would be if the banker had been asked, months or possibily years earlier, to suggest the firms or individuals to be employed as "experts." It may be shocking to systems analysts who have succumbed to the doctrine that "general systems theory" encompasses all knowledge, when an experienced senior manager finds a comprehensive computer model an insufficient basis for decision; but there are true "limits" to computerization: Even in an up-to-date computerized society such as we are developing in Massachusetts, most people still prefer to have their appendix removed by a surgeon, not by a computer scientist. To live in a "knowledge-based" community does not mean that information must always be about information: At some point, somebody must know how to drive in a nail, milk a cow, or at least adjust the wiring of the automated nail-driving machine or milking machine. An "information society" without basic trades is an unfeasible idea. Nor is there such an individual as a "feasibility expert."

Within each profession, temperamental differences as well as differences in conviction and approach must be taken into consideration. Some eminent legal authorities like to enumerate long lists of problems in order to discourage innovators or— more charitably—to display their own erudition. Confronted with such exercises, it may be best to change attorneys promptly! In the channel tunnel affair, we were fortunate to find open-minded, innovative, problem-solving rather than problem-raising legal advisers; among the former I ought to mention John Ferguson (later United States Ambassador to Morocco), George W. Ball (later Undersecretary of State and Ambassador to the United Nations), and of course my older brother Alfred, who in addition to his official positions had the added distinction of winning—with his partner—a doubles championship in tennis, at the age of seventy, rewarded by a cup presented to the tournament winners by the British tennis and cricket club hidden in the woods of Meudon near Paris.

For macro-engineering ventures, the early steps may be the most difficult. To find venture capital and—more vital at the outset—venture *time*, one may have to rely on one's friends of long standing. "Venture capital" is another of those phrases that will bear close scrutiny: Even the more ardent "venturers" do not really like to lose money, and the portfolios of "venture capital companies" may include, accordingly, some rather familiar corporate and institutional names. For the novice, I think I would still recommend two 1970 reports printed up by the United States Department of Commerce: *Financing New Technology Enterprise* and *A Guide to Venture Capital Financing*. I had the experience of serving on the Technical Advisory Board's Venture Capital Panel, which drew up the reports, and I can testify that they were prepared with tender loving care and attention.

For people who think of themselves as "intellectuals," it can come as something of a shock to find that bankers and financiers can be as brilliant and "cultured" as college professors or professional authors. Having had to put together several consortia to offer finance for large-scale undertakings, I can report that the world of "Wall Street" and "the City" is full of surprises. It is, admittedly, a somewhat "archaic" world, where questions of precedence and prestige count for a great deal. I remember spending several days trying to arrange a meeting between the heads of two leading investment banks that, as it happened, had never worked together previously as co-managers. Fortunately, the chairman of the senior bank had injured his leg recently, thus presenting the chairman of the "junior" bank an excuse to walk the long block and pay "his respects" without loss of "face." Couve de Murville, the enigmatic former French minister of foreign affairs, is said to have followed the rule of "never being *demandeur*," that is, of never asking a favor; I suspect that contemporary diplomats are less antiquated in their interpersonal relationships than are the leading denizens of Wall Street. But our bankers, in addition to supporting opera and the ballet quite generously, are *very good* at their business. Valid major technology projects will find them inventive and loyal partners.

The world of finance now consists of a variety of institutions whose exact roles are undergoing puzzling changes due to the competition to offer and market new "financial products." But for the United States, it will be well to bear in mind the distinction between commercial and investment banks. By and large, there was no legal distinction thus limiting the types of business in which a licensed bank could engage until the 1935 Glass-Steagle Act. During the Depression, when many "widows and orphans"—and professional investors as well—lost money because of unwise placements of funds by commercial banks, it was decided that there was too great a danger of "self-dealing" if the same institution could offer securities to the public, and then buy those same securities for its own account or for its customers. Firms such as J. P. Morgan & Company were then required to spin off their investment banking activities; as I recall it, Mr. Junius Morgan stayed with "the bank," now known as Morgan Guaranty Trust Company of New York, while Mr. Henry S. ("Harry") Morgan headed up the new investment house, Morgan Stanley & Company.

Since the days when I would more or less regularly dine on Wall Street, the largest brokerage house in the land, Merrill Lynch, Pierce, Fenner, and Smith, has entered the arena of investment banking and has become a "top house," not at all astonishing in view of its financial capabilities and its control of the world's largest network of brokerage offices: The job of the investment banker is, after all, one of "packaging" deals for sale to institutions and the public, and the ability to "market" an issue swiftly and expertly gives an important edge to a firm with its own "outlets."

Even the World Bank—more stodgily titled the International Bank for Reconstruction and Development—has its own subsidiary for joining with private investment banks in offering finance for Third World development projects. My brother Alfred ran the Paris headquarters of the bank's International Finance Corporation (IFC) for several years; I obtained a firsthand impression of IFC's standing when I routinely invited my brother to speak with any Sloan School students interested in contacting him and found that the room I had reserved was much too small: We had to carry in at least fifteen extra seats from across the hall to accommodate the clusters of students, mostly from the developing countries, who arrived with long yellow pads in order to take notes on any opportunities they might learn about for obtaining money, through the World Bank or its affiliates, to accelerate the normal pace of development in their homelands.

The distinction between commercial and investment banking is not, however, absolute: An exception known as the Edge Act, passed during World War I, allows American commercial banks to establish investment banking subsidiaries abroad. As Gilbert and Sullivan pithily expressed it in *H.M.S. Pinafore,* "Things are seldom what they seem." And to an American abroad, it is important not to be taken in by seemingly unambiguous phrases, such as the Bank of England or the French National Railways! The Bank of England, I learned, is governed by a board representing the leading "private" banks in the land. Once, when visiting the governor at his impressive office on Threadneedle Street, I was delighted to find in the seat of honor and power a distinguished banker whom I had known in the City—and who has served also as an ambassador to the United States! While this close interlinking of public and private duties goes contrary to traditional American preoccupations with "conflict of interest," perhaps the British tradition of mutual trust has something to recommend it, after all, especially in a period when it is important to harmonize public and private policy.

Although France is, from time to time and depending on elections, an aberrantly "socialist" country, the "nationalization" process has frequently been less drastic than outsiders have been led to believe. When the railways were "nationalized," for instance, a bloc of shares was reserved for the old Chemins de Fer du Nord, the Rothschild family's nineteenth-century company, which developed railway service to Deauville. Although the investment bank of the Rothschild family has, in turn, been nationalized by the government of President Mitterrand, it is interesting to observe the number of "capitalists" who have come out in support of France's new socialist experiment. Whether socialist or capitalist, France continues to be governed by the former students—the *anciens élèves*—of the *Grandes Ecoles: Plus ça change, plus c'est la même chose!*

Even the word "engineer" is only a first approximation, if one is operating in a different cultural and educational environment. In the United Kingdom, when my friends and I first bobbed up in 1957, there was a rather rigid "class distinction" between consulting engineers, who seemed to "rule the roost," and contractors. Of course, many contractors were far wealthier than the consultants; nonetheless, owners tended to rely on consulting engineers to oversee and inspect work, and to review contractors' proposals with a jaundiced and remote eye. The leading consulting engineers appeared to decide which of their colleagues had the right to carry on professional activities in the coveted U.K. market, and which firms had to "earn their spurs" by working abroad. I was much interested therefore to learn that a recent government-sponsored study of construction delays in industrial projects, ordered by former Environment Secretary Michael Heseltine, castigates the old practice of awarding separate contracts for design and construction.

In the United States, major contractors often have subsidiary consulting organizations; Morrison Knudsen Company of Boise, Idaho, had a highly regarded consulting arm, International Engineering Company, a California firm whose president, when I worked with the firm, was the late Charles Dunn, who had probably managed more major tunneling jobs than anyone on earth. Mr. Dunn's reputation was international; he was a short man, always impeccably turned out, and I was present on several occasions when his views, expressed tersely and not without humor, would instantly subdue a quarrelsome group of important engineers who however lacked his experience and powers of analysis and summation. In retrospect, it is amazing that no school of engineering honored itself by offering Mr. Dunn an "honorary degree." It was Mr. Dunn's advice that made international agreement rapidly possible on the detailed program for core borings in the English Channel; and he was flanked and fully supported by the distinguished French and British senior engineering advisers, Monsieur Malcor and Mr. Harding, and their associates and staffs.

There are so many legal, diplomatic, and technical steps in the approval of a major modern engineering project, particularly where there is an international dimension, that even the very highest levels of government can be confused or "caught up" in the process. At one point, when the Channel Tunnel Treaty seemed to have been "agreed on," there was a congratulatory exchange of messages between the president of the French Republic (General Charles de Gaulle) and Her Majesty the Queen (Elizabeth II) of the United Kingdom. *The Sunday*

Times (London) reported on February 9, 1964, the text of a telegram from the general: ". . . the French are deeply aware of the historical importance of the decision to build a channel tunnel . . ." and the queen's gracious reply: "I am sure that the carrying out of this important project will have happy long-term results for the people of our two countries . . ." The "sticking point" at the present moment is the British government's reluctance to provide a "guarantee" for the bonds to be sold to the public; the Common Market officials seem to be ready to help with such a guarantee, but the negotiation of these arrangements could be quite time-consuming.

It is a truism that guarantees are most readily provided when they are demonstrably unnecessary. The Port Authority of New York, which had difficulty in financing its first projects in the 1920's, developed such a fine reputation for care in estimating costs and revenues and for efficiency in the supervision of construction, that its bonds were eventually very salable despite the absence of a guarantee by the states (New Jersey and New York) that constituted the Port Authority in the first place. Inasmuch as politicians who are asked to approve "full faith and credit" guarantees realize that the political costs are apt to be severe if the guarantees are in fact called upon, every care in negotiation must be taken to see that the risks are allocated in such a manner that it is highly unlikely that the guarantee will be called upon. All these matters can seem rather dull, but they are nevertheless absolutely central to the willingness of essential parties in large ventures to proceed from the stage of studies and forecasts to the quite different terrain of commitment and construction. This is why the better schools of business management emphasize seminars, texts, and casebooks dealing with "security devices."

The world has entered an era where its engineering abilities far outstrip its traditional experience in analysis and organization. As public policy adjusts to the new situation, governments will increasingly look for advice to the small group of investment bankers and financiers who are accustomed to structuring the very largest projects. Everywhere government budgets are under severe pressures from military, educational, and social improvement programs. Even Soviet Russia is now looking abroad for help in developing the huge resources of Siberia. As a concomitant to a disarmament agreement that the United States feels is truly in its interest and in the interest of its NATO allies, it seems likely that both the United States and the Soviet Union will wish to explore genuine opportunities for mutually useful investments. If peace becomes an operationally feasible alternative to the arms race, the phased, deliberate delineation of cooperative major engineering undertakings may become an attractive method of reemploying resources hitherto dedicated to the expectation of war.

In any event, it is not too soon to endorse international assessment of such portentous suggestions as the GIF proposal for a major hydroelectric dam across the Bering Straits. Northwest Siberia, Northern Japan, Alaska, and Canada are all likely to be affected by any climatological effects of such a venture. Maitra has suggested that "the straits might be seen as a great laboratory for experimental mapping of the physics of the earth's climate."

That the capital markets of the free world retain their resiliency was demonstrated, not so many years ago, when Imperial Chemical Industries (ICI) found that an issue it offered for sale on the London exchange was oversubscribed, on a single day, about forty times: If each prospective purchaser had been allowed to buy the number of shares bid, some ten billion dollars of ICI shares would have had to have been offered. While many of the prospective purchasers in this case knew that the issue would be oversubscribed, the example is pertinent as a demonstration of the technical strength of the London market. And Wall Street has at least an equal capacity for raising large sums of money.

In the United States, the states themselves have had a big stake in delineating innovative methods for financing what are essentially public works, through the instrumentality of private investment. Thus, state legislatures, individually or on occasion in concert with other states, have authorized a series of public authorities to borrow money from the private capital markets. A problem may arise when the managements of public authorities, having established a good credit record, stretch their mandate to its outermost limits and compete with legitimate private business for access to the capital markets. An example of this aberration is thought by some observers to have occurred when the Port Authority of New York raised hundreds of millions of dollars for the World Trade Center in downtown Manhattan. For many years, the two giant towers comprising the center obviously reduced substantially the opportunities of the real-estate industry to attract tenants to privately financed office buildings.

Municipal corporations, with their ability to issue tax-exempt bonds because they are, from a legal point of view, elements of the state and therefore under the Constitution exempt from federal taxation, have used this special position as a device to attract investors for whom the tax-exemption feature is specially advantageous. For instance, the state of Mississippi established a municipal corporation, several years ago, to build a large shipyard (at Pascagoula) for Lytton Industries. Lytton Industries was thereby enabled to obtain a large contract for the construction of vessels for the United States Navy. And it should be noted that, as an exception to the prohibition against investment-banking activities by commercial banks, such U.S. banks are specifically empowered to underwrite securities of municipal corporations. Thus, a macro-engineering promoter may after all find it useful to call on a leading *commercial* bank either to develop a project attractive for municipal finance or because the bank's "Edge Act company" may be able to help abroad.

Even in England, where the legal line between investment (or, as they say, merchant) banks and commercial banks is not at all so clear, there is nonetheless a distinction in fact: The large banks of deposit, such as Barclays, Martins, and Lloyds, do not customarily undertake the promotional role familiar to the great merchant banking houses. Although the merchant banks in England can accept deposits from their clients, the merchant banks themselves do not have the aggregations of capital available to the commercial banks with their thousands of branches. To this day, there is something very personal about the London merchant bank; the partners will on occasion risk their own funds in new ventures, thus playing a role akin to that performed by venture capital companies in the United States. Most major London houses have strong links with investment or commercial banks in the United States; with Britain's ambivalent but increasing integration into the Common Market, London will no doubt be more and more useful as a financial center for operations throughout Europe.

If the Suez Canal were proposed today, could it be financed privately? One must doubt that it could, unless solid undertakings were made by sovereign governments. Venture capital has been invested in "public utilities," but usually under conditions that are thought to offer a rate of return that, if not "insured," is virtually "assured." In the United States, the most sought-after security is a guarantee backed by "the full faith and credit of the United States." The World Bank also has a statutory authority to guarantee investments, but thus far has been reluctant to make use of this little-noticed standby power. The most exacting task facing the macro-engineer as promoter is to reduce the risks of investment by obtaining binding commitments having the effect of fixing both costs and minimum revenues. With respect to costs, it is sometimes possible to obtain from reputable contractors a promise to complete a job on a fixed time schedule and at a definite price. In such cases, there can be rewards for early completion and for economies that reduce costs below the estimates. Frequently, there are penalty clauses so that overruns in time or money are effectively discouraged.

Large construction firms vary enormously in the reliability of their estimating departments. Some firms seem to hit the nail on the head year after year. Other firms have a record of intermittent overestimates of the cost of projects. I seem to recall that the Mont Blanc Tunnel cost roughly twice as much as the early estimates contemplated.

In the building of the early American railroads, big profits were often made by farsighted contractors. Even today, by far the major costs of railway construction are in the building and equipping of the roadbed, not in the rolling stock. Thus, if we are to succeed in building a new generation of up-to-date railtype systems, whether emphasizing the flexibility of a pallet on a guideway or the high-speed potential of an evacuated tube, a creative role will have to be played by experienced construction firms so that costs can be measured in advance with sufficient accuracy to command the confidence of investing institutions.

Assuming that costs can be controlled by an astute selection of construction firms and by careful drafting of contracts, is there any way to assure adequate revenues, in the absence of a government guarantee? The pipeline industry has developed the ingenious device of a "throughput" agreement, which in effect promises the investors that a certain volume of traffic, paid for on a stipulated basis, will be available during the entire time the investment is at risk. In similar fashion, ships are often chartered before they are built; the "charter party," signed by reputable, credit-worthy individuals or institutions, can be brought to a bank as a basis for borrowing money to build the ship. Similarly, large office buildings are often financed in advance of construction by leasing a substantial number of floors to reputable tenants. The lease agreement then forms the basis of a "sale and lease back" underwritten by insurance companies or other sophisticated institutional investors.

The insurance industry has experimented with "use and occupancy insurance" as a means of guaranteeing the investor that revenues will indeed be sufficient to cover amortization and interest charges on a large project: Such a clause facilitated the financing of the Chesapeake Bay Bridge-Tunnel project; and, despite their obvious difficulties, the creative imagination evident in such clauses is a prime requisite if worthwhile plans are to become brick and mortar.

If macrofinance is a necessary corollary of macroengineering, it is equally true that experienced lawyers have a most vital role to play: George Ball, Lloyd Cutler, Robert Bridges (in San Francisco), and Colin McFadyean (in London) have made essential contributions to many major engineering ventures. The institutional aspects of engineering are beginning to attract systematic attention, especially as new ventures in the oceans and outer space pose new legal and political problems. The lawyer has a legitimate and necessary function as "institutional engineer"; that Napoleon III's great prefect, Georges Haussmann, was a lawyer need not be pooh-poohed or downrated: The legal profession is one of the world's great professions, and engineers make a fundamental error if they feel its experience, as exemplified by its leading practitioners, can be sidestepped. On the contrary, engineers' education must be upgraded by at least elementary training in constitutional and administrative law so that they will be capable of interacting maturely with experienced lawyers.

We have indicated that macro-engineering projects of the future will be increasingly financed and sponsored on an intersectoral basis; that is, private and governmental investment will share the risks and rewards of many large projects. In the United States, with its strong antitrust tradition, we are only beginning to form public corporations such as COMSAT and AMTRAK, which are deliberately contrived to provide a role for private participation and finance: There are residual suspicions that make it difficult for government and industry to cooperate fully and on a basis of mutual confidence and respect. However, it is precisely the absence of habits and methods of fruitful cooperation that has placed the international trading position of the United States in apparent jeopardy. While we have successfully exported management science (in an extreme case, the Bank of England quite recently changed its organization under the aegis of a consulting report prepared by McKinsey & Company), we must now *import* a bit of management technology if we are to face up successfully to "*le défi Européen*," to say nothing of "*le défi Japonais*."

This will be something of an uphill battle: With the success of the European Business School established at Fontainebleau under the wise guidance of General Georges F. Doriot (a former professor at the Harvard Business School) and with the NATO Science Committee seriously urging other continents to combine resources to establish "M.I.T.'s" abroad, it comes as a surprise to Americans to learn that, for many of our most important decisions, we do not have appropriate methods or machinery. In Europe, there is a large admixture of government in industry, especially since the wave of nationalizations promulgated and enacted under President Mitterrand in France. We have cited "Le Plan" as a successful example of intersectoral consultation in the formation of national objectives for specific industries and regions; indeed, the brilliant futurism piloted by Jacques Monod and his enthusiastic young team at Le Plan has permeated the thinking of leaders of both government and industry. In Japan, established procedures of consultation have long made it possible to develop effective agreements on national programs of industrial development.

Heretofore, the accent has been mainly on civil engineering projects. The moment we move into the more volatile field of mechanical engineering, a further complication is introduced into the development process. Broadly speaking, one can move directly from the drawing board to the construction of a road, tunnel, dam, bridge, or even a skyscraper of conventional design. But with novel systems for elevators, trains, airplanes, and rockets, it is necessary to build, test, and improve a prototype. Many excellent designs of valuable new systems lie rotting in the files of corporations, government agencies, and research institutes for the sole reason that no one was found—or sought—to move from the stage of design and patenting to the decisive stage of construction, testing, and commercialization.

Hardy indeed is the entrepreneur who will stake his all on his own design. Of course, Howard Hughes staked a great deal on his hunch that he had correctly designed a gigantic seaplane early in World War II, and it did indeed fly—several feet above the ocean. In some cases, it is possible to simulate the functioning of a larger system through the use of scaled-down models; it is now common practice, for instance, to build three-dimensional models of new refineries as a step beyond the (two-dimensional) blueprints.

Differing institutional approaches to the problem of prototype finance may be illustrated by the case of the air-cushion train (or *aérotrain*). Monsieur Bertin, founder of the distinguished engineering firm that bears his name, was among the first engineers to realize that the British invention of the Hovercraft might find its most important application as a land-based guideway system. To demonstrate the point, he proposed building a three-mile test track near Paris on which he would place a prototype with air cushions instead of wheels for support and with the forward motion supplied by an airplane engine bolted on the top of the vehicle. In a matter of months, an intersectoral consortium was formed. It included the French National Railways (the famous SNCF), the Paris Airport Authority, Rothschild Frères, the Schneider-Creusot company, and more than a half-dozen other leading public and private institutions. This powerful combination succeeded not only in underwriting a test track, but in obtaining a commitment of funds from the French government for the construction of a demonstration line.

The more socialistic British (even under a Conservative government!) proceeded differently: The National Research and Development Corporation (an arm of Her Majesty's Government) established a subsidiary, Tracked Hovercraft, Ltd., brilliantly managed by the late Dennis Hennessey. Taking advantage of the pioneer work on linear electric-induction motors accomplished by Professor Braithwaite of Manchester University, Hennessey and his remarkable chief engineer, Tom Fellows, constructed a one-mile prototype track near Cambridge (some might call it "the other Cambridge," that is, the English Cambridge). Extrapolations from the first trial runs of the test engine indicated that a smoothly running air-cushion vehicle could be developed for normal operating speeds of up to three hundred miles per hour. I was privileged to watch one of these early test runs: There is no doubt that it was a brilliant achievement.

The United States appeared to adopt a third method of funding this development. Through the Department of Transportation, the device of a *subcontract* was used to have a prototype track and test vehicles built for later evaluation. Although subcontracting has proved reasonably efficacious in the military and aerospace fields, it has not always proven satisfactory in improving civilian technologies. In fact, all three initiatives described above have been shelved—French, British, and American—and innovation in wheelless transport has been left, willy-nilly, to the Japanese. And the Germans too have built a full-scale prototype.

What is needed, in this whole area of macrofinance and implementation, is a spirit of entrepreneurship that combines sensitive awareness of all relevant factors with an almost romantic desire to see a correctly appraised project succeed. Isambard Kingdom Brunel confided to his diary just before the Thames Tunnel works were prematurely closed down in the wake of a fatal accident: "Tunnel is now, I think, *dead*. The Commissioners have refused on the ground of want of security. This is the first time I have felt able to cry at least for these ten years . . . However *nil desperandum* has always been my motto—we may succeed yet."

With respect to the plight of America's basic industry, I am in agreement with the general viewpoint expressed by Robert B. Reich in his very useful book *The Next American Frontier*. Professor Reich—of the Kennedy School of Government at Harvard—reminds us that "the American industrial system that reached its full flower in the postwar era was organized around the principles of high volume and standardization," whereas the new frontier that beckons us is "flexible-system production . . . characterized by technological innovation, precision manufacturing, and customization of products."

I would add just a few points to the above analysis, which Dr. Reich has developed in convincing detail. First of all, even the most flexible system of production needs basic supplies of water, electricity, raw materials, and people: in other words, an efficient national or continental infrastructure. Second, if we are to stimulate the desired kind of dynamic entrepreneurship and participation by "all ranks" in the production process, we shall need to provide focal points for effort, enthusiasm, and investment. By opting for a limited number of major technological programs that combine high technology with the American knack for large-scale organization, we may provide incentives, rewards, and a *raison d'être* for producers of specialty steels, vehicles tailored to exacting scientific standards, and a work force that is "on its toes" because it will know that this country has again surged ahead—perhaps a generation ahead of its competition—by translating the best of modern technological capabilities into the steel, concrete, and motive power of systems that will merit the admiration of the world.

To implement this objective, it is not necessary to turn the whole country into a test-bed for innovations that are unproved. But where mechanical engineering, for instance, requires that prototypes be built and tested, we shall have to find the means, the steadiness, and the initiative to put together the required study groups and laboratories. I find it very admirable that the Japanese have been able to complete their Seikan Tunnel after eleven years of what must often have been disheartening effort; of course, they must still build the landward approaches and install the trains that will make it operational, but Americans ought to know that this venture, which has met with serious opposition from time to time in Japan, cannot be justified by our usual criteria of cost accounting; but a nation that plans to stay in business for a long time cannot afford to be without appropriate infrastructure. One must look at the patient, methodical development of the magnetically levitated supertrain with the same *optique:* Where the three leading powers of the West lost patience and failed to develop the internal teamwork of which the project was worthy, the Japanese have gone forward bravely and brilliantly. The correct American response is to acknowledge insufficiency where it has existed, to regroup for a better infrastructural and industrial effort, and to move forward in a manner that will preserve the openness of international markets.

I think the Congress of the United States, well advised by the best minds in the country, can assist whatever administration may be in office during the coming crucial decade by setting up and funding a group of public corporations chartered to carry out specific mandates in fields vital to the safety and prosperity of the Republic. In such an endeavor, the legislative and executive branches can count on support and encouragement from the vast and variegated "third sector": the not-for-profit part, if you will, of American private enterprise. Our universities, independent research institutes and laboratories, professional associations, and privately endowed libraries are among the types of institution that can provide knowledgeable assistance in the formulation and facilitation of high policy. The public corporation or "authority" framework can be tailored to the needs of particular programs and can provide for private as well as public finance and participation.

The independence conferred by corporate status seems to me preferable to the encouragement of short-term seesaw policies that would result from treatment under the departmental or agency approach adopted, for instance, for our on-again, off-again program on synthetic fuels. We do not need more government programs to please either the gloomy or the cheerful batch of fashionable forecasters: If the Republic is to stay in business, we know in advance that there will be good times and bad times, and what the public desires is a series of programs that make sense in the long run (even if we do stockpile oil during a temporary glut!).

One of the fears underlying the nation's present hesitations is a fear of the success that this book attempts to outline: We do not wish—nor should we—to give up social and environmental gains in pursuit of a myth of industrial or technological plenty. What is not adequately understood is that without prosperity we shall be unable to afford the very social and environmental benefits that latter-day Luddites seek to defend. In the Route 128 area outside Boston with which I am familiar, I can report from personal observation that the success of the local "high tech" industries has brought about a substantial increase of support for environmental groups, an increase in country dancing, sailing, horseback riding, and backpacking, and a surprising resurgence in educational and social concern. We cannot have it both ways: Either we are afraid to succeed, or we fear an effort that might fail. In my view, fear of success is as much a problem for the American future as fear of failure.

Although the history and forecasting of "value changes" could be regarded as one of the quagmires in social research, this is an area germane to our topic and it is best that we air it, despite the difficulties and embarrassments involved. In the 1960's, a wave of disenchantment with traditional habits and institutions swept over an entire generation. The "hippies" and their drug culture were but the most extreme form of a movement that, often inarticulately, represented a search for greater emphasis on personal development and a more caring and sensitive approach to social and environmental affairs. In the general confusion, the value of work—all work—was "downgraded," and play became such a disproportionately important part of consciousness that it ceased to be pleasurable: It led directly not only to excesses of drugs, alcohol, and other forms of personal indulgence, but also to disarray in the schools and universities, and not infrequently a breakdown in the self-confidence of the older generation, which succumbed to feelings of guilt and inadequacy.

This is, has been, and will remain an imperfect world. But a society that cannot work, we now know, will not savor its leisure; and without study and deliberate change and improvement, work itself will remain sterile and self-defeating. There is no escape from the old Greek preference for balance, equilibrium, and reason. The United States has paid the penalty for years of stagnation and neglect: It is time to move forward; and providing millions of young people with the opportunity for outdoor, healthy work that is technically correct both in design and supervision and that has for its goal immediate as well as long-term environmental enhancement is not a step backward, it is a step forward. If we are to sustain our position in "high tech," we need to balance this new thrust into the future with a selective reinforcement of "low tech" skills as well. Not everyone can aspire to a career in higher mathematics or computer science. Even computer scientists must wear shoes, brush their teeth, and drive to work. If we deprive the essential "low tech" occupations of all honor and reward, the much-advertised "service society" of the present and future will turn into a nightmare. Even in France, the famed *Ecoles Ménagères,* which teach household arts, and the *Ecole Boulle,* which, named after a seventeenth-century sculptor, instructs young people in the finest traditions of cabinet making, seem to be "bucking the current" set in motion by fascination with "high tech." All the more honor to the promoters and founders of the school for cooking founded several years ago in Hyde Park, New York, and which finds its graduates in the fortunate posture of entering a "seller's market"!

The late Alan Chadwick sensed the "new wind" when he opened, without benefit of endowment or diplomas, an informal course for intensive horticulture on eight acres near a small mountain sacred to local Indians, in Round Valley (Covelo), California. I was privileged to stay at Round Valley for a few days and to observe the complete dedication with which the young men and women attracted by Chadwick's teaching responded to his strictures: "You may think that you are making the garden," he said, "but the reality is that the garden is making you." And the "graduates," after one year of unremitting, dawn-to-dusk labor, were swamped with job offers from corporations, municipalities, estate owners, and federal agencies that needed reliable and trained people to tend lawns and gardens.

In fact, a small garden involves a great deal of "tech," and whether it is "high tech" or "low tech" I must leave to future historians. What is already clear is that the passion for work and for visible physical accomplishment is a tremendous step in the right direction. It should not take nearly as great a "psychological leap forward" for Americans to overcome the traditional, if unexpressed, feeling that engineering is a "low class" occupation, and that management is somehow "above" the nitty-gritty that seems to be an inescapable part of technology, high or low. Even the Finniston Report, Great Britain's monumental survey of the engineering profession to which I referred in an earlier chapter, speaks of better "employment" of engineers by managers. The idea that the managers themselves ought to have training in engineering as the basis of their own education has not yet been put forward with conviction in the Anglo-Saxon world.

Some of my good friends have been presidents of liberal arts colleges. I regret to say that they have not, to my knowledge, liberalized the old notion of a liberal education: Science and engineering are still regarded as "beyond the pale," even if they do take us to the moon and the planets and beyond! This deliberate refusal to look squarely at the preparation that future lawyers, bankers, and statesmen will need if they are to understand their world and serve usefully as leaders cannot inure to the benefit of the Republic. One small beginning might be to introduce basic courses in system dynamics, to provide a "language bridge" between the social and the physical sciences. Another idea would be to merge or "twin" a liberal arts college with an institute of technology.

Our leading technology institutes have been more flexible— some people think *too* flexible—in introducing liberal arts subjects into curricula specially tailored for future engineers and scientists. Even without the structural changes suggested in these chapters, technologists will discover, as Kenneth Olsen did when he started Digital Equipment Corporation, that they are being pushed by circumstances into positions of management and authority. And a leader in industrial and community affairs *must* have an overview of more than technical matters: If engineers are to be our managers, then they must be steeped in history, sociology, law, and the other subjects that hitherto had been targeted at the "gentlemanly" professions!

In 1980, the deans of the School of Government and the Graduate School of Business Administration at Harvard University jointly wrote a foreword to an unexceptionable book, *Business and Public Policy,*[1] which pleaded for a more constructive and cooperative relationship between government and business. John T. Dunlop, the editor, began his own chapter by pointing out that "the last decade has seen a vast expansion in the scope and detail of government regulation of business decisions, beyond those of the New Deal era." In a chapter entitled "Educational Challenges in Teaching Business-Government Relations," the Business School's Hugo Uyterhoeven reasonably asked, "In the decade ahead, will business and government be able to work together in formulating cohesive strategies for some of the country's major industries? . . . can the country afford to let its steel industry slowly slide downhill . . . ?"

The two deans had insisted, in their foreword, that "the present adversary relationship between business and government does not serve society's interest." George P. Shultz, in his highly readable chapter "The Abrasive Interface," illustrated this point with a bit of recent history concerning Sohio's attempt to move oil inland by pipeline from the West Coast: "Sohio began in January 1975 the process of securing necessary permits and governmental approvals: a total of approximately 700 permits were required from about 140 local, state, federal, or private agencies. On March 13, 1979, fifty months later, the decision was reached to abandon the project. In the interim, Sohio had spent $50 million and managed to secure only 250 of the 700 permits. . . . What's left is government regulating a pipeline that doesn't exist."

The two deans are, of course, right in their castigation of the lack of cooperation between government and industry. But part of the problem lies, alas, within the structure of the university, which, with the most benevolent of intentions and owing to a series of endowments and understandings that grew up over a long period of time, fostered *two separate schools of government and business*! Despite professions of mutual esteem—genuinely intended—the very structure of many of our oldest and finest universities encourages the formation of competing elites, one destined for "public service" and the other for "private enterprise." Yale's School of Organization and Management, a recent accretion to the institutional galaxy, has avoided the government-business dichotomy by using the overarching term "management"; but this leaves out what I think is an essential dimension in management, the professional acquaintance with engineering and a modicum of science! I think, therefore, that Alfred P. Sloan was profoundly right when he situated the Sloan School of Management within a technological institution; but all schools that prepare future managers must now enlarge their horizons so that a generation facing the unprecedentedly expanded potentials of engineering feasibility will be capable of making the decisions, and implementing them, that can once more restore a sense of unity and purpose to national affairs.

It is no aspersion on the excellent and dedicated staffs of existing management schools to point out that their underlying terms of reference may be "part of the problem." Were the country not facing issues that require rapid response and realignment, the plethora of institutions of learning linked inevitably with narrowly sectoral career paths would hardly constitute a serious impediment. But "ethos" *is* important, and we should be careful that we do not separate our young people into structured groups, which will then be propelled forward by their own inner dynamic, linked to government *or* industry, or to a management philosophy that either has too little connection with the essential technological base of all economic activity or too exclusive a dependence on computer models and an exaggerated faith in the omniscience of systems analysis. I suspect that mature managements of the leading management schools are well aware of these semantic and institutional dilemmas; but "mergers" among academic institutions, although not unknown, are harder to bring about than mergers in business; and to start a school that would have, for the diversified American polity, the standing of the Zürich Polytechnikum in Switzerland seems, at the moment, beyond our grasp.

Individuals may, however, succeed where institutions have failed. Ignace Paderewski, perhaps the greatest pianist of his age, became not only prime minister of Poland but a world-renowned statesman. Thomas Jefferson, as Dumas Malone has properly reminded us in his stunning series of books, was a competent lawyer, agricultural manager, violinist, architect, and statesman. Young people have the option of concentrating in one field—for instance, engineering—in college, and in another—for instance, law or business management—in graduate school. We may become "polytechnic" to an extent without attending what is officially designated as an "*école polytechnique.*" But at some point, I believe the United States will wish to have a national academy to which entry is available only through merit as established by rigorous competitive examinations; such an academy will not replace existing institutions, but it will serve as a standard against which their achievement will be measured.

What we are confronted with in American education is a situation of entropy aggravated by affluence and the politics of "local control." While there is no disposition to displace the states from their constitutional responsibility for education within their respective borders, there is much that the federal government can and should do to encourage higher standards. Assistance to locally endorsed "voucher" plans, so that parents can choose either public or private schools for their children, is one possibility often discussed; another idea would be further encouragement of specialized regional high schools for science and technology, jointly funded by federal and state agencies and by private foundations and individuals. Perhaps a Central Academy for Engineering and Management might be inaugurated, with federal and private support, as a postgraduate school for the training of those engineer-managers destined for leading responsibilities in government and in private industry alike. I remember, on one occasion when my father allowed me to accompany him on a visit to President Roosevelt in the White House, that the President—in short sleeves and very cheerful—expressed the hope that the Vanderbilt estate (near his own Hyde Park property) might be acquired some day by the federal government and transformed into a staff college for the Civilian Conservation Corps and for the improved training of natural resource planners.

Macro-engineering can assist those who think of themselves as environmentalists by adding technical innovation and authenticity to programs that could otherwise wilt for want of practicality. I was delighted to read, very recently, of a program publicized in California by Christopher Swan for a "Suntrain," a solar-powered passenger railway suggested for the "Eighty Corridor" route from San Francisco to Reno. The concept of powering the engines by hydrogen manufactured with the help of solar power at stations along the route strikes me as worth looking into. When I was in Osaka less than two years ago, Mr. Iwatani explained to me that he had learned how to handle hydrogen during World War I, when of course Japan was an ally of the United States; now Mr. Iwatani sells hydrogen even in the United States! And his great company, which participated in the experimental "hydrogen automobile" in Japan, would doubtless be ready to discuss cooperation with Mr. Swan's group in California. What is encouraging about the varied teams interested in the "Suntrain" idea is that they are ready to *do* something, not just to criticize and oppose existing methods which, we all know, will somehow be superseded.

Rail service to Reno—whether solar-powered or otherwise—may not appear to carry within it the seeds of a national renaissance; but we would be bypassing established facts if we did not acknowledge the new and growing impact of tourism as an element of the American economy. New York's principal income, I once learned from that city's commissioner of cultural affairs, derives from visitors to the city who spend their dollars not only on hotels and restaurants but also on museums, concerts, and theater, as well as the attractive shops and boutiques of the metropolis. The technical ability to conduct all our work (or almost all) from an isolated home equipped with the latest in automated office equipment—from computers to word processors—will not compensate for humankind's inveterate penchant for gregariousness. City and country are warp and woof of human existence: They reinforce each other, and even—or especially—our rapidly urbanizing world will wish technology's help in keeping the countryside as pristine as possible—and within easy reach!

If I am right in my judgment that we are on the verge not only of a resurgence of rail-type passenger transportation, but of very high-speed commuting, then real-estate values in the United States, Canada, and Mexico—as elsewhere on the planet—will be dramatically transformed. Even at the 300 mph speeds already proven by Mr. Kyotani and his staff in Myazaki, London will be one short hour from Paris; and it will be perfectly possible to commute for work from Tunbridge, Vermont, to Boston, or from Santa Cruz to Los Angeles. Peter White, one of my gifted classmates, has long commuted on the Long Island Railroad from his home near Smithtown on the three-hour run to Manhattan. With modern equipment, the trip will be easily accomplished in half an hour or so, and I think that as word spreads that there is indeed a much "better mousetrap," the world's commuters will insist on up-to-date transportation from home to office. Mr. Swan's "Suntrain" may charm the tourists who wish a slow ride to Reno; I think that state-of-the-art "high tech" has a better chance of attracting the dollars of harassed commuters to and from our leading metropolitan areas. I have always regarded Peter White as one of the heroes of our epoch: six hours of commuting per day! That he and his splendid wife have succeeded in raising a family of more than a dozen children, and with good humor and wise judgment, seems to me one of the great unreported success stories of my generation.

C. Northcote Parkinson has long observed that "a Civil Service expands by an inexorable rule of growth, irrespective of the work (if any) which has to be done . . . 1914 represented the culmination of an arms race, when 4,366 officials could administer what was then the largest navy in the world, 1967 represents the point at which we have become practically powerless, by which period over 33,000 civil servants are barely sufficient to administer the navy we no longer possess."[2] Parkinson's severe if humorously stated criticism of British public administration might, I suppose, be transposed with very little amendment to the situation of most industrialized or "developed" nations, whether of West or East. In good times and bad, the real-estate boom in and around Washington, D.C., seems curiously even: When the business cycle is down, Washington, D.C., may still count on the accretion of government agencies in an ever-optimistic nation that still expects the government to tackle, even if it cannot solve, our most pressing problems.

Bruner, Goodnow, and Austin, in *A Study of Thinking*,[3] devote a chapter to "The Process of Concept Attainment." They begin with the somewhat startling assertion, "It is curiously difficult to re-capture preconceptual innocence." I imagine they are referring to something like our American penchant for organizing new government departments whenever a new crisis or problem is perceived: Having provided the nation with a new Department of Education, I suppose President Carter not only satisfied a large constituency but led many disinterested citizens to feel that now "something was being done." If institutions were indeed purposive, logically organized "systems," then the reformer could feel that, having made his or her point, the matter could then be dropped or put aside. I confess to mild astonishment when I finally perceived that the United States Department of Transportation was not, in sober fact, doing anything fundamental to improve prospects for ground transportation in the United States. But reducing regulatory intervention and letting private industry "take up the slack" is only a half-answer: If government controls engineers, rights-of-way, powers of approval or refusal, and (lest we forget) money, then government must participate in what is planned, or, for want of government as a partner, large affairs will tend to lapse. Even the most "anti-interventionist" government is a government nonetheless, and the immobilization of one of the great machines for progress and improvement is hardly a prospect "devoutly to be wished."

But those of us who do not have to deal with the mountains of paper work inflicted every working day on the heads of all government departments—state, federal, or municipal—should have a degree of compassion and understanding for the travails of the modern bureaucrat. In a free and diverse society, initiatives *ought* to come from those of us who are still "out there" and not in Washington. When we bring "ideas" to those in high office, it will be charitable to have them thought through carefully, drafted up in simple but clear language, and endorsed by at least some of the persons whose opinions on the matter at issue are respected both inside and outside government. It is in this spirit that I expect government, private industry, and the "tertiary" sector to be invited to a series of workshops or seminars during the next two or three years, to explore such major national opportunities as trans-isthmian shipways, macro-engineering education, the outlines of a sustainable, expanded space program, and the beginnings of a modern transcontinental underground transport system for the United States.

This matter of government-industry collaboration really must cut both ways. With respect to the space program, I have the strong feeling that it is the *private* sector that must now be brought in, on realistic terms that will effectively multiply the resources available for a number of vital programs. With respect to underground transportation, it is the *government* that has been "spinning its wheels" and must now be brought in as a partner and cosponsor, with reputable private interests, to prove out new initiatives that are absolutely vital for the nation's security and prosperity.

I take it as very encouraging that Cordell Hull opened a special macro-engineering lecture series on April 29, 1983, held at M.I.T. under the joint auspices of the Sloan School of Management and the School of Engineering. This series, named in honor of Isambard Kingdom Brunel, will provide students from M.I.T. and its sister institutions in Cambridge, Massachusetts, with an opportunity to hear national macro-engineering issues discussed by people whose experience has been intimately intertwined with the definition and development of very large engineering schemes. We cannot wait for an "ideal" institutional matrix when grave issues face the Republic. Imperfect as institutions may be, the individuals whom they comprise can surmount parochial concerns; when a good case has been made, Americans are "second to none" in drawing up specific technical and organizational plans to improve the nation's quality of life and to restructure our physical environment not only for "the best of times" but, if need be, "for the worst of times."

Conceptualization may not "grab" the reader as a very exciting sort of activity, but it is absolutely indispensable if the public and the professions are to be prepared for the efforts that will be entailed in building tomorrow's large technological systems. But we must be wary. As Robert Sinai has put it in an *Encounter* article entitled "What Ails Us and Why" (April 1979), "At all times we see man's thoughts turned into acts and these transformed into their opposite; and his dreams when translated into deeds attain that which he least dreamed of." In other words, much human activity is, in Forrester's phrase, "counter-intuitive": Unless we study carefully the impacts of our acts, however well-intentioned they may be, the result can be not only unexpected but disturbing. But at a time for action, although feedback loops must be given due deference and all proper precautions must be taken, a society that is too filled with self-doubt will find that its wellsprings of vitality and action are, like Hamlet's, "sicklied o'er with the pale cast of thought." It is not a prescription for ultimate wisdom to sit on our hands, while other and more resilient societies build the infrastructures and the industries first blue-printed in our own laboratories. Or do we wish to travel down the road that will lead, in a decade, to a "Marshall Plan" in reverse, with bright young bureaucrats from Singapore and Göteborg buying up the best apartments in Washington and New York, so they may funnel resources into the ailing economy of a once-proud nation that, through carelessness, lost its leadership and its luster?

We are, to an extent, a jaded society. Unlike our Victorian ancestors, we are not greatly impressed by vast undertakings—even when they are dramatic and economically viable. A generation surfeited with vicarious trips to the moon legitimately seeks deeper meaning and greater fulfillment in the personal dimensions of life. In such a world, can there be sustained support for artificial islands at sea, for new guideway systems on land, even for the mining and development of lunar resources?

In fact, there is an excellent case for just such a point of view. And it can be put forward on grounds of environmental protection, the saving of scarce resources, and the enhancement of personal and cultural values.

In certain societies, there was a tradition and even a mystique surrounding public works. In ancient Rome, it was not unusual for wealthy citizens to build public baths or libraries, much as today's philanthropists endow research foundations or university chairs. Alexander the Great, as a conqueror with an articulated purpose of founding a new world-civilization, used public works—and new cities—as a deliberate method of establishing the multinational society that he envisaged. In France, there is still an ingrained enthusiasm for *les grands travaux*, reinforced by the high social position of the engineer.

Today it is necessary to remind public-spirited people that, when they acquire wealth or power, physical structures can add much to the quality of American life—and to the reputation of sponsors and patrons. It is a matter for wonderment that the largest city in the United States does not have a proper science and technology museum! Nor do our public plazas customarily have the adornment of water fountains and sculpture.

Of course, American philanthropy has done a great deal: the Frick Gallery, the Morgan Library, Carnegie Hall in New York; the Rothko Chapel in Houston; the various DuPont legacies in Delaware, all have delighted and instructed the public. What I am referring to, however, is a "reconceptualization effort": philanthropists, in and out of government, should now turn their attention to such possibilities as an interstate bikeway system, both to save lives and to promote a healthy outdoor activity and reduce dependence on muscle-stunting means of locomotion. Americans must make a conscious effort to be *less passive* physically, emotionally, and intellectually, lest the television screen and the movie theater become agents of demoralization and decadence.

Much is made of returning power to the states, but the states will be unable to reassert their "sovereign" role if governors, legislatures, and officials have no concepts in their heads that can attract conspicuous interest and support. Many governors have some form of *science* advisory body, but there should be much more activity in the field of conscious state leadership of *engineering* programs that might provide unique benefits for the various regions of our country. For instance, there is as yet no American research cluster or institute that has made a specialty of any of the following problems: tunnel technology; shipway design; levitated transport; steelmaking; intensive horticulture; solar power from space; asteroid mining; the design of rocket engines; the design and propagation of bikeways; the building of a prototype housing project or new town based on the pioneering United Nations work of Professor Peter Land; the design and testing of offshore artificial islands for energy supply, port development, or manufacturing.

There is no inherent reason why such projects (and the reader can make up alternative lists to suit personal convictions or tastes) must be promoted by or *with* the *federal* government. I have the impression, from my visits in the White House during a variety of administrations, both Democratic and Republican, that most people in "the corridors of power" are overworked, under intense pressure, and doing the best they can to bring some order into public business. I remember being amazed that Arthur Schlesinger, Jr., could be curious about the latest news of the channel tunnel project, when he was serving as an adviser to President Kennedy; I enjoyed my brief visits to Washington to brief Peter Flanigan in the Nixon White House, Douglass Cater during President Lyndon Johnson's tenure, and so on. With the best will in the world, there is only so much any human being can do. If "decentralization" is a worthwhile banner, then perhaps one of the first things to do is to bring more "bright ideas" to the "state houses," which are somewhat less subject than Washington, D.C., to importunation from innovating intellectuals and engineers. There is no reason that I can think of that would prevent a conscientious governor from convening a meeting of engineers, businessmen, and bankers to discuss the best means of "differentiating" the state's "engineering output": With suitable authorization, a state government could work directly with public and private universities and research institutions to establish joint study groups, programs, and laboratories in specialties whose improvement appears helpful to a state's economy and quality of life.

What I am suggesting is that habit and routine exercise a much greater dominion over us than we usually care to admit. Architects have been specifying traditional elevator systems for several generations, partly because they are tested and available and known to be reliable and reasonably economical, but partly also because of a lack of initiative and curiosity. Now we shall see such seminal ideas as Gabriel Bouladon's escalator-elevator combination surprising us in the megastructures of Japan and Europe! No wonder that the late Harold D. Lasswell proposed a "Museum of the Future," so that citizens could walk down alternative halls and see, in three-dimensional models, the systems that science and engineering could provide, depending on popular and official preferences. Nor must new ideas, to be serviceable, embody only "high tech" elements. The ancient institution of the Roman Baths, brought up-to-date by a bit of modern "physical medicine," may yet improve the social climate and the mental and physical health of urban populations. But how many of our architects and planners have, even inside their heads, a concept or picture of what tomorrow's city might be?

The United States as a society is characterized by literally thousands of voluntary associations that engage in activities to protect, enrich, and improve our social life. There is every reason to expect that some of this energy and enthusiasm, once the reasons are explained, can be attracted to the redesign and improvement of the *built environment*. This is *not* tantamount to a plea for large, dehumanizing projects. Quite the contrary. I know of no person who has had a more decisive impact on community life than Harold S. Williams, the soft-spoken rangy president of the Institute on Man and Science, who has rescued several *small towns* from obliteration and who has now set up shop, with the help of a young philanthropist, to help other attractive and delightful communities threatened with collapse because of forces they were unable, unaided, to control. Hal Williams made himself a nationwide reputation when he persuaded citizens of Stump Creek, Pennsylvania, when they were literally in the process of moving out, that if they cooperated with each other, the town could be restored and made viable. Discouragement had spread because the town's major employer, a coal mine, had shut down; and in Appalachia, this was very bad news indeed. But the trustees of the small Institute in Rensselaerville came to the rescue, and the families that decided to "stay on" actually built a whole new infrastructure of water supply and so on, making of Stump Creek an example to small towns everywhere.

'   From a conceptual viewpoint, there is not so much difference between *caring* for the future of a small community and *caring* about the future and safety and prosperity of that larger community that is the nation. It happens that for *some* (not *all*) of the new engineering possibilities that could spell convenience and economic opportunity in the future, a national or continental scale will be necessary. Within communities, we may very well choose to emphasize walking, bicycle riding, skating, and horseback riding. But for longer trips, greater speed will actually reinforce the values of family and community living: Business trips away from home that now mean long overnight absences will be accomplished in a matter of hours or less. And by *taking care* in advance, we can assure our existing towns and cities of a future supply of fresh water and other basic supplies. I shall never forget the "world turned upside down" feeling in my own family when one of our sons returned home unexpectedly, because the town where his college was located had suddenly run out of water, and the students were told to go home until the water crisis was over!

Much has been made of the "rapid deployment force" now under development at the Pentagon. Should there not be a civilian counterpart, perhaps with logistical support from the armed forces, so that when disaster strikes at any human community, Americans can respond more effectively and more promptly? I remember visiting, several years ago, a communications center established in Washington to expedite the flow of relief supplies to distant places in need of emergency aid because of fire, flood, earthquakes, or other sudden catastrophes. There is now a considerable literature on such disasters.[4] Perhaps a "readiness force" for peaceful temporary service abroad, on the model of the famous ship *Hope,* which has traveled the seven seas offering medical services, could help bring about that synergy of civilian and military effort that must be the hallmark of our society in times when macro-engineering has become a feature not just of peace, but of war as well.

No one can write a book at this moment on the future of technology without taking into account—if only by omission—the awesome possibility of nuclear warfare. Americans have shown by the overwhelming congressional support for rearmament that, at whatever cost, the nation's independence will be maintained and that commitments to our allies will be honored; at the same time, the American public, like the Russian public and like all members of the human race everywhere, will support rational efforts leading to verifiable mutual dismantling of atomic weapons and long-range delivery systems. Having said this much, and having lived through the relatively modest inferno of World War II in northwest Europe, I have to admit that the worst *does* sometimes occur, whether by design or by accident; and it happens that environmental, aesthetic, and social needs correspond with what could bring about a realistic improvement in American readiness for the worst imaginable sequence of events. I am referring to the new capabilities for underground construction of our transport and logistical facilities.

Already, communities that can afford to do so have buried unsightly telephone, water, and gas lines, and more recently power cables have been buried beneath the surface; with the new high-speed capabilities of rail-type transport, it is simply common sense to accelerate the improvement of tunneling capabilities so that long-distance transport may occur fifteen hundred feet or so beneath the surface. And while we optimize use of subterranean space, we should also push forward the development of new, more cost-effective rocket engines so that a beginning can be made on the conduct of industrial activities on the moon and in outer space. In this sense, Professor Gerard O'Neill's attractive vision of the earth as a park or garden, with unpleasant industries located "up there," may ultimately coincide with reality!

There is much to be done. It is comforting to recall instances where a single decision-maker, at the right time and in the right place, was able to galvanize human energies on a vast scale in order to accomplish some great work for human betterment or protection. The decision by Alexander the Great to establish Alexandria, which for a thousand years remained the principal *entrepôt* and center of culture of the Mediterranean world, must rank among these great decisions. Along with this example, I think history will place President John F. Kennedy's decision to send astronauts to the moon, and perhaps François Guizot's extension of free elementary school education throughout the length and breadth of early nineteenth century France. But many decisive improvements in the human condition have occurred "outside official channels." Individuals who have seen a need have simply gone to work to define and dramatize a problem, to secure support, and to obtain approval—sometimes very reluctant approval—of those in authority who are sometimes mislabeled "decision-makers." Thus, Florence Nightingale won her uphill battle against many "Establishment" figures to bring decent medical care to soldiers in the Crimean War and eventually to the British public at large. Thus, Isambard Kingdom Brunel, in whose honor a special lecture series has just been inaugurated at the Massachusetts Institute of Technology, decided, with his father's very active help and participation, to complete the world's first underwater tunnel—under the Thames in London. Similarly, hundreds of human beings—more accurately, thousands—have initiated projects that rightly or wrongly the world regards as worthy monuments to human accomplishment.

The person who perceives a new public need and then acts to meet it is often called, somewhat derisively, a "promoter." In fact, such people are self-chosen leaders, and without them, society could not function. At a certain point, when the public recognizes the legitimacy of a self-motivated public effort, the promoter is garbed with official character. Thus, the young Cecil Rhodes, who arrived penniless and in a sickly condition in Southern Africa, became a prime minister; Vicomte de Lesseps was the most sought-after private citizen in Europe *after* he had successfully completed the Suez Canal; and Riquet de Bonrepos was given the additional title of "Baron of the Canal of the Two Seas" when work was well launched on *his* project, which still links the Atlantic Ocean and the Mediterranean Sea.

But the implementation of important ideas, whether in construction or in the less tangible realms of education and legislation, requires "fertile soil": a public opinion ready to recognize new imperatives and responsive to authentic leadership, official or unofficial. Alvin Toffler has correctly identified the "new wave" industries that will lead America's economy forward; the very existence of these industries testifies to the efficacy of thousands of "self-starters" in our population, people who have both the technical and the promotional ability to start companies, produce up-to-date artifacts and market them.

Meanwhile, we must encourage that special breed of promoter who is attracted by fundamental improvements in infrastructure, by the complex dynamics of heavy industry, and by the new frontiers of ocean and outer-space development. While retaining and even increasing our faith in the indispensability of research, we must—for a time—shift the focus from research to development, from evaluation to construction, from planning to implementation.

In July 1983, I visited an old friend who has devoted nearly his entire working life to the various campaigns of the International Red Cross; he and his attractive wife live on the shores of Lake Geneva in a new and stunning apartment complex. Before escorting me along well-lit corridors to his own "flat," my host pointed out, with a touch of sadness, the extensive air-raid shelters now required in new housing projects in Switzerland. Human error or vindictiveness *could* unleash a severe and unprecedented catastrophe that would threaten the air even over "neutral" countries: This is the reality with which we must somehow learn to live. Those who design and decide upon new infrastructure arrangements in North America need not be mesmerized by a sense of impending doom; but the contingency of the new warfare must be regarded as one of the hazards of the future. An educated and responsible American public will wish to implement those blueprints that provide not only for prosperity and convenience, but also for health and reasonable safety in good times and bad times alike.

The seven locks of Fonserannes are often cited as the most spectacular works of the Canal des Deux Mers (Canal of the Two Oceans), built in the time of Louis XIV to link the Mediterranean Sea and the Atlantic Ocean. The magistral staircase of water has its own independent water supply.

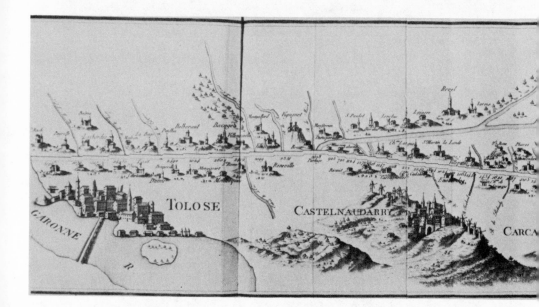

The above map was commissioned by Pierre-Paul Riquet in 1664, just before the start of construction. This intrepid entrepreneur had built miniature waterworks on his own estate, and succeeded in persuading the king's great minister, Colbert, that he should have the royal permission to build a canal much discussed since the reign of François I. But first Riquet had to build a scale model of the canal along the entire route from the Gironde to the Aude river, showing that the reservoirs on high ground could indeed be filled with water. Only in October 1666 was the king's edict forthcoming. Construction was completed in 1681, just one year after Riquet's death. Over the 257 km route there are 65 locks, still serviceable. To the right of Riquet's portrait is a view of the town of his birth, Béziers, on the river Orb, "the wine capital of the south." The Canal des Deux Mers (or Canal du Midi) was finished by Riquet's son, Jean-Mathias. The cost of the work has been reported as 15,249,399 livres, of which 7,484,051 was granted by the king, 5,807,831 by the province of Languedoc, and 1,957,517 by Riquet himself. It took more than a century for his descendants to pay off the debt. A grateful monarch had, however, made him Baron de Bonrepos.

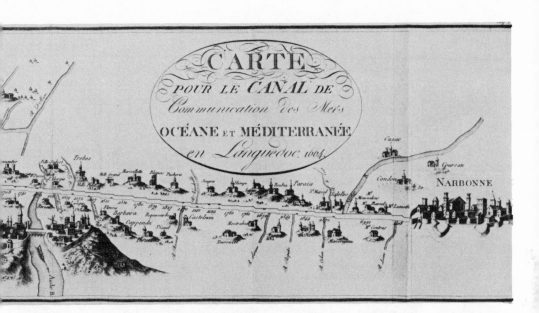

CARTE
POUR LE CANAL DE
Communication des Mers
OCÉANE ET MÉDITERRANÉE
en Languedoc: 1664

NARBONNE

Today the Canal des Deux Mers runs through modern Toulouse; it has provided the city with a splendid waterside boulevard. In the time of Henri IV, it had been the Bishop of Toulouse who presided over a special commission to examine the project. And when Riquet was at the outset of his promotional efforts, it was the friendly Archbishop of Toulouse, Monseigneur d'Anglure de Bourlemont, who encouraged the fifty-three-year-old entrepreneur to send his famous memorandum to Colbert. Contemporary Toulouse is a "high tech" center, the site of the famous School of Aeronautics and Astronautics—and of a distinguished branch of the National Veterinary School. But in its own time, the canal involved the most advanced technology then available; it remains a monument to managerial and technical audacity.

This *Vanity Fair* cartoon portraying Ferdinand de Lesseps appeared on November 27, 1869. The simple caption is "He suppressed an Isthmus." Lesseps had a harder promotional task than Riquet because the Suez Canal was of interest to several sovereign states, and in one way or another he needed broad assent for his undertaking. The canal was in fact opened to traffic in 1869, and the fanciful painting copied below shows the Indian Ocean and the Mediterranean Sea embracing as the chief monarchs of Europe look on. Lesseps had received his concession in 1854. When he formed his company, some eyebrows were raised when he placed on the Board of Directors, as vice-president, an American banker from Boston, Paul Forbes.

Isambard Kingdom Brunel (right) was the greatest engineer-entrepreneur of the nineteenth century. With his father, Sir Marc Brunel (former chief engineer of the Port of New York), he built the world's first tunnel under a navigable river—the Thames. Upper left: The oil painting depicts Sir Marc being welcomed by his son to a congratulatory banquet in the tunnel. Two months later, as the Goodall watercolor reveals, all was almost lost in a sudden inundation of the works. The etching at the left shows how the situation was retrieved by the use of a diving bell to repair the damage done on the fateful 18th of May, 1827. Upper right: We observe the passageway open to the public.

The two photographs above show Brunel's brilliant but ultimately bankrupt seven-foot gauge "Great Western Railway," which provided rapid and safe service between Bristol and London. Unfortunately, the rest of the country had adopted standard gauge, and locomotives like the *Rover* (top) and the *Flying Dutchman*, shown passing Worle Junction in 1891, had "nowhere else to go.". . . The two lithographs shown top right and center right are from a much admired series of Great Western Railway scenes, the top one depicting the west portal of the Box Tunnel and the other the Maidenhead Bridge. Lower right is the Clifton Suspension Bridge as completed by Brunel's fellow engineers after his death.

Launched on January 31, 1858 (a Sunday), the S.S. *Great Eastern* was five times the size of the largest vessel then afloat. The ship was 693 feet long, built to accommodate 4,000 passengers, with a 22,500-ton displacement. It was 120 feet wide—too broad for the Panama Canal which would not open for traffic until 1914. Above right, we see the first attempted broadside launching from the river bank (no existing drydock was large enough to contain the ship's skeleton); below right, the luxurious appointments of the public salons are plainly visible. The ship could carry enough fuel to sustain a voyage around the world. But its owners went bankrupt repeatedly, perhaps because the entrepreneurs of the day did not have the advantage of "traffic engineering" firms which, had they existed, would have emphasized the profit potential in catering to the masses of emigrants who sought passage to America. Catering only to the "classes," the ship was underutilized. On the charter voyage from France in 1867, Jules Verne was, inevitably, one of the passengers. Napoleon III had hoped the vessel would bring thousands of Americans to the Paris Exposition; only 191 passengers signed on for the return voyage. The ship remained a center of curiosity, and when it docked in Liverpool in 1886, half a million people scrambled aboard to visit. In May 1889, it was broken up for scrap. The first ship to be larger than Brunel's was built in 1906; it was named the *Lusitania*.

Early in 1865 the S.S. *Great Eastern* was stripped of her elegant fittings and made ready for the rough job of laying the first transatlantic cable. Smaller vessels had been employed on this business and failed. Top: A barge from Greenwich loads cable onto the *Great Eastern* at Sheerness. Bottom: The ship can be seen paying out cable at sea.

While the deck was replete with apparatus for cable laying, cleared space was maintained below so that cable line could be brought up unhindered. The S.S. *Great Eastern* failed in one attempt during 1865, but in 1866 a submarine cable was successfully laid across the 1,800-mile stretch from Ireland to Newfoundland. Queen Victoria and President Andrew Johnson exchanged enthusiastic messages. But in fact, Cyrus Field's patient promotional work had years before secured congressional assent and the support of President Franklin Pierce.

Above, an aerial view of the *Proyecto Experimental del Vivienda* (PREVI) shows the intimacy and high density of this pioneering demonstration of clustered housing. Note that all but peripheral streets are for pedestrians, and that the entire housing project, while certainly large, meets the practical and psychological criteria of "human scale." The great variety of national styles suggests that this U.N.-sponsored experiment can in fact be applied in a wide variety of social and cultural settings. The house at upper right embodies the flexibility Professor Land insisted upon: As families increase in size and resources, they can add additional stories without exorbitant expense. Lower right: The system of interlocking concrete blocks provides both ease and security of construction. PREVI has been planned for an ultimate population of 12,000. The message of this project will take some "learning." Peter Land insists that lot sizes should be *reduced*, that pedestrian streets should be narrow, and that energy can be saved by grouping houses in high-density clusters. Social, educational, and commercial facilities are linked by "alamedas," central walking streets down the middle of each neighborhood. It is worth noting that Professor Land's theories would help reduce the costs—and the social disarray—in communities that may be established on offshore islands. But lawmakers take note: In many areas, zoning regulations will need adjusting if high-density, low-cost clustered housing is to become a reality in the foreseeable future.

This attractive plaza (above) and village thoroughfare (left) form part of the *Proyecto Experimental del Vivienda* (PREVI) of which Professor Peter Land was managing architect. This large-scale model housing project, sponsored by the United Nations, was officially launched in 1968 with the signing of an international agreement. Construction began in 1970–1971; more than 500 houses were built, each with its traditional patio and with room for later expansion. Architectural teams from thirteen countries participated, each team designing its own village under Professor Land's overall direction. This large project on the outskirts of Lima, Peru, convinced many observers that sensitive attention to detail could make cluster housing practical for urban renewal on a scale suitable for the crowded metropolitan centers of both the developed and the third worlds. While PREVI came under construction, Peter Land also managed the reconstruction of two villages destroyed by the major 1970 earthquake; recourse to "self-help" made these dwellings dramatically inexpensive. Some PREVI houses were finished by self-help, but the basic preparatory labor was furnished by contractors.

CHAPTER 7

Neoindustrialization: Engineering for a Healthier, More Livable Environment

THE UNITED STATES HAS BEEN ON A "HIGH TECH" BINGE. PUN-dits and politicians alike have led the country to rely on the "sun-rise" industries of computer science, robotics, telecommunications, and bioengineering to bring on a "new wave" of affluence and power. And fascination with fantasies of the future—some doom-laden, some cornucopia-strewn—have riveted public attention on dimly perceived horizons to such an extent that even mature opinion-leaders have neglected that sine qua non of all serious policy assessments: a sense of balance.

That expectations of employment opportunities in the "high tech" industries were overdrawn has been documented by a number of special reports such as a feature article in the March 28, 1983, *Business Week*. Accepting the Bureau of Labor Statistics definition of "high tech" firms as those having twice as many technical employees and twice the R & D expenditures of other coded firms, *Business Week* surmised that, over the next decade, "While high-tech industries . . . will generate 10 times the number of jobs expected from the rest of industry, it will still amount to only 730,000 to 1 million jobs. And most of these will be in traditional occupations, not in technical ones." Meanwhile, the

United States has lost two million jobs in manufacturing in the last three years. A program to put the United States in a leadership position in industry must stress excellence in all sectors, not just in the "glamorous areas" that have high visibility because of their novelty and the substantial market opportunities that they are successfully exploiting.

We tend to think of "high tech" as an isolated series of firms or processes. In fact, the advanced methods now winning general acceptance are important precisely because they will transform the situation of what we used to call "basic industry" and of that considerable congeries of methods and installations known as "infrastructure." From a macrohistorical perspective, the key contribution of the new technological methods may turn out to be their augmentation of the range, impact, and speed of service of macro-engineering ventures. This is why I have chosen the term "neoindustrialism" to describe the discussion presented in this chapter: All of us know in our bones that we shall not restore the old industrial system established in the nineteenth century, nor do we wish to. What will emerge is a new synthesis of the familiar systems and the new technologies. A "neoindustrial" society, as I perceive it, will have an agenda that can command nationwide assent: the reorientation of education so that technology and science will move toward the center rather than remaining on the periphery; a concerted effort to preserve vital natural resources such as forests, topsoil, and clean air and water; a redesign of urban neighborhoods to promote the ubiquity of cleanliness, personal safety, and the aesthetic and social values associated with low-rise clusters as well as reconceptualized larger agglomerations; provision, through interregional arrangements, of assured supplies of water and energy; the establishment on a phased basis of transcontinental high-speed underground rail service; the intersectoral and intersectional pooling of talent and resources so that basic industry can be upgraded as part of a program of national resurgence.

The neoindustrial outlook sketched above can reconcile those whose main concern is a successful economy with the groups that still fear further industrial efforts, however labeled, because of their assumed deleterious effects on the environment or public health. As we gradually surmount the rather naive posturing that has characterized the discussion of environmental issues during recent years, the country will show a surprising unanimity in insisting that the best available scientific advice guide decisions that affect the public health and safety; experiments in "urban agriculture" and in the planting of fruit trees along urban streets point in a sane direction. And the new science of environmental medicine, with its careful accumulation and weighing of evidence, should help depoliticize an issue that is too grave to be left to chance. Science itself is one of the most rapidly changing fields of endeavor; but if mistakes are to be minimized in environmental matters, at least the very best scientific advice now available should be brought to bear whenever the public feels that its safety and health are at risk.

Although we shall be very respectful of science, particularly as our people become better acquainted with its methods and precepts, it is important not to "go overboard" in deference to symbols or shibboleths, even when they are presented to the public as artifacts of the latest advanced thinking in science and technology. I believe that Professor Harvey Sapolsky, whose wit can on occasion be fairly devastating, has rendered an important public service by evaluating the impact of the novel management and control system known as PERT on the effectiveness and costs of the United States Navy's Polaris missile-submarine system. In a book entitled simply *The Polaris System Development*,[1] Sapolsky demonstrated that the navy, in an adroit manner, used PERT as much for its effect on Congress and the public as for management of the system! The "Program Evaluation and Review Technique" was valuable because it freed Admiral Raborn and his able staff from interference: They could point to the "system" as a guarantor of good performance; it was quite similar to the CPM ("Critical Path Method") devised in the DuPont Company but never allowed to interfere with DuPont's effective managers. Sapolsky explains that the Polaris Program was successful because its managers knew what they were doing and were in close personal touch with each other and with field operations: If they really needed information, they would go and talk directly to the people involved. PERT's importance as a management tool was, in the final analysis, a function of its usefulness in public relations.

I find Sapolsky's "straight from the shoulder" analysis refreshing and perceptive. The decision to use PERT may have been a correct decision, all things considered, in the Polaris case; Sapolsky does indicate its very high costs, however, and he has warned us against too implicit a confidence in new managerial software "systems" that may be somewhat less "systemic" than they are made to appear.

In a similar vein, it would not be difficult to gather together a volume or two with forecasts by very eminent authorities on what "will" happen in the next year or decade. While a few statements hold up, there is an astonishing number that do not. In the early days of atomic energy, some statements that now appear very silly indeed were made by eminent people about the low monetary costs of nuclear power. While "think tanks" were busy on such matters as future lifestyles and the imminent arrival of superprosperity, the "energy crisis" burst upon an unsuspecting world. "Analysts," however, were as untroubled as the thick-skinned and amiable people who give us daily weather forecasts over the radio: They trimmed their sails and then forecast more energy shortages until the present (and perhaps temporary!) "oil glut" took over the headlines. I think the late Herman Kahn has been right to come up with three alternative future scenarios instead of one: There is a better chance he will "look good," regardless of whether events bear out "optimistic," "surprise-free," or "pessimistic" models of the future. But for serious planning and decision-making, the main point is to design programs that have an enduring value, in good times and bad, "through thick and thin."

Of course we *want* and *need* as much legitimate "high tech" as we can get, both for civilian and for military purposes, assuming a reasonable balance is maintained in terms of budgetary requirements for all essential goods and services. Without a computerized guidance system, there could not have been an Apollo Program. I remember visiting "Doc" Draper in his modest M.I.T. office a year or two before he "retired"; he kept his small office in a run-down building that looked to me like an abandoned warehouse. Charles Stark Draper, whose name is now emblazoned on the modern laboratory complex that is the independent successor to the former "instrumentation laboratory" of

M.I.T., had agreed to chat about prospects for developing a marketable electric car. He stressed the importance of finding a technically competent manager who would make this problem his main concern for a period of time. I have always remembered the quiet, absolutely accurate statements that "Doc" Draper made on this occasion: no frills, no embroidery; very pragmatic; very direct.

This "no-nonsense" style, combined with complete openness and ease of communications, is one of the features that I have come to value during my twelve or so years at M.I.T. Some of my European friends have been shocked by the "management style" at M.I.T., where hundreds of entrepreneurs, most of them highly specialized scientists and engineers, develop curricula and research programs, and then, with the benign advice of the "front office," are turned loose (if their ideas are approved!) to find the necessary funding. Although M.I.T., like virtually all American universities and graduate institutes, has its own development office (under the direction of a salty amateur mountaineer, Don Severance, and his wise-beyond-her-years associate, Edith Nelson), I think it fair to say that almost a majority of the professors and senior research associates at M.I.T. spend a goodly portion of their time, explicitly or implicitly, fundraising. Curiously, this necessary connection with the "real world" has helped to keep M.I.T. relevant and on its toes.

A number of M.I.T. department heads and senior professors have had more than a casual brush with very large-scale engineering projects. After working on the original "Whirlwind" computer under Dean Gordon Brown, Jay W. Forrester designed and managed the SAGE Air Defense System, an intricate, automated early-warning system that was for long vital to the nation's defense against aerial attack. Ernest Frankel, who assisted with a detailed evaluation of some suggestions I developed with J. Vincent Harrington to save time and money in the construction of subsea tunnels, has now been "taken aboard" by the World Bank as a full-time adviser on marine systems and port development. David Gordon Wilson, after tinkering with pallet guideways to reduce the toll of highway accidents, has actually designed a new-technology bicycle, after concluding that the recumbent position provides more leverage on the pedals! Sarah

Jane Neustadtl, a former managing editor of *Technology Review,* will soon publish a major report on mountain deforestation and its remedies, with the enthusiastic sponsorship of the Appalachian Mountain Club and its dynamic director, Tom Deans. Well, they are a lively bunch—and constantly shuttling back and forth between classes and consulting assignments; recently, I have found it hard to pin down my young associate in the Macro-Engineering Research Group, "Larry" Meador, who seems to spend nearly half his time in Singapore, Bangkok, and other far places. I suppose that when supersonic ground transport comes up for a "vote," M.I.T. staff members will be disqualified on the basis that their "self-interest" in more rapid planetary transit disqualifies them as impartial judges!

I have proposed the term "Neoindustrial Society," not because I think it is original—which it probably is not—or even euphonious, but because I think we should bury the idea that industry must be spoken of henceforth in the past sense, and also because I think that the "critique" of traditional industrialization and urbanization has now reached a point of virtual consensus. It ought to be possible to put into understandable language what nearly all Americans now wish to obtain, with the help of both private and public instrumentalities. With IBM continuing to outsell its Japanese competitors *in the Japanese market,* it seems to me that we can avoid becoming too fixated on Japan's role as a competitor; other competitors, and formidable ones, are arising elsewhere, and somehow we shall just have to study and work harder and more effectively, without erecting a high protectionist barrier around a beleaguered "Fortress America": Our competitors are also trading partners and allies; it is time for us to learn their languages, to visit in their dazzlingly different countries, and to form those friendships and associations that are the surest guarantee of future good relations.

One of the successful new industries that I have watched proliferate in the last few years is the "think tank." Although two M.I.T. graduates founded Arthur D. Little, Inc., more than a century ago as a normal business corporation, and offered consulting services initially on chemical engineering problems and ultimately on nearly everything, the "think tank" now, of course, has more of a "not-for-profit" connotation. The Battelle Memorial Institute, established in the 1920's under the will of Gordon Battelle, has generated the most intricate set of subsidiaries and affiliates in the business; the Battelle and Mellon Institutes together advised the president of Stanford University on the formation and design of Stanford Research Institute, and today there are hundreds of small and large institutes and centers in all parts of the country engaged in what is called "contract research."

So far so good. But there is one peculiarity about all these fine organizations that keeps them fully as routinized as any government "bureaucracy": The engine that drives these institutions is money, and if there is no "market" for a research product, it is unlikely to be hawked. In ordinary times, this is a perfectly reasonable situation. But in unique times—and I think we are, as a country, at such a critical moment—the research "establishment" doesn't do much advanced policy thinking because, quite simply, the contract research institutes have not been given that kind of contract! To put it differently, the fact that all those "deep thinkers" are sitting in research institutes doesn't necessarily mean that there is a constant flow of operationally useful ideas and schemes for the betterment of the Republic. The "average citizen," therefore, must, however diffidently, scratch his or her head and try to decide what the country really needs. If the public, for instance, decides that a supersonic subway is a pretty good idea, then, if convincing dollars are mobilized, the "deep thinkers" will go to work.

Meanwhile, although many of my good friends are professional thinkers, I am not sure the net outcome spells salvation for the nation's future. Either the contracted thinking is about very narrow matters such as the likely demand for electric power in X county during the next six years (a perfectly reasonable question to look at, by the way), or there is a Delphi study of the most probable lifestyle of youths aged fourteen to nineteen in the period 2000–2020 A.D.—also a reasonable enough question to study, if that happens to be what you're concerned about. But if the problem is how Americans should devote their energies and resources *now* so that the country will be in better shape ten and twenty years down the road, then I think there is a shortage of constructive, well-considered ideas and programs.

But thanks to "champions" in and out of government—indeed, in and out of organizations in general—I think there are lists to choose from, and certainly there is a great deal to do. Dr. Edward K. David, a former science adviser to the President of the United States, has stated the issue bluntly enough: ". . . we are battling for survival against other nations in such work-a-day technologies as steelmaking, shipbuilding, mining, metal refining, transit and railroad technology and other less glamorous necessities." Dr. David ascribes part of the blame for this situation to our singling out aerospace and electronics as the places for bright people to work, in the late 1950's and the 1960's. In short, a lack of balance and distribution in the award of scholarships, research assignments, and development contracts. The difficulty has been that once such a one-sided preference is authoritatively expressed, the thousands of "thinkers" who ought to help restore equilibrium are themselves caught in the web: They go, as practical people, to where the contracts are, not to where they aren't.

A few evenings ago, I was idly thumbing through some speeches of the late Harold Wilson, which he delivered before becoming prime minister. What startled me was the close similarity of the issues he discussed, precisely two decades ago, to the issues that currently exercise American commentators and office-seekers. Following are some remarks made by Mr. Wilson when he opened the science debate at the Labour party's annual conference held at Scarborough in 1963:

> It is of course a cliché that we are living at a time of such rapid scientific change that our children are accepting as part of their everyday life things which would have been dismissed as science fiction a few years ago. We are living perhaps in a more rapid revolution than some of us realise. The period of 15 years from the last time we were in Scarborough, in 1960, to the middle of the 1970s will embrace a period of technical change, particularly in industrial methods, greater than in the whole industrial revolution of the last 250 years. When you reckon, as it is calculated, that 97% of all the scientists who have ever lived in the history of the world since the days of Euclid, Pythagoras and Archimedes, are alive and at work today, you get some idea of the rate of progress we

have to face. . . . Let us be frank about one thing. It is no good trying to comfort ourselves with the thought that automation need not happen here; that it is going to create so many problems that we should perhaps put our heads in the sand and let it pass us by. Because there is no room for Luddites in the Socialist Party. If we try to abstract from the automative age, the only result will be that Britain will become a stagnant backwater, pitied and held in contempt by the rest of the world.

When Mr. Wilson in due course became prime minister, one of his enduring achievements was the establishment of an Open University, that is, a university whose courses were broadcast on radio and television so that people who could not attend normal classes might, nonetheless, by hard work and correspondence, earn a degree. I was heartened last year when Dr. James Breedon, one of the brilliant young planners brought into the Boston school system during the all-too-brief superintendency of Dr. Robert C. Wood, told me he was considering the option of working with friends to bring about an American version of such an Open University. Although "bits and pieces" of such a possible institution already exist, there is no general national support for such an idea; and yet it is an idea whose time is, I should think, overdue.

What I have been implying, and shall now try to state more forthrightly, is that our think tanks, betterment associations, and discussion clubs ought to develop the habit of *specificity:* We can produce warehousefuls of reports and documents, many of them well prepared and cogent, but if they lead only to more documents and reports we shall end up like the hero of the Anatole France short story who, managing to open the door to his study, backed in with a final armful of books and papers, succeeded in closing the door after him, but suffocated to death because he had not left himself a means of egress.

If every think tank would plant one tree, build a model house, offer a science course in a nearby grade school, or erect a neighborhood swimming pool, our "quality of life" would zoom upward at an exponential rate! The passion for jogging has, I know, won addicts among the "thinkers," and that is, in a double sense, a "giant step" forward. William James put the matter, as usual, in a good perspective: "Individuals, daily more numerous, now feel . . . civic passion. It is only a question of blowing on the spark till the whole population gets incandescent. . . ."

I think we must deal forthrightly with the charge that very large civic undertakings smack of "monumentalism," that they make the individual feel less important, that they destroy the values of neighborhoods and other groupings that retain a sense of "human scale." This is, I believe, where civilized maturity and judgment must guide the selection of projects: Small *is* beautiful, and where human scale can be preserved and fostered, let us by all means adopt appropriate technologies! To establish industrial parks on offshore islands—with all proper safeguards against ocean pollution—does *not* seem to me a bad idea in principle. And if an extensive dike system involving thousands of laborers and literally billions of dollars (or guilders) must be built to safeguard or enlarge the territory of Holland or Belgium, is this contrary to personal or group well-being? But not all small projects are *good!* Just as some "organic" foods are highly poisonous, so evil can reside in small, intermediate, and large-scale manifestations. Charles Dickens wrote a whole series of novels about the tyranny of small institutions and small-minded people over innocent victims; the remedy lay in the macropower of a whole society to react to diverse tragedies by the enactment of humane laws and regulations. We had better get it out of our heads that there is any vice or virtue in scale *as such.* As Mr. Schumacher rightly put it, "It all depends on what you are trying to do."

I think, therefore, that we must treat large-scale engineering systems, present and proposed, as cases to be examined on their merits. This sort of exercise is not to be regarded as a mere contractual opportunity for a "think tank," but as a means of breathing new life into the American economy. If, instead of only copying systems already proven abroad, we can leapfrog a generation of effort by building and testing prototypes, let us assemble the necessary resources of people and money and machinery; to "reindustrialize" on the pattern of the past is to invite defeat; this is why I have proposed, *faute de mieux,* the rather awkward term "neoindustrialism"; at least it conveys the intention to branch out on a new tack, to work with all the new methods and apparatus of "high tech" but without deluding ourselves into thinking that the new gadgetry is an end in itself.

I confess to a certain uneasiness with the overextension of the word "software." I quite recognize that it is intended to be the opposite of "hardware." But I remain old-fashioned enough to protest when the word "software" is defined as inclusive of law, religion, scholarship of all kinds, and literature. Just as I think that society must defend itself against the more absurd pretensions to omniscience of a certain tendency in "systems science," so I think people who value the more traditional values of our not-altogether-failed society must protest when "software" experts, however persuasive or attractive they may be, try to convince us that all of life can be understood as consisting either of "hardware" or "software." The outward reach of technology itself is forcing us to stretch our sympathies and our understanding, as planet-wide systems bring hitherto remote societies within the web of modernity. The "software" of foreign languages, cultural appreciation and understanding, anthropology, comparative law, and sociology must all be brought into play as the United States, if it decides to promote some of the larger systems "invented here," thrusts its citizens into dynamic interaction with groups of people whose religions and habits are known to us only in the vaguest and most theoretical terms.

Even some of our more civilized and best-thought-out sociological artifacts may be inappropriate for instant and universal export. With deforestation and desertification now officially certified as major planetary problems, what could be more logical than internationalizing the concept of a civilian conservation corps? To bring together millions of young people who are unemployed or underemployed with land that is eroding for want of attention must seem superficially attractive to Western "experts." But in many Eastern societies, there remain rather formidable caste systems that effectively prohibit members of several of the principal castes from performing manual labor at all. Nor need this mean that countries such as India are unable to generate "grass roots" movements to halt deforestation: The Chipco movement, which encouraged villagers to protect trees marked for destruction by the lumber industry, stands as a case in point. And in neighboring Nepal, the community forestry movement has inspired entire settlements to participate in the upgrading and preservation of local woodlands: Where the Cartesian logic of a Western "organization" arouses only misunderstanding and resentment, efforts consonant with indigenous culture and established lines of leadership and communication have worked quite well indeed.

Sarah Jane Neustadtl, whose perceptive and well-written study of current life in threatened mountain environments will soon be published by the Appalachian Mountain Club, has explained to me her hope that community forestry and similar initiatives will gradually bring the hill people of many Nepali villages into the "market economy": If this should happen, that is, if a *surplus* of wood and of crops can be made available for sale, then a new medium of exchange, money itself, will be available to the hill tribes. Then and only then will they be able to benefit from hydropower, for what use is electricity if a family cannot afford to buy the stoves, light bulbs, and other items without which electric power is useless? The sudden "solution" that, after a brief *coup d'oeil*, may appear logical and sufficient, needs therefore to be placed in a more complex perspective: Yes, hydroelectric power is a good idea; but no, not immediately everywhere, not until macro-engineering has been meshed with the other skills needed in all large affairs, and then only after the most careful preparation of the "social and cultural soil."

M.I.T.'s macro-engineering research group has been fortunate to have had several visits from Miss Atsuko Takashima, a professor of comparative culture in Tokyo, who has encouraged intellectual interest in root problems of Asian and Western mutual comprehension. The United States has reason to be pleased with its own crop of young and adventurous anthropologists, many of whom are more at home with the languages and cultures of Himalayan hill tribes than are residents of the region's major cities. The turmoil in Iran has alerted the general public to the very real risks posed by a modernization process that does not take into sufficient account local traditions and preferences. Macro-engineering's reach *will* extend to the most remote regions, but the interdisciplinary teams that design and schedule very large projects will be well advised to include as fully empowered members anthropologists and writers who have had direct experience with the societies to whom we are offering the somewhat mixed blessings of modernity.

This is why, if we are eventually to create a special cadre of engineer-managers for "superprojects," I would like to see them shipped off, for a few months at least, to a relatively primitive society where they can observe the effects of even small technological improvements on village life and customs. When in the summer of my freshman year at college I was sent to Mexico by my father, who was then serving as president of the Society of the Friends of Mexico, I had the great good fortune to meet the famous archaeologist and sociologist Manuel Gamio. Professor Gamio, who played a major role in restoring the Temples of the Sun and the Moon in Teotihuacán, told me that he had been appalled by the absence of any fresh air in the huts in which the native Indians were living; Dr. Gamio decided that the best way to "market" the idea of windows was by example. He therefore moved into a hut himself, and slowly built an opening for a window. This aroused great curiosity, and Dr. Gamio made himself available to answer questions as to why he had made an opening for a window, how the window was constructed and inserted, and how it was operated. When opinion had matured from hostility to skepticism to acceptance and finally to the desire to "try it out," Mexico's foremost archeologist of the day then set up a little business to sell windows!

Similar wisdom was shown by the Pérez brothers when they decided to establish a school for Indians in the Andean region of Bolivia. Enrique de Lozada described this episode in an article written for the April 1939 issue of *The Quarterly Journal of Inter-American Relations*, established by a journalist of deep culture and broad sympathies, John I. B. McCulloch. Lozada describes movingly how the example set by Elizardo Pérez and his brother proved infectious:

> Before two weeks had passed, the news that a school was being built spread throughout the whole region. This was not simply, so Pérez announced, a school devised by the white man for the Indian, but a school *of and for the Indian*. The purpose was not to teach the Spanish "a-b-c," but to instruct

children in making things for the house. By the end of the first month, the work was going ahead with amazing speed, for the Indians were willing to collaborate enthusiastically on a school which would really belong to them. . . . Results obtained at Huarizata were such as to excite the interest of the general public and the national government. . . . Huarizata . . . has gradually developed into a central nucleus which projects its influence over thirty new schools.

One problem with travel to far places and cultures that seem to us exotic is that we, as members of complex industrialized societies, are thereby allowed to feel "superior," for the reason that we have ignored what is going on, so to speak, in our own "backyard." This criticism can certainly not be leveled at the group of young biologists and doctors who launched, to make a biological assessment of the family, a "pioneer health center" in Peckham, in 1926. I cannot recommend too highly one of the resulting studies, *The Peckham Experiment,* published in 1945 by the Yale University Press. The investigators found, among other startling bits of information, that the average family in this not atypical section of London's metropolitan area, had virtually no social contacts apart from routine relationships at work! By providing a swimming pool and cafeteria in a setting that attracted numerous families, social contacts were fostered and, in fact, hundreds of marriages took place, which, the analysis revealed, could not possibly have occurred without the existence of some such center for communication and leisure.

The August 15, 1982, *New York Times Magazine* carried a well-researched cover story, "ALONE: Yearning for Companionship in America," which documented the connection between loneliness and disease, and chronicled the long list of social conditions that have led to the isolation of so many individuals from the consolations and comforts of family and friends.

There is a role, in all this, for imaginative, innovative social and physical engineering: The revival of conviviality can, in fact, serve as both a purpose and a result of a number of correctly conceived macro-engineering programs. Although the Peckham Experiment went "out of business" when World War II scattered the staffs and families who had constituted the center, its lessons remain, and fortunately there are books and records for those who wish to take the trouble to find them. We have now learned that the pursuit of a healthy community life is not merely a matter of "medical" care; health can and should be pursued actively *and socially*. The distinguished founder of macro-engineering studies in Japan, Dr. Manabu Nakagawa, was coach of the winning Japanese university crew (Hitotsubashi University's), which earned the right to represent Japan at the Olympic races a few years ago. I owe it to Dr. Nakagawa that, during a recent visit to Massachusetts with three members of his current crew who wished to participate in the great annual Head of the Charles Regatta, I had the opportunity of getting to know Edward J. Smith, Jr., and his dedicated colleagues at the Cambridge Boat Club. Athletic groups of all sorts are providing not only physical exercise, but also rewarding social contacts for millions of Americans united in a common enthusiasm for a sport or hobby. We need engineering programs that can make such activities more available and more enjoyable.

In the Boston area, where the maritime tradition persists in the form of a sport despite the decline of Boston as a commercial harbor, I was delighted to learn of the extent to which yachtsmen are willing—even eager—to teach schoolchildren and others the mysteries of navigation and sailing. A school board fully alive to its opportunities can develop friendly linkages with boat owners and their associations; and local politicians would be amazed by the favorable response if they sought advice from the area's part-time sailors and fishermen on how government agencies might participate in a program to use optimally Boston's extensive waterways: for commuting, commerce, and recreation.

One developer who has known how to marshal both public and official support is Mr. Rouse, the initiator of the new town of Columbia, Maryland (strategically sited between Baltimore and Washington, D.C.). Mr. Rouse has sensed the general desire for centers of conviviality in an atmosphere provided by a historic setting maintained immaculately and with good taste. The Faneuil Hall market near Boston's port has been acclaimed as one of the success stories in postwar urban redevelopment. Mr. Rouse has achieved a comparable result in Baltimore, where the sister ship of the famous S.S. *Constitution* (anchored in Boston Harbor) has been brought in for the charm and authenticity it provides for a setting where very new buildings had to be constructed. Perhaps the Baltimore Harbor redevelopment is not technically "macro-engineering"; that is not really the point: It is a very large-scale, coherent group of physical structures and facilities, and stands, I think, as a model for the design of further urban complexes that will benefit not only the convention-goer and the casual tourist, but the local economy as well. Mr. Rouse has launched a counterattack against the isolation and distress brought about by megastructures that have had the effect of de-humanizing urban life.

For those who need convincing on this matter, I would like to recommend essays by two noted psychiatrists who contributed to the 1979 Macro-Engineering Symposium held in Texas in connection with the annual meeting of the American Association for the Advancement of Science. Cynthia Oudejans Harris, a faculty member of Case Western Reserve University's School of Community Medicine, said, "We live on a planet which has turned MACRO in our lifetime, we live in a MACRO world. What does this do to us at the gut level? How can we find our way amidst the immensities surrounding us?" Dr. Harris stresses the importance of choice, of being able to say no or yes to a large project; and she develops the interesting notion that people must feel a sense of pride and "ownership," not in the legal but in the psychological sense, if they are to be happy with "bigness."

Dr. Hans R. Huessy, for his part, emphasized that successful macro-engineering of any kind requires the development of a "macromorality" in which responsibility for the impacts of macro-engineering is not shunted aside. Dr. Huessy is a professor of medicine at the University of Vermont's College of Medicine. It was his father, Eugen Rosenstock-Huessy, who founded the voluntary work camp movement in Germany during the Weimar Republic, and who in 1912 had suggested the use of German Army units in civilian public works. I regard the young Dr. Huessy as possessing unusual qualifications—by background, experience, and education—to assess the subtle problems of group dynamics that are implied in any major restructuring of social organization. Dr. Huessy spoke categorically of "large-scale mistakes made in our attempts to provide efficiency and good living through macro-engineering. This country built huge subsidized low-cost housing projects for multiproblem families. We have had to abandon many of these projects because, to our surprise, hundreds of multiproblem families housed in one area didn't stop having problems. From all we know of how groups work, we should have been able to predict this . . ."

Dr. Huessy continues with an informed critique of new towns in both the United States and the United Kingdom. He finds that these "planned utopias" attract, to begin with, mostly transient families; that with many mothers working, and with the older generation almost completely absent, children come home to empty neighborhoods. "One curious aspect found among these inhabitants was an over-use of medical facilities. Apparently the doctor's waiting room, not the neighborhood or work room, was a good place to meet people, even though an expensive one."

But all of us have experienced large-scale organizations where both Dr. Harris and Dr. Huessy would feel that the principles of social psychiatry had been met and satisfied: the general human need for leadership, social support, positive expectations, adequate information, anticipatory guidance, and opportunities for constructive participation. I notice this sense of well-being, for instance, when I travel on the excellent passenger trains of the French National Railways (the SNCF). Even under stress, the railway staffs seem to take great pride in their work. I remember an incident when my wife and I were traveling with our small children on a train in Normandy during the stormy interim before General de Gaulle was called to the presidency: A waiter in the dining car, serving us a delicious hot meal while the train raced on impeccably, turned to my wife and said, "*Vous voyez, Madame, tout n'est pas pourri en France.*"

In Holland, the whole population takes pride in the great system of dikes that protects the nation from the sea; and without the constant readiness of the "dike army," this macro-engineering project—to my mind the most dazzling on the planet—could not function as it does, year after year and century after century. I sense a similar sense of pride when speaking to almost any American about the achievements of our astronauts and of the devoted engineers and scientists who have provided the indispensable backup for their exploits. And I foresee immense opportunities lying just ahead, if we can learn to select, with that necessary combination of wisdom and boldness, the major projects of the future. Such projects will require "high tech," but also "low tech" and "intermediate tech"—plus a whole range of qualities that are beyond technology itself and have to do rather with such matters as integrity, courage, persistence, compassion, and judgment.

In myriad ways not particularly well covered by newspapers and television, individuals in government, research institutes, and the universities have been engaged in specific voluntary initiatives with a view to assisting educational institutions and other vital agencies of society to do a better job. I have been lucky in having been associated with some of these efforts in and near communities where I have lived and worked. There is a depth and density of leadership ability in the typical American community that outsiders have been slow to appreciate. I think that the mind-boggling options now presented to us as a nation by macro-engineering challenge local leadership to begin thinking in national and continental terms. Meanwhile, the web of voluntary activities continues to help public and private organizations function despite the net of self-serving bureaucracies and outdated objectives that plague all human institutions, and probably always will.

No single, quiet effort that I know of has had a more beneficent effect, or has been mounted with more of a sense of public obligation and service, than the Institute for Educational Services, incorporated in Massachusetts a decade ago. This institute was an outgrowth of various discussions between Thomas J. Burns of the United States Office of Education and John A. Evans, a staff associate of Robert R. Everett of MITRE Corporation (an acronym for M.I.T. Research and Engineering). These men were concerned by such problems as the lack of a coherent approach to collecting information on already successful educational practices so that such techniques could be disseminated where appropriate—but the list of their concerns was a lengthy one! The upshot was a series of innovative services, several of which have now been taken over by other organizations. One of the early achievements was a service to a large number of communities for a central listing of employment opportunities in the public schools and a corresponding listing of teachers seeking employment: Curiously enough, until this arrangement was made, both school superintendents and job-seekers lost a lot of time, the superintendents because they were asked about job openings that did not exist, and the teachers because—in ignorance of which job openings were available—would waste time (and gasoline) traveling to school districts where there were no openings in the desired special fields.

When Proposition 2½ was enacted—the tax-limitation law inspired by California's Proposition 13—Massachusetts communities did not have an information system that permitted them—and the state—to evaluate where painful staff cuts could or should be made. John Evans, assisted by Kathleen M. Lestition and C. Lawrence Meador, devised a computerized decision support system that made it possible to compare the situations of the various school districts and communities, so that the shrinking resources made available through federal and state agencies could be allocated on the basis of fairness. The three authors of the system reported on this effort, "Toward a Public Service Data Utility," in a book published in 1981 by the American Institute of Aeronautics and Astronautics, *Macro-Engineering: The Rich Potential*, reflecting papers prepared for the 1980 macro-engineering symposium cosponsored by the AIAA and the AAAS in San Francisco in connection with the AAAS annual meeting.

I would not be surprised if other states were tempted to investigate the format developed by MITRE Corporation for this model public-service data utility. Without some such instrumentality, it is difficult to allocate resources wisely. Especially when there is a financial "crunch," it is important that the bargaining procedure between communities and school boards, on the one hand, and their police, firemen, and teachers, on the other, be based on reliable and objective data. The Institute for Educational Services started out with the state's commissioner of education (Dr. Neil V. Sullivan) on the board; the Massachusetts Teachers Union was represented by its principal officer, and the

Association of School Superintendents was also represented. Mr. Allan R. Finlay, a respected banker who had served the state as chairman of the board of higher education, became chairman of the institute's board of trustees, which included Dr. Childress of the Educational Testing Service, and other knowledgeable citizens, including Mr. Everett, the president of MITRE Corporation, who sustained the long research and development effort to the point where it was relied on by many of the leading personalities of the state.

The effort very briefly described in the foregoing paragraphs was significant, it seems to me, because it represented a contribution by some of the most highly regarded "high tech" people in the commonwealth to the performance of public schools throughout the state. In the nature of things, an effort so "technical" could hardly hope to capture the public imagination or earn the usual rewards for public service of a very high caliber. But the episode illustrates, I think, the immense potential for cooperative effort among individuals in federal, state, and local agencies to work loyally with staffs of not-for-profit research institutes and with representatives of community groups. Richard Gardner, the Columbia law professor who recently spent four years as United States Ambassador in Rome, has often spoken of the need of our country for a highly educated citizenry that can project American values and traditions abroad; surely no efforts should be spared that carry the hope of improving the performance of our beleaguered school systems, whether they are public, private, or parochial.

Dr. Kathleen Lusk Brooke of the Oliver Wendell Holmes Institute has written that "large-scale enterprises . . . originate as solutions to problems." The Club of Rome, under the energetic guidance of Dr. Aurelio Peccei, started a planetary dialogue on what it called "the world problématique." The United States, as still the world's most affluent nation in the aggregate, shares many of the social and environmental enigmas described by Dr. Peccei and his colleagues. There is a difference, however: The United States, if its citizens agree on what the problems are and which programs can best remedy them, has the capability of concerted action. Nor is this a chimera of someone's imagination. Europeans who visit the United States find it curious that there are so few ideological or even practical differences between our two main political parties. There are enormous differences between the styles and interests of competing individual candidates. But we can be thankful that our differences are minimal, that our constitutional tradition is a strong one, and that we are not perpetually seesawed by the divisiveness that has been typical of European politics for the past two centuries. In short, the task for American leadership is a *manageable* task. And in a nation with a tradition of pragmatism, it should not be too difficult to list and select those programs most likely to provide us with a prosperous, pleasant neoindustrial society. And this does not mean appointing a national prefect with an army of bulldozers under his command; what it does mean is a series of meetings and, if they go well, the formation of some study groups and possibly one or two interdepartmental committees.

What would be the effect of a concerted decision to proceed with major engineering programs? At first, the effect on the national economy would be negligible. It takes many years to gear up for even a single large-scale technological program. In some cases, there must be a preliminary period of several years for the design, building, and testing of prototypes. And where current state-of-the-art technology is to be used, there is the delay factor caused by the need to assemble authorizations from a number of different levels and departments of government. Even with goodwill on all sides and in the absence of significant political opposition, an effort to put our best foot forward on land, at sea, and in aerospace would probably require a decade of preparation.

But the preparation should be put in hand! It is not a matter of casting blueprints "in concrete," but rather of propagating a frame of mind conducive to large, carefully studied common enterprises. And the study groups must be set up. If it is felt that resources should be allocated for a new-generation rocket engine, then appropriate resources and influence must be assembled in something akin to the "decision seminar" suggested originally by Lasswell and referred to in earlier pages of this book. It will not be sufficient to have meetings of experts. People with "clout" in finance, industry, labor, and government must get used to the idea of joining study groups focused clearly on defined programs and projects.

We are lucky, it seems to me, that so much has already been done. Although not all of us will agree with all the conclusions and prescriptions, it is just as well for us that the country has been through the phase of highly generalized studies such as those conducted by the Commission on the Year 2000, the Club of Rome, and more recently the Report to the President on the Year 2000. We have heard a great deal about pollution, congestion, and alienation; we know that cyclical behavior is part of the picture of the future, but we also know that precise pinpointing of future macroevents is beyond the capability of even the most confident think tanks.

Following the "very big picture" studies and forecasts, we have had the "one-problem" studies, of which perhaps the best examples are those carried out under the direction of the late and much-missed Carroll L. Wilson, with the assistance of Robert P. Greene. *Man's Impact on the Global Environment; Inadvertent Climate Modification; ENERGY: Global Prospects 1985–2000,* and *Coal—Bridge to the Future* (a 1980 Report of the World Coal Study)[2] have "straightened us out" on some of the main policy considerations as we progressively "zero in" and move from the realms of policy formulation to the more pragmatic terrain of program and project selection and design.

In the field of macroproject proposals, we have had some challenging suggestions and studies by talented and tenacious champions. We are fortunate to have made a beginning on the assembling of information concerning some of the options for engineering on a large scale during the coming decades. But the next step must surely be to ensure that our list is a more complete list; here we owe a debt of gratitude, I think, to Dr. Kathleen Murphy and her associates, who have begun a systematic, computerized look at macroprojects, particularly in Third World countries. We shall have to go through a series of "data bank" exercises, hopefully in cooperation with journals and associations of the construction industry and the banking fraternity, to develop a reliable, constantly updated system of reporting and compiling information. In this task, the recently formed societies devoted to large-scale engineering can be immensely helpful.

And the numerous conferences, congresses, and conventions on the subject, such as the *Colloque International sur la Gestion des Grands Projets* (International Colloquium on the Management of Large-Scale Projects) held in Lyon, France, in September 1983, will be sources of information and evaluation for the new data banks, and for the study groups established to pursue particular projects or programs.

In addition to the "macroscopic" activities outlined above, a number of steps must be taken to enhance realistic consideration of those ventures that survive detailed interdisciplinary scrutiny and emerge as the "best bets" for the improvement of the nation's infrastructure, industrial posture, and general amenity and security. With respect to canal modernization, there is new construction experience as well as innovative design and invention to be included in an up-to-date assessment. With respect to subterranean transport tunnels, we must gather together in one place an assessment of what has been accomplished in tunneling techniques and also in the separate field of guideway and vehicle development. My own view is that we ought to proceed, as rapidly as resources permit, to the development of a prototype for a complete system that will incorporate the most promising and reliable elements of automated tunneling and electro-magnetic levitation. And I think we should analyze several of the so-called "sunset" industries such as steel and shipbuilding, to see what hopeful possibilities may have been provided by new developments in "high tech," including advanced metallurgical and control technologies.

The study groups formed to consider these separate topics ought to be composed of the best engineering talent in each field, together with management, labor, finance, and government representatives of the right stature; also, it seems to me important that public-interest groups be invited to participate from the outset, so that environmental and social impacts are considered *ab initio,* and not as an afterthought or because it is wise "public relations" to do so. Public relations and legal counsel should also be brought in "early in the game": The entire team should confront the decisions to be taken at each successive step. In this manner, all concerned will be educated together and simultaneously: The whole show will not have to be stopped because one of the necessary partners was not "in the picture."

Although politicians and political parties ought to be encouraged to join in the discussion of macro-engineering issues, project study teams ought to be nonpartisan: The central interest is in the long-range welfare of the Republic, not in short-run political advantage. But government, at the very highest level, should be urged to take part in the central deliberations and to assist the process of selection, study, and development.

Jay W. Forrester, in a prescient address to a symposium of the National Academy of Engineering in 1967, said, "It is now time to examine the entire engineering social system and set a new direction for the year 2000." In particular, Professor Forrester recommended a new and higher category, a "sociotechnical systems engineer" or, more succinctly, an "enterprise engineer." In an explanation of the functions of such a "new model," Forrester said:

> The kind of engineers most needed can harness the resources of the country and the world for results most beneficial to society. Such men couple science, economics, and human organizations. They act as the interfaces between compartments of human endeavor. . . . Such a man is judged not for his plans and proposals but for his accomplishments. He is not excused when "human factors" defeat his technical objectives; instead, his reputation rests on how well he blends plans and politics. . . . He is a doer. He understands theory as a guide to practice. . . . In private as well as public research and development, such men must find ways to reverse the deterioration of ethics and efficiency. . . . In the public sector they must show the level of wisdom and leadership that can coordinate great engineering projects with politics.

After stressing in further detail the need for engineers with a capacity for leadership, Forrester suggested "an entirely different kind of engineering institution," which would "anticipate the needs of society and build toward the future." He recommended that the National Academy of Engineering assume a key role in defining and nurturing such an institution.

In the years that have elapsed since the stirring address by

Professor Forrester, the construction industry has had to develop, on its own and without any help from the universities and technology institutes, cadres of engineer-managers ("enterprise engineers," in Forrester's trenchant phrase) in order to face the avalanche of unprecedentedly large engineering projects that came "on stream" in the seventies. There is a more obvious need now than there was then for new methods of selecting and training the "one in fifty" engineers destined for macromanagement. But the country as a whole must begin to be interested in its physical future, in the way our cities, suburbs, and countrysides will appear and function in the year 2000 and beyond. Whole communities should become as involved in designing their future environment as my Canadian regiment was in the game of chess, after our colonel had outsized chess sets made for each squadron by the regimental carpenter in 1945: It is a question of leadership.

When I was a cadet in Ontario, our instructors taught us a method of thinking that we were advised to use when, under the stress of battle, we had to make decisions. The "appreciation of the situation," as taught to generation after generation of British officers, still has much to commend it. There are only four steps, as I recall the matter now: first, defining the object or purpose; second, enumerating the factors bearing on accomplishment of the object; third, the alternative courses of action that are considered feasible; and fourth, the plan selected. This sequence seems to me a pretty adequate "rough and ready" summary of systems analysis. At any rate, I argue that we have not chosen, in our minds, a correct national object: Our judgment has been clouded by references to economic theory, when we should have kept our eye on the target: namely, how to increase and maintain the country's wealth while at the same time safeguarding the public health and safety. If we think directly about the wealth-producing capacity of the nation, then we are brought into contact with realities that can be assessed by ordinary citizens; policy ceases to appear so complex that several higher degrees seem necessary before one can even formulate a tentative opinion. But once we know that prosperity depends on the efficient production of goods and services, then we can focus our minds on those industries and ancillary facilities without which there can be no economy—and no services to ourselves or anyone else.

If my crude statement of a national policy purpose can, for the moment, be accepted, then the "courses open" are fairly clear: Either we leave the modernization or "optimization" of our basic plant and equipment—including the topsoils on which agriculture must be based and the water that is equally necessary for both agriculture and industry—to the mysterious workings of a "market economy" that we know is subject to cyclical fluctuations, *or* we ask government to join with private enterprise and with the not-for-profit institutions that play such a large and useful role in our country—to build in partnership the basic installations that our leading specialists and statesmen regard as important for the nation's future. I have skipped the second—or "factors"—step, because all of us have had to become acquainted with the obvious role played by our competitors in trade and industry and by our rivals in the field of military and ideological affairs. Now what is the plan?

Not a detailed "blueprint," but simply a "way forward": the series of consultations, studies, prototypes, already suggested in these pages, and ultimately the construction of macrosystems carefully tailored to our needs and our style of living.

Engineering—and architecture and urban design and planning—should be able to deal with some of the most recalcitrant problems of American society, such as crime and less-than-par health in our large cities. If the French in the 1860's were able to carry through a complete transformation of their capital city, are we to regard ourselves in the 1980's as less determined and less able to design and implement a program to deal with problems that everyone knows about? There are now books that discuss on the basis of actual experience the relation of behavior to the planning of neighborhoods; should we not test some relatively new ideas, such as Peter Land's, that on the basis of pilot models appear to offer a healthier, more attractive, more human-scale environment than we can obtain in our monolithic high-rise agglomerations? The restructuring of a modern city is, make no doubt of it, a *macro*project; but the overall magnitude of the task does not mean that components of a larger system must themselves suffer from giantism! On the contrary: It is the existence of a general plan to ameliorate the conditions of a city that will make possible the kind of "human scale" that our best commentators, including social psychiatrists and architects, regard as optimal.

Oscar Newman has pointed out, in his challenging book *Defensible Space—Crime Prevention through Urban Design,* that "poorly designed buildings and projects have crime rates as much as three times higher than those of adjacent projects housing socially identical residents at similar densities." Newman's book was funded by the National Institute of Law Enforcement and Criminal Justice of the United States Department of Justice, and has had a notable impact on urban planning and design. In Boston, a substantial redevelopment of the core of the city was carried out under the enlightened administration of Mayor John F. Collins, now a consulting professor at M.I.T.'s Sloan School of Management. Enlightened planning and architecture have already brought about substantial improvements in many areas of the city; but much remains to be done, and redesign of slum areas on a "macro" scale will have to be tackled, sooner or later. Perhaps, somewhere in the United States, there should be a *Proyecto del Vivienda* equal in quality to what has already been accomplished—and brilliantly—in Lima, Peru! But who is to take the initiative for such a "new beginning"?

I suspect that, as always in the history of our country, it will be a matter of self-appointed "champions"—people who can define the problem, visualize the needed improvement, and communicate the drama of the enterprise to the necessary members of the professions and the public. I think that the presence on the scene of an American Society for Macro-Engineering may ultimately be helpful; but no organization can replace the catalytic effect of individual commitment to a new vision of the future.

This chapter is about "neoindustrialism," and indeed the whole book has attempted to discuss two closely interrelated topics: the infrastructure and industry. What precisely is the crux of the connection between the two subjects? The point is a very simple one: Industrial plants cannot function without access to water, energy, and transportation. Transportation costs have been said to absorb 25 percent of the Gross National Product. One in six American workers is reputed to be dependent on the automobile industry alone. And water must be supplied not only to industry (without water development, coal slurry pipelines cannot function at all) but to agriculture and to our metropolitan areas as well. Having survived an "energy crisis," the United States is busily dismantling the various programs that were designed, during the emergency, to make us less vulnerable to the next energy "crunch": One is tempted to cite the old saw to the effect that "the only thing we learn from history is that we never learn from history."

An infrastructure designed, built, and maintained with the best minds in the country assigned to the task will measurably improve the terms of trade for American business. A generation ago, "only 8 percent of the U.S. economy was subject to foreign competition," Robert Reich has estimated; but today imports comprise "more than 30 percent of American manufactured goods." Both imports and exports must move through our antiquated ports or—in a much smaller percentage—through our airports. There is no American equivalent of Rotterdam's Europoort, equipped to handle deep-draft vessels and possessing the full array of modern machinery for handling all types of vessels and cargos. Automation *is* affecting the shipping industry, as Ernest G. Frankel has demonstrated in his authoritative series of texts;[3] but America needs not only to proceed systematically with port improvement, but also with the interface arrangements that can minimize delays and costs in transferring goods from ship to train, truck, and air modes. The United States remains the world's largest single market under one jurisdiction. By upgrading transport methods and facilities, the costs of imports will be reduced and, to that extent, the American exports that include (increasingly) imported components will be reduced in price; corresponding reductions in the costs of our exports will help make U.S. manufactured products and raw materials more competitive on world markets.

The design and construction of strategically placed intermodal transfer centers should be studied as one promising approach to the reduction of transportation time and costs. But such centers should be located where they can take advantage of upcoming new systems for rapid long-distance travel and transport. The idea of an "air cargo hub" was evaluated positively by a

Wilbur Smith and Associates report for the Illinois-Indiana Bi-State Authority, published in 1979, recommending a location at the Lawrenceville-Vincennes site. To the extent feasible, inter-modal centers should be designed with a view to accommodating expected developments in all forms of transportation, and should be linked with storage and processing facilities utilizing the most advanced "high tech" methods that combine reliability and genuine economy. A specialized cargo airport may seem to be the "last word" in logistics, but the true logistical centers of the future must be *multimodal*, that is, they must accommodate all forms of transportation, and one of the key arguments for the Lawrenceville-Vincennes location is its proximity to rail, high-way, and water transport facilities.

A system of infrastructure improvement on a macroscale will require a level of coordination and discipline that would be unusual for the peacetime United States. But we can take com-fort from the experienced judgment of Clemenceau, France's great premier in World War I: "True freedom is the right to discipline oneself in order not to be disciplined by others." I con-fess I owe this quotation to the 1983 illustrated calendar of Out-ward Bound's fine Hurricane Island School. A further quotation from the same source—in this case attributed to William Shedd—is not without relevance: "A ship in harbor is safe, but that is not what ships are for."

I hope that my friends in the fraternity of economics will not misunderstand me when I say that macro-engineering can sup-plement their "optique" by looking at many of the same prob-lem-areas but from a different perspective. For instance, in one of the standard texts on macroeconomics, I did not find, in the very comprehensive and careful index, any reference to the words "infrastructure," "water," "energy," or "transportation." This is *not* said in a spirit of criticism or denigration: It is simply a fact that economists construct their system of observation and analysis in a different manner and emphasizing variables that, confessedly, macro-engineering does not include in its purview, except by reference.

For instance, I remember dining many years ago at a Lon-don club at the kind invitation of the Honourable William Buchan. Regrettably, I arrived a bit late, and occupying the one remaining empty chair, I introduced myself to the trim, well-turned-out guest on my right; he gave me his name, and when I asked what business he was engaged in, he said he made money. "Oh, yes," I replied, "but how?" When he gave me the same answer, I fumbled as to how to repeat the question a second time when it suddenly dawned on me: He did, in fact, "make" money: The American dollar bill was at that time manufactured on machines of the gentleman's London firm! I would say that his approach to "making money"—and he made a great deal, even in the terms used by economic textbooks—closely approximates the manner in which macro-engineering views the economic system. Nor do macro-engineers pretend that they have all the answers: Truth, especially that kind of truth with which economics and politics must deal, is inherently *interdisciplinary*.

One problem that bobs up now and then when cost-reduction enters a conversation is the escalating cost of paper work; according to one recent study of the construction industry, the "software" or *paperasserie* contributed by architects, planners, lawyers, accountants, and others amounts to as much as 30 percent or more of the total cost of building a new home or a new office building or factory. This is an area where men of genius, such as Mr. John Bemis who has guided Acorn Structures, Inc., to such success in the marketing of prefabricated wooden houses, can make their mark; and I suspect that if Peter Land were turned loose on an *American* housing project where zoning regulations had been modified to permit optimal design, there would be an equally dramatic decrease in the paper-work cost of construction. But not all money spent on "administration" is wasted.

It has been said that Napoleon would have won the Battle of Waterloo if he had been able to recall his reserve: the thirty-two thousand men and ninety-six guns detached under Marshal Grouchy to pursue the Prussians defeated on the previous day at Ligny. But the messenger sent to Grouchy never reached his destination. Napoleon did not have the assistance, at Waterloo, of his ultrareliable chief of staff, Marshal Berthier, prince of Neuchâtel and Wagram, vice-constable of the empire who, had he not died a few days before the battle, would surely have sent off not one messenger, but a whole fleet of aides-de-camp to retrieve poor Grouchy, who marched back and forth uselessly while the Prussians managed to rejoin Wellington and thus carry the day for England and victory.

The anecdote about Waterloo not only illustrates the importance of staff work but the complexity of the decision process itself: Decisions must be *implemented,* and the mere giving of orders and directions is an exercise in futility if a decision does not bring about *decisive* results. This is why we must examine closely the pretensions of conferences and seminars addressed to "decision makers." As John Kenneth Galbraith has pointed out in *The New Industrial State,* corporate decision-making involves a whole "technostructure" of specialized individuals and staffs. And in government, there are few occasions when even a President can exercise an absolutely decisive control over events. Subordinates are apt to "tailor" instructions from the top or, on occasion, to ignore them. I remember my own astonishment when, as a young man, I conveyed a memorandum from President Roosevelt to an appointee who was asked by the President to constitute a special committee; the subordinate took no action for several days (or was it weeks?) and I finally had to negotiate my way back to the President himself: The second memorandum was of course obeyed instantly.

This whole matter of "decision" and "decision makers" is so misunderstood and understudied that I was delighted to learn that Martin Krieger, a research fellow in the Program of Science, Technology, and Society at M.I.T., has announced a seminar on "Great Decisions." Without the capacity for decision-making that is followed by actual construction, the whole future of macroengineering as an element of public policy would be jeopardized. Louis Armand used to say to high officials who were reluctant to take a position on the channel tunnel question that "no important career was ever made by opposing a great project which will benefit the public." Of course, modern publics have had to learn that not all "great projects" are as "great" as forecast, and there is a tremendous weight of suspicion and doubt when exaggerated claims are made for novel programs; but choice in human affairs is inevitable, and a systematic negativism will only mean that the American future—including the American environment—will suffer. All life involves dichotomies: good and evil, up and down, analysis and synthesis, entropy and harmony. It happens that the present moment in history requires an effort at integration, rationalization, and construction. This may offend those (valuable!) individuals in our midst who are temperamentally inclined to tergiversate, overanalyze, indulge in orgies of introspection. But the prince of Denmark memorialized by Shakespeare is *not* the right model for the American economy or for American politics. Governor De Witt Clinton would be a better choice, if we are prowling for serviceable models from history!

Ramón Barquín, in addressing the 1979 AAAS macro-engineering symposium "On Large-Scale Undertakings and Human Values," asked the following question: "In our willingness to do battle with nature and build a massive Grand Coulee or a Boulder Dam . . . or construct the Itaipu by diverting the Paraná River for four years into a man-made cut . . . are we not in effect underwriting or emphasizing self-reliance, self-fulfillment, rationality, and power?" Dr. Barquín, an executive with IBM World Trade Corporation in Hong Kong, also asked: "Do large-scale engineering projects cause value changes?" and he answered, "In many cases, probably yes," citing the effect of enhanced mobility brought about by the railroad as a factor in loosening the ties of family life and the traditional preference to live in one's home town. Values *are* changing, but technology is changing, too; the new communication and computer technologies essentially enhance the capacity of society to channel change in a direction that better accords with fundamental values. And this in turn is a problem of definition and design.

Sir Peter Parker, the successful businessman who has chaired the British Railways Board since 1976, wrote a charming article entitled "A Vision of Design Management"[4] for *Technology in Society,* my favorite quarterly journal. Sir Peter seems to see "design management" as the key to industrial success or, in his words, "a declaration of interdependence of all the functions in any corporate success. But its full significance transcends the techniques. The author's definition tries to go beyond that of the specialist function of industrial design and its coordination, because that specialism at its best becomes a creative force unifying the character and action of an enterprise. It becomes the spark in the generation process of making change happen. The concept should go forward with the sweep of Lord Caldecote's definition: 'Design is the process of converting an idea into information from which a product can be made.'"

So regarded, the word "design" can be regarded as a term applicable, in the largest sense, to the elusive task of "managing" the choice of investments in which a whole nation may best place its faith. This much is certain: Without a design in somebody's head, somewhere, it is not going to be possible to translate lofty goal statements and purposes into the steel and concrete of physical structures. This book has put forward a set of suggestions for arriving at a "design process" capable of leading to major physical improvements that are: a) feasible and b) desirable from the viewpoint of public policy.

In essence, the interdisciplinary groups that I have suggested might be regarded as "design teams"; inasmuch as designs that cannot be carried out are quite useless, I have insisted that responsible management people, from industry and government, join at an early stage with financial and legal and other experts, so that centers that are involved in "decision making" will have shared in the design of those "products"—in this case, the products are really projects or programs—which are to be the subject matter—the raw material if you will—for "decision." Put more pithily: If we wish to avoid "noise" and "delay" in the macroenvironment of contemporary decision-making, we had better bring the decision people into the design process—there is more likelihood one will approve a proposal if one has helped develop it oneself!

How can such generalities be applied to the "nitty-gritty" of basic United States industries? The men managing "sunset" industries are not necessarily more stupid or less devoted than the managers of avant-garde industries, but they *are* coping with more severe problems; first of all, there is apt to be more *unaccustomed* competition to cope with; second, labor and materials costs are likely to be more inflexible; third, the cost of capital improvements may appear prohibitive; fourth, recommended new "rescue technologies" may have their own problems; fifth, in order to readjust for long-term economic health, it may be necessary to disappoint shareholders who will not wish to forgo their next quarterly dividend checks.

Thus far, the response of the federal government to the distressed condition of industries under pressure from foreign competition has been to retreat into protectionism: Japan was persuaded to limit its exports of steel to the United States, for instance. The trouble with this policy is that it meant an almost automatic increase in the cost of domestically produced automobiles; thus, Japan had to be induced, also, to limit its exports to the United States of automobiles as well. And of course competition comes not just from Japan, but also from South Korea, Europe, and elsewhere.

For the steel case, as in other instances, there is no substitute for seeking the best technological, marketing, and industrial real-estate advice, and indeed advice from the legal and accounting fraternity as well. Once it is determined that the maintenance of a steelmaking capability of substantial size is a matter of national interest, every effort should be made to assist that industry to adopt the most modern methods and to place itself—geographically and otherwise—in the best position to make money. Nationalization is *not* a solution, and would in any case fail to receive public acceptance if it were proposed. It is doubtful if the protectionist reaction of the federal authorities will really "protect" steelmaking: If Professor Reich is correct, it has had the effect of pushing foreign competitors into the higher-priced "specialty steels," just as limitations on the numbers of cars that can be imported have had the effect of motivating foreign car manufacturers to upgrade their products so that they can better slice into the more profitable part of the market represented by larger-sized cars. It would have been better for the federal government to have eschewed this chipping away at free trade and therefore at the health of the world economy, and to have launched instead a carefully conceived program to support modernization of facilities and, where appropriate, removal of plants to locations that would tend to reduce costs of transportation.

One advantage of a rational program of macro-engineering investments is that it would provide a foreseeable market for industrial outputs of basic products for many years to come. While such a program would hardly constitute the major economic event in the United States in a manner comparable to the impact of the great hydroelectric scheme in Sri Lanka already described in these pages, nonetheless, macro is macro, and there would be a "kicker" effect on the national economy. But the argument for such projects does not rest on Keynsian hypotheses alone, but on the stark physical need for the services that only an up-to-date infrastructure can deliver.

That the United States has formidable competitors should not be taken as bad news. No American would like to see the rest of the world in the pathetic situation in which most of the world's countries found themselves in the aftermath of World War II. Moreover, prosperity and success abroad imply substantial and enduring markets for American goods. But many people who have been "coasting along" will have to go back to work. At every level of society, people will have to be retrained for the rigors of a competitive, rapidly changing techno-economic environment. "Lifelong education" is no longer an idle phrase. And just as executives and engineers and skilled laborers will have to go back to school from time to time, the staffs and faculties of universities will have to keep in closer touch with the day-to-day realities of business and industry.

The new industrial society that is beginning to emerge will not only be more "high tech," it will direct its engineering energies so that the environment is preserved and enhanced, and so that all Americans will find that the quality of their lives has been improved and not degraded. "Human factors engineering," broadly conceived, will come to the fore. We are beginning to learn how to design safer and more enjoyable neighborhoods, how to provide transportation facilities that are rapid, unobtrusive, and virtually nonpolluting. Nor will a sensible neoindustrialism ignore the challenges and opportunities of the oceans and of space.

To accomplish these attainable goals, real work will have to be accorded a more deferential place in our value structure. Schooling must include, for everyone and not just for a specialized caste, a thorough grounding in basic science and technology. We shall also have to widen our contacts and our sympathies. When leaders such as William M. Mahoney, the innovative superintendent of the Hingham (Massachusetts) public schools, succeed in establishing "immersion centers" where high school students can study a foreign language not only during classroom periods but during lunch and during sports as well, then we know that this country is on its way: We mean "business," and we are not about to be mere hewers of wood and drawers of water for more "advanced" societies elsewhere.

This French battle plane near Villers in World War I illustrates the new ubiquity of technological developments. In an age of instant electronic communication and of widespread travel, knowledge "levels upward."

Test flights made by Lieutenant H. J. Brow indicated a speed of 230 or even 240 miles per hour for this U.S. Navy Curtiss Racer. To generations that have looked aloft for feats of ultra high speed, it may be disorienting to learn that even higher speeds may soon be attainable through subterranean transport.

The *Christopher Columbus,* flagship of Pan American Airways, was one of a fleet of twelve trimotor passenger planes when the airline industry appeared to be the uncontested leader in a new era of industrial growth.

This American Airlines DC-3 received her number (NC 17331) on February 13, 1937. Few aircraft have proved as enduring and serviceable as this Douglas product, examples of which may still be seen in the skies.

Above: The Lockheed XF-90, a U.S. Air Force heavy-penetration fighter, was test-flown in May 1949. Lower right: An Air France Concorde supersonic transport. A joint project between England and France, it was launched in November 1962, and saw commercial flights established in the mid-1970's. Each Concorde costs some $70 million to build, seats 100 passengers, and has a range of 3,500 miles. The controversy that surrounded the plane's impact on noise pollution and on the depletion of the ozone layer indicates the sensitivity of macro-engineering projects to environmental and social critiques. It is somewhat surprising that no international joint ventures have announced plans for an improved supersonic airplane service to the Far East.

Boeing 707 prototype stratotanker-stratoliner during its initial flight on July 15, 1954. Some stratoliners were equipped with Pullman-like berths for transoceanic flights, and thus momentarily broke the linkage between high speed and extreme discomfort. Immediately below: A De Haviland Comet III on its maiden flight on July 21, 1954, over the countryside of Hertfordshire, England.

The space shuttle *Columbia* blasts off a few seconds past 7 A.M. on April 12, 1981. NASA hailed the event as the "dawn of a new age of space flight." In fact, federal policy has not yet defined the role of competitive, privately financed technology in the "new age"; the question remains open whether the NASA bureaucracy is the most effective and economical route for the maintenance of American leadership in astronautics. How are we to encourage the *next* generation of rocket engines? Below: A design for an "Erector Set" type of solar-power satellite to be assembled in space. Right: A "mass driver" is accelerating some materials from the surface of an asteroid, thereby changing the orbit of the asteroid to make it more easily accessible to earth-launched rockets.

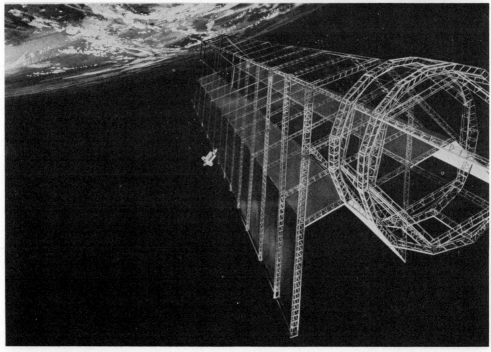

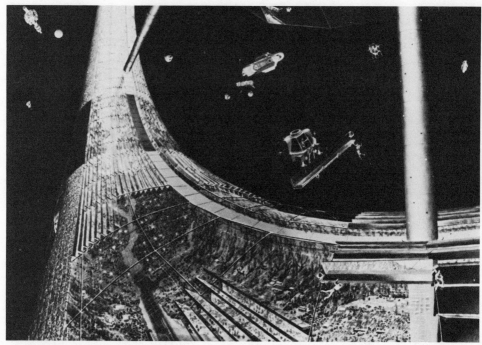

A segment of a torus-shaped space colony for 10,000 inhabitants, as developed in a ten-week-long Ames/Stanford summer study. Farming sections are interspersed with populated areas; artificial gravity would be provided. The diameter is 150 yards.

A closer view of the space-colony interior, based on a more ambitious hypothesis: a colony with a diameter of 4 miles, a length of 10 miles, and the ability to support several hundred thousand people. The bridge is similar in size to the San Francisco Bay Bridge. BUT—would it not be easier to colonize the moon first?

Coalition and Consensus: A New Paradigm

THE ACCEPTED PARADIGM OR MENTAL MODEL THAT LONG AC-
cepted mere quantitative increases in the production of goods
and services as evidence of human progress no longer commands general allegiance. While the strictures of the Club of
Rome are not universally accepted as social gospel, nonetheless
most people now agree that many of our problems derive from
past technological successes: Mass production and monolithic
housing have led to alienation; the automobile and rapid transit
produced congestion; industrial prowess multiplied pollution.
But even a relatively mild bout with a world recession has restored a sense of balance: It turns out that "flexible manufacturing" is needed to maintain the United States' competitive
position, and that this in turn requires a more highly skilled and
better motivated work force; technology itself has provided us
with the means for building safer and more convivial neighborhoods; industry can be designed and sited so that it is not a blot
on the landscape.

In short, the neoindustrial paradigm includes the discovery
that technology must, after all, be linked to articulated purposes
and that if appropriately directed it can improve the human con-

dition. Whether it does so or not is not a function of scale but of the match of purpose to means. If the person in the street is skeptical of the impartiality of the scientific method, that may mean another change in the traditional paradigm; but James Bryant Conant himself was careful to debunk the myth of "a scientific method" two generations ago: "There are only," wrote Dr. Conant, "the methods of scientists." [1] It is now accepted that human beings are part of nature and utterly dependent on nature's bounty: We are not, despite William James's great essay, in a permanent "war against nature." And where an earlier generation concentrated on the meticulous "division of labor," ours is challenged to set new precedents for teamwork, synthesis, and mutual comprehension.

The United States, with its complexity, its multitudinous problems and opportunities, cannot focus for any considerable length of time on a single grand object such as the persistent Dutch battle against encroachment of the sea. For a short time, the public may be fascinated with "space spectaculars" or other dramatic feats of engineering, but for the longer haul, there must be a balanced, rational series of programs tailored to perceived necessities and using to the full the resources of private enterprise as well as the public purse. In Governor Clinton's time, a single engineering project—the Erie Canal—made it possible for our developing nation to "leap forward" and to compress into a short space of time developments that otherwise might have dragged on over scores of years. Supersonic underground transit *might* constitute a comparable focus in the decades immediately ahead of us; but there are also urgent tasks in outer space, in the oceans, and on the surface of our own territory. The next "giant step" must therefore be seen as a nexus of separate but conceptually interrelated projects.

If the paradigm suggested above does indeed command something approaching a new national consensus, then an event of some importance has occurred or is in the process of occurring: There is a latent but genuine constituency for long-range policies, for the equal protection of the economy and the environment, and for balanced attention to the requirements of defense and the overarching need to seek an end to the continual threat of mutual incineration. If this indeed is a correct reading of the climate of American opinion, then the nation is ready to take those specific steps that alone can translate such a new determination into the physical, educational, and institutional improvements that must now be the main objects of attention of public and private authorities alike. A task of our national leadership is to select those few objectives that can attract and retain substantial public support over the long run.[3] Once several major efforts that are clearly in our economic, environmental, and security interests are observably under way, there will be a good momentum for overhauling attitudes, curricula, and even institutional arrangements.

When people's basic wants are satisfied, when no dire threats loom on the horizon, an incremental approach to life is generally accepted as normal and desirable. It is only when our security or status is subject to threat or attack that we sharpen analytical powers, demand higher levels of performance from high and low alike, and expect community-wide cooperation under charismatic or at least logical leadership. The United States, like other nations, is a product of incremental growth interrupted by the bursts of legislative enthusiasm that occur in times of stress; it is therefore quite understandable that in this era of multiple risks we should look more deeply at our problems and hope for more "systematic" thinking as part of an effort at coherence and perspective. Can there be an operationally viable focus for such a discussion?

The gigantic array of hydroelectric projects presently under construction near James Bay—at a total cost of upward of fifteen billion dollars—shows that North America is capable of long-range planning and action. Although schedules have been "stretched out" because of the present easing of the energy supply crisis, the Province of Quebec has demonstrated its ability to persist with a major undertaking despite cyclical problems and temporary marketing difficulties. The greatest of all Western Hemisphere dam projects, however, is in South America, on the Brazil-Paraguay border. The March 19, 1983, *Economist* reported that, with its 12,700 megawatt hydroelectric plant, Itaipu will be "the largest in the world when it is fully operative in 1988. It will generate more electricity than Britain's six largest power stations."

The Paraná, South America's second largest river after the Amazon, has been rerouted to facilitate the project; forty thousand workers were employed during construction—and forty thousand people were removed from their homes when fourteen thousand square kilometers of farmland and forests were flooded. Itaipu will appreciably reduce Brazil's vulnerability should there be another wordwide oil shortage; meanwhile, Brazil will have *excess* energy capacity. That this is indeed a world-class project may be gleaned from the comparison with the Grand Coulee Dam in the United States, which has a generating capacity of 10,800 megawatts.

Because of the urgency of flood protection and irrigation, China has the world's most extensive network of dams—more than 13,500 according to the *Economist*, that is, more than twice the number of large dams as the United States. Five of the world's highest dams are still under construction, and despite increasingly severe criteria, the World Bank continues to finance very large dams in developing countries where social and economic benefits are believed to outweigh costs that can be identified in advance.

It will be remembered that the decision of President Nasser to nationalize the Suez Canal was provoked by the reversal by Secretary of State Dulles of the United States plan to provide financing for the Aswan High Dam. Here is an instance where macro-engineering not only affected world diplomacy but led to open warfare (when the United Kingdom, France, and Israel jointly invaded Egypt after the takeover of the canal). The dam was built with Soviet assistance in the 1960's, but it has proven to be at best a mixed blessing: Although the twenty-one-hundred-megawatt plant does provide electricity and irrigation has been extended, Lake Nasser, the third largest reservoir in the world, has itself required the removal of a sizable farm population, and there has been damage to fisheries (notably the sardine industry) and to soil because of increasing salinity, and there have been the ravages of the Bilharzia parasite. The ease with which President Sadat expelled the Russians from Egypt was not unrelated to disillusionment with the Soviet-backed High Aswan Dam.

Wilson Clark, in his comprehensive book *Energy for Survival*,[2] comments on the "increase to epidemic proportions of a slow-killing disease called schistosomiasis, or bilharziasis, which is carried by a certain type of snail found in the Nile and other rivers of Africa. In years past, the annual Nile floods have washed enough of the snails out to sea to keep the snail population to manageable proportions. The calm, gentle waters of Lake Nasser, however, provided the environment the snails need to establish a real foothold and multiply without restraint. The snails serve as an interim host to the larvae of a blood fluke that, upon entering the human body, attacks the liver, stomach, heart, and lungs. The recorded death rate from the disease is high, and no one is certain how many additional deaths from heart attacks, kidney failures, and other organic disorders may actually be caused by it. An increase in dam construction in Rhodesia has also mirrored the increase in bilharziasis, and construction of the Sennar Dam in Sudan brought the same deteriorating health conditions there."

Clark then cites, very aptly, the conclusion of a scientist at Washington University in St. Louis, Missouri:

> The tremendous, continuing increase in the incidence of bilharziasis is one more manifestation of a biological dilemma: The basic vulnerability of an artificial ecosystem. Disease and suffering for millions of people are a direct outcome of the attempt to control the processes of nature with the simplistic solutions that modern technology offers in the form of simple, managed ecosystems in place of the intrinsically complex natural systems.

There *are* promising ways forward, but they will involve expertise that resides in professions other than civil engineering: This is precisely why M.I.T.'s Macro-Engineering Research Group has, from the outset, recommended interdisciplinary, interprofessional, intersectoral, and—where appropriate—international teams to evaluate and design large-scale engineering projects. For those particularly interested in the hydroelectric alternative to deforestation and soil erosion in developing countries, the *New Scientist* of April 9, 1981, carried an article well worth perusing: "Saving Nepal's Dwindling Forests." Fabian Acker, in this careful report, urged cross-flow turbines to bring mills closer to the consumer. "Wood supplies 85 per cent of Nepal's total energy," he affirmed. "Each citizen consumes an average of 600 kg a year. But the country's forests grow only around 80 kg per person a year. . . . The Nepalese use water power mainly to drive mills for grinding grain, but it would be fairly simple to install a generator to provide electricity for light and perhaps even for cooking." Acker also applauds the growing use of biogas generators fueled with cow dung.

What all this indicates is not only the need for interdisciplinary knowledge, but the need for a deep knowledge of social patterns as well: The introduction of new technology, even if it is not "advanced" or "macro," is an act of social engineering. By assembling and studying actual cases—life that has been lived—macro-engineers of the future will be enabled to make more appropriate suggestions when they operate outside the bounds of the societies with whose habits and constraints they are familiar. In our own country, we should not find it too burdensome to acquire relevant information before making detailed plans or proposals: That there have been "bloopers" in past uses of macrotechnology is well known; but unless we are inherently stupid, there is no reason to assume that mistakes must be repeated: The essence of a free society is its constitutional ability to correct its own errors.

Especially if we are on the verge of a group of major technological enterprises, it is well to confront the problem of societal risk squarely and without embarrassment. On the initiative of two very bright students, Stephen Ehrmann and C. Lawrence Meador, I was induced—because of some remarks made at an informal lunch at the Faculty Club at M.I.T.—to launch a seminar entitled "Failure of Human Systems." Meetings of the seminar became quite popular events, perhaps for the reason that some very well-known faculty members, learning about the course, volunteered to speak openly about failures in their fields of specialty. I remember a fine talk by the chairman of the Department of Aeronautics and Astronautics, René Miller, on the subject of failures of aircraft; Herbert Hollomon, director of the Center for Policy Alternatives and a former president of the University of Oklahoma, spoke eloquently of the role of failure in the various situations in which he had found himself, in academia and in Washington, D.C., where he had served as Assistant Secretary of Commerce for Science and Technology; and we had the constant coaching of the judicious Dr. Merton Kahne, professor of psychiatry at both M.I.T. and Harvard, and chief of the Psychiatric Services of the Massachusetts Institute of Technology.

What we learned in all of this—and the course announcement stated that students were invited to join a field of inquiry that as yet had no acknowledged existence—was that failure experiences are valuable, that they teach us the limits of what can or should be done. The individuals and institutions that can treat failure as a *learning experience* rather than as a harbinger of disasters to come are those that will most likely earn the rewards of success. In warfare, it is often the nations that suffer grave losses at the onset of hostilities that, if they have time and will to recuperate, prove to be the winners in the end. Surgeons and even judges have been known to make mistakes; but that does not mean that we condemn the practice of surgery or the rule of law as norms for social behavior. Sir Robert Jackson has pointed out to me the close connection between the failure of the Ground-Nuts scheme and the launching of major (rather successful) hydroelectric projects in Africa in the years closely following World War II.

My own observations of research and development in the United States have led me to the conclusion that we are not prepared, at this time, to undertake a "crash program" of macro-engineering, even if we wished to do so and even if the highest authorities in the land, in industry and in government, were in agreement that this is a correct and necessary policy. While there is a great deal of interesting and valuable work going on, it is insufficiently focused; we have not done the particular homework that must be accomplished if we are to undertake vast new programs with adequate confidence that they will achieve their objectives and not result in unforeseen and undesirable impacts. However, the homework can be identified once there is agreement on the specific topics and programs to be studied. And the design teams or study groups could be formed in short order, and with every prospect that they would come up with solutions that would assist measurably in improving the nation's infrastructure, industry, environment, and security. Let me cite a few examples.

If the United States wished to develop a railway service superior even to the "maglev" high-speed trains undergoing full-scale testing in Japan, a competent engineering group would have to be recruited and authorized to build a prototype; the final design of the prototype would have to be reviewed, and a choice made between surface and underground emplacement. If underground tunnels were decided upon, it would be necessary to build and test full-scale models of tunneling machines capable of long-distance service at reasonable cost and with sufficient reliability. At the moment, there is no diversified tunneling laboratory in the United States, and no center for the design and testing of electromagnetically levitated trains. The further matter of designing and testing controls that would operate reliably at ultrahigh speeds would constitute a third field for research and development. Altogether, five to ten years would be needed to "prove out" the system.

Consultants emerging from prestigious business and management schools have found a ready market for studies of "strategic planning." No doubt this is a valid and serious topic for American and other firms and for government agencies at every level. But we should be a bit careful lest first-class talent be dissipated on a great many small projects that have very little long-term strategic value for American society as a whole. For perhaps twenty million dollars a year over a period of five years, I would surmise, the United States—if public and private abilities were pooled—could design and start testing a transit system that could be a generation ahead of our international competition. But to date, the leaders of the transportation industry, segregated as they are into separate compartments labeled "aerospace, rail, highway, shipping, pipelines," etc., have not been able to consider the one primordial question: What can the best talent in transportation and allied disciplines come up with that will place the United States in a leadership position with respect to the ease and pace of long-distance travel and transportation?

I have been impressed by the fact that Dr. Kyotani has sent one of his very bright students to M.I.T., where the young man is studying *aeronautical* engineering before returning to his post with Japanese National *Railways!* In the United States, there are few incentives for our best engineering students to enter the field of railway technology, which has been shamelessly abandoned by government and industry alike. Of course, the argument can be made that highway travel is now so sophisticated that the nineteenth-century type of rail system is outmoded, that arguments for the resuscitation of an American railroad industry are sentimental, impractical, and too expensive. But I am not talking about the revival of the Yankee Clipper, outstanding though that train was in its day. I am suggesting that we should be planning not just to evaluate, but also to design and test a system that operates at close to supersonic speed.

There are, in addition to the technical problems, the vital questions about system costs and revenues. And here, let me state my biases: Traffic and revenue potential ought to be studied, at least in a preliminary manner, by the firms whose opinions on long-distance rail and air travel are customarily relied upon by investment banks. If a first study is made by a bright graduate student or an amateur accountant, let us have the people who have made their livelihoods for years by making traffic and revenue forecasts review those preliminary estimates and come up with a believable range of income that will be available to a mature, completed system. The input of professional traffic engineers will be essential to the planning group, because the system must be designed to attract traffic, not to amuse the media.

As for costs, the big expense will be the tunneling effort; despite improvements in methods, tunneling is still a very costly affair, and the very best engineering minds in the field must be brought together to select equipment to be tested, to design necessary prototypes, and to carry out tests under varying conditions of terrain. The mining industry digs many hundreds—if not thousands—of tunnels every year, and mining engineers should be part of the team. If ultimately it proves feasible to establish a high-speed grid of freight and passenger trains operating reliably underground, the benefits to this nation's environment, economy, and security would be enormous. I have no doubt that such a system would lead, in due course, to intercontinental links of great value to the United States and its trading partners.

It is not too early to interest leading investment bankers in the idea of a nationwide high-speed underground or surface transport grid, interfaced at "strategic" intervals with intermodal transfer, storage, and processing facilities. Such a system would require macrofinance, and there would have to be assurances of funding despite awkward aberrations in business and other cycles. The World Bank provides just such assured long-range finance for developing countries. The United States is by far the largest contributor, and I think rightly so, to the World Bank. But I fail to understand why it is logical for the American taxpayer to underwrite billions of dollars of investment in basic infrastructure abroad and to refuse, rather prissily I think, to form an institution with similar powers and duties at home. Felix Rohatyn, the banker who has helped keep New York City from going over the deep end financially, has proposed some interesting institutional innovations; the governor of New Jersey, Thomas Kean, has suggested an "infrastructure bank" to operate within his own state, and I am sure the country has the financial and legal talent to enable it to set up, with proper safeguards, an institutional fabric that will insulate infrastructure investments from the vicissitudes of politics and short-term business cycles. If a full faith and credit guarantee can be made available by Congress to ailing automobile and aircraft firms, perhaps such a guarantee should, with all reasonable safeguards, be provided for a fund to make possible the financing of selected major projects that will, with proper leadership, improve America's wealth, health, and safety.

The tiny nation of Holland has managed to finance an enormously expensive dike-building program in the last few years; the British, with all their problems, have nearly completed a billion-dollar barrier to defend the London region against the Thames floods that on occasion can be very menacing indeed; France's railway system, with TGV (*trains de grande vitesse*—trains of great speed) service now extended to Lyon, Geneva, and shortly other key destinations as well, makes huge capital improvements year after year. Should not our country combine its aerospace prowess with the not-to-be-despised abilities of our

leading engineering organizations in order to design a ground—
or underground—transportation system that will be second to
none?

This is in no sense a plea for a reckless, headlong, spend-
thrift rush into untested systems. What I do plead for is a
phased, sober, professionally guided interdisciplinary program
to begin to design, test, and evaluate about half a dozen innovative macrosystems that could have a "triggering effect" on our
economic and environmental health. We have reached a point
where no serious person disputes the necessity for rigid environmental safeguards whenever new—or old—technological systems are to be built; costs that in "neanderthal" times were
blithely imposed on the community must now be absorbed by the
activity that creates the problem in the first place. But an underground transport system would, if carefully and correctly designed, be of more help to the American environment than,
conceivably, a dozen additional "environmental organizations."
In fact, the next step in the environmental movement, I think,
would be to study alternative macrosystems and to play an active
role in their assessment and selection.

The vital step of constituting research and development
groups that are working on specific engineering systems rather
than on vague, general assessments is one that I trust will not be
too long delayed. Especially with the addition of "high tech" capabilities, it is important that there be a true "combined operation" including all the various skills and disciplines so that each
team may evolve its own morale and momentum. I think we can
learn a great deal from the episode of dirigibles; the German
dirigibles had fewer accidents in proportion to the number of
flights than the dirigibles of other countries, and my cursory
reading of the history of this technology leads me to conclude
that the sense of pride and continuity developed at the hangars
established by Count Zeppelin was the key factor in the excellence of the German product. Professor Francis Morse at Boston
University's College of Engineering and other experts have recommended a "new model" macrodirigible; it is an idea worth
exploring, but I think if it is to be accomplished it should be
proposed as a joint venture with the North German groups and
families that retain an affection for this technology and the sense

of quality production and loyal teamwork without which little that is lasting can be achieved.

Much criticism has been leveled at the "multinational corporation," as if it were somehow sinful to operate in more than one national environment. In fact, it seems to me that combinations with like-minded groups in other friendly countries to develop technologies of mutual interest should be regarded as nonexceptional and intrinsically desirable. The laws of each nation can provide safeguards against abuses and irregularities of all kinds; but if there were multinational interest in a supersonic underground transport system from Montreal to Mexico City, with local stops in Washington, D.C., Chicago, and Dallas, should this not be encouraged?

No doubt for the next generation or two, infrastructure will not be subject to dramatic change. For one thing, the highways, airways, pipelines, shipping routes, and railways now in place were very costly, must somehow be amortized, and the people whose livelihoods are intertwined with their perpetuation will not willingly see them scrapped and superseded. But I think the new paradigm to which I referred earlier includes—or will soon include—a realization that we must provide the procedures and instrumentalities for retraining people; once this is accomplished, improved methods of work will arouse less hostility and will in fact be welcomed. Other countries and cultures have proved that they can adapt to change, and I do not really think that Americans have grown so crotchety that they will automatically resist innovation. If we wish to retain a national surplus so that the finer arts of living can be cultivated, we should favor a neoindustrial society that can earn its own way: The experience of Italy's Renaissance seems to indicate that affluence is favorable for architecture, painting, music, and literature; without patrons and sponsors, the arts languish. If it is urged that an all-powerful state can also be a patron, I would simply point out that Solzhenitsyn prefers to live in Vermont, and the daughter of Stalin emigrated to the United States.

Along with improvements to our earthly infrastructure, I trust that public opinion will insist on an American space program that is more extensive, more realistic, and better funded on a long-term basis than the present NASA program. In April

1982, when I attended an annual meeting of the American Institute of Aeronautics and Astronautics in the attractive setting so ably redeveloped by the Rouse organization, I was struck by one fact: the absence of young men and women, except for a few individuals who were actually conspicuous in the crowd because of their relative youth. We had the privilege of being addressed by the novelist James Michener, who noticed this fact from the podium and commented on it. One cannot blame the young: Why should they risk years of study when there is no "career path" assured by a steadfast national commitment to space industrialization and development?

For space development, as for land-based infrastructure programs of major dimensions and for substantial ocean technology commitments as well, I think we shall have to give serious thought to the funding of independent public authorities that would function very much as Port Authority and Toll-Road Authority organizations have done, and with such notable success, during the past forty years and more. Such publicly constituted bodies obtain their funding from the capital markets of the private sector, but with the advantage of legally binding undertakings by public agencies that they will provide assistance—by deeds of commission and omission alike—that will protect the authorities' mission.

At sea, once the uncertainties surrounding the Law of the Sea Treaty have been dealt with, the United States will wish to push forward with the aggressive development of new capabilities in the growing field of ocean engineering. Twenty years ago, I was involved in conversations with some leading offshore oil-drilling companies and others on proposals for the extended use of subsea methods in oil recovery from the continental shelf. More recently, owing to the megadevelopments of the North Sea oil fields, the British and others have actually built submarines that carry out inspection and repair activities at very great water depths. Thanks to the United States Navy program of submarine building, there is a great deal of experienced talent with the capability for designing, building, and operating sophisticated undersea facilities of all kinds, and it is important to us as a nation to see that this capability is fully exploited. In the beginning, activities such as mining and oil exploration and recovery from the bottom of the sea are apt to be expensive: There is a learning curve, plus the capital costs of new equipment and systems. But as a net importer of energy and minerals, there is every reason for the United States to be in the forefront of developments: It is not sufficient to monitor the progress of others. The cadre of experienced people that now exists should pass on its skills to a new generation of dedicated specialists. But as with space, recruitment for ocean engineering will lag unless there are programs and industries that can offer employment and the prospect of an active career.

It is no denigration of the need and value of alternative energy sources to mention the continuing market for conventional energy sources as well. Looked at from the viewpoint of national strategic planning, the United States should be in a position to transport oil and compressed gas via submarine tankers, to undertake mining from submarine facilities on the sea bottom, and to haul bulk cargoes and personnel in freighter submarines that would be available in times of crisis as auxiliaries to the fleet. Five-sixths of the earth's surface is covered by the waters of the ocean; the world population is still growing exponentially, and industrialization continues to be employed by developing countries as their main "ace-in-the-hole" against overwhelming poverty. These are facts, and although many intelligent people might wish them otherwise, a continuing demand for raw materials will push the search for them to the subsea territories that remain untouched and virginal with the single exception of the relatively shallow seas of the continental shelves.

American prowess in ocean engineering will not be assured by the mere collection of data, useful and necessary though this may be. What is needed is a carefully thought out program capable of yielding a monetary return: A merely military or scientific approach will not, in my judgment, receive the long-term public support needed for major programs. America's great strength, in the final analysis, lies in the free exercise of its people's talent and dedication, and historically the free-enterprise approach— aided and abetted by wise governmental policy—has proven the most successful method of eliciting sustained accomplishment. If we return again to the case of the Erie Canal, it is important to remember that although the work was carried out by the state of

New York and its contractors, the money was raised by bonds sold to the public (and very promptly repaid!) The "mixed-economy" corporation, the public authority, the intersectoral joint venture are all possibilities that, together with other forms of association and agreement, should be fully investigated as methods open to us once priorities and programs are defined and there is an official, publicly approved decision to proceed.

The construction of artificial islands, either "free standing" or based on seamounts, seems to me a field in which the United States should participate actively. An American engineer who had headed the Hudson Institute team that in the sixties recommended an artificial series of "Great Lakes" in South America—Robert Panero—devoted several years recently to an effort to develop a modern port and transshipment complex in the western Pacific. Now that Ernest Frankel has endorsed the idea of "movable ports," perhaps this alternative of "floating artificial islands" that can be relocated in accordance with the shifting requirements of international trade will prove more acceptable both socially and environmentally. There is no reason to interfere with settled societies of a type described so vividly by Herman Melville, when we have, *due to megatechnology*, the option of building whatever is required in the empty spaces of the ocean and in a manner most serviceable to the requirements of commerce.

A further reason for a programmed "thrust" into ocean space may be provided by jurisdictional considerations: If a settlement is established on a firm basis, at least some of the attributes of sovereignty will follow. In international law, this is a rather complex and technical question, concerning which authorities such as J. D. Nyhart and Milton Katz would be better qualified to pontificate than I; but it seems clear that some extension of United States sovereignty into ocean areas not yet "parceled out" by treaty or custom may prove useful. Here again, a decision to proceed with a given program ought to flow from a thoroughly *interdisciplinary* team, including (in this case) "proctors in admiralty" as well as specialists like Neil Ruzic who, having written *The Case for Going to the Moon* long before the Apollo Program, is now busy developing a (nonartificial) "Island for Science" in the tropics.

If "artificial islands" should strike anyone as a "bizarre" idea, it is well to remember that, for most of its people, Holland is an "artificial country." Except for the above-sea-level portion of its territory where only a minority of its population dwells, the Netherlands (aptly nomenclatured!) must be regarded as essentially a network of linked artificial islands. Even "natural" islands can disappear or "pop up," as Surtsey reminded us, when volcanic activity under the sea suddenly produced it in 1965, five hundred miles northwest of Scotland. Whether the first artificially contrived "sea-city" should be built within territorial waters or in waters regarded as international may depend more on specific economic opportunities than on considerations of law and jurisdiction; however, the anticipated legal regime affects the economics to such an extent that, here again, it would be prudent to invite a good international lawyer to the first meeting. And government interests are so palpably evident that the first meeting ought to be "intersectoral," too.

One reason it may be useful to settle upon "macro-engineering" as a generic term for so many diverse types of activity is that there are important dynamic interactions between and among the subsets I have mentioned. For instance, there is an obvious and immediate relationship between a decision to proceed with large infrastructure developments and the provision of the industrial complexes—for steel, concrete, and other materials—needed to assure supplies for construction. Similarly, advances in the "high tech" elements for space exploration or military systems can be of great assistance to the communications and transport technologies that form so large a part of the category known as infrastructure.

This linkage explains, for instance, the importance that Ian McGregor, recently chairman of the British Steel Corporation, has attached to an Anglo-French official decision to proceed with a permanent transport link between the United Kingdom and France.

There is a significant linkage, also, between the evolution of earthbound infrastructure capabilities and humankind's ability to develop the resources of the moon and other heavenly bodies. Automated tunneling, an achievement that will probably be within reach within a decade or two, will immensely facilitate mining on the moon and the building of permanent settlements there. A great deal is now known about the composition of the outer crustal layer of the moon, and in view of low lunar gravity compared to that of the planet Earth, it appears likely that the lunar surface will be used as a launching platform for the various artifacts and installations that will be designed for operations "in orbit." Likewise, it will be economic to use lunar materials rather than materials that must be transported from the gravitational field of the earth at much higher costs. As better space transport engines are devised, financed, and built, we may expect the mining of the asteroid belt and the moon to come within the range of what investment bankers can consider as reasonable. Meanwhile, it is not only a sound national investment to retain and expand our capabilities in space exploitation and development, it would be imprudent to fail to finance those preliminary steps that can help the United States and its trading partners to gain actual experience with new technologies as they become available.

If we can indeed move on to a new plateau of agreement on essentials, then the *technology component* of specific programs can be accelerated: The Apollo Program involved innovations and risks far more demanding, for instance, than called for by Dr. Salter's idea of a supersonic subway. In conversations with senior colleagues at the Massachusetts Institute of Technology, I found far less doubt about the nation's ability to accomplish the technological improvements that would be needed than about the economic and social justification of a scheme that would permit coast-to-coast travel and transport in an hour or less. In macro-engineering planning, I think it is a good rule to ask specialists about questions in which they are expert; for instance, engineers should be asked to answer questions on technology; when it comes to finance, feasibility questions should be addressed to senior bankers, insurance executives, or government officials having policy-level responsibility for financial decisions. Similarly, questions about social and environmental impacts should be directed to sociologists, social psychiatrists, experts in environmental medicine, and so on. It will not be possible to take advantage of the nation's enormous capabilities in engineering if policy decisions—such as whether to commission a preliminary study at all—are left in the hands of unidisciplinary specialists, however eminent they may be.

The reason there is something of a "club atmosphere" in macro-engineering discussions is that, in the nature of things, only a relatively small number of executives and experts can play a critical role in the associated processes of decision-making and control. Looking back on the complex series of events that re-launched the channel tunnel project as a "live" subject for debate and decision after World War II, I think that a key "confidence building" event, at least so far as I am concerned, was the terse "yep" of Mr. George Brown, when he was asked if the twenty-one-mile undersea link could in fact be built. Brown & Root had just completed the Roberts Tunnel, which brings water to Denver across the Great Divide. Mr. Brown seemed to be sure that if his team could build a twenty-mile tunnel on land, one mile more under the sea would not make that much difference: Land under the sea is land nonetheless.

There is a further distinction to be made, and while it may seem obvious once it is mentioned, in fact a great deal of public business is transacted as if the distinction really didn't exist—or count. I refer to the distinction between a "policy" decision and an operational "project" or "program" decision. In the one case, an attitude and constraints or options may have been set up to guide future meetings on the same set of issues. In the latter case, dirt begins to fly. It is relatively easy and inexpensive to make a policy decision: It can be changed, explained away, or allowed to die and be forgotten. Very different is the atmosphere of a group that knows that there is a job to do, a row to be hoed.

This book, for instance, while it has argued the possible merits and demerits of various projects and programs, has above all pleaded for a national policy broad enough to include macro-engineering as an element of intersectoral activities, indeed as a *key element* in the processes of information acquisition and decision-making. If we do not really expect to build large technological systems, then of course there is little incentive to take the preliminary steps that are necessary, such as information acquisition and institution-building. Once a national policy is established and believed in, however, there can be a host of useful and often indispensable measures that will contribute to our capacity to undertake tasks for which, in fact, few other nations are as well prepared.

Cooperation with Canada has been so continuous and obvious for very many years that the relationship, at least on the official level, has been allowed to slacken and even deteriorate. Canada has had severe internal problems because of its bilingualism; at the same time, there has been a rise in national assertiveness, a quite normal phenomenon in view of the fact that our northern neighbor has become an industrial power in its own right. Canada resents the implication that it should be a mere supplier of raw materials to the more populous nation to its south. On the other hand, the two nations share a long frontier—the longest undefended border in the world—and a host of common concerns about environmental health, resource development, and economic growth. In the field of transport and energy, there is the prodigious and successful example of cooperation for the St. Lawrence Seaway and Power Project.

More broadly, there should be contacts on a routine basis, and not just when something special comes up, between officials at the policy level and between members of the Parliament in Ottawa and their "opposite numbers" in the Congress sitting in Washington, D.C. There ought to be a constant airing of problems that arise between the two countries and above all of programs on which they can cooperate to their mutual betterment. The development of Canadian resources is necessarily a *Canadian* affair, but where Canadian policy favors joint financing or international marketing arrangements, the United States should have consultative machinery *in being* so that we need not "reinvent the wheel" every time something new comes up. American and French interests played an important and constructive role in the finance and management of the Churchill Falls Hydro-Electric Project. The market for electricity in New England and New York has been a positive factor in the James Bay hydroelectric program. But new projects must have their "seed time," and more frequent meetings, even in the absence of critical issues or disputes, can be very helpful by giving the participants an opportunity to know each other better and to become more conversant with the different problems that face policy-level people on the two sides of the border.

Dr. Arthur J. Cordell, economic adviser of the Science Council of Canada, presented a critical survey of the "Socio-Economics of Technological Progress" in a talk before Carleton University in Ottawa, on February 23, 1972. He concluded, "The tendency to prescribe more technology to solve some of the specific and easily identifiable ills is, in my view, a wrong approach." To those who labor in the construction industry and who see in humankind's engineering proclivities a positive force, Dr. Cordell's strictures may come as something of a shock. But he, too, is looking beyond mere technology, beyond mere economics, for a new paradigm that can reintroduce quality, compassion, and beauty into a civilization that has been overfascinated by quantity, interchangeability of parts (and of people), and the drabness associated with mass production. It seems to me that the emerging paradigm that casts technology as a servant and companion of environmental improvement is the proper response to concerns—legitimate and important concerns—that grew out of the studies of the Club of Rome, the Stockholm Conference on the Environment, and other pioneering efforts to counter the carte blanche previously accorded industrialization, even in intellectual circles. Having come this far, however, I do not think that either the Science Council of Canada or the National Science Foundation of the United States would exclude technology as a method of addressing specific social—and environmental—problems. The idea of limiting all industrial and economic growth had great appeal while world opinion—particularly in nations already industrialized—coped with the studies of the Club of Rome. Those studies, which changed basic attitudes to a remarkable degree, have increased sensitivity to issues that had been insufficiently recognized; the present disposition is to transform the methods and impacts of industrialization so that the environment and the public health may be *improved*; and in this new endeavor, "high tech" is a powerful potential ally.

We have, in recent years, undergone a number of "challenges," commencing perhaps with Jacques Servain-Schreiber's curious *Le Défi Américain* (which sold quite well in the United

States, as also in France) and, in 1980, from the same author, *The World Challenge*. For Americans, however, I suspect that the real challenge is to ourselves: Are we to remain in a dead-end of self-deprecation and self-doubt, or are we to treat past mistakes and failures as a learning experience? It has often been pointed out that Japan's steel industry, which has chalked up such stunning successes in its competition with the American steel industry, must pay for even more stringent environmental regulations than those imposed in the United States. The debate between "environmentalists" and "industrializers" may be prolonged by those who have not been able to learn a new vocabulary or to discern a growing convergence of economic and environmental thinking, but our problem, essentially, is to use the next "wave" of industrialization as a powerful new tool in the service of drastic environmental improvement.

People in positions of power and influence *can* amuse themselves, in ways that most of us would be surprised by, perhaps for the very reason that their reactions are so human and so understandable. If one is very attached to a particular decision or project, however, which depends utterly on the casual opinion of a person with the real power of decision, the exogenous variable represented by personality quirks may become a subject of concern. I know that historical events—or nonevents—ought to turn on more weighty considerations; but for the principal players in the game of power politics, even a macroproject may seem to be "small potatoes." What must still command great admiration in the story of the Suez Canal, in this connection, is the adroitness and thoroughness of Lesseps when confronted with difficult personalities in high places: That he correctly sized up the pasha of Egypt was confirmed by the episode when Lesseps, at the end of a long day in the desert, jumped his horse over a high wall, thus gaining the unstinted admiration of the pasha, who on that very evening signed the concessionary documents for the Suez Canal.[4]

A less exogenous variable, but a troublesome one nonetheless, is presented by situations where governments are in office for a very short time. Some delightful and stable small countries nonetheless keep changing their governments; this surely has inconveniences for the domestic population, but it makes it ultradifficult to conclude long-range international agreements concerning major programs: Ministers are simply not in office long enough to form an educated view on matters brought to them; very often, by the time a government is ready to make up its mind, it is on the way out. This may have been a factor in the frequent delays and postponements of what some commentators call "the Danish national project," i.e., the proposal to build a bridge across the Great Belt and thus link together the island on which Copenhagen is situated with the other part of Denmark, which occupies the northern half of the Jutland Peninsula.

I think that enough has been written in these pages to make it perfectly clear that we shall see more and more of cross-water linkages within and between countries, and even between continents. Moreover, if, as, and when tunneling becomes less hazardous and more economical, we shall see not just a domestic but a *global* shift to long-distance tunnel transport modes. If this bit of futurism can be accepted, it changes the framework within which discussions have been conducted concerning—among other projects—the channel tunnel. Such a linkage must thenceforward be viewed not as a strange aberration in surface land transportation, but as the first step in a future very high-speed system capable of linking London with Paris by a direct, London-Paris tunnel. Most of the technology for the fast trains—or guided vehicles—already exists and has been tested; but tunneling technology is still too costly for such enterprises to be bankable; ten or twenty years may make a vast difference, however. What can be said with some confidence even at this early date is that the nation that first succeeds in introducing and operating a businesslike underground transport system that can reliably perform at high speeds (600 mph and upward) over long distances will have established a major international market for a new industry.

In the 1920's and the 1930's, when the pipeline industry was in its infancy, railroad magnates had the opportunity of capitalizing on their rights-of-way by entering the pipeline industry themselves or by teaming up in joint ventures with the pipelines; instead, the railroads chose the path of an outright competitive war, a war that still continues and intensifies as coal slurry and analogous pipelines struggle for the right to cross the nearly ubiquitous railroad rights-of-way. I think a similar crossroads now confronts the aerospace industry. Leading aerospace companies, it seems to me, have the talent and the technology needed for the "flight" of levitated trains through a tunnel or tube; these are precisely the companies that should be designating small groups of specialists to prepare underground transport systems of the future. Of course, L. K. Edwards, who proposed "gravity-vacuum" flight in the sixties, came from Lockheed Aircraft; and Mr. Foa, who worked on early models of a tunnel system using evacuated air, came to the subject with the benefit of the aerodynamics background of the Rensselaer Polytechnic Institute. But a new coalition is needed now, one that will include civil engineering contractors of the old school together *with* aerospace companies. I doubt if such groupings can be formed from within the engineering profession; but with leadership from innovation-minded investment bankers and perhaps a friendly nudge from government—including one from a Department of Defense that finds even *its* huge budget insufficient for all the games that must be played, I think that the *right* kind of conference could be held; such a meeting, if attended by policy-level executives determined to get results, could deserve the appellation "historic."

In 1972, Patrick Beaver concluded his *History of Tunnels* by asserting, "The tunnelling machine of the future will be fully automated, capable of digging, mucking, lining and, if necessary, grouting in one single coordinated operation." I was privileged to observe, hundreds of feet below the Tsugaru Straits, that the Japanese have already developed an operational grouting system that is fully automated. Other steps toward automation have been taken elsewhere. If the device of a special tunnel research institution, which I suggested earlier, seems too creaky and time-consuming, there is always an alternative: If a creditworthy agency announces that it will pay a fixed price to the firm that offers to dig a tunnel along a specific route, using a fully automated machine, and within a stated time-frame, then an incentive will have been provided, directly to industry, to roll up its sleeves. Here is a case where "high tech" must be brought to bear on a technology—tunneling—that goes back to prehistoric times. It is an appropriate illustration of the macro-engineering of the future, which because of advanced technology will multiply the reach of large-scale engineering until the earth becomes, in Marshall McLuhan's phrase, a "global village."

In 1970, when I first joined the M.I.T. staff as a senior research associate, I was happy to see a familiar figure across the Faculty Club dining room. It was my old college friend Louis Sutro, who did look as if he had not been outdoors for quite a while. Louis quickly explained that he had been working for over twenty years on the design of a "Mars rover" or, more particularly, on the visual and sensory apparatus without which no remote-controlled vehicle could function effectively. Sadly, Louis recounted that funding was sometimes on, sometimes off. Louis Sutro is one of a large group of first-class scientists who will be indispensable, once a *long range* space program is set in place. If we are not going to invest in a manned expedition to Mars, I assume that we shall, in due course, send a surrogate mission in the form of an automated Mars rover. Whether James Oberg's idea is valid—"terraforming" Mars— that is, transforming its climate so that the "red planet" will be habitable by humankind, I am not competent to say; but we must be grateful that such conundrums remain for future generations to deal with; I find that our immediate prospects are quite exciting and difficult enough!

One observation that I have made, in the course of a few years of acquaintanceship with large technoventures, is that more seems to depend on individual actions than I had been led to believe by my teachers. I had been told that Carlyle exaggerated the role of the "great men" he admired, and that both "hero-worship" and "devil theories" were poor guides to historical truth. In fact, I think people who write history, and this remark must include some writers who specialize in the history of technology, like to find logical patterns for events; and there may be uneasiness at the thought that a small intervention at a critical moment might have upset a whole series of "causes" that appeared to lead ineluctably to the outcome that in fact occurred. The great Duke of Wellington himself said, after the Battle of Waterloo, that "it was a damned close-run thing." It is not that people make *a* difference. They make *the* difference.

If an accident had not deprived Napoleon of Berthier's solid staff assistance at Waterloo, would not Grouchy have been successfully recalled with his critical thirty-two thousand troops? If Lesseps had followed his son's advice and raised twice as much money as he thought was needed to complete the Panama Canal, would the French have succeeded in completing it? Could the Northeast Corridor now have a railway service comparable to the French or the Japanese high-speed systems if the Department of Transportation had opted for a state-of-the-art construction program instead of an endless process of research and demonstrations? No one really knows the answer to such questions, but in all three cases—and many more—the answer *could* have been a resounding yes. And were it not for the "what if" factor in history, there would be little incentive to run the risks that large and small enterprises entail.

Gordon S. Brown, formerly dean of engineering at the Massachusetts Institute of Technology, wrote a landmark article for *Technology Review* in January 1973, in which he asserted: "Engineers must federate with people from other disciplines to upgrade the 'software' of tomorrow's socio-economic system. They must actively participate with economists, politicians, lawyers, business executives, sociologists, and the like, in the planning process. They do not do this today to anything like the extent that is necessary."

Dean Brown continued, "The engineers who conduct these activities will make their tasks much easier if they apply their skills in simulation and system dynamics to make possible a deeper understanding of the structure, interactions, dislocations, and modes of behavior of the social system. They will thus provide a framework wherein society can test hypotheses and select trade-offs while options are still open. Participation in this work will in turn permit these engineers to guide their own professions on what to build, how to build it, and what to do with it after it is built."

Drawing on a lifetime of experience in the forefront of engineering developments, Gordon Brown's perspective is worth reflecting on: "In other words, to inject technology into our society has anthropological connotations which, depending on how we plan and what we do, can be either subversive or benign . . . Because of all this, I contend that engineers are revolutionists:

they bring great change not only to their own profession, but also—and more than any other profession—they are the primary instigators of social, economic, and political change in the society in which they live."

Especially in a discussion of the largest, most influential technological projects—the macroenterprises that form the topic of this book—it must be obvious that, in Professor Brown's moving terms, they can be "either subversive or benign." The fact that there is this risk—which extends to *every* field of human activity (including cooking)—has induced neo-Luddites to oppose all large schemes automatically, without examining details of each case, really without thought.

But to achieve the kind of "neoindustrial" approach that I have suggested as the linchpin of a new paradigm for the American future, all professions will have to make a sincere effort in the direction of mutual comprehension. Victor Papanek, the gifted dean of the School of Design at the California Institute of the Arts, has reminded us that "design is the conscious effort to impose meaningful order." Papanek's preoccupation is the maintenance of "human scale," which of course ought to be a central concern of all who participate in the design and development of macrosystems. I resonate to his statement that "in a dramatically changing world society that is (tremblingly) afraid of change and that educates its young into ever-narrowing areas of specialization, the integrated, comprehensive, anticipatory designer is a dedicated synthesist." This plea is very much in conformity with Buckminster Fuller's call for "a comprehensive, anticipatory design science"; indeed, such a development is a logical outcome, also, of the "human factors" emphasis in recent design and engineering education: If airplane seats are to be increasingly designed for the comfort and convenience of the passengers and the crew, it is not such a great conceptual leap to include the "human factors" outside the airplane itself, such as noise and air pollution, within the engineer's expanding purview.

A "macroscopic" view of American infrastructure is bound to turn up inconsistencies and inconveniences that interfere with economic functioning in an era when the nation's prosperity is increasingly bound up with the avoidance of excessive system costs. For instance, it is a curiosity that coast-to-coast trucking is often a more rapid means of delivering goods than rail or even—as professors Roger Curran and Peter Jenkins of Keene State College (N.H.) pointed out to me—than air! The rationalization of transportation systems within North America offers evident opportunities to analysts of new business opportunities. This is, also, a question deeply "affected with a public interest." It deserves the attention of experts like M.I.T.'s fine systems analyst, Richard de Neufville, whose landmark work, *Airport Systems Planning*, raises a number of questions for those who are interested in intermodal transfers and the design of the continental and intercontinental transport systems of the future.

Kenneth E. Boulding, in *Beyond Economics*, contributed a chapter entitled "A Conceptual Framework for Social Science" that is germane to any general discussion of a new interdisciplinary field of study such as macro-engineering. "It may well be," Boulding wrote, "that we move fastest along our narrow specialized trails. Still, the trails are converging. There are three signs of this convergence. One is the development of hybrid specializations. In the natural sciences, for instance, physical chemistry developed between physics and chemistry some three or four generations ago. . . . The second sign of convergence is the development of applied fields which cut across the specialized disciplines. Labor relations, for instance, is a field which cuts across economics, sociology, social psychology, psychology, law, political science and engineering. . . . In the process of contributing to an applied field the specialized disciplines can hardly avoid contributing to one another. Finally, even in pure theory there are signs of increasing dissatisfaction with the narrow models of the pure disciplines."

A backward glance at the interdisciplinary and interprofessional history of large-scale engineering must make us aware that even some of the more thoughtful attacks on technology are not really to be "swallowed whole." Norman Mailer, in *Pontifications*, asserted ". . . the technological society looks to destroy any idea of the heroic." A quick perusal of Samuel Smiles's nineteenth-century *Lives of the Engineers* stands as a refutation of that! But we must take to heart Mailer's warning: "The citizens of a technological society are as powerless as an Oriental peasant.

Their standard of living may be vastly superior, but their social impotence is similar: they command less and less; they are manipulated more and more." However, is not society itself, at least since the origin of civilized life in established settlements, a product of technology? What Mailer means, I suggest, is that modern technology, particularly the advanced technologies that lead to automation and "remote controls" of all sorts, is somehow more threatening than the earlier and more familiar technologies of the Middle Ages and the pre-Victorian era. That the disruptions caused by *rapid* technological change are very real, no one should attempt to deny. How to guide technological change wisely, and how to use it to enhance the individual and the environment, constitutes the problem that now faces all societies, industrialized or nonindustrialized.

As accelerating automation occurs and proliferates, there will be new pockets of unemployment. To deal with this enormous social question effectively, at least two approaches suggest themselves. First of all, our skills and outlook must constantly be upgraded: If production itself will continue to be handled more by machines and less by people, then we are bound to have the kind of exodus from the factory that we have already had from the farm. American universities now employ a larger population than all who remain on America's farms, according to a readable, recent, and useful book, *Mega-Trends;*[5] in such a situation, the retraining option will not cover "all azimuths" of the question. We must have a more creative approach to the fact that fewer and fewer people can provide for the basic necessities —and probably the "basic luxuries"—of a majority of the population.

That unconventional thinker Eugen Rosenstock-Huessy came up with a useful metaphor when he likened the unemployed to the reserves of an army: unemployed, yes, but always able to be employed at the "critical point" in a battle or war. If the military analogy may be pursued, this means that we should have permanent services that can be expanded as needed to direct people into activities of public benefit where the "market economy" does not function. The experience with the Civilian Conservation Corps during the Depression of the 1930's illustrates this type of activity. But the older generation, too, needs opportunities for service, and health care and teaching may be among the fields where "extra" help may be appreciated. David Rockefeller and others, in founding an Executive Service Corps, succeeded in recruiting very valuable talent in an effort parallel to the Peace Corps itself.

If the *épanouissement* and health of the individual human being are to be central to the structure of neoindustrial society, macroprojects can make a genuine, thoughtful contribution. Bikeways, local and interstate, are one obvious illustration; urban and suburban centers for participative sports are another. With respect to farming, we should heed the warnings of James McHale and others that present methods, while producing impressive food-production figures, risk major depletion and loss of topsoil. If topsoil conservation is to be viewed increasingly as a serious element of national policy, then we may see a more labor-intensive type of agriculture expanding its reach, even as the trend to automation and labor-saving continues its dynamic thrust. And to mount a major program of conservation, there will have to be a series of macroprograms, both high tech and low tech.

Forty miles north of the Port of Dhahran is Madinat Al-Jubail Al-Sinaiyah, perhaps the largest civil engineering project of the century. Five years ago, the land around the tiny fishing village of Jubail was unrelieved desert. Today, fifty thousand people are at work in the new industrial city; the population could reach three hundred thousand or more by the year 2000. Production has already begun at a steel factory and rolling mill, a methanol plant, and a fertilizer facility; more than a dozen additional industrial units are to commence operations within the next two years. The Royal Commission for Jubail and Yanbu, in charge of development at these two macrosites, has employed American firms such as the Bechtel Corporation and the Ralph M. Parsons Company to assist in planning and supervision. Of the top twenty "worldscale" projects sponsored by developing countries in the 1970's and analyzed in Dr. Kathleen Murphy's *Macroproject Development in the Third World*,[6] more than half were managed by leading United States companies. Thanks to this practical experience in the management of very large-scale projects and programs, American firms have achieved a degree of engineer-management competence that should be viewed as a precious national asset, to be employed not only abroad but at home as well.

Because of the very long lead-time necessarily involved in macro-engineering enterprises, the time to start—if we are, as a country, serious about upgrading our infrastructure and our industry—is now. Processes of consultation must be initiated that can lead directly to the formation of study groups for the principal topics such as water supply, waste disposal, transport, energy, steel, shipbuilding, aerospace, and so on. Where the most desirable networks involve continent-wide facilities, the necessary contacts should be undertaken—on a private as well as a governmental basis—with decision centers in Canada and Mexico. Nor will it be sufficient to assess only engineering options as a subject separate from political, legal, and environmental considerations. "Technology assessment" is now so embedded in our institutional structure that the public is no longer aware of the very dramatic choices that the nation now faces, as candidates for public office debate technological options that are already defined but fail even to mention those major steps forward that could mean so much to the health, the prosperity, and the security of the nation.

Only when exceptional events impinge on the public consciousness do we concentrate on those traditional "four horsemen of the Apocalypse": flood, famine, pestilence, and war. A more contemporary list might include drought, surfeit, overpopulation, and, some might add, the ravages of a long peace! But flood remains a grim reality in the Gangetic Plain of India; famine has stalked the Sahel in middle Africa; disease is not only an ever-present danger in crowded slum areas of Asia and Africa—Western medicine has been blamed for producing the population crisis by exporting too much modern hygiene and medicine. William James pleaded for maintaining "the martial virtues" even in peacetime; and how can we contradict him, when in the 1960's an entire generation appeared to be "at risk" because of overpermissiveness, a lack of coherence, and the absence of a sense of worthwhile public purposes that could command widespread respect and devotion? If the world could now match the Roman achievement by defeating the onward march of the Sahara Desert both in North Africa and in the Sahel; if at least some of the refugees from the Middle East and Asia could be offered permanent havens constructed, after the manner of the indomitable Dutch, on artificial islands in the oceans; if American cities could be rebuilt *on a human scale* but with the generous resources made available to Baron Haussmann when he rescued and restored Paris more than a century ago; if our countryside could be freed from at least a portion of the airports, highways, and railroads that disfigure it by developing high-speed subsurface transport networks—a feat well within the technological abilities of the United States—would this not represent a worthy beginning, not only for the reconstruction of industry and infrastructure, but also for recapturing a measure of self-control for the human future?

Quis custodiet custodes ipsos?—Who shall guard the guardians themselves?—has been, since Roman times, the key conundrum of politics. In the United States, with power deliberately divided among executive, legislative, and judicial branches, and with fifty partly sovereign states sharing power with the federal government, large undertakings have always required broad coalitions so that the creaky machinery of government is activated: Such coalitions have included our principal political parties, "pressure groups" of various dimensions, and voluntary movements on behalf of any number of causes: from the March of Dimes, which helped wipe out infantile paralysis, to the impressive financial association that built Lincoln Center in New York. It is thanks to these volunteer efforts of individuals and groups, and not only to the structure of government, that the United States has weathered the numerous crises and changes in the course of the longest period of stable government enjoyed by any major power on earth.

I remember very well the excitement of the process of forming a new coalition in the political field, when my father joined with a small group of friends to organize the City Fusion party, which mobilized the independent Democratic vote to join the small Republican party in New York on behalf of the election of Fiorello H. La Guardia as mayor in the early 1930's. But today, although honesty in government remains as important as ever, the overriding issues are not always identified or discussed in political campaigns: The choice among alternate engineering systems may be the key if unacknowledged issue of our times. If this be true—and I have argued that there is at least a large measure of truth in the statement—then many of the decisive coalitions of today and tomorrow will revolve around particular technological ventures, just as New York politics, in the first decades of the nineteenth century, revolved around the issue of the Erie Canal and its obstinate champion, De Witt Clinton. Small wonder that as many towns and streets have been named after Governor Clinton as have been named for Washington, Lincoln, or Jefferson!

Science and technology have in fact succeeded, quite literally, in "making a silk purse out of a sow's ear"; there is little that is unfeasible, if people of intelligence and conviction wish to make the effort. It is, in the main, a question of purpose and steadfastness. There is also the matter of compassion—and intelligence: I find it hard to believe that the public will forever accept such a high accident rate on congested highways, when David G. Wilson and others have designed fail-safe guideway systems that would beyond doubt save many lives and much suffering. Here, it should be added, is a modern technology that can benefit from the latest advances in computers and communications, and that would have as its principal outcome the saving of that most precious commodity of all: life itself.

But can we afford—even with the present "oil glut"—to risk scarce energy resources in the construction of new macrosystems? Here indeed is a proper subject for informed debate and—in due course—an informed consensus.

Let us be forewarned: Macroprojects, however well selected and designed, will not usher in a risk-free society. William H. McNeill of the fine history department at the University of Chicago has wisely summed it up: ". . . one can properly think of most human lives as caught in a precarious equilibrium between the microparasitism of disease organisms and the macroparasitism of large-bodied predators, chief among which have been other human beings."[7]

About two millennia ago, the Romans built a hundred-mile aqueduct to carry water from the Jebel to Leptis Magna (now a ruin surrounded by the sands in Libya). The aqueduct also carried olive oil, which was poured into the water at Jebel and skimmed off at Leptis, where it was placed in suitable containers for export. Is the scheme of Professor Debanné to pipe Rhone water under the Mediterranean Sea and over the Atlas Mountains really more costly and difficult in our times than the feats actually accomplished by the 3rd Augusta legionnaires in theirs? Does not Masaki Nakajima's plan for a Global Infrastructure Fund point a sensible way forward for humankind in an epoch when macro-engineering and megatechnology will either be harbingers of a harmonious era of peaceful construction or of a catastrophic episode of the macroparasitism identified by Dr. McNeill?

In *general* terms, the idea of massive investment in wealth-creating projects in the third world might have a very wide appeal were it not for the current crisis in international debtor-creditor relations. I mentioned the problem to Allan R. Finlay, who in addition to his interests in education remains one of America's most astute financial analysts; he came up with a surprising answer: Why not a tax-exempt foundation with an internationally respected board of governors? This device might have *worldwide applicability* in the context of macro-engineering if worked out in close consultation with the International Monetary Fund and other governmental and intergovernmental bodies. Perhaps a practical next step would be the appointment of an interdisciplinary commission to examine the role and structure of such a foundation and to recommend guidelines under which it could operate.

I owe to W.H.G. Armytage[8] the report that on March 3, 1956, A. Markin, a Soviet engineer, broadcast over Moscow radio a plan to link Siberia and Alaska by means of a dam that would "bar the Arctic from the Pacific" and provide for the pumping of the warm Pacific water into the Arctic Ocean, thereby transforming the climate of the northern territories of Asia and North America. At some point in the evolution of international emotions, the discussion of such joint technological undertakings and of the likely impacts and implications could supply a welcome alternative to meetings exclusively concerned with missile counts and megatonnages. Hazardous though some macro-engineering projects may appear, they do constitute a major alternative topic for the international agenda, one that humankind can, on the basis of experience and knowledge, view with a judicious optimism.

During the period 1881–1883, companies formed by railway promoters pushed the channel tunnel nearly a mile under the sea from
each coast. The work was halted because of the strenuous objections
of the adjutant-general of the British Army, Sir Garnet Wolseley, the
officer who had been too late to rescue Gordon at Khartoum. Sir
Garnet, in a famous misjudgment about his country's future foreign
alignments, announced his fears of a French invasion through the
tunnel. Winston Churchill later expressed the view that had the tunnel been completed, World War I might have been won two years
earlier, because of the greater ease of supplying the Allied armies in
France. After 1957, the "old bores" were used for geophysical tests
and were found to be dry and generally in excellent condition.

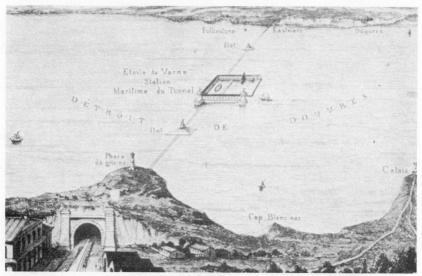

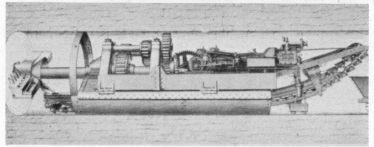

The top picture illustrates the 1856 plan of Thomé de Gamond for a twin railway tunnel under the English Channel. The large island in the middle background would have been built on the submerged Varne bank. Several other artificial islands were proposed (in his *Étude pour l'avant-projet d'un tunnel sous-marin entre l'Angleterre et la France*, Paris, 1857, Victor Dalmont, éditeur), so that the time of construction might be reduced by having a number of working faces in midchannel. The center sketch, of a bridge proposed in 1890 by Schneider Hersent & Cie, was never a serious competitor. Bridge projects have been the graveyard of many great reputations, including that of Jules Moch, the minister of the interior who represented the last but vital thread of legitimate authority before Charles de Gaulle accepted the presidency of the Republic. Directly above is Colonel Beaumont's efficient boring machine.

Directly below is the French survey vessel *Ajax*, employed in 1875–1876 for a remarkable program of seabed sampling carried out in the channel by Lavalley, De Lapparent, and Larousse. Using Colonel Beaumont's mechanical tunneling machine, pilot headings, each a mile long, were driven out to sea in 1882. The machine was worked by compressed air and was reputed to excavate 40 feet of chalk every 17 hours. Bottom: Above-ground installations of the Channel Tunnel Company in the early 1880's.

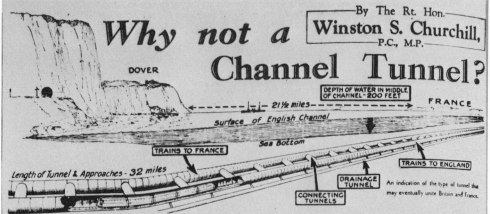

Why not a Channel Tunnel?

By The Rt. Hon. Winston S. Churchill, P.C., M.P.

DOVER

DEPTH OF WATER IN MIDDLE OF CHANNEL - 200 FEET

21½ miles

FRANCE

Surface of English Channel

Sea Bottom

TRAINS TO FRANCE

Length of Tunnel & Approaches - 32 miles

TRAINS TO ENGLAND

DRAINAGE TUNNEL

CONNECTING TUNNELS

An indication of the type of tunnel that may eventually unite Britain and France.

The severe weather of this week has turned the minds of many people to the question of a Channel tunnel.

In this article Mr. Winston Churchill discusses also the political and economic possibilities of the proposal.

THERE are few projects against which there exists a deeper and more enduring prejudice than the construction of a railway tunnel between Dover and Calais.

Again and again it has been brought forward under powerful and influential sponsorship. Again and again it has been prevented. Governments of every hue, Prime Ministers of every calibre, have been found during successive generations inflexibly opposed to it. To those who have consistently favoured the idea this ponderous and overwhelming resistance has always seemed a mystery.

Anyone can see that the economic and commercial arguments are by no means one-sided. At present we have the bulk of the sea-borne trade between England and the Continent.

With a tunnel there could be no more than equality.

At present we have a great mass of cross-Channel shipping which could play its part, and did play its part, in moving British forces to the Continent, and which forms a substantial portion of our Mercantile Marine.

"island" argument, wittily expressed by Lord Randolph Churchill in his speech against the tunnel which so greatly amused the House of Commons in 1889, that "the reputation of England has hitherto depended upon her being, as it were, virgo intacta."

Nevertheless, it is not upon such arguments or sentiments that the issue has been so often decided. National safety has been the paramount thought. The immunity from invasion we have enjoyed for nearly a thousand years is held to be compromised, if not destroyed, by the making of a tunnel. It is upon strategic grounds that successive Governments have based their resistance, and it is these very grounds that deserve a cool examination in the light of modern war conditions.

It Could be Flooded

BEFORE the Great War I formed the opinion that the tunnel would be an additional strength and not a danger to our strategic security.

The First Sea Lord of the Admiralty, Prince Louis of Battenberg, and the Chief of the Imperial General Staff, Sir John French, both shared this view. It was, of course, insisted that the tunnel should have a shaft to a lighthouse in the sea by which, if all else failed, it could be flooded by the Navy.

This lighthouse would at all times be under the control of the strongest sea Power, and could at any time be used by that sea Power to close the communication. Thus the dangers of a surprise or treachery before the declaration of war, which would leave the tunnel open to an invading army, would be decisively removed. Security would be absolute as long as we continued in supreme control of the

a tunnel in addition to our other means of transport became obvious.

In the early months of 1917 the destruction of tonnage by German submarines became so enormous that if it had continued the Allies would have had to face defeat and the British Isles subjugation.

If the construction of a tunnel had been a matter of months instead of long years, I cannot doubt that it would have been undertaken, and would have come about as naturally and as inevitably as Daylight Saving, against which similar prejudices existed. Thus I cannot feel that the experiences of the war stultified those who, upon strategic grounds, favoured the scheme.

But what has happened since the war?

How do all the latest developments in the air affect the problem?

It would seem that they enormously strengthen the case for the tunnel. The danger which modern Britain has to face is not invasion but starvation.

Feeding London

IT would be extremely difficult, if not impossible, to feed London if the estuary of the Thames were made too dangerous for shipping.

We are, in our present air weakness, vulnerable as we have never been before, and as is no other country now. When I think of the dangers to which we are exposed, I marvel at the illogical standard of values of those who dwell complacently under the air menace, and yet would be sincerely alarmed at a Channel tunnel. Indeed,

it seems the perfect case of swallowing the camel and straining at the gnat.

Therefore I still remain of my prewar opinion that a tunnel would be no strategic danger, and that there would be no difficulty in closing it if necessary. On the other hand, if it existed and could be kept open, it might prove an invaluable aid to our safety. It would, however, be much easier to ensure its being closed than to ensure its being kept open, and therefore the argument which has been set forth above must be stated with moderation. I plead, however, that it should be weighed in scales free from preconceived bias or by prejudices the foundations of which have been sapped by science.

We Must Rule the Sea

BUT at any given moment every scheme of national defence must be weighed against every other. In any question of priority the Channel tunnel would not now hold a high place. More pressing dangers than those against which it would assist us, and other means of coping with them, claim precedence. We must never resign the mastery of the narrow seas. We have held it for centuries by seapower. That power we must in all circumstances maintain. But the need of superior air force has now become paramount. It should take the first place in all our thoughts and arrangements.

We have preserved our island by being the first of sea Powers. We can only preserve our existence in the future by air defence, which in our home land and home waters must be at least equally trustworthy and dominating.

On February 12, 1936, the Right Honorable Winston S. Churchill, P.C., M.P., published an article in the *Daily Mail* strongly advocating the channel tunnel project. He rejected the witty 1889 assertion of his father, Lord Randolph Churchill, that "the reputation of England has hitherto depended on her being, as it were, *virgo intacta*." Citing the views of Lord Battenberg and Sir John French, the younger Churchill pronounced the project an asset to national defense. At right is a sketch, reproduced from a 1964 brochure of the Channel Tunnel Study Group, of the loading area for piggyback trains at a channel-tunnel terminal.

By 1957, although the project was again attracting significant attention in Britain and on the Continent, there was no source of detailed planning and funding. Technical Studies, Inc., was founded to help fill the void. At right are the original three officers: Arnaud de Vitry, chairman; Frank P. Davidson, president; and Cyril C. Means, Jr., executive vice-president. Technical Studies, Inc. promptly joined with the Suez Canal Company, and with the companies formed in the nineteenth century, to establish the Channel Tunnel Study Group. The British Railways Board, as a principal shareholder of the Channel Tunnel Company, Ltd. (a member of the group), built an automated model, a portion of which is shown below right, to explain to the public the actual functioning of the marshaling yards and terminals on the British side. The French Railways (owning half the shares of the *Société Concessionaire du Chemin de Fer Sous-Marin entre La France et l'Angleterre*, also a member of the group) built a working model of the French terminal area. Its model was exhibited atop the Galeries Lafayette, in Paris.

INTERNATIONAL COMPETITION PERMANENT TRAFFIC LINK ACROSS THE GREAT BELT . DENMARK

NYBORG
KNUDSHOVED
SPROGØ
HALSSKOV
KORSØR
THE FERRY ROUTES

The idea of a permanent traffic link across Denmark's "Great Belt" is referred to, at times, as "the Danish national project." That this should be so is the result of both geography and history: Copenhagen, the capital, is situated on the island of Zeeland, which is separated from the other half of Denmark—the Jutland peninsula lying just north of Germany's Schleswig-Holstein—by the more than 13 miles of the Great Belt. Water depths are so shallow that either a bridge or an immersed tube could easily be envisaged, but the front runner thus far has been a plan for a combined road-and-rail bridge. The traffic and revenue, which have been examined by such reputable firms as De Leuw, Cather & Co. of Chicago, appear to be ample and reliable. But Danish cabinets, in the postwar period, have not enjoyed very long tenure, and the lack of political continuity has combined with a debt-laden national budget to introduce a series of delays. On October 18, 1966, a company to build the link was formed with the distinguished assistance of Per Markussen, frequently a Danish representative at NATO and other European conferences. The Danish Parliament has expressed a preference for building the Great Belt link ahead of a link—on the other side of Zeeland—with Sweden. Perhaps the next step will be the formation of a financial consortium strong enough to assure completion of the work without the intervention of government guarantees. Danish engineering firms such as Christiani & Nielsen are quite able to take care of construction, but no doubt there will be discussions of wider associations as the project moves closer to reality. A piggyback rail service through a tunnel or tube may be an option worthy of closer examination. In the same vein, a causeway to connect Prince Edward Island with Canada was a lively topic for years, but with the severe weather endemic in northern climes, there may be reasons for the Canadians to consider afresh the possible advantages of a tunnel connection across the Northumberland Straits.

Since 1869, when Laurent Valdeuil first proposed a tunnel across the Strait of Gibraltar, there has been desultory activity on the alternative possibilities for a fixed link. Although the strait is only 9 miles wide at its narrowest point, all engineering plans have been complicated by the great depths of water (350 meters along the favored route), by the seismically active structures beneath the sea bottom, and by the swift tides and currents. A test-drilling program is now under way, and Spain and Morocco are cooperating in a study program.

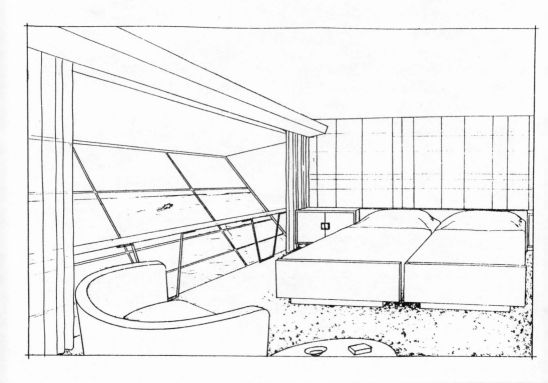

This large rigid airship proposed by Francis T. Morse would have an overall length of 1,900 feet, a payload—at a 6,000-mile range—of upwards of 1,750 tons, and could carry 3,500 passengers. Professor-emeritus Morse, who is a licensed architect as well as an engineer, drew the sketches at left to demonstrate the spacious accommodations a large airship could provide. As early as a 1979 presentation before the American Association for the Advancement of Science, Dr. Morse pointed out that "an airship's ratio of useful lift to gross lift far exceeds that of its heavier-than-air counterpart." Probably a new surge of investment awaits improvements in the technology of financing as much as it does a transfer of new high-tech methods to the old art of airship construction. A large airship might be chartered to carry automobiles directly to the inland point of import, thus avoiding transshipment charges and the delays incident to other available means of shipping cars across ocean distances. For passenger travel, staterooms could be sold on a condominium basis, much as skyscrapers are financed, long before they are built, by the device of lease-back arrangements.

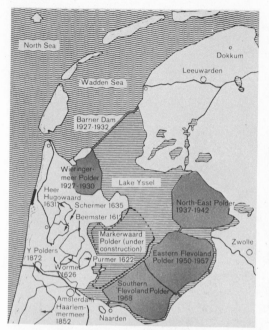

Map labels:
North Sea
Dokkum
Leeuwarden
Wadden Sea
Barrier Dam 1927-1932
Wieringer-meer Polder 1927-1930
Heer Hugowaard 1631
Schermer 1635
Beemster 161?
Lake Yssel
North-East Polder 1937-1942
Markerwaard Polder (under construction)
Zwolle
Y Polders 1872
Purmer 1622
Eastern Flevoland Polder 1950-1957
Wormer 1626
Southern Flevoland Polder 1968
Amsterdam
Haarlem-mermeer 1852
Naarden

This map shows the accomplishment of a macro-engineering scheme for creating agricultural land out of the Zuyder Zee. Conceived by a civil engineer, Cornelius Lely (1854–1929), early in the present century, the project involved damming off the large inlet called the Zuyder Zee, reclaiming 215,000 hectares to form five new polders (land reclaimed from the sea), and leaving 120,000 hectares to form Lake Ijssel. Below: The building of dikes near Enkhuizen in Southern Flevoland and Markerwaard polders. Top right: The construction of the Barrier Dam, a 30-kilometer dike between the provinces of Friesland and North Holland. Begun in 1927, the great dike was closed on May 28, 1932. Bottom right: The four-lane highway that runs across the dike. . . . Other polders on the map go back to the early 1600's.

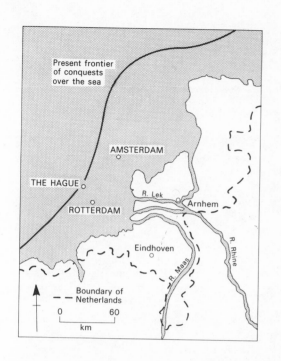

More than 60 percent of Holland's population lives on land reclaimed from the sea. The map shows the enormous accomplishment of the Dutch in building a nation by reshaping the natural environment in a benign manner. Below is an aerial view of the "Block van Kuffeler," a pumping station that drains the area of the future Southern Flevoland Polder. Pumping stations are built simultaneously with the dikes around the future polders, just as windmills were employed earlier to pump the water out of soggy ground. First made for drainage, the pumping stations will be used at later stages of the work to keep the completed polders dry. The picture at lower left indicates how lakes, varying in size, have been left between the old land and the new polders. At various points along the banks of the lakes, we can discern the beaches and marinas deliberately sited for recreational use. Correctly regarded, even agricultural and pasture land are part of humankind's "built environment." To restructure portions of the earth need not, therefore, be classified as an aversive or destructive activity. Vierlingh, who authored the first book on the art of dike building, in 1570, wrote to Prince William of Orange, "The sea must be won with sweetness," but added, after reflection, "Although the Dutch are a peaceful nation, diking against Neptune is like waging war and therefore we must be warlike!" In 1754 the office of Director General of the Nation's River and Sea Works was established. Ever since, the powerful Waterstaat has planned and led the nation's hydraulic program. The dikes form an 1,800-mile system that protects Holland from inundation; they are the country's basic infrastructure, the sine qua non of all other activities, however worthy. The *coup d'oeil* that planted the system of dikes in the consciousness of the lowlanders was the result of four centuries of Roman occupation that began under Drusus in 15 B.C. Roman technology transfer included not only dike building but the selective breeding of cattle and the introduction of cabbages, lentils, radishes, and plum trees, all of which enter into the modern Dutch menu. And the windmill? It is regarded as an Arab invention.

Described in *Fortune* as "future sentinels of Holland's lowlands," these gigantic piers will form part of "the largest storm-surge barrier in the world," to be completed in 1986. After the piers are finished, the cofferdams in which they were fabricated are to be flooded so that a specially designed ship can be floated in to lift the piers and transport them one by one to their places in the barrier. The five-mile dam stretching across the Eastern Scheldt will cost $1.8 billion. This project is one of four designed to protect the country against storm tides from the North Sea. In the past century alone, the dikes have suffered seven major breaches. In 1953, 1,800 people were drowned. Piers in the barrier are up to 135 feet in height and 165 feet in length. To preserve the ecology of the estuary, the gates will be raised above sea level during normal weather, allowing the tides to flow between the estuary and the sea. But when storm tides threaten, the gates will come down like guillotines, severing the bay from the surging onrush of the North Sea. The British recently completed a similar barrier on the Thames River; they were induced to take action by the same 1953 storm.

Notes

CHAPTER 1

1. E. F. Schumacher, *Small Is Beautiful* (New York: Harper Torchbook, 1973).

2. See Jack Preiss, *Camp William James* (Norwich, Vermont: Argo Books, 1978), p. 39 *et seq.*

3. National Research Council, Committee on Satellite Power Systems, *Electric Power From Orbit: A Critique of a Satellite Power System*, (Washington, D.C.: National Academy Press, 1981).

4. See Samuel Hopkins Adams, *The Erie Canal* (New York: Random House, 1953) p. 78.

5. Robert West Howard, *The Great Iron Trail—The Story of the First Transcontinental Railroad* (New York: Bonanza Books, 1962).

6. Robert M. Salter, "Transplanetary Subway Systems: A Burgeoning Capability," Chapter 7 in Part II (CASES FOR THE FUTURE) in *Macro-Engineering and the Infrastructure of Tomorrow*, Frank P. Davidson, L. J. Giacoletto, and Robert Salkeld, eds., AAAS Selected Symposium 23 (Boulder, Colo.: Westview Press, 1978).

7. *Ibid.*

8. J. Peter Vajk, *Doomsday Has Been Cancelled* (Culver City, Cal.: Peace Press, 1978).

9. See Prologue, "Lunch at Luchow's," in Joseph Gies, *Adventure Underground* (London: Robert Hale Limited, 1962), p. 13 *et seq.*

10. David Fromkin, *The Independence of Nations* (New York: Praeger, 1981).

CHAPTER 2

1. David Fromkin, *The Independence of Nations* (New York: Praeger, 1981).

2. See David H. Pinkney, *Napoleon III and the Rebuilding of Paris* (Princeton, N.J.: Princeton University Press, 1958), p. 21.

3. Robert A. Caro, *The Power Broker—Robert Moses and the Fall of New York* (New York: Knopf, 1974).

4. Vivian Rowe, *The Great Wall of France—The Triumph of the Maginot Line* (New York: Putnam, 1959).

5. *The Official Journal of the European Communities*, Vol. 20, No. C-183, August 1, 1977, p. 15, reported "the motion for a resolution on the construction of a tunnel under the English Channel." This followed *Debates, Report of Proceedings* of the European Parliament, Luxembourg, April 7, 1977.

   In 1979–80 the EEC commissioned a report by Coopers & Lybrand Associates, London, and SETEC Économie, Paris, on "The Nature and Extent of Possible Community Interest in the Construction of a Fixed Link across the Channel." This report concluded that ". . . the Community overall has a clear interest in encouraging the project to go forward."

6. *The Global Infrastructure Fund (GIF)—a Progress Report*, submitted by Masaki Nakajima, chairman of the board, Mitsubishi Research Institute, Inc., Tokyo, Japan, April 1981.

7. See David McCullough, *The Path Between the Seas, The Creation of the Panama Canal, 1870–1914* (New York: Simon and Schuster, 1977), p. 126.

8. Thomas Whiteside, *The Tunnel Under the Channel* (New York: Simon and Schuster, 1962) recounts the history of this project with meticulous care; the book first appeared in *The New Yorker* in serial form.

9. See "Submerged Caisson System: an Evaluation," by E. G. Frankel, Inc., a report made in April 1983, to Mid-Channel Access Corporation.

10. Sheila Kitzinger, *Women as Mothers* (London: Fontana Books, 1978).

11. *Man's Impact on the Global Environment*, Report of the Study of Critical Environmental Problems (SCEP), Assessment and Recommendations for Action (Cambridge, Mass. and London, England: M.I.T. Press, 1970). See also *Inadvertent Climate Modification*, Report of the

Study of Man's Impact on Climate (SMIC) (Cambridge, Mass.: M.I.T. Press, 1971).

12. *Coal—Bridge to the Future*, Report of the World Coal Study (Cambridge, Mass.: Ballinger Publishing Company, Harper & Row, 1980).

CHAPTER 3

1. Alan Wood, *The Groundnut Affair* (London: Bodley Head, 1950). See also Annual Reports of the Overseas Food Corporation, (London: H. M. Stationery Office, 1948 *et seq*).

2. Conference of Ministers of African Member States Responsible for the Application of Science and Technology to Development, *Results of a UNESCO Delphi Survey on Technologically Feasible Futures for Africa,* (Paris: UNESCO, December 7, 1973). See Annex VII, page 3, "Helium-Filled Airship for Large Loads."

3. Nikos Papadakis, *The International Legal Regime of Artificial Islands* (Leyden, the Netherlands: Sijthoff Publications on Ocean Development, 1977).

4. See Chapter by George Kozmetsky, "Evaluation of Macro-Systems: Models and Case Analysis" in Frank P. Davidson, C. Lawrence Meador, and Robert Salkeld, eds., *How Big and Still Beautiful? Macro-Engineering Revisited* (Boulder, Colo.: Westview Press, 1980), p. 40 *et seq.*

5. V. Giscard d'Estaing, *Démocratie Française* (Paris: Fayard, 1976).

6. Emmanuel G. Mesthene, *Technological Change—Its Impact on Man and Society* (New York: Mentor Books, 1970).

7. Samuel Smiles, *Lives of the Engineers*, in three volumes (London: Murray, 1861).

8. Frontinus, *Aqueducts*, i, 16, cited by Will Durant, *Caesar and Christ* (New York: Simon and Schuster, 1944), p. 326.

9. Joseph G. Debanné, "Proposal for a Trans-Mediterranean Aqueduct," *Technology Review*, Vol. 78, No. 1 (Oct./Nov. 1975), p. 48 *et seq.*

10. G. Bouladon and P. Zuppiger, *A New Form of Vertical Transport for Skyscrapers* (Geneva, Switzerland: Battelle Memorial Institute, International Division, 1963).

11. Philomena G. Grodzka, "A TVA For Space? Practicalities for Near-

Term Decision," Chapter 12 in Frank P. Davidson, L. J. Giacoletto, and Robert Salkeld, eds., *Macro-Engineering and the Infrastructure of Tomorrow* (Boulder, Colo.: Westview Press, 1978).

CHAPTER 4

1. *Engineering News Record*, February 10, 1983, p. 113.

2. *Engineering News Record*, March 18, 1982, p. 51. See also *ENR*, February 17, 1983, p. 30 re: Hochtief, AG, Essen (West Germany) project.

3. See William D. Mulholland, "Churchill Falls: A Manager's View of an Energy Project with Continent-wide Impacts," *Macro-Engineering and the Future: A Management Perspective*, Frank P. Davidson and C. Lawrence Meador, eds. (Boulder, Colo.: Westview Press, 1982), p. 103 *et seq.*

4. George N. Kates, *The Years That Were Fat: The Last of Old China* (Cambridge, Mass.: M.I.T. Press, 1967). Copyright Harper, New York, 1952.

5. *Engineering Our Future—Report of the Committee of Inquiry into the Engineering Profession*, Chairman: Sir Montague Finniston, FRS (London: HM Stationery Office, Cmnd 7794, January 1980).

CHAPTER 5

1. A. Lawrence Lowell, "Foresight in Foreign Affairs," *Before America Decides: Foresight in Foreign Affairs*, Frank P. Davidson and George S. Viereck, Jr., eds. (Cambridge, Mass.: Harvard University Press, 1940).

2. Peter Drucker, *Management* (New York: Harper & Row, 1973), p. 104.

3. Pitirim A. Sorokin, *Social and Cultural Mobility* (New York: Macmillan, 1959), p. 29.

4. Lester Thurow, "The Productivity Problem," *Macro-Engineering and the Future*, Frank P. Davidson and C. Lawrence Meador, eds. (Boulder, Colo.: Westview Press, 1982), p. 100.

5. Kathleen J. Murphy, *Macroproject Development in the Third World* (Boulder, Colo.: Westview Press, 1983).

6. Peter Hall, *Great Planning Disasters* (Berkeley: University of California Press, 1980).

7. See "The Great Recycling and Northern Development (GRAND) Canal Concept" by Thomas W. Kierans, P. Eng., in Robert Salkeld, Frank P. Davidson, and C. Lawrence Meador, eds., *Macro-Engineering: The Rich Potential* (New York: American Institute of Aeronautics and Astronautics, 1981).

8. Vajk, *op. cit.*

9. Brian O'Leary, *The Fertile Stars* (New York: Everest House, 1981).

10. See *Technology Review* article entitled "People on Mars?" Vol. 85, No. 7 (Oct. 1982), p. 77.

11. James Grier Miller, *Living Systems* (New York: McGraw Hill, 1978) p. 40.

12. Jay W. Forrester, *Industrial Dynamics* (Cambridge, Mass.: M.I.T. Press, 1961).

13. Charles Beatty, *De Lesseps of Suez* (New York: Harper, 1956), pp. 81–83.

14. Rebecca McCann, *Complete Cheerful Cherub* (New York: Covici Friede, 1932), p. 19.

15. Hall, *op. cit.*

16. Vajk, *op. cit.*

CHAPTER **6**

1. John T. Dunlop, ed., *Business and Public Policy* (Cambridge, Mass.: Harvard University Press, 1980).

2. C. Northcote Parkinson, *The Law of Delay* (New York: Ballantine Books, 1970), pp. 1–3.

3. Jerome S. Bruner, Jacqueline J. Goodnow, and George A. Austin, *A Study of Thinking* (New York: Wiley, 1956), Chapter 3, p. 50 *et seq.*

4. See, for instance, Gilbert F. White and J. Eugene Haas, *Assessment of Research on National Hazards* (Cambridge, Mass.: M.I.T. Press, 1975) and J. Eugene Haas, Robert W. Kates, and Martin J. Bowden, *Reconstruction Following Disaster* (Cambridge, Mass.: M.I.T. Press, 1977).

CHAPTER 7

1. Harvey M. Sapolsky, *The Polaris System Development—Bureaucratic and Programmatic Success in Government* (Cambridge, Mass.: Harvard University Press, 1972).

2. *ENERGY: Global Prospects 1985–2000*, a report of the Workshop on Alternative Energy Strategies directed by Carroll L. Wilson (New York: McGraw Hill, 1977). For the other reports referred to in the text, see Notes 11 and 12 cited above in Chapter 2.

3. Ernest G. Frankel, *Management and Operations of American Shipping*, and *Regulation and Policies of American Shipping* (Cambridge, Mass.: Auburn House, 1982).

4. See "The Innocent Eye—A Vision of Design Management," by Sir Peter Parker, *Technology in Society* (An international journal published by Pergamon Press and with editorial offices at the Polytechnic Institute of New York) Vol. 2, No. 3 (1980), p. 303.

CHAPTER 8

1. James B. Conant, *Science and Common Sense* (New Haven: Yale University Press, 1951), see especially p. 45.

2. Wilson Clark, *Energy for Survival* (New York: Anchor Books, 1974).

3. "Our collective passions constitute the history of mankind." Eugen Rosenstock-Huessy, *Out of Revolution* (New York: Morrow, 1938), p. 3.

4. S. C. Burchell, *Building the Suez Canal* (New York: Harper and Row, 1966).

5. John Maisbitt, *Mega-Trends* (New York: Warner Books, 1982).

6. Murphy, *op. cit.*

7. William H. McNeill, *Plagues and Peoples* (New York: Anchor/Doubleday, 1976).

8. W.H.G. Armytage, *A Social History of Engineering* (London: Faber & Faber, 1961), p. 334.

Selected Readings

Armytage, W.H.G., M.A. *A Social History of Engineering*. London: Faber & Faber, 1961.

Bascom, Willard. *A Hole in the Bottom of the Sea—The Story of the Mohole Project*. New York: Doubleday, 1961.

Baxter, R. R. *The Law of International Waterways, with Particular Regard to Interoceanic Canals*. Cambridge, Mass.: Harvard University Press, 1964 (a study undertaken by the Harvard Law School at the suggestion of the Suez Canal Company).

Beatty, Charles. *De Lesseps of Suez*. New York: Harper, 1956.

Beaubois, Henry. *Airships—Yesterday, Today and Tomorrow*. New York: The Two Continents Publishing Group, 1976.

Berton, Pierre. *The Impossible Railway: The Building of the Canadian Pacific—A Triumphant Saga of Exploration, Politics, High Finance & Adventure*. New York: Knopf, 1972.

Bobrick, Benson. *Labyrinths of Iron—A History of the World's Subways*. New York: Newsweek Books, 1981.

Borgé, Jacques, and Viasnoff, Nicolas. *Le Zeppelin*. Paris: Balland, 1976.

Bruner, Jerome S., Goodnow, Jacqueline J., and Austin, George A. *A Study of Thinking*. New York: Wiley, 1956.

Cohen, Edward, and Birdsail, Blair, eds. *Long-Span Bridges*. O. H. Amman Centennial Conference, Volume 352, Annals of the New York Academy of Sciences, 1980.

Davidson, Frank P., Giacoletto, L. J., and Salkeld, Robert, eds. *Macro-Engineering and the Infrastructure of Tomorrow*. Boulder, Colo.: Westview Press, 1978.

Davidson, Frank P., and Meador, C. Lawrence, eds. *Macro-Engineering and the Future—A Management Perspective.* Boulder, Colo.: Westview Press, 1982.

Davidson, Frank P., Meador, C. Lawrence, and Salkeld, Robert. *How Big and Still Beautiful? Macro-Engineering Revisited.* Boulder, Colo.: Westview Press, 1980.

Davidson, Frank P., and Viereck, George S., Jr., eds. *Before America Decides: Foresight in Foreign Affairs.* Cambridge, Mass.: Harvard University Press, 1938.

De Camp, L. Sprague. *The Ancient Engineers.* New York: Doubleday, 1963.

Les Descendants de Pierre-Paul Riquet de Bonrepos. *Histoire du Canal de Languedoc.* Paris: Crapelet, 1805.

Dugan, James. *The Great Iron Ship.* New York: Harper, 1953.

The Global Infrastructure Fund, A Progress Report. Submitted by Masaki Nakajima, chairman of the board, Mitsubishi Research Institute, Inc., Tokyo, 1981.

Goldman, Marshall. *Environmental Pollution in the Soviet Union.* Cambridge, Mass.: M.I.T. Press, 1972.

Gresser, Julian, Fujikura, Koichiro, and Morishima, Akio. *Environmental Law in Japan.* Cambridge, Mass.: M.I.T. Press, 1981.

Hadfield, Charles. *The Canal Age.* New York: Praeger, 1969.

Hagen, Victor W. von. *The Roads That Led to Rome.* Cleveland and New York: World Publishing Co., 1967.

Hill, Ernestine. *Water Into Gold.* Melbourne: Robertson & Mullens, 1940 (the story of the development of the Murray River valley in Australia).

Horwitch, Mel. *Clipped Wings—The American SST Conflict.* Cambridge, Mass.: M.I.T. Press, 1982.

Howard, Robert West. *The Great Iron Trail: The Story of the First Transcontinental Railroad.* New York: Bonanza Books, 1952.

Jackson, Robert. *Airships—A Popular History.* New York: Doubleday, 1973.

Kiers, Luc. *The American Steel Industry: Problems, Challenges, Perspectives.* Boulder, Colo.: Westview Press, 1980.

Lampe, David. *The Tunnel—The Story of the World's First Tunnel Under a Navigable River Dug Beneath the Thames 1824–42.* London: Harrap, 1963.

Léger, Alfred. *Travaux Publics aux Temps des Romains.* Nogent-le-Roi: Jacques Laget, 1979.

Lovell, Sir Bernard. *The Story of Jodrell Bank.* New York: Harper & Row, 1968.

Lynn, Leonard H. *How Japan Innovates: A Comparison with the U.S. in the Case of Oxygen Steelmaking.* Boulder, Colo.: Westview Press, 1982.

McCullough, David. *The Path Between the Seas: The Creation of the Panama Canal, 1870–1914.* New York: Simon & Schuster, 1977.

Michener, James. *Space.* New York: Random House, 1982 (a novel).

Mostert, Noel. *Supership.* New York: Knopf, 1974.

Murphy, Kathleen J. *Macroproject Development in the Third World.* Boulder, Colo.: Westview Press, 1983.

Nathan, Adele Gutman. *The First Transatlantic Cable.* New York: Random House, 1959.

Needham, Joseph, F.R.S. *Science and Civilisation in China* (especially Vol. IV:3). Cambridge, England: Cambridge University Press, 1965.

Newman, Oscar. *Defensible Space—Crime Prevention through Urban Design.* New York: Collier Books, 1973.

O'Leary, Brian. *The Fertile Stars.* New York: Everest House, 1981.

Papadakis, N. *The International Legal Regime of Artificial Islands.* Leyden: Sijthoff, 1977.

Pearse, Innes H., and Crocker, Lucy H. *The Peckham Experiment—A Study of the Living Structure of Society.* London: Allen and Unwin, 1943.

Pim, Commander Bedford, R.N. *The Gateway of the Pacific.* London: Lovell Reeve & Co., 1863.

Pinkney, David H. *Napleon III and the Rebuilding of Paris.* Princeton, N.J.: Princeton University Press, 1958.

Preiss, Jack. *Camp William James.* Norwich, Vermont: Argo Books, 1978.

Rosenberg, Nathan, and Vincenti, Walter G. *The Britannia Bridge: The Generation and Diffusion of Technological Knowledge.* Cambridge, Mass.: M.I.T. Press, 1978.

Rowe, Vivian. *The Great Wall of France.* New York: Putnam, 1961.

Salkeld, Robert, Davidson, Frank P., and Meador, C. Lawrence, eds. *Macro-Engineering: The Rich Potential.* New York: American Institute for Aeronautics and Astronautics, 1980.

Shepherd, C. W. *A Thousand Years of London Bridge.* London: John Baker, 1971.

Smiles, Samuel. *Lives of the Engineers* (in three volumes), with portraits and numerous illustrations. London: Murray, 1861.

Smith, Delbert D. *Space Stations—International Law and Policy.* Boulder, Colo.: Westview Press, 1979.

Spier, Peter. *Of Dikes and Windmills.* New York: Doubleday, 1969.

Steinman, D. B. *Famous Bridges of the World.* New York: Random House, 1953.

Strage, Mark. *Cape to Cairo: Rape of a Continent.* New York: Harcourt Brace Jovanovich, 1973.

Talese, Gay. *The Bridge: The Story of the Verrazano-Narrows Bridge Linking Brooklyn and Staten Island.* New York: Harper & Row, 1964.

Tough, John M., and O'Flaherty, Coleman A. *Passenger Conveyors, An Innovatory Form of Communal Transport.* London: Ian Allan, 1971.

Wade, Wyn Craig. *The Titanic—End of a Dream.* New York: Rawson Wade, 1979.

Wendt, Herbert. *The Romance of Water.* New York: Hill & Wang, 1963.

White, Edward, and White, Muriel. *Famous Subways and Tunnels of the World.* New York: Random House, 1953.

Winslow, Thacher, and Davidson, Frank P., eds. *American Youth: An Enforced Reconnaissance.* Cambridge, Mass.: Harvard University Press, 1940.

Index